Arbitration and Mediation in International Business

International Arbitration Law Library

Series Editor Dr. Julian D.M. Lew QC

In the series *International Arbitration Law Library* this book,
Arbitration and Mediation in International Business,
is the second edition of the fourth title.

The titles published in this series are listed at the end of this volume

International Arbitration Law Library

Arbitration and Mediation in International Business

Second Edition

Christian Bühring-Uhle

and for the Second Edition

Lars Kirchhoff and Gabriele Scherer

A C.I.P Catalogue record for this book is available from the Library of Congress.

ISBN 90-411-2256-7

Published by Kluwer Law International,
P.O. Box 316, 2400 AH Alphen aan den Rijn, The Netherlands
sales@kluwerlaw.com
http://www.kluwerlaw.com

Sold and distributed in North, Central and South America by
Aspen Publishers, Inc.,
7201 McKinney Circle, Frederick, MD 21704, USA

Sold and distributed in all other countries by
Turpin Distribution Services Ltd.,
Stratton Business Park,
Pegasus Drive, Biggleswade,
Bedfordshire SG18 8TQ, United Kingdom

FSC

MIX

FSC® C103993

Foreword to the Second Edition

Professor William W. Park
Boston University

What a delight and privilege to receive a preview of the Second Edition of this fine book, which now profits from the thinking of not one, but three, distinguished scholars: the original author, Dr. Bühring-Uhle, and his colleagues Lars Kirchhoff and Dr. Gabriele Scherer.

At the time of my first Foreword, *Arbitration and Mediation in International Business* was a precious rarity among works on Alternative Dispute Resolution. The book provided an empirical analysis of how both arbitration and mediation were conducted in a cross-border context, along with a normative guide to the relative costs and benefits of these two methods of non-judicial dispute resolution.

A decade later, the authors' scholarship has become even more exciting. The new edition of the work has been enhanced by discussions of innovative tools for settlement negotiations, and analysis of practical techniques by which to integrate mediation and arbitration in international business.

The law's evolution has also given the book an added significance to trade and investment. No longer arbitration's stepchild, mediation has come into its own as an independent discipline. Legislation has been enacted,[1] directives drafted,[2] and institutional rules adopted,[3] all with the aim of promoting efficiency in the non-binding resolution of commercial disputes.

---

[1]   See e.g., Austria's new Mediation Act (*Zivilrechts-Mediations-Gesetz*), entered into force by publication in *Bundesgesetzblatt für die Republik Österreich*, 6. June 2003, Teil I, No. 29, pages 123-133 (BGBl.I Nr. 29/2003).

[2]   On the draft European Union Mediation Directive, see Alexander Petsche & Gottfried Schmutzer, "Der Entwurf der Mediations –RL", *Ecolex, Fachzeitschrift für Wirtschaftsrecht* (JUNE 2005, NO. 6) page 493.

[3]   International Chamber of Commerce, ADR Rules in force as from 1 July 2001, ICC Publication 809. For the ICC, the reference to "ADR" signifies "Amicable Dispute Resolution"

In commenting on a book, reviewers normally attempt to call into question some aspect of the work, if only to make their remarks more interesting. Alas, there is little with which to quibble in this superb treatise.

For the next edition, however, the authors might consider further examination of how arbitral jurisdiction operates in relation to multinational corporate groups. Increasingly, arbitrators have been asked to join companies that never signed the arbitration clause, but which (under theories such as agency or estoppel) remain vitally implicated in the dispute, often as *de facto* guarantors for undercapitalized respondents.[4] In weighing adjudicatory alternatives, consideration must be given to such challenges, including the multifaceted notion of *Kompetenz-Kompetenz* (an arbitrator's "jurisdiction to determine jurisdiction") and the separability doctrine by which the legitimacy of an arbitration clause may withstand the invalidity of the main agreement.

Readers of the Second Edition will find rewards in each succeeding chapter. Like a fine wine, *Arbitration and Mediation in International Business* has become richer with age. For scholars and practitioners alike, the book holds intellectual joy and practical utility, making it a "must" for every international lawyer's library.

Boston, 27 October 2005

---

rather than "Alternative Dispute Resolution", reflecting a conscious choice to exclude the binding decision-making constituted by arbitration.

[4]   See e.g., *Peterson Farms Inc. v. C&M Farming Ltd.*, [2004] EWHC 121, [2004], 1 Lloyd's Rep 603, 2004 WL 229138 (4 February 2004, Q.B. Div., Commercial Court); *Contec Corp. v. Remote Solution Co. Ltd.*, 398 F.3d 205 (2d Cir. 2005); *Sarhank v. Oracle Corp.*, 404 F.3d 657 (2d Cir. 2005). For the grandfather of this line of cases, see *First Options of Chicago, Inc. v. Kaplan*, 514 U.S. 938, 943 (1995).

Contents

CONTENTS

CONTENTS

Preface by the Authors

When *Arbitration and Mediation in International Business* came out about ten years ago, no one expected it to have much of an impact. The success, both in sales numbers and in critical acclaim, led to numerous requests for a second edition.

About four years ago, we decided that working on a second edition, and producing something more than just an update, would be a worthwhile enterprise. Why? Over the last decade, a number of new developments, in particular with respect to hybrid mechanisms of alternative dispute resolution, have led to significant changes within the field of conflict research in general and Alternative Dispute Resolution (ADR) in particular. Sophisticated methods of conflict management have made their way into many business contexts formerly little receptive to them. Simultaneously, on the scientific level, research on conflict theory has progressed significantly.

Therefore, some of the insights presented as provocative – or at least new – in the first edition are now part of the common understanding of practitioners and scholars. ADR has developed, and so has the attitude towards ADR.

A second edition, by definition, is a tradeoff between preserving the relevant "old" thoughts and integrating new elements. The challenge consists in adding updates and insights without changing the character of the book entirely. The path we have chosen was that of leaving the old structure largely intact, bringing it up to date, conducting an entire new empirical survey, and integrating numerous other new elements and approaches that we hope will increase the practical usefulness of the book. We have also taken care to streamline the book, making it more user-friendly and less academic.

The result is practically a new book, an endeavor that was made possible through an expansion of the team. Lars Kirchhoff and Gabriele Scherer therefore came on board as co-authors for the second edition.

The authors would like to thank Constantin Olbrisch for his contribution to Chapter 7, as well as Alexander Steinbrecher, Tobias Mischlau and Yvonne Gogoll for their excellent research assistance.

Christian Bühring-Uhle, Lars Kirchhoff and Gabriele Scherer
Hamburg/Berlin, December 2005

Abbreviations

AAA	American Arbitration Association
ABA	American Bar Association
ACDC	Australian Commercial Disputes Centre
ADR	Alternative Dispute Resolution
Art.	Article
BATNA	Best Alternative to Negotiated Agreement
Brussels Convention	1968 European Convention on the Jurisdiction of the Courts and the Enforcement of Judgments in Civil and Commercial Matters
CAM	Arbitration Centre of Mexico
CCPIT	China Council for the Promotion of International Trade
CEDR	Centre for Effective Dispute Resolution
CIETAC	China International Economic and Trade Arbitration Commission
CPR	International Institute for Conflict Prevention and Resolution (formerly Center for Public Resources)
CRCICA	Cairo Regional Centre for International Commercial Arbitration
DIS	Deutsche Institution für Schiedsgerichtsbarkeit e.V. (German Institution of Arbitration)
DRB	Dispute Review Board
FIDIC	Fédération Internationale des Ingénieurs-Conseils (International Association of Consultant-Engineers)

Geneva Convention	1961 European Convention on International Commercial Arbitration
HKIAC	Hong Kong International Arbitration Centre
IACAC	Inter-American Commercial Arbitration Commission
IAMA	Institute of Arbitrators and Mediators Australia
IBA	International Bar Association
ICC	International Chamber of Commerce
ICC Court	ICC Court of International Arbitration
ICCA	International Council on Commercial Arbitration
ICDR	AAA International Centre for Dispute Resolution
ICSID	International Centre for the Resolution of Investment Disputes
ICTE	International Centre for Technical Expertise
LCIA	London Court of International Arbitration
Lugano Convention	1988 Lugano Convention on the Jurisdiction of the Courts and Enforcement of Judgments in Civil and Commercial Matters
NAI	Netherlands Arbitration Institute
New York Convention	1958 New York Convention on the Recognition and Enforcement of Foreign Arbitral Awards
Orange Book	FIDIC Conditions of Contract Design Build and Turnkey, Test Edition December 1994
Panama Convention	1975 Inter-American Convention on International Commercial Arbitration
PON	Harvard Program on Negotiation
PSS	Post-Settlement Settlement
Red Book	FIDIC Conditions of Contract (International) for Works of Civil Engineering Construction, 4th Edition 1987
SIAC	Singapore International Arbitration Centre
SCC Institute	Arbitration Institute of the Stockholm Chamber of Commerce

SCC	Standards Council of Canada (SCC)
SNT	Single Negotiating Text
UMA	Uniform Mediation Act
UNCITRAL	United Nations Conference on International Trade Law
Washington Convention/ ICSID Convention	1965 Washington Convention on the Settlement of Investment Disputes Between States and Nationals of Other States
WATNA	Worst Alternative to Negotiated Agreement
WIPO	World Intellectual Property Organisation
ZCC	Zurich Chamber of Commerce
ZOPA	Zone of Possible Agreement
ZPO	Zivilprozessordnung (German Code of Civil Procedure)

Introduction

International business disputes pose a formidable challenge to the law and the legal profession as well as to international actors. In recent decades, it has become ever more apparent that the sole reliance on traditional legal concepts and structures is frequently insufficient to meet the needs of the participants in international trade and investment. Interdisciplinary research and innovative practitioners have joined efforts to develop a modern "technology" of conflict management. Some of the techniques developed have become known under the term "alternative dispute resolution" (ADR). Many of these techniques, in essence, represent modern versions of the ancient settlement technique of *mediation*. Based on the hypothesis that these techniques can significantly improve the practice of dispute resolution, this book tries to explore their potential in the settlement of international business disputes.

Part One of the book (Chapter 1) serves as an introduction. It looks at the economic background and the growing need for effective conflict management in international business. It also demonstrates that litigating international disputes in national courts has serious shortcomings.

Part Two of the book (Chapters 2 to 4) deals with international commercial arbitration. Chapter 2 explains how most of the deficiencies of transnational litigation can be overcome in the legal framework of international commercial arbitration. The sequence of international commercial arbitration procedures is explained in a detailed fashion in Chapter 3. Chapter 4 describes and analyzes the results of the surveys conducted by the authors in 1996 and 2004. When the first edition of this book was published, it was the first time that the process of international commercial arbitration had been the subject of comprehensive empirical research. The recent survey provides contemporary data on some of the key questions of the original survey, as well as some additional points dealing with mediations in the context of international commercial arbitration.

Alternatives to arbitration are discussed in Part Three (Chapters 5 to 8). It starts with an overview of the interdisciplinary roots of modern conflict management (Chapter 5) and continues, in Chapter 6, with an in-depth examination of mediation and other ADR techniques as well as their actual and potential applications in international business. Chapter 7 introduces tools and techniques which can support business mediation, with a focus on litigation risk analysis. Chapter 8 looks at the legal issues raised by the use of alternative techniques in the context of multi-jurisdictional disputes.

Part Four (Chapter 9) contains the synthesis of the book and concludes that some of the difficulties encountered in dealing with international business conflicts can be avoided by integrating mediation into the legal framework of international commercial arbitration. After analyzing various ways of combining the benefits of mediation and arbitration, the authors propose a dynamic system for dispute resolution process design.

The book concludes that mediation and arbitration have to be viewed as complementary elements of an integrated system and that the key to successful dispute resolution in international business is the conscious and creative design of conflict management processes.

PART ONE:
CHALLENGES OF CONFLICT MANAGEMENT

Need for Conflict Management in International Business

"Recht zu haben ist nicht die Aufgabe eines Erwerbsunternehmens"
("to prevail at law is not the task of a business enterprise")[1]

This section first looks at a number of developments that characterize the economic background for contemporary international business disputes and their management: the progressive integration of world markets and the related increase in transborder economic contacts, and a shift in the nature of international business transactions from a preponderance of comparatively simple exchange contracts to long-term arrangements faced with considerable complexity and uncertainty.[2] An overview of the risk factors that make international business relations particularly vulnerable – with an emphasis on the problemes of litigating international disputes in national courts – illustrates the particular need for adequate conflict management in international business.

I. GLOBALIZATION OF THE WORLD ECONOMY

The world is becoming smaller as national boundaries are becoming more permeable and are gradually losing their economic significance. The volume of world trade is steadily increasing. Modern technologies and the continuing shift toward market economies and free trade are creating an increasingly globalized world economy. In addition, the regional integration of markets in trading blocks is changing the parameters of business activities.

Faced with the growing internationalization of competition and the escalating costs of research and development, global companies increasingly engage in "strategic alliances" joining forces to develop sophisticated new technologies or

---

[1] Interview with Hans-Georg Haeseler, February 14, 1992.

[2] Bartlett & Goshal, *Managing Across Borders* (2nd ed 2002); Brett, *Negotiating Globally: How to Negotiate Deals, Resolve Disputes, and Make Decisions Across Cultures* (2001); see also Bjorklund, Coe & Park, "International Commercial Dispute Resolution", 37 *International Lawyer* 445 (2003).

to manufacture and distribute their products. But even smaller companies and individual entrepreneurs increasingly deal with customers, suppliers, competitors and potential partners from many different countries.

The rapid pace of the globalization of markets is not matched by an equally quick adaptation of the individuals and organizations involved: And since conflict is inherent both in competition and cooperation, the potential for transnational business disputes inevitably rises.

II. VULNERABILITY OF INTERNATIONAL BUSINESS RELATIONS

1. Increasing Complexity of International Business Transactions

The last decades have seen a dramatic increase in the sheer size and complexity of international business transactions. In contrast to more traditional forms of international trade consisting of discrete transactions such as the sale or transportation of merchandise, these transactions typically expand over long periods of time, deal with complex technologies, and frequently include more than two parties. Sophisticated financing schemes often provide lenders with considerable influence on the transactions. And governments are often involved, sometimes directly as parties or through state owned entities, or they closely follow and influence projects that are seen to touch vital national interests such as a country's national security, its industrial policy, or the exploitation of its natural resources.

Complex international business transactions include, e.g., more or less closely integrated distributorships, long-term "take or pay" supply arrangements, manufacturing joint ventures, high-technology licensing agreements, natural resource development projects, large scale infrastructure development schemes, or "strategic alliances" between two or more industrial conglomerates to develop complex technologies, or to manufacture and distribute goods in third countries.

2. Particular Vulnerability of International Business Relations

International business relations are particularly vulnerable to change and therefore carry an even greater potential for conflicts than domestic exchanges because a number of factors increase the level of uncertainty threatening international business relations and limit the effectiveness of both legal and nonlegal regulation. The factors responsible for added uncertainty include economic, financial, political, legal, and interpersonal factors. Some of these factors constitute the parameters of classical "political risk analysis" or "country risk analysis", others are more concerned with the dynamics of the particular relationship.

a. Economic Factors

Evidently, international business transactions are based on a different valuation of the elements of the transaction. The difference in the valuation of each party's contribution is frequently a function of the economic circumstances in the parties' respective home countries. The balance between the contributions exchanged can be affected by changes in prices, actual and opportunity costs and other factors of valuation in any of the countries involved and in the world market as a whole.

b. Financial and Monetary Factors

International transactions are exposed to financial risks such as the cost and availability of capital in a number of countries and, again, to the world financial markets. More importantly, the exchange has to be valued in money, and international parties will have to base their calculations on their own home currency. Fluctuations in exchange rates can therefore have a tremendous impact on the economic balance of an international business transaction. In addition, commonly at least one party depends on the convertibility of its currency or the availability of foreign exchange. And foreign investors typically rely on the possibility of repatriating their profits.

c. Political Factors

International business relations are particularly vulnerable to political developments within any of the countries involved and in the relationship between these nations. Typical political risks include war, revolution, civil disturbance, closed trade routes, nationalization, trade embargos and inconvertibility of local currency. But less "catastrophic" changes of governments or of government policies can have a profound effect on business, too. Not infrequently, a government – directly or through state owned entities – is itself a party to the contract and subordinates its contractual behavior to political goals. Government can indirectly influence contractual exchanges by exercising pressure on the local party. And sometimes the government directly affects the deal by issuing new legislation or regulations. The extreme example is outright nationalization, but similar effects can be caused by a creeping nationalization through changes in the legal environment.

d. Legal Factors

Both the exchange as such and the parties acting internationally are frequently subject to several jurisdictions. The multiplicity of laws can lead to the delicate situation that someone is confronted with mutually exclusive obligations. A well known historical example is the jurisdictional conflict between the United States and several European countries relating to the participation of European firms in the construction in the Soviet Trans-Siberian pipeline. Enforcing a trade embargo against the former Soviet Union, the U.S. government prohibited the European subsidiaries of American firms from executing existing supply contracts while several European governments tried to force these companies to honor their commitments.[3]

e. Interpersonal Factors

In all relationships, the future behavior of one party is a risk factor for the other. In international business, this risk is increased by information deficiencies and a number of barriers to effective communication. Typically, parties to an international business exchange have added difficulties in understanding, predicting and monitoring the other side's behavior because they are not familiar with its background and are hampered in their efforts to know more about the other side by cultural and language disparities and logistical problems.[4]

Language. In most international business relations at least one party will have to communicate in a foreign language. Even where the language abilities of the actors or the services of the interpreters are exceptionally good, the potential for miscommunication is large because subtle nuances get lost in the process of translation and because everybody will understand certain notions and concepts from the vantage point of their own social and cultural background. In addition, language problems exist even where both sides speak the "same" language: as George Bernard Shaw said, "England and America are two countries separated by a common language".

Communication in business often involves *legal terms* such as "property", "contract", "bond", "waiver", "patent" etc. The exact meaning of these words can only be determined by reference to a particular system of law. Since different systems frequently give different meanings and connotations to the same terms (or their linguistic equivalent in another language), business people and lawyers may think they agree while in reality they have a materially different understanding of the substance of their conversation.[5]

---

[3] Cf. the accounts in: Basedow, "Das Amerikanische Pipeline Embargo vor Gericht", 47 *Rabels Zeitschrift* 147 (1983); and Morse & Powers, "U.S. Export Controls and Foreign Entities: The Unanswered Questions of Pipeline Diplomacy", 23 *V. J. Int'l L.* 537 (1982); courts dealing with the pipeline embargo include the District Court for the District of Columbia in: *Dresser Industries, Inc. v. Baldridge*, 549 F. Supp. 108, 77 *Am. J. Int'l .L.* 626 (1983); and the Rechtbank Den Haag in: *Compagnie Européenne des Pétroles S.A. v. Sensor Neerland B.V.*, 22 *Int'l Leg. Mat.* 66 (1983), 77 *Am. J. Int'l .L.* 636 (1983).

[4] For further details, see von Schlabrendorff, "Resolving Cultural Differences in Arbitration Proceedings", *International Financial Law Review* 38 (Mar 2002).

[5] For example, American law distinguishes "real property" and "personal property" while French law distinguishes "immovable" and "movable" property. Behind the seemingly similar terms lie different concepts: for instance, immovable property under French law encompasses farm animals and agricultural machinery while real property in most American jurisdictions does not. Hence, when a French and an American negotiate the sale of a farm

Culture. All International business exchanges are the product of cross-cultural communication.[6] Cultural differences are a double risk factor in international business relations for they are a not only a frequent source of conflicts, but they are also a barrier to effective conflict management. Cultural groups are not necessarily identical with nations and are often determined by ethnic, religious and regional groups within nations and across their borders. In many ways culture operates as mental programming or "software of the mind"[7] and determines how the world is perceived, how the self is experienced and how life is organized. Language is only one of a number of cultural systems, and frequently the spoken words can be understood only in the context of their cultural background.[8] Other cultural systems are gestures and other forms of non-verbal communication, fundamental values and attitudes, but also the varying concepts of time and space, the symbolic value of certain material things or the meaning of friendship.

An important source of conflict and instability in cross-cultural business relations are differing concepts of what constitutes a binding *agreement*.[9] Economic exchanges can be based primarily on detailed technical rules that are spelled out in writing, or on more or less explicit unwritten moral practices and informal customs. Accordingly, not all cultures have the same notion of the binding force of a written contract and of the importance of detailed regulations. In some cultures, an established relationship between businessmen or "a man's word" may traditionally have greater weight in creating morally binding obligations than a written instrument. These discrepancies in the "language of agreements" can result in misconceptions about whether or not certain understandings in business relationships have binding force in the eyes of different partners.

---

in France and agree on the transfer of all immovable property, they may actually think of quite a different set of assets.

[6]   For an anthropological analysis of intercultural communication see Hall, *The Silent Language* (1959); see also G. Fisher, *Mindsets: The Role of Culture and Perception in International Relations* (1988); G. Fisher, *International Negotiation: A Cross-Cultural Perspective* (1980); Bergemann & Sourisseaux, *Interkulturelles Management*, (3rd ed. 2002) and Salacuse, *Making Global Deals* (1991).

[7]   Cf. Hofstede, *Cultures and Organizations: Software of the Mind* (1991).

[8]   For example, when an American says "that's difficult" in response to a request, against the backdrop of a "can-do" culture that places a high value on persistence and that teaches its youth not to take no for an answer, it may well imply that the matter is open to negotiation. For someone coming from a culture like the Japanese where open confrontation is considered embarrassing and an explicit "no" might be regarded as impolite, "that is difficult" may be a diplomatic way to express a clear and final rejection.

[9]   With regard to other differences of legal cultures, see Bernardo Cremades, "Overcoming the Clash of Legal Cultures: The Role of Interactive Arbitration", 14 *Arb. Int.* No. 2 (1998), at 157.

Culture has an important organizational dimension because national cultures influence internal structures and organizations tend to develop their own, organizational, culture. Both aspects are risk factors in international business. Differences in the lines of command, the methods of decision-making and internal consultation, and in the time needed for these processes, may make it difficult to understand the other side and to communicate effectively. When two disparate organizations have to work together very closely, as in a strategic alliance, effective cooperation can be prevented by discrepancies in corporate cultures, i.e. in the priorities, values and methods required and rewarded in employees, in the way employees are taught to think, work and solve problems.

> In the British-Japanese alliance between computer makers ICL and Fujitsu, ICL planned to purchase a Fujitsu keyboard for one of its computer systems. Engineers at ICL requested that Fujitsu test the quality of the keyboard by hitting the same key 50 million times. Since this number by far exceeds any imaginable usage of a keyboard, the engineers at Fujitsu were upset and protested against the "unreasonable" demand which might have been the product of overly concern for safety but which might be perceived to imply a measure of distrust or disrespect. The conflict could only be resolved when an executive with years of experience in the ICL-Fujitsu alliance intervened as a mediator.[10]

Logistical Difficulties. Communication and information deficits are magnified by the geographical distance that has to be bridged and the costs associated with all forms of long-distance interaction. The development and maintenance of a continuous working relationship and the "smoothing out" of the inevitable differences occurring in the course of a business exchange is rendered more difficult when person-to-person meetings require international travel of at least one of the participants or when contacts have to be relegated to other means of communication. Communication in writing, over the internet or in its traditional fashion, or over the telephone, and even via video conferences is necessarily "poorer" than direct meetings because it lacks the context and the full arsenal of verbal and nonverbal communication often indispensable for true understanding. Also, these methods reduce the scope of the communication to the core substance on the agenda and do not allow for the peripheral social interaction (coffee breaks, meals, time "lost" with conversations on non-business matters etc.) that is often essential to building and maintaining relationships. And when direct meetings do occur, the fact that the meeting necessitates international travel conveys a sense of formality and urgency that might stand in the way of informal problem solving.

---

[10]   Cauley de la Sierra, "How MNCs Handle Disputes in Strategic Alliances", *Business International* (June 15, 1992).

III. REDUCED EFFECTIVENESS OF CONTRACTUAL PLANNING

The importance of contractual relationships for international business disputes warrants a brief look at the function contracts have as an instrument to regulate economic exchanges. The analysis of contracts as a socio-economic phenomenon provides some insights of a more general nature in understanding the background for many international business disputes.

Despite the great diversity of economic constellations, complex international commercial contracts have common traits: they are affected by a significant level of uncertainty and an inherent tension between the goals of contractual risk distribution and the need to maintain flexibility to adjust to inevitable change.[11] Contractual exchanges are governed by a complex interplay between legal and non-legal mechanisms. Long-term contracts tend to be *relational* in nature and are faced with considerable *uncertainty* and the need to manage the inevitable change occurring during the life of the contract. Therefore, contracts projecting exchanges into the future have to strike a balance between the inherently incompatible goals of distributing and allocating risks and providing for necessary adjustments to accommodate change.[12] Contracts are necessarily incomplete because in addition to the inherent limitations of planning under uncertainty, the actual level of completeness in contractual planning is further reduced by the need to rationalize the cost of contracting as well as by the tendency of businessmen to avoid dealing with legal details and to rely chiefly on extra-legal control mechanisms.[13]

The preservation of cooperation is facilitated by social norms, the desire to maintain a good business reputation and by what Adam Smith has called the "discipline of continuous dealings".[14] But the effectiveness of this type of social regulation depends in large measure on the coherence of the social context (between the parties and within a larger group context, e.g. in an industry) and on the continued expectation of future dealings.

Another factor influencing the stability of the cooperation is the correlation between the duration of the concrete contract to the duration of the overall business relationship. When contractual exchanges are relatively transactional in nature, e.g. sales contracts, and occur in the context of longstanding business relationships between suppliers and purchasers, the stabilizing effect of the discipline of

---

[11]   See also Frick, *Arbitration and Complex International Contracts* (2001).

[12]   See Scott, "Conflict and Cooperation in Long-Term Contracts", 75 *Cal. L. Rev.* 2005 et seq. (1987); see also Scott, "Risk Distribution and Adjustment in Long-Term Contracts", in: Nicklisch (ed.), *The Complex Long-Term Contract* 51 et seq. (1987).

[13]   See Macaulay's empirical work on contracting behavior in business, Macaulay, "Non-Contractual Relationships in Business: A Preliminary Study", 28 *Am. Sociological Rev.* 55 (1963).

[14]   Smith, Adam, *The Wealth of Nations* 700 (E. Cannon ed. 1937) (1776), cited after Scott, "Conflict and Cooperation in Long-Term Contracts", 75 *Cal. L. Rev.* 2005, 2009 (1987).

continuous dealings has the strongest impact on the individual contract. At the other end of the spectrum are long-term contracts occurring in non-repetitive business relations, e.g. in an international construction project where the parties have to cooperate closely for the duration of the project but might never have to deal with each other once the project is completed.

Both legal and nonlegal control mechanisms will tend to be less effective in international business. Legal standards and legal enforcement mechanisms are indispensable – albeit not sufficient – to secure cooperation. The effectiveness of legal mechanisms, however, is hampered by the dilemma between the goals of risk distribution and adjustability, as well as by the ambiguity of legal devices that can deter opportunism but can also be exploited for opportunistic maneuvers. In addition, both legal planning and legal enforcement generate costs, including potential harm to the relationship.

IV. PROBLEMS OF LITIGATING INTERNATIONAL DISPUTES IN NATIONAL COURTS

An *international* tribunal for the resolution of commercial disputes does not exist and is not likely to be created in the near future. Therefore, international commercial litigation has to be conducted in the *national* courts of some country. Frequently, as we shall see below, litigation takes place in the courts of several countries at the same time. The fact that in any cross-border litigation several legal systems are involved creates a number of specific legal complexities that increase the uncertainty and transaction costs (costs, delays, disruptions) associated with litigation in general.[15]

The following groups of legal issues can be distinguished: which court has jurisdiction over the dispute? (1.), how will it conduct the procedure? (2.), which rule will apply to the substance of the dispute? (3.), and which effect will its judgments have abroad? (4.)

1. Jurisdiction

The rules under which the courts assume jurisdiction over a dispute vary from country to country and frequently lead to conflicting results. Since courts can base their jurisdiction on such different grounds as the residence or corporate headquarters of the defendant, the nationality of the plaintiff, or the occurrence of the liability-creating event, to name just a few, plaintiffs often have to choose between a number of jurisdictions when deciding where to bring suit.

---

[15] For more detailed discussions, see Lowenfeld, *International Litigation and Arbitration*, (2nd ed. 2002); Weintraub, *International Litigation and Arbitration: Practice and Planning*, (3rd ed. 2001).

This choice is often motivated by tactical considerations like the desire to take advantage of particular procedural or substantive rules, an expected bias in favor of the plaintiff, or the likelihood of a very high damage award, or simply to get before a neutral forum, which is why this process is sometimes called "forum-shopping". American courts have been frequently confronted with plaintiffs from distant parts of the world presenting claims that had no real connection to the United States.

Since uniform international standards about the assertion of jurisdiction do not exist, different bases of jurisdiction and different interpretations of the same bases can lead to multiple lawsuits in different jurisdictions when the defendant decides to launch a counter-suit in a different forum. This problem is aggravated by the fact that the mere pendency of a lawsuit in another country is not generally an accepted ground for a stay of proceedings. Therefore, it is entirely possible and indeed occurs not infrequently that the same dispute is subject to parallel lawsuits in the courts of two or more countries.

A dramatic example is the US$ 1.1 billion treble damage antitrust suit by the liquidator of the transatlantic discount air carrier *Laker* Airways against several European and American Air Lines who allegedly drove Laker out of business by fixing predatory prices and pressuring Laker's banks to withdraw their funding. Both British and American Courts asserted jurisdiction and the resulting conflict escalated into a battle of several rounds of anti-suit injunctions in the two jurisdictions (followed by several levels of appeals[16]) where each court would prohibit the parties from participating in litigation in the other court.[17] The dispute occasioned enormous transaction costs, and when finally the parties were prepared to enter into a settlement, a major stumbling block was the claim by the plaintiff's American lawyers for USD 60 million in (contingency) legal fees.[18]

---

[16] The British lawsuit went up to the House of Lords, *British Airways Bd. v. Laker Airways*, 1985 A.C. 58 (1984). That decision was preceded by a "blocking order" by the British government based on the 1980 Protection of Trading Interest Act, prohibiting all persons doing business in the United Kingdom, except American air carriers, from complying with United States antitrust measures arising out of Laker's action, see *Laker Airways, Ltd. v. Sabena, Belgian World Airlines*, 731 F.2d 909, 920 (D.C. Cir. 1984).

[17] Cf. the account in *Laker Airways, Ltd. v. Sabena, Belgian World Airlines*, 731 F.2d 909, (D.C. Cir. 1984).

[18] See Moore, "Laker Settlement Stalled by Demand for USD 60 Million Fee," *Legal Times* 1 (June 10, 1985); in the final settlement the lawyers received USD 12.5 million; Donne, Michael, "Laker Creditors 'to be paid by Christmas'", *The Financial Times* 1 (September 7, 1985).; other contested issues were Sir Freddie Laker's demands for free transatlantic air passes from the defendant air lines and access to crucial documents needed for his memoirs, as well as the refusal of Laker's attorneys to agree not to use information gained in the case when representing other clients in antitrust matters.

Conflicts like the Laker "saga" are difficult to preclude when an economic activity affects several countries, and falls into the scope of the economic legislation of several jurisdictions, e.g. laws dealing with competition, securities markets, or export controls. Parties to disputes in these areas will often see their best chances in the courts of different countries (Laker's liquidator may not have had any claim at all in the United Kingdom and in any event could never have claimed treble damages), and will therefore each try to force the other side into the forum of their choice. Unless one of the courts declines to exercise its jurisdiction under the doctrine of "*forum non conveniens*", the courts are pitted against each other in a jurisdictional conflict.

Parallel litigation in different countries can cause considerable costs, delays and uncertainty. Even where one of the actions has little prospects for success and even where the jurisdictional conflict is in the end resolved by a clear decision in favor of one jurisdiction, having to defend against a parallel action in a foreign court can be costly, especially when – as in the United States – the chances for the winning party to recover its attorney's fees are marginal. This, in turn, opens the door for extortionary maneuvers exploiting the "nuisance value" of a parallel suit in order to exact favorable settlement terms.

> The parallel proceedings in the Armco cases in England and the U.S. arose out of a management buy-out of English insurance companies owned by Armco of the U.S., in September 1991.[19] In 1998, Armco brought suit against the purchasers in the Southern District of New York alleging Common Law fraud, conversion, breach of fiduciary duty, and RICO violations. The defendants filed motions to dismiss for lack of personal jurisdiction, improper venue, and *forum non conveniens*.[20] In the subsequent English proceedings in 1999, defendants sought to enjoin the U.S. litigation based on exclusive jurisdiction clauses. The English trial court found that the clauses only bound some of the defendants and that England was not the "natural forum" for the litigation.[21] Subsequently in 1999, the New York District Court denied the motions to dismiss, because the forum selection clauses did not cover the pending litigation relying on the English trial court opinion to demonstrate that the U.S. was the proper venue.[22] On appeal of the defendants in 2000, the Court of Appeal in England reversed the lower trial court and issued an antisuit injunction against the Armco entities from proceeding in the U.S. holding that when there is an exclusive jurisdiction clause there must be

---

[19] See Wilmore & Teitz, "Parallel Proceedings – Sisyphean Progress", 36 *Int'l Law* 423, 426 et seq. (2001).

[20] 68 F.Supp.2d 330.

[21] *Donohue v. Armco Inc. and Others*, 2 Lloyd's Rep. 649 (Q.B. 1999).-

[22] 68 F.Supp.2d 330 and 342.

strong reasons for not granting an antisuit injunction.[23] At the end of 2001, the House of Lords reversed the Court of Appeal's injunction; it found that England was not the natural forum for the proceedings and that the defendant, as to the Armco entities with whom he had exclusive jurisdiction clauses, had the right to expect not to be sued in New York and even more critically, not to be subject to RICO claims that would be impossible in England.[24]

One way to prevent multiple litigations is through stipulation of an unambiguous *choice of forum* clause. This possibility, however, exists only in the context of contractual disputes – except in the rare case where the parties to an existing dispute are able to reach an agreement on where to litigate. As the Armco case illustrates, parties to a choice of forum clause cannot be certain that the chosen forum will indeed accept the jurisdiction – it may refuse to do on so the basis of *forum non conveniens* or related doctrines, with the possible consequences of leaving the parties with no forum at all. Nor can the parties be assured that all other courts will respect their forum selection and refrain from exercising their own jurisdiction. Hence, the danger of competing parallel lawsuits cannot be excluded entirely.

This, however, may be different under international treaties. The most important agreement in this area is the 1968 European Convention on the Jurisdiction of the Courts and the Enforcement of Judgments in Civil and Commercial Matters ("Brussels Convention"),[25] now in force as the "Brussels I Regulation".[26] It is the only multilateral convention of significance covering the original jurisdiction of courts. Other judicial conventions exist but they are generally limited in their scope to the recognition and enforcement of judgments. Within its range of application, the Brussels Convention/Regulation virtually eliminates the danger of parallel litigation. Jurisdictional conflicts are avoided by providing uniform rules on jurisdiction and obliging the member states to respect the jurisdiction of the courts in other member states as well as written choice of forum clauses. With narrow exceptions, it applies to practically all civil and commercial matters.[27] In addition, it provides for the enforcement of judgments. The system established by the Brussels Convention/Regulation has been extended to a number of additional

---

23 *Donohue v. Armco Inc. and Others*, 1 Lloyd's Rep. 579 (C.A. 2000).

24 *Donohue v. Armco Inc. and Others*, U.K.H.L. 64, ¶ 15, 21 and 24.

25 Signed Sept. 27, 1968, entered into force Jan. 1, 1973, EC 46 (1978), 21 O.J.Eur.Com. (No. L 304) 77 (1978); 8 *Int'l Legal Materials* 229 (1969).

26 Council Regulation (EC) No 44/2001, of December 2000 on jurisdiction and the recognition and enforcement of judgments in civil and commercial matters (Official Journal L 12 of 16.01.2001) ("Brussels I Regulation"), between all Member States except Denmark; the relations between Denmark and the other Member States continuing to be governed by the Brussels Convention in its original form.

27 For the scope of the Regulation cf. its Art. 1.

states[28] through the 1988 Lugano Convention on the Jurisdiction of the Courts and the Enforcement of Judgments in Civil and Commercial Matters ("Lugano Convention").[29] An important advantage of the Brussels/Lugano system over other international conventions is that in addition to having a uniform set of standards, it ensures a uniform court practice through the European Court of Justice, competent in matters concerning interpretation of EU-Regulations.[30] In addition, some states have concluded bilateral agreements that cover jurisdictional and/or enforcement questions. The Unites States, however, is party to no such agreement.[31]

2. Conduct of Procedure

The conduct of transnational litigation has a number of particularities. For instance, certain *judicial acts* may have to be taken *outside the jurisdiction* of the court before which the dispute is pending, e.g. when process has to be served on a defendant residing in another jurisdiction,[32] or when certain evidence can only be found abroad.

In this subsection we will first take a brief look at the issues of the neutrality of the forum (a.) and then highlight the most important differences in the practice of civil procedure (b.), before turning to judicial conflicts connected with taking evidence in transnational litigation (c.).

---

[28] The system now encompasses Austria, Belgium, Denmark, Finland, France, Great Britain, Greece, Germany, Iceland, Ireland, Italy, Luxembourg, Netherlands, Norway, Portugal, Spain, Sweden, Switzerland.

[29] Signed Sept. 16, 1988, reprinted in 31 O.J.Eur.Com. (N8.L 319) 9-48 (1988).

[30] Where a country is not encompassed by the Brussels I Regulation, the Convention calls on the European Court of Justice to rule on questions of interpretation arising out of the application of the Convention.

[31] A treaty negotiated between the USA and Great Britain and initialled in 1976 never entered into force, reportedly due to pressure from the British insurance industry; cf. Vagts, "Dispute-Resolution Mechanisms in International Business", 203 *Recueil des Cours* 17, 59 (1987-III); the text of the United States-United Kingdom Convention on the Reciprocal Recognition of Judgments in Civil Matters is reprinted in 16 *Int'l Legal Materials* 71 (1977).

[32] Service of process cannot be by-passed because under most laws it is an absolute requirement in order to establish personal jurisdiction. And since service of process in most countries is regarded as an official act falling into the exclusive domain of the state's sovereign powers, foreign courts have to rely on the cooperation of local authorities. Traditionally, the granting of judicial assistance to foreign countries is based on the "comity of nations" and lies in the full discretion of the state asked to render the assistance. However, the Hague Convention on the Service Abroad of Judicial and Extrajudicial Documents in Civil and Commercial Matters has brought some progress, streamlining the procedures and obliging the authorities of the contracting states to respond to a properly presented request.

a. Neutrality of Forum

A major concern with the procedure in transnational litigation is the *neutrality of the forum*. The litigation of international disputes in national courts inevitably forces one party (the "foreign party") to deal with laws, procedures and practices which are unfamiliar to that party and its regular legal advisors. The prospect of having to litigate in the home courts of the opponent is perceived as one of the major disadvantages of transnational litigation. The concern about neutrality is not only due to the suspected biases of a "hometown justice" where judges will tend to rule in favor of the local party. Such biases may exist, and they may have more or less subtle manifestations. But the fear of hometown justice will often simply be the result of prejudices and a certain degree of xenophobia. However, even where, as in most cases, the judge is perfectly impartial, the fact that the suit will be conducted according to a procedure and in a language that is unfamiliar to one party creates an *inherent bias*: in order to convince the local judge the foreign party will have to learn the rules and skills of the local "game". Also, transaction costs are divided unevenly because one of the parties will have to hire local counsel in addition to its home counsel and will have to defray the costs of translating documents and transporting parties, home counsel and witnesses to the venue of the trial.

b. Fundamental Differences between Civil Law and Common Law Procedure

The *taking of evidence abroad* has been the source of a number of *judicial conflicts* between legal systems. These conflicts are rooted – apart from certain political and economic considerations that have played a role in some highly publicized disputes – in philosophical differences over what are proper procedures for the judicial finding of the truth.[33] The most dramatic judicial conflicts occurred between the United States and various European countries and had to do with certain characteristics of American civil procedure that stand in vivid contrast to the practice in most European countries, most notably the American practice of pre-trial discovery.

A very brief summary of some distinctive traits that distinguish Common Law, and particularly American, litigation practices from those of most Civil Law countries might be of help not only for an understanding of the judicial conflicts that arise in the context of international litigation but also as a background for certain recurrent issues in the practice of international commercial arbitration. The following discussion is based on the familiar distinction between the legal traditions of "Common Law" and "Civil Law". "Common Law" comprises the legal systems of Britain, the United States, and the former colonies of the British Commonwealth, whose principles of civil procedure historically go back to the practice in the Courts of England. " Civil Law" comprises the "legal families" in

---

[33] For a discussion of this topic cf. Wirth, "Ihr Zeuge, Herr Rechtsanwalt! – Weshalb Civil-Law-Schiedsrichter Common-Law-Verfahrensrecht anwenden", 1 *SchiedsVZ* 9 (2003).

the zone of influence of the French Civil Code of 1804 and of the German academic thinking of the 18th and 19th century. These two main schools of Civil Law, which differ considerably among themselves, have inspired the legal systems of most countries in continental Europe and Latin America, and of a number of Asian and African nations. Despite the great differences within the Civil Law and Common Law traditions, the fundamental differences in attitudes and practice between these two traditions justify to treat and compare them as groups.

(1) General Differences

Perhaps the most significant differences relate to the role of the judge and the division of tasks between the judge[34] and the parties.[35] It is generally said that Common Law follows the archetype of "adversarial" procedure whereas Civil Law is said to follow the "inquisitorial" model. In the adversary system, the parties present alternative versions of the facts and interpretations of the law to the judge who mainly listens and ultimately chooses one of the two versions. The judge does not make his own inquiries into the facts and does not adopt conclusions, of facts or of law, which have not been proposed by either party. In the inquisitorial procedure, the judge, in cooperation with the parties, conducts his own inquiry into the factual and legal issues. Inquisitorial procedures are "judge controlled" whereas adversarial procedures are "party controlled".[36] None of these two archetypes today exist in their pure form, but the *ideal types* of adversarial and inquisitorial procedure still have great force in shaping the minds of lawyers and are helpful in explaining the contrasts encountered in the practice of different nations. In the *Civil Law* tradition of "inquisitorial" procedure the judge plays a very active role in conducting the proceedings and finding the facts. The procedure is structured as a sequence of written exchanges and hearings where legal arguments and the facts are developed in a process of continuing interaction between the judge and the parties.

In the German tradition, the centerpiece of this *"trial by colloquy"* is a discussion where the judge tests the arguments of the parties and expresses preliminary views of the relative strengths and weaknesses of each party's case (*"Rechtsgespräch"*). The hearings tend to be brief – rarely longer than half a day – and usually concentrate on procedural matters and legal arguments. After the dispute has been crystallized through written exchanges, the judge may issue a ruling as to what proofs will be admitted (*"Beweisbeschluss"*), thereby excluding the taking of evidence on any facts that are not both contested and relevant (on the basis of the judge's preliminary

---

[34]   Which term is to include panels of several judges.

[35]   Which term is to be understood to include the lawyers.

[36]   For a comparative discussion of the two types see Reymond, "Civil Law and Common Law Procedures: Which is the More Inquisitorial? A Civil Lawyer's Response", 5 *Arb. Int'l* 357 (1989) and Staughton, "Common Law and Civil Law Procedures: Which Is More Inquisitorial? A Common Lawyer's Response", 5 *Arb. Int'l* 351 (1989).

determination of the legal merits). To the extent that this type of generalization is possible, the process is more focused on legal considerations than on the finding of facts, and the process of establishing the facts relies more heavily on documentary and physical evidence than on oral testimony. In many Civil Law systems, the judge is also held to work with the parties with the aim of achieving an amicable solution.[37] The broad powers over the conduct of the proceedings enjoyed by the Civil Law judge are used not so much in order to conduct an exhaustive "inquisition" into the truth but rather to structure and streamline the procedure. Particularly in the German tradition, the parties are obliged to bring forward in their initial pleadings all factual allegations and all items of proof they wish to rely on and will be only allowed to supplement their pleading if they can rely on a valid excuse for not having previously advanced the new allegations. They are forced to "lay their cards on the table".

In the classical *Common Law* procedure, the judge has more of an observer role while the actual proceedings are in the hands of the lawyers who in a dialectical process develop the facts in front of the mainly passive judge.[38] Common Law procedure has been decisively influenced by the existence of jury trials, and even where – as in England – juries have been largely abolished in civil matters, many of the old attributes still prevail. The most important of these attributes is the principle of orality. Since historically the "common man" on the jury could not be expected to be literate, all evidence had to be presented orally. And even as people became more educated, the principle was maintained: for a long time jurors where prohibited from seeing documents or from taking notes.[39] The trial is the focal point of the entire procedure. It is conducted – since juries are difficult to reconvene – as one continuous hearing which usually lasts for several days or weeks in a row. The written preparation of the trial is much less intensive than in Civil Law litigation and pleadings are said to be of a "skeletal" nature.[40] The procedure is much more focused on the facts and follows the ideal of an exhaustive examination of the truth. By giving each side a full and fair opportunity to present its case, the trial is

---

[37]   Cf. Art. 21 of the French New Code of Civil Procedure: "*Il entre dans la mission du juge de concilier les parties.*" – "It is part of the task of the judge to reconcile the parties." (translation by the author). Or see Sec. 278 para 1 of the German Code of Civil Procedure: "*Das Gericht soll in jeder Lage des Verfahrens auf eine gütliche Einigung des Rechtsstreits oder einzelner Streitpunkte bedacht sein.*" ("The court shall, during all stages of the procedure, consider efforts to reach an amicable solution to the dispute as a whole or individual contested issues" – translation by the authors.)

[38]   And/or the jury, see at end of paragraph. Unless otherwise indicated, the term judge will be used in the following to cover both judge and jury, where applicable.

[39]   For an explanation see Wilberforce, "Written Briefs and Oral Advocacy", 5 *Arb. Int'l* 348 (1989).

[40]   Smit, "Substance and Procedure in International Arbitration: The Development of a New Legal Order", 65 *Tul. L. Rev.* 1309, 1313 (1991).

supposed to spread out, at a single "moment" in time, all aspects of the case in front of a detached and impartial "trier of facts" (in the United States frequently still a jury) who will then establish "the truth". The Common Law style of civil procedure places very high emphasis on the detached impartiality of the decisionmaker. This impartiality is feared to be compromised by a proactive role of the judge who takes the investigation in his own hands. Thus, even when in some cases a more proactive role might advance the course of justice, the priority will be given to the preservation of the judge's impartiality. It is out of this concern for impartiality that settlement attempts by the judge are viewed with such suspicion.

The Civil Law procedure can be said to be, in essence, "deductive" in that it takes the demands of the parties, looks at the legal provisions that might support them, and from the relevant legal norms deduces which facts have to be established, and to which extent the parties' factual allegations differ. It is only on the basis of this deductive determination of the relevant facts that evidence will be considered. In contrast, the Common Law procedure might be considered more "inductive" in nature since it first establishes the facts and then looks to the law to establish the legal consequences of these facts.

(2) Characteristics of American Pre-Trial Discovery

Probably the single most important source of conflict and misunderstandings between judicial systems is the American practice of pre-trial discovery. In its basic form, pre-trial discovery is a standard feature of all Common Law systems. What sets apart the American practice is the scope of private evidence gathering it permits. The fundamental maxim of discovery is that "mutual knowledge of all the relevant facts gathered by both parties is essential to proper litigation."[41] The idea behind discovery is to give both parties an equal opportunity to conduct their own investigation of the case and to give each party access to evidence controlled by the other side. In practice, discovery "battles" seem to encourage "poker" tactics. As one Australian lawyer put it:

> "... especially common-law advocates have a bias against showing one's cards prematurely; they prefer shotgun ambush tactics."[42]

Discovery also has the purpose of preserving evidence that may not be available at a later moment, e.g the inspection of perishable goods; a macabre example is the testimony of a dying victim in an action for liability for injuries. Last but not least, the exchange of information occasioned by discovery is often a valuable basis for settlement discussions.

---

[41] *Hickman v. Taylor*, 329 U.S. 495, 507 (1947).

[42] Interview with Ezekiel Solomon, January 14, 1992.

The *methods* of pre-trial discovery correspond to the basic distinction between oral and physical, especially documentary, evidence. The personal knowledge of witnesses (including parties) can be discovered through written "interrogatories"[43] which have to be answered in writing, or by means of oral "depositions"[44]. Here, the witness will be examined and cross-examined by the lawyers from both sides or will orally answer a written interrogatory in front of an officer taking the deposition. In addition, parties can be requested to affirm or deny certain allegations presented to them by the other side in form of a "Request for Admission".[45] Physical evidence – whether in the possession of a party or a third party – is discovered through "requests for the production" of documents or other pieces of physical evidence and through "inspections" where lawyers from one side have to be granted entry onto the premises of the other side to conduct their own investigations.[46] The parties are required to cooperate with discovery requests and the courts have a wide arsenal of sanctions against non-cooperation which include default judgments and fines for "contempt of court".[47]

Truly unique is the *scope* of discovery available in the United States under the Federal Rules of Evidence. The requirement that the information sought be "relevant" to the "subject matter involved in the pending action"[48] is designed to prevent lawyers from conducting outright "fishing expeditions" inspecting the files of a potential defendant under the pretext of a fabricated complaint in order to search for grounds for a lawsuit. However, the applicable standard of "relevance" still allows for very extensive discovery. The only test a request for discovery has to meet is that "the information sought appears to be reasonably calculated to lead to the discovery of admissible evidence".[49] Coupled with the possibility of "blanket" requests that simply furnish a general description of the information sought rather than an item-by-item listing, this standard of relevance allows for very broad intrusions into the sphere of the other side.

The extraordinary scope of pre-trial discovery carries with it the danger of *excesses and abuses*. In an extreme example, discovery took five years and produced 64 million pages of documents.[50] And although one of the advantages

---

[43] Fed. R. Civ. P. Rule 33 ("Interrogatories to Parties").

[44] Id. Rule 30 ("Depositions Upon Oral Examination") and Rule 31 ("Depositions Upon Written Questions").

[45] Id. Rule 36.

[46] Id. Rule 34 ("Production of Documents and Things and Entry Upon Land for Inspection and Other Purposes").

[47] Cf. Rule 37 Fed. R. Civ. P.

[48] Fed. R. Civ. P. 26(b) (1).

[49] Id.

[50] "On Trial, Survey of the Legal Profession", Supplement to the *Economist* 12 (July 18, 1992).

of the discovery process is said to be that it facilitates voluntary settlements by allowing the parties to gauge their strengths and to better understand the facts, the enormous cost of discovery makes it a very effective instrument to achieve settlement by extortion: the prospect of having to spend hundreds of thousands, if not millions, of dollars in defence of a suit may serve as a strong incentive to "buy out" the plaintiff even if the suit is not believed to have merit. Discovery is said to account for 60% of the time and money spent on lawsuits in the United States, and according to a survey a large majority of litigators for both plaintiffs and defendants said that discovery is used as a weapon to increase a trial's cost and delay to the other side (nearly half said lawyers use it to drive up their own charges).[51] Although a legal institution should not be judged only by looking at the excesses and abuses it makes possible, the sense of crisis in the American legal system is pervasive, and many calls have been made for a reform or even outright abolition of discovery.

(3) Presentation of Evidence

The different concepts of the roles of lawyers and judges lead to important differences in the way evidence is presented at trial. In a continental European trial[52], for instance in a French or German court, the taking of evidence rests under the exclusive control of the judge and is limited in scope. Comparatively little emphasis is placed on direct oral testimony, the decision of the dispute rests primarily on written materials submitted in preparation of the trial. Only in unusual circumstances will the written evidence include documents that were not submitted voluntarily by one of the parties. Although a party may ask the court to order the other party to produce a document, this is rarely done and it is possible only if the requesting party (1) provides a concrete description of the document requested and (2) establishes to the court's satisfaction that the document is in the other side's possession and that it is likely to constitute evidence directly relevant to the final decision.[53] The production of documents is usually not enforced by coercive means but only indirectly, through adverse inference regarding the alleged contents of the document. When oral testimony is held, witnesses are considered to be "the court's witness" – not a witness of any particular party. It is the judge who invites

---

[51]   Id.

[52]   See Reymond, "Civil Law and Common Law Procedures: Which is the More Inquisitorial? A Civil Lawyer's Response", 5 *Arb. Int'l* 357 (1989); for a brief overview see Lecuyer-Thieffry & Thieffry, "Negotiating Settlement of Disputes Provisions in International Business Contracts", 45 *Bus. Law.* 577, 583-585 (1990).

[53]   Cf. French New Code of Civil Procedure, Arts 138-142; the German Code of Civil Procedure ("*Zivilprozessordnung*" – ZPO) is even more restrictive, requiring a basis in substantive law and an acknowledgment by the other party that it is in possession of the document, ZPO sec. 421-425.

the witnesses, and it is his decision whether to follow the lawyers' proposals as to who will be asked to appear. When witnesses appear, it is generally the judge who poses the questions. Direct contact before or during the trial between a lawyer for one of the parties and a witness is severely restricted. In France it is categorically prohibited and may lead to serious sanctions for professional misconduct, whereas in Germany it is permitted as long as any appearance of an attempt of influencing the testimony is avoided. If experts are appointed, they are the experts of the court and have to provide neutral testimony, usually in writing, but in the court's discretion an expert can be asked to appear in court to explain his findings.[54] The parties themselves cannot appear as witnesses, they may only testify in a different capacity, as parties, and in some countries only at the request of the court or with the opposing party's consent.[55]

By contrast, in a Common Law trial, the gathering of evidence is conducted by the parties and is very broad in scope. Much more emphasis is placed on the actual hearing and on oral testimony. Through the process of pre-trial discovery, the lawyers have access to the physical evidence in the possession of the other side. Both sides appear with "their" witnesses, including the parties who have the same status as witnesses and may be called to swear an oath. Usually, the lawyers will have interviewed the witnesses before the trial and may even have "rehearsed" with the witnesses the testimony to be given in court. Witnesses are interrogated by the lawyers, first by counsel for the party who presented the witness (direct examination), after which opposing counsel has an opportunity to challenge the testimony by posing his own questions to the witness (cross-examination). The judge supervises this process and may intervene, at his own initiative or – more likely – at the objection of opposing counsel, when he deems particular questions improper (e.g. "leading questions" or questions directed at "hearsay" knowledge). Experts are also presented by the parties and will be subjected to direct and cross examination. Often, both parties will present experts who will give conflicting assessments of the technical facts at issue, which often prompts the courts to appoint a third, "independent" expert. Traditionally, the judge hardly interferes in examination of witnesses and experts but simply watches the spectacle in front of him and in the end makes up his mind based on the evidence the lawyers have laid out before him.

---

[54] Lecuyer-Thieffry & Thieffry, "Negotiating Settlement of Disputes Provisions in International Business Contracts", 45 *Bus. Law.* 577, 584 (1990).

[55] Cf. for Germany Fischer-Zernin & Junker, "Between Scylla and Charybdis: Fact Gathering in German Arbitration", 4 (2) *J. Int'l Arb.* 9, 25 (1987); for France: Lecuyer-Thieffry and Thieffry, "Negotiating Settlement of Disputes Provisions in International Business Contracts", 45 *Bus. Law.* 577, 584. (1990).

Another difference relates to the method of recording testimony: the Common Law tradition calls for literal transcripts of the entire testimony whereas in Civil Law systems, the judge will usually dictate a summary of the testimony.[56]

c. Judicial Conflicts of Gathering Evidence Abroad

The dramatic differences between legal systems in the methods and scope of evidence gathering in civil litigation led to significant practical problems and frictions in the conduct of transnational litigation. Conflicts between legal systems emerged primarily when American courts decided to by-pass the bureaucratic channels and used their personal jurisdiction over foreign litigants as a basis for ordering discovery to be held in foreign countries. In most cases, discovery conducted without the consent of the local authorities represents a violation of the local country's sovereignty and of its laws[57] because in most countries the taking of evidence is regarded as an official function within the exclusive domain of the courts.

The desire to set up a system to bridge differences between the Common Law and Civil Law approaches to the taking of evidence abroad and to provide a set of effective, streamlined procedures for judicial assistance led to the development of the Hague Convention on the Taking of Evidence Abroad[58] which was ratified by the United States, Britain, France, Germany and a number of other significant trading nations. The Convention embodies a diplomatic compromise by which countries with very extensive methods of evidence gathering consented to respect the judicial sovereignty of countries with more restrictive policies, whereas the latter countries agreed to assist with discovery requests that require the conduct of procedures alien to its judicial traditions.

However, resort to the Convention has been limited. American courts frequently by-pass the Convention and issue orders for discovery abroad based on the personal jurisdiction over foreign litigants. As a result, the Hague Convention has not been able to prevent conflicts between the judiciaries to the extent it had been hoped for. If anything, judicial conflicts, mainly between the United States and other countries, including the United Kingdom and Canada, have increased in the last decades. Several countries have enacted "blocking statutes" specifically designed

---

[56] Reymond, "Civil Law and Common Law Procedures: Which is the More Inquisitorial? A Civil Lawyer's Response", 5 *Arb. Int'l* 357 (1989).

[57] Cf. Art. 271 of the Swiss Penal Code: "Whoever, on Swiss Territory, without being authorized to do so, takes on behalf of a foreign government any action which is solely in the province of a [Swiss] government authority or a [Swiss] government official ... shall be punished by imprisonment, in serious cases in the penitentiary" (translation taken from Vagts, "Dispute-Resolution Mechanisms in International Business", 203 *Recueil des Cours* 17, 48 n86 (1987-III)).

[58] Hague Convention on the Taking of Evidence Abroad in Civil and Commercial Matters, opened for signature June 1, 1970, entered into force October 7, 1972, 8 *Int'l Leg. Mat.* 37 (1969), 847 UNTS 231.

to defend a country's judicial sovereignty against what is viewed as an exorbitant reach of extra-territorial jurisdiction coupled with excessively intrusive discovery methods. The consequence of these conflicts between judicial systems is that often the foreign litigant in an American lawsuit is placed in the unenviable situation of being squeezed[59] between the potentially serious punishments imposed by his home country for cooperating with the American discovery request made outside the Convention and the potentially equally serious sanctions the American court can impose in case of non-cooperation[60]

3. Substantive Law

Another source of uncertainty in international litigation is the multiplicity of substantive laws that might compete for application to the dispute. Absent a clear and unmistakable contractual stipulation of the applicable law, national courts will apply their own choice of law provisions in order to determine which law to apply. Often, this will be a difficult decision because many transnational disputes have connections with several legal systems. Even where the determination of the applicable law is fairly straightforward or has been effectuated by the parties, it may be hard to predict any outcome when a national court has to apply foreign law. Contracts, statutes and judicial precedents may have to be translated and experts may have to be hired to testify as to how a foreign law would be applied to the case at issue, and even an enlightened court may in the end lack the background knowledge to comprehend the essence of a law embodied in an unfamiliar legal tradition.

4. The Effect of Foreign Judgments

Due to the territorial limitations of jurisdictions, a court judgment has no force outside the jurisdiction where it is rendered. In a foreign country, it can only have an effect if it is recognized by the competent authority, usually the courts of that country. This is of great practical importance because in a foreign jurisdiction, *recognition* is a requirement both for the *finality* of a judgment and for its *enforcement*. A foreign judgment will only have the effect of a final decision (*"res judicata"*) and the power to preclude re-litigation of the same claim if it is recognized in that jurisdiction. And it is only through the competent local authorities that a foreign judgment can be enforced.

Absent treaty obligations, however, states are under no obligation to recognize foreign judgments. The mutual recognition of judgments and other official acts

---

[59]   The term "squeeze" is taken from Salacuse, *Making Global Deals* 104 (1991).

[60]   These can include imprisonment for contempt of court, financial penalties, restrictions on the ability to defend its claim or, in the extreme case, a judgment by default; cf. Fed. R. Civ. P. Rule 37.

has to rely on the comity of nations ("comitas gentium", "courtoisie"), a loosely defined notion by which states (voluntarily) afford recognition to the legislative, executive and judicial acts of another nation, as long as this creates no conflict with their own interests. The practice in most countries is to recognize some judgments and to reject others, after a case-by-case examination of factors such as the original jurisdiction of the court that issued the judgment, due process, and the absence of any discrepancy with important public policies (*ordre public*) of the recognizing state. How generous or restrictive the practice turns out, varies not only from country to country but also among various jurisdictions within a country. Some countries insist on reciprocity and require that the party seeking recognition shows that comparable judgments from the jurisdiction where recognition is sought would be recognized in the country where the judgment at issue originated. Other countries require that the judgment be in harmony with its own conflict of laws provisions, and some even review the substance of the judgment and refuse recognition if it is incompatible with local law ("revision au fond"). In some cases, enforcement of foreign judgments may even be prevented or reversed by "blocking statutes" (see above at p. 24).

A notable exception is the practice established in Europe under the above mentioned Brussels I Regulation obliging the member states to recognize and enforce judgments entered into by courts of other signatory states. Only a few limited grounds for refusal are specified. These are (1) lack of jurisdiction, (2) improper service in case of default judgments, and (3) violation of the recognizing state's fundamental *international* public policy.[61] A few other multilateral conventions exist but have little practical significance.[62] A few bilateral treaties deal with the enforcement of judgments, but their relevance has never been great and was in part superseded by the Brussels Convention/Regulation. As mentioned, the United States is party to no such agreement.

---

[61] The Regulation further reduces uncertainty by establishing clear standards for jurisdiction, thus practically eliminating the potential for refusal on jurisdictional grounds, by spelling out the procedures and competent authorities, and by securing uniform application of the Regulation through the European Court of Justice's final authority of interpretation.

[62] For instance, the Hague Convention on the Recognition and Enforcement of Foreign Judgments in Civil and Commercial Matters, reprinted in 15 *Am. J. Comp. L.* 362 (1967) which was only adhered to by Cyprus, the Netherlands, and Portugal; another example is the 1979 Montevideo Convention on the Extraterritorial Validity of Foreign Judgments and Arbitral Awards (English text reprinted in 18 *Int'l. Leg. Mat.* 1211 (1979)) which has had very little effect partly because the Convention failed to specify the exact criteria according to which the "recognizing" court should determine the validity of jurisdiction of the judgment court.

V. CONCLUSION: NEED FOR CONFLICT MANAGEMENT

In a globalized world, international business transactions are increasing in number, size and complexity. Complex economic exchange relationships are faced with considerable uncertainty. They are governed by a web of legal and non-legal rules and sanctions. The inherent limitations of nonlegal governance mechanisms make legal mechanisms indispensable in achieving stability.

Resolving international business disputes by means of litigating in national courts, however, is confronted with many risks:

1. It may already be difficult to find an appropriate forum; if the courts of several countries claim jurisdiction over the same dispute, simultaneous litigation in several jurisdictions can ensue; as a result, litigants will have to defend themselves in two or more courts at the same time and may get caught in a battle of conflicting anti-suit injunctions; if the jurisdictional conflict is not resolved, courts may issue conflicting judgments in the same matter.

2. During the procedure, litigants will be concerned with the neutrality of the court and may be forced to seek and present evidence or tolerate the taking of evidence by the other side through unfamiliar methods; due to certain fundamental differences between legal systems, litigants may even be caught in judicial conflict that can result in a squeeze between discovery orders and blocking statutes.

3. Additional uncertainty results when national courts have to select the applicable law and possibly have to apply foreign laws.

4. And a judgment may not be of much worth outside the jurisdiction where it was obtained.

Evidently, not all of these potential risks and problems will arise in any given case, and good litigation planning/management may avoid some of the pitfalls of transnational litigation. However, a high dose of uncertainty is inevitable, and it is the deficiencies of litigating international disputes in national courts that have been the major factor for the rise of international commercial arbitration to being the "preferred" means of dispute resolution in international business.

PART TWO:
INTERNATIONAL COMMERCIAL ARBITRATION

In light of the problems associated with transnational litigation in national courts and since international commercial tribunals are still to be created, arbitration has become the "preferred" mode of dispute resolution in international business. In the words of an experienced practitioner:

> "... we've come pretty far with having a straightforward means of dispute resolution: the courts are no longer the place for international business, it's international commercial arbitration, with all of its flaws; at least it's recognized, it's uniform, it's enforceable, it's in place and about as fair as you can make it ..."[63]

Part Two examines how international commercial arbitration works and how its legal framework copes with the problems of litigating in a multi-jurisdictional context (Chapter Two) and presents the process and the cost structure of the process as well as recent trends in the field of international commercial arbitration (Chapter Three). Finally, Part Two introduces and explains the results of surveys conducted by the authors in 1996 and 2004, aiming at defining the contemporary status quo of both arbitration and settlement (Chapter Four).

---

[63]   Interview with Gerald Aksen, January 21, 1992.

Chapter 2

Background, Legal and Institutional Framework

I. BACKGROUND

Arbitration, as a response to the specific demands of commerce,[64] is a private process for the binding resolution of a dispute through the decision of one ore more private individuals selected by the parties to the dispute. Compared to other methods of third-party intervention, it is distinguished from court adjudication through its private nature and from mediation or conciliation[65] through its binding character. Some scholars include the rendering of a non-binding opinion in the term "arbitration", but for the purposes of this book, the term shall be limited to procedures leading to a binding decision.

1. History

Together with mediation, which denotes dispute settlement through the intervention by a third party not empowered to render a binding decision, arbitration is probably the oldest means of peaceful dispute resolution in humanity. It certainly preceded adjudication through state courts, and in all likelihood archaic forms of arbitration preceded the existence of states themselves. Together with mediation, from which it was originally not clearly distinguished, it can be seen as the natural form of dispute resolution within social groups: if two members of the group are unable to reach agreement they will turn to another member who enjoys the trust of both and who is asked to find a solution. And again naturally, mediation would blend into arbitration because the third party would normally first try to reconcile the two disputants and help them to reach an agreement before resorting to his ultimate authority to spell out a binding solution.

Commercial arbitration is probably as old as commerce itself. In the Anglo-American world, mercantile dispute resolution through merchants can be traced back to the 13th century where they sat as private judges in "piepowder courts",

---

[64]   Drahozal, "Commercial Norms, Commercial Codes, and International Commercial Arbitration", 33 *Vanderbild Journal of Transnational Law* 79-134 (2000).

[65]   In accordance with the prevailing international practice, the terms are used synonymously in this book.

staple courts and on tribunals of the merchant guilds and trading companies.[66] In the 18th and 19th century commercial and maritime arbitration was developed under the auspices of trade associations, mercantile, shipping and stock exchanges, chambers of commerce, and toward the end of the 19th century, specialized arbitration institutions. The first international arbitration institution with a global reach was the Court of Arbitration of the International Chamber of Commerce (ICC).[67] The ICC is a non-governmental "world business organization", founded in 1919. From its inception, the ICC offered assistance in the organization of conciliation and arbitration procedures. The Court of Arbitration was established in 1923 at the seat of the headquarters of the ICC in Paris.

Since the foundation of the ICC Court of Arbitration ("ICC Court"), the history of arbitration has been characterized by a dramatic expansion of the caseload, by rising stakes and increasing complexity of the disputes, by growing participation of governments and of parties from non-European countries, and perhaps most importantly by a change in the nature of the procedures away from an informal "merchant's justice" towards professionalism, legalism and proceduralization. During the first 20 years of its existence, the great majority of cases administered by the ICC were disposed of by conciliation.[68] In 2003, the proportion of conciliation/ADR cases had sunk to 1,4%.[69] And whereas traditionally commercial arbitration was handled by "commercial men", and today still is in certain specialized types of arbitrations, in ICC arbitration nowadays the number of lawyers acting as arbitrators has been estimated at 97%.[70]

2. Attributes of International Commercial Arbitration

Arbitration can be defined as private adjudication based on an agreement between the parties. These elements, as well as the terms "international" and "commercial" shall be explained briefly.

---

[66] Mentschikoff, "Commercial Arbitration", 61 *Col. L. Rev.* 847, 854-856 (1961).

[67] Craig, Park & Paulsson, *International Chamber of Commerce Arbitration* (2000).

[68] Eisemann, "Conciliation as a Means of Settlement of International Business Disputes: the UNCITRAL Rules as Compared with the ICC System", in: *The Art of Arbitration* (Liber Amicorum for Pieter Sanders) 124 (1982).

[69] Eight requests for ADR were filed in 2003, as compared to 580 requests for arbitration, statement by Mr. Emmanuel Jolivet (General Counsel International Court of Arbitration ICC), April 30, 2004.

[70] Informal ICC estimate cited by Ulmer, "Winning the Opening Stages of an ICC Arbitration", 8 (2) *J. Int'l Arb.* 33, 40 n21 (1991); a 1983 study of 100 ICC arbitrations, conducted under a number of legal systems, had revealed a degree of 94%. According to Mr. Jolivet (cf. previous footnote above), most arbitrators are lawyers, but people with other backgrounds have served as arbitrators in 2003 as well, e.g. a manager or an executive in the hotel or insurance industries.

a. Adjudication

Adjudication is a process in which disputants present proofs and arguments to a neutral *third party* who has the power to hand down a *binding decision*, generally based on objective standards. The two prototypes of adjudication are litigation in the courts (public adjudication) and arbitration (private adjudication).

b. Private

Arbitration is private adjudication because it is based on and governed by a private agreement, it is conducted in a private setting, the decision is entrusted to a private individual, and the parties are either private individuals or entities, or they are public entities acting in a commercial capacity. However, strictly speaking, arbitration has a *hybrid character* because it is a private process that depends for its effectiveness and validity on the support of the public legal system, and because it has *public effects* comparable to the judgment of public court.[71]

c. Agreement

Arbitration is of a hybrid nature in a second way: it depends on the consent of the parties but once this consent is given, the parties are bound by the decision regardless of whether they accept it. In selecting arbitration, the parties agree to submit their dispute to a private tribunal[72], to exclude the jurisdiction of the public courts, and to abide by the decision of that tribunal. The arbitration agreement also serves to lay down the rules of procedure to the extent permitted by the law of the state in which the arbitration takes place (*"lex fori doctrine"*). Two types of arbitration agreements exist, the submission of future disputes through an *arbitration clause* (*"clause compromissoire"*) that is included in or annexed to the principal contract, or the submission of an existing dispute to arbitration by means of a *submission agreement* (*"compromis"*). The majority of international arbitration today is conducted on the basis of a contractual arbitration clause.[73]

d. Commercial

No universal definition exists for "commercial" transactions, disputes or arbitrations. The term has significance for international arbitration because under the laws of some states, only "commercial" disputes can be submitted to arbitration, a fact that is recognized by international conventions such as the 1958 "New York

---

[71] Cf. Redfern & Hunter, *Law and Practice of International Commercial Arbitration* 11 (3rd ed. 1999).

[72] Unless otherwise indicated, the terms "tribunal" and "arbitrator" are meant to include both arbitrators acting alone and tribunals of several, normally three, arbitrators.

[73] Redfern & Hunter, *Law and Practice of International Commercial Arbitration* 6 (3rd ed. 1999).

Convention" (see below at p. 57 et seq.) that allows states to exclude disputes from its application which are not regarded as commercial under their internal laws[74]. In addition, the term commercial is used to denote acts of sovereigns that are not covered by sovereign immunity and to distinguish between "international commercial arbitration" (governed by private law) and "international arbitration" of disputes between states under public international law.

e. International

"International" can be defined with regard either to the *nature of the dispute*[75] or to the *nationality or residence of the parties*.[76] In order to avoid confusions stemming from the synonymous use, commonly encountered in the English language, of "international law" and "public international law", the term "transnational" is sometimes used to denote incidents which in some way transcend national boundaries.[77] For the purposes of this book, the terms international and transnational will be used synonymously, under a broad definition covering occurrences that are related to international trade either through their nature or through the fact that they involve nationals or residents, including corporations, of different countries.

3. Types of International Commercial Arbitration

Within international commercial arbitration, four important distinctions can be made. One is between general arbitration and specialized arbitration, in particular industries such as commodities trade and shipping, another is between institutional and ad hoc arbitration, the next is between arbitration in law, "amiable composition", and arbitration in equity, and the last is between judicial arbitration and contractual arbitration for the adaptation or the filling of gaps in contracts.

a. Specialized Arbitration

In sheer numbers, specialized forms of international arbitration surpass non-specific commercial arbitration by a wide margin. Maritime, insurance and commodities trade arbitrations are held by the thousands in cities like London or New York. They are conducted mostly in an ad-hoc fashion or under the auspices of a particular trade association or mercantile exchange, according to specialized arbitration rules, typically by experts from the trade, and frequently at the exclusion of lawyers both

---

[74] Art. I (3) of the New York Convention ("Commercial Reservation").

[75] Cf. Art. 1492 of the French Code of Civil Procedure: "… involves the interests of international trade".

[76] Cf. Art. I 1(a) of the European Convention of 1961: "… international trade between physical or legal persons having, when concluding the [arbitration] agreement, their habitual residence or their seat in differing Contracting States."

[77] Cf. Jessup, *Transnational Law* (1956).

from the tribunal and from the representation of parties. Specialized arbitrations take place in a universe of their own. And although they doubtless are international, commercial, and arbitrations, they are commonly not covered by the general literature on international commercial arbitration. Since they are highly specialized, they will not be further dealt with here.

b. Institutional and Ad Hoc Arbitration

Historically, the parties used to spell out the procedures in the arbitration agreement, and when the dispute arises jointly select the arbitrator(s) and work out the details of the procedure together with the tribunal which under most laws is empowered to devise its own procedure. This type of customized procedure is called "ad hoc" arbitration. By default, the way in which arbitrations are conducted is "ad hoc" unless the parties agree to employ the services of an arbitration institution.[78]

Arbitration institutions provide model arbitration clauses and, most importantly, ready-made arbitration rules – often in many different languages[79] -, drafted by experts and in many cases continually refined over the course of decades of experience. In addition, the institution helps with the selection of the place of the arbitration, the appointment and – where necessary – replacement of the arbitrator(s), and offers several other forms of assistance with the proceedings such as the fixing and processing of the arbitrators' fees or the administration of time limits. Finally, many institutions also render logistical support like the transmittal of written pleadings and documents, or the selection and reservation of hearing rooms. Among the major institutional providers[80] figure the International Chamber of Commerce (ICC), the London Court of International Arbitration (LCIA) and the American Arbitration Association (AAA) whose procedures will serve as illustration and references throughout this book. All three institutions have recently revised their rules in order to maintain the attractiveness of international commercial arbitration by, inter alia, reducing delays and allowing for more flexibility in the conduct of the procedures.[81]

---

[78] For empirical insights about perceived differences between ad hoc and institutional arbitration, compare the recent study *Patterns and Discontinuities in International Commercial Arbitration: The Global Center Survey of Practicioners* (May 24, 2005), at Chapter VI; the webpage of the Global Center for Dispute Resolution Research can be found at www.globalcenteradr.org.

[79] The ICC Arbitration Rules are available online in fourteen languages (Arabic, Brazilian Portuguese, Chinese, Czech, Dutch, English, French, German, Italian, Japanese, Polish, Russian, Spanish and Turkish) at www.iccwbo.org/court/english/arbitration/rules.asp.

[80] For an overview see Redfern & Hunter, *Law and Practice of International Commercial Arbitration* 50-52 (3rd ed. 1999); contact details including the respective websites can be found in the appendix of this book.

[81] Cf. Lalonde, "The New LCIA Rules", in: Barin, *Carswell's Handbook of International Dispute Resolution Rules* 71 (1999); Bond, "The Rules of Arbitration of the International

Perhaps the most important advantage of institutional arbitration is a certain measure of *convenience, security and administrative effectiveness.*[82] Before a dispute has arisen, it is generally very difficult to ascertain what the exact nature of the dispute will be, what kind of procedure will be most appropriate, what contingencies will have to be taken into account and whether both sides will cooperate to get the matter resolved. Negotiating and drafting an arbitration clause that covers all these considerations is a difficult, time-consuming and costly exercise. The use of recognized model arbitration rules ensures that the process will take place, that it will be reasonably fair and efficient, that it will lead to a decision, and that this decision will be enforceable.

Another very important advantage of institutional arbitration is that the prestige and the track record of the institution strengthen the *credibility of awards* and thus facilitates both voluntary compliance and enforcement.[83] In the case of ICC arbitration, confirmation of the terms of reference and scrutiny of the draft award further enhance this credibility because a court deciding over the validity or enforceability of the award will have the assurance that a neutral and competent authority has supervised the procedure and has certified the existence of a prima facie agreement to arbitrate and that the procedure complied with the rules, and was therefore "in accordance with the agreement of the parties" (Art. V 1 (d) New York Convention).[84]

The *disadvantages of institutional arbitration* are mainly the additional cost of the administrative fee[85] and the delays from the sometimes cumbersome administrative procedures. The ICC has also drawn criticism both for requiring the terms of reference and for the institutional review of awards because in each case the procedure may be delayed. As a consequence, the ICC has modified the requirements concerning the Terms of Reference slightly. Another problem in institutional arbitration can be the standardized time limits for responding to the request for arbitration, in case of the ICC, the LCIA and the AAA 30 days.[86] Especially governments with bureaucratic command lines and a naturally slower response time have difficulty in complying with these limits and although extensions are granted fairly liberally

---

Chamber of Commerce" 37, in: *Carswell's Handbook of International Dispute Resolution Rules* (1999).

[82] Compare, for example, the recent study *Patterns and Discontinuities in International Commercial Arbitration: The Global Center Survey of Practicioners* (May 24, 2005), at 57.

[83] Id.

[84] Cf. *Carte Blanche (Singapore) Pte., Ltd. v. Carte Blanche International, Ltd.*, 888 F.2d 260 (2d cir. 1989).

[85] For details on the calculation of fees in international arbitration see below at p. 91 et seq.

[86] Cf. Art. 5.1 ICC Rules, 2.1 LCIA Rules, 3.1 AAA Rules.

by the institutions, it puts the respondent in the unfavorable situation of having to ask for a derogation from the rules.[87] Finally, the advantages of guidance by the institution only materialize where the institution is not later contradicted by a state court which vacates the award or refuses its enforcement:

In the much-discussed "Pyramids Arbitration",[88] a crucial preliminary issue was whether the Egyptian government, through the Minister of Tourism, had become a party to a contract between the developer S.P.P. and the Egyptian General Organization for Tourism and Hotels (EGOTH). The contract had envisaged the construction of a resort complex near the Pyramids of Giza and was later canceled by EGOTH in light of vehement protests in Egypt and abroad against a "Disneyland" near the archaeologic site. At the closing of the agreement, which contained a dispute resolution clause calling for ICC arbitration in Paris, S.P.P had insisted that the Minister sign the agreement. The agreement itself did not mention the Egyptian Government as a party. The words "approved, agreed and ratified by the Minister of Tourism" and the Minister's signature led the ICC Court to confirm the prima facie existence of an arbitration agreement binding the Egyptian government. The arbitration tribunal assumed jurisdiction over the Egyptian Government and ordered it to pay USD 12.5 million in damages plus interest and cost to S.P.P. The Government contested the jurisdiction of the arbitration tribunal throughout the proceedings and later successfully attacked the award in the French Courts. The Cour d'Appel in Paris vacated the award on the grounds that the Minister's signature merely ratified EGOTH's entering into the agreement but did not make the Government a party.[89] On the same day, the District Court of Amsterdam arrived at the opposite conclusion and granted leave for enforcement.[90] The claimants in

---

[87] Redfern & Hunter, *Law and Practice of International Commercial Arbitration* 46 (3rd ed. 1999).

[88] *S.P.P. (Middle East) Ltd. and Southern Pacific Properties Ltd. v. The Arab Republic of Egypt and the Egyptian General Organization for Tourism and Hotels*; award published in 22 I.L.M. 752 (1983); the judgment of the Court of Appeal of Paris of July 12, 1984 is reprinted in English in 23 I.L.M. 1048 (1984); the case is discussed in Park, "National Law and Commercial Justice: Safeguarding Procedural Integrity in International Arbitration", 63 *Tul. L. Rev.* 647, 691-692 (1988); Redfern, "Jurisdiction Denied: The Pyramid Collapses", *Journal of Business Law* 15 (1986); Salacuse, *Making Global Deals* 110 (1991); and Wetter, "The Conduct of the Arbitration", 2 (2) *J. Int'l Arb.* 7, 29-30 (1985).

[89] The decision was later confirmed by the French Cour de Cassation, judgment of January 6, 1987; English version in 26 I.L.M. 1004 (1987).

[90] Reprinted English in 24 I.L.M. 1040 (1985). The Dutch action was ultimately dismissed after confirmation of the annulment by the French Cour de Cassation; see Park, "National Law and Commercial Justice: Safeguarding Procedural Integrity in International Arbitration", 63 *Tul. L. Rev.* 647, 692 n. 154 (1988).

the end initiated a new arbitration procedure under the ICSID Convention.[91]

Another case where a decision of the ICC Court was rendered obsolete and an award was canceled at the end of a complete arbitration procedure is the *Sofidif* arbitration. The case involved three related contracts dealing with supplies of enriched uranium from a French company to the Iranian government. There was a certain overlap between the four parties to the three contracts but in no case was the constellation identical. The dispute resolution clauses were not coordinated: one contract provided for French substantive law and ICC arbitration in Paris, another provided for French substantive law and ICC arbitration in Geneva, and the third contract only provided for ICC arbitration but specified neither the applicable substantive law nor the situs of the arbitration. Against the objection of the defendants the ICC Court consolidated the dispute and ordered all three contracts to be arbitrated before a sole arbitrator in Paris. The ensuing award was canceled by the Cour d'Appel in Paris on the basis that the consolidation of arbitral procedures had to be left to the contractual arrangements of the parties.[92]

These may be isolated incidents and in general, the "ICC stamp" does enhance the prospects of achieving a lasting and internationally enforceable award, but the cases show how intricate the legal issues are that arise in the course of transnational arbitration and that the "ICC insurance" is an imperfect one: there will always be a measure of uncertainty over the durability of any results achieved. This uncertainty will be less significant in institutional arbitration than in ad hoc arbitration, and it will be less significant in international commercial arbitration than in transnational litigation but it will always have to be borne in mind when calculating the "legal risks" of international business relationships.

The *advantages of ad hoc arbitration* include the higher amount of party-control over the procedure, greater flexibility to tailor the proceedings to the particulars of the dispute, and savings in terms of the costs and delays associated with institutional arbitration. The advantages of ad hoc arbitration are greatest when the arbitration agreement is made after the dispute arose because then the parties know the requirements for effective dispute resolution. Ad hoc arbitration is frequently used for disputes between governments and foreign corporations. With skilled legal advice, a process can be designed that leads to satisfying results in less time (e.g. through simultaneous rather than sequential exchanges of pleadings) and at lower cost, and fee arrangements with arbitrators can be made that free the parties and the arbitrators of the uncertainty connected with the wide discretion many institutions have – and need – in fixing the fees.[93] However, all these advantages

---

[91] Montagnon, "World Bank Steps Into Egyptian Tourism Row", *Financial Times* 4 (August 5, 1988).

[92] Decision of the December 19, 1986, reprinted in *Rev. Arb.* 359 (1987).

[93] The ICC fixes the fees within a bracket determined by the amount in dispute, cf. Appendix III to the ICC Rules of Arbitration.

are dependent on a certain amount of *cooperation* between the parties both in structuring the procedure and in constituting the arbitral tribunal. This cooperation is often difficult to achieve when the parties are in the midst of a dispute. Hence the *dilemma* of drafting dispute resolution clauses: before the dispute arises, the parties lack the necessary information about the dispute to really cover all aspects that might become relevant – unless they want to cover *every* contingency which, if it is not impossible, will be too expensive to do. And once the dispute has materialized, the parties are often too much at odds with each other – and may be too preoccupied with tactical considerations – to reach agreement about the many issues that have to be covered.

Institutional arbitration comes a long way in solving this dilemma in that it provides a set of rules that can be easily incorporated by reference, and are detailed enough to cover the most important contingencies but sufficiently general to give the parties and the tribunal the flexibility to adapt the proceedings to the particularities of the dispute. And, most importantly, it provides for a neutral authority that warrants the establishment of the tribunal and resolves all deadlocks and disputes about the procedure. Also, many of the logistical services rendered by the institution must be performed by someone and have to be paid for in any event (in major ad hoc arbitration usually a secretary is hired expressly for the administration of the arbitration). The advantages of institutional arbitration may therefore in most cases be well worth the additional expense.

A compromise solution sometimes chosen when the parties do not want to or cannot agree to employ the services of an arbitration institution has been made available through the promulgation in 1976 of the *UNCITRAL Arbitration Rules*.[94] Sponsored by the United Nations, drafted by eminent scholars and practitioners, and available in the six official languages of the United Nations,[95] they offer a detailed, culturally and ideologically neutral set of rules that has found widespread acceptance all over the world. Many arbitration institutions have adopted them in whole or in large part (e.g. the Inter-American Commercial Arbitration Commission), and through the practice of the Iran-United States Claims Tribunal[96] a solid body of published arbitral precedents exists. In addition, the UNCITRAL Rules provide for a procedure to resolve deadlocks in the nomination of the tribunal: the Secretary General of the Permanent Court of Arbitration in The Hague selects an appointing authority which in turn makes the necessary appointments. Finally, most arbitration institutions are offering a reduced service alternative at a substantially reduced

---

[94]   Cf. www.uncitral.org/english/texts/arbitration/arb-rules.htm.

[95]   English, French, Spanish, Arabic, Chinese, and Russian.

[96]   The Tribunal was established in The Hague pursuant to the "Algiers Accords" in the aftermath of the Iranian hostage crisis in order to process claims of American and Iranian nationals that arose after the Iranian Revolution and that operates under the UNCITRAL Arbitration Rules; for general information cf. www.iusct.org.

fee where they serve merely as appointing authority for ad hoc arbitration under the UNCITRAL Rules (e.g. AAA, ICC, LCIA, NAI, SCC). Thus, by agreeing to arbitration under the UNCITRAL Rules and nominating an appointing authority, the parties achieve two of the most important aims of institutional arbitration, namely a set of detailed procedural rules and the certainty that the tribunal will be established.

c. Arbitration in Law, Amiable Composition and Arbitration Ex Aequo et Bono

Unless otherwise specified, arbitration will be held according to rules of law. In cases where the parties fail to specify the applicable law, the arbitrators either choose the law they deem appropriate or proceed on the basis of choice of law rules. Most national laws and many arbitration rules, however, accept the possibility for the parties to grant the arbitrators the powers to decide as amiable compositeurs or according to principles of equity, i.e. *ex aequo et bono*.

Amiable composition is a frequently misunderstood institution of French law that has been adopted by many other Civil Law systems. *Amiable compositeurs* are authorized to disregard certain non-mandatory rules of statutory law. It is important to note that the arbitrator acting as *amiable compositeur* is not free to simply ignore the law[97], he can only disregard non-mandatory provisions, i.e. the provisions which the parties themselves may derogate by contract, and only if he has come to the conclusion that their application would lead to an inequitable result.

Arbitration in equity[98] or *ex aequo et bono* – an institution originating in public international law – is sometimes defined synonymously with *amiable composition* and sometimes understood to grant additional leeway to the arbitrators, allowing them to disregard even the mandatory provisions of law, as long as they respect international public policy.[99] Where this option is contemplated, it is therefore advisable to spell out exactly what the mandate of the arbitrators is.

d. Contractual Gap Filling / Adaptation by Arbitral Tribunals

Since contracts are necessarily incomplete and often provide inadequate solutions for new, unexpected circumstances, it frequently occurs that contractual arrangements have to be completed or that existing provisions have to be adapted in order

---

[97] If he does, the award may be set aside or refused recognition for being beyond the scope of the arbitral agreement (cf. Art. V 1(d) of the New York Convention).

[98] "Equity" in this context refers to what the arbitrators, in good conscience, deem to be "equitable" and has nothing to do with the common law distinction between "law" and "equity". For a discussion of the various definitions of this notion of equity see Redfern & Hunter, *Law and Practice of International Commercial Arbitration* 127-128 (3rd ed. 1999).

[99] Lecuyer-Thieffry and Thieffry, "Negotiating Settlement of Disputes Provisions in International Business Contracts", 45 *Bus. Law.* 577, 592 at n. 75 (1990).

to adequately cope with the new situation. If the parties are unable to agree, the issue is whether arbitrators may substitute their decision and change the substance of the contractual relation, thereby creating new substantive provisions.[100] Under many national legal systems, a distinction is made between judicial arbitration for the resolution of disputes, and contractual arbitration where the substance of the contractual relation is determined by a third party. Creating new substantive rules through contractual adaptation or the filling of gaps is frequently regarded to be outside the scope of judicial arbitration, as it is also outside the mission of state judges. This can be of crucial importance in the enforcement of the award because it might be refused the status of arbitral award and the accompanying benefits like recognition and enforcement under the New York Convention.[101]

It is helpful to distinguish between overt and "veiled" contract adaptation or gap-filling. Where the parties have *expressly granted adaptation powers* it depends on the place of the arbitration or the procedural law under which the arbitration is conducted[102] whether the arbitrators can actually exercise this power without endangering the status of their decision as a regular arbitral award. It is important therefore to verify this point before according these powers (from the parties' perspective) or using them (from the arbitrators' perspective). Where the parties have made no express stipulation, it could be argued that reference to institutional arbitration rules can create such powers. With most rules this is not the case, e.g the ICC has made clear that its rules do not confer such powers.[103] An indirect way to confer adaptation powers may be by means of bestowing *amiable compositeur* status on the arbitrator. It has been argued that a certain "modification capacity" (which does not go so far as to authorize a "revision" of the contract) is inherent in the concept of *amiable composition* but the issue is hotly debated and, again, extreme caution is recommendable.[104]

---

[100] This situation has to be distinguished from the mere "rectification" of technical mistakes in the contract where the form (the actual wording) is brought in accordance with the agreed but not accurately recorded substance (the parties' intention) of the contract; cf. Redfern & Hunter, *Law and Practice of International Commercial Arbitration* 369 (3rd ed. 1999).

[101] Peter, "Arbitration and Renegotiation Clauses", 3 (2) *J. Int'l Arb.* 29, 39-45 (1986).

[102] Since it is this law that determines the status and validity of the award, cf. Art. V 2.(e) New York Convention.

[103] Redfern & Hunter, *Law and Practice of International Commercial Arbitration* 369 (3rd ed. 1999).

[104] For a detailed discussion under French law see de Boisseson, *Le Droit Français de l'Arbitrage – Interne et International* 317-321 (1989).

II. LEGAL FRAMEWORK OF INTERNATIONAL COMMERCIAL ARBITRATION

As mentioned above, arbitration is a private process with public legal effects. In order to have these public effects private arbitration needs the support of the public legal system, and *international* arbitration will invariably need the support of more than one national legal system. International commercial arbitration is governed by the private regime of the arbitration agreement, which includes any arbitration rules incorporated by reference, the powers conferred upon the arbitral tribunal and any additional powers granted an arbitration institution, and by the public regime of national legal systems and international conventions. Through a highly complex interaction, national legal systems and international conventions combine to provide the framework within which international arbitration is conducted. It is important to understand this context in order to understand the process of arbitration and the motivations of the parties selecting it.

Before dealing with the process itself (see Chapter 3), we will therefore take a brief look at the legal framework surrounding international commercial arbitration. We will first look at national laws and then at the coordination of these national laws achieved through international arbitration conventions.

1. National Legal Systems

As mentioned above, three levels of legal regimes are governing international commercial arbitration: the contractual arrangements of the parties, the various national legal systems that have an impact on the arbitration, and international agreements between states. Among these levels of governance, the national legal systems are of central importance because it is the national legal systems that determine the validity and the effect of the arbitration agreement, and it is also the national legal systems that incorporate and implement any pertinent international conventions. Or put inversely: as a practical matter, the private arbitration agreement as well as any international conventions will only have the effect that national legal systems confer upon them.[105]

a. The Limits of "Delocalization"

The dependence of international commercial arbitration on national legal systems is sometimes seen as an obstacle to dispute resolution in international trade. Over the last decades, scholarly discussion dealt with the notion of a truly international, "delocalized" system of international commercial arbitration which operates

---

[105] States have adopted different methods, and different scholarly theories exist, with respect to the effect that international agreements have on the internal legal order of states. For the purposes of this book, however, it is sufficient to acknowledge that in practice it is up to each national legal system to implement the norms spelled out in an international agreement.

independently of all national legal systems, or at least independently of the national law of the place where the arbitration is held.[106] This may (or may not[107]) be a desirable aim, and in the limited field of investment arbitrations between states and private investors this aim has, to a limited extent, been achieved under the mechanism established by the ICSID Convention. However, outside of this strictly limited field, the reality of international commercial arbitration is still dominated by national legal systems and in particular by the law of the "situs" of the arbitration, and it would take considerable time and effort to achieve a truly "denationalized" system of international business dispute resolution.[108] Thus, some commentators conclude that the delocalization development has ended in failure.[109]

In a more limited sense of the word, the parties can to a certain extent "delocalize" the arbitration through the selection of the law applicable to the procedure. Generally, the law applicable to the procedure will be the local law of the place where the arbitration is conducted and, to the extent permissible under *that* law, the procedural rules agreed upon by the parties and, failing such agreement, the rules determined by the arbitral tribunal. Part of the choice open to the parties – but not to the arbitrators if the parties fail to agree – is the possibility to "delocalize" the arbitration by having the procedure governed by the national law of a country other than the situs of the arbitration. This possibility is expressly contemplated by the New York Convention[110] and a number of national arbitration statutes.[111] Such a choice may have advantages in that it permits to choose a procedural law that is

---

[106] For a discussion of the "delocalization theory" see Park, "The *Lex Loci Arbitri* and International Commercial Arbitration", 32 I.C.L.Q. 21 (1983), and the response by Paulsson, "Delocalization of International Commercial Arbitration: When and Why it Matters", 32 I.C.L.Q. 53 (1983); see also Lecuyer-Thieffry and Thieffry, "Negotiating Settlement of Disputes Provisions in International Business Contracts", 45 *Bus. Law.* 577, 599-622 (1990) and Redfern & Hunter, *Law and Practice of International Commercial Arbitration* 89-92 (3rd ed. 1999).

[107] A forceful defense of a minimum of local court control over international arbitrations can be found in Park, "National Law and Commercial Justice: Safeguarding Procedural Integrity in International Arbitration", 63 *Tul. L. Rev.* 647 (1988); see also Reisman, *Systems of Control in International Adjudication and Arbitration: Breakdown and Repair* 107 et seq. (1992).

[108] For some interesting and innovative suggestions, centering around the institution of a supranational "International Arbitral Court of Appeal" see Rubino Sammartano, *International Arbitration Law* 510-512 (1989).

[109] Cf. Redfern & Hunter, *Law and Practice of International Commercial Arbitration* 89 (3rd ed. 1999).

[110] Cf. Art. V. New York Convention: "Recognition and enforcement of the award may be refused ... if ... (e) The award ... has been set aside or suspended by a competent authority of the country in which, or under the law of which, that award was made."

[111] E.g. Art. 1493 of the French Code of Civil Procedure.

especially well fitted to the anticipated needs of the particular arbitration procedure but it creates complications that may warrant second thoughts. Choosing a foreign procedural law (from the perspective of the situs) may make it more difficult to obtain the assistance of local courts e.g. for interim measures of protection.[112] The influence of the local courts on the arbitration can only be limited to the extent that the local law permits. And even countries that are very liberal with international arbitrations held in their territory do not completely renounce control. Finally, where a foreign procedural law is chosen, another forum is created where the award may be vacated.[113]

b. The Interaction of National Laws

Every international arbitration is impacted by at least two, and potentially many more, national legal systems. These are:

- the law governing the parties' capacity to enter into an arbitration agreement;[114]

- the law governing the arbitration agreement;

- the law of the situs of the arbitration;

- the procedural law, if any, chosen to govern the arbitration (which does not completely supersede the impact of the law of the situs);

- the law applicable to the substance of the dispute;[115]

- the law of any country where provisional remedies or judicial assistance with the gathering of evidence is requested;

- the law of any country where recognition and enforcement of the award is sought;

- the law of any country where competing judicial proceedings are initiated;

Obviously, this multiplicity of laws creates the potential for significant uncertainties, comparable to the pitfalls encountered in transnational litigation. And, as is the case with transnational litigation, the rising stakes at issue and the increasing

---

[112] If, for instance, local courts can decline jurisdiction over interim measures when arbitration is to be held abroad, they might well do the same where the arbitration is held locally but under express exclusion of the local procedural laws.

[113] Cf. Art. V 1 (e) New York Convention.

[114] State entities are sometimes restricted in this capacity, e.g. in France, Belgium and Saudi-Arabia; for details see Redfern & Hunter, *Law and Practice of International Commercial Arbitration* 146-147 (3rd ed. 1999).

[115] This may or may not be a national law since parties sometimes specify that their relations be governed e.g. by "the principles of international trade law".

sophistication of parties and lawyers have facilitated the development of a large arsenal of tactical maneuvers that exploit the frictions between multiple legal systems to help unwilling defendants evade their obligations.[116] In general, however, the legal framework of international arbitration is superior to that of transnational litigation because certain developments in recent decades have helped reduce, if not eliminate, many of the hazards arising out of the multi-jurisdictional context. The most important factors are the 1958 New York Convention on the Recognition and Enforcement of Foreign Arbitral Awards (the "New York Convention") and the trend in national legislation and court practice around the world towards favorable treatment of international commercial arbitration.

c. The Liberalization of National Arbitration Laws

In a large number of countries, over the last decades fairly liberal arbitration laws have been enacted which to a large degree respect the autonomy of the arbitral process from court intervention and supervision.[117] Of particular importance for the practice are the reforms in France, Switzerland and the United Kingdom because these three countries traditionally have been the seat of the majority of international arbitrations. But even countries that were traditionally hostile to international commercial arbitration are changing their policies. For instance, many Latin American nations have in recent times turned their back on the notorious "Calvo Doctrine" that traditionally forced foreign investors to pursue their claims against host government through the courts of that same state[118] and have enacted new legislation and/or ratified international arbitration conventions. Although there are considerable differences among these laws, most of them provide for:

- ready enforcement of arbitration agreements;

- court assistance with the conduct of the arbitration proceedings;

- fewer mandatory procedural rules and less court interference with arbitration proceedings;

---

[116] For a detailed analysis with colorful examples see Craig, "The Uses and Abuses of Appeal From International Arbitration Awards", in: Southwestern Legal Foundation, *Private Investors Abroad – Problems and Solutions in International Business* Ch. 14 (1988).

[117] Many of these countries adopted the UNCITRAL Model Law on International Commercial Arbitration in whole or in part. Where this was not the case, the Model Law has at least been examined in the drafting process, cf. Roth, "The UNCITRAL Model Law on International Commercial Arbitration", in: Weigand, *Practitioner's Handbook on International Arbitration* 1165 (2002).

[118] For a brief explanation of the "Calvo Doctrine" see Eyzaguirre Echeverria & Siqueiros, "Arbitration in Latin American Countries", in: Van den Berg (ed.), *ICCA Congress Series No. 4*, 81, 83-84 (1989) and Verdross & Simma, *Universelles Völkerrecht* 879-880 (3rd ed. 1984).

- a limited scope of judicial review of arbitral awards rendered within the jurisdiction;

- limited grounds under which local courts can refuse the recognition and enforcement of foreign arbitral awards.

The trend towards granting the arbitral process a larger measure of autonomy has been enhanced by the UNCITRAL Model Law on International Commercial Arbitration in 1985. The Model Law, which facilitates the conduct of arbitration within its ambit and enhances the enforceability of foreign arbitral awards, has been adopted in whole or in part by a large number of jurisdictions.[119]

In addition, national courts have displayed an increasingly favorable attitude towards international arbitration, a tendency exemplified by the decisions of the United States Supreme Court expanding the scope of subject matters that can be submitted to international arbitration into areas that traditionally had been regarded as prerogatives of public policy, such as securities[120] and antitrust[121] law.[122]

d. The Impact of National Legal Systems on Arbitration

As in transnational litigation, the impact of the multiple national legal systems is manifested in several respects: the *jurisdiction* of the arbitral tribunal determines whether the process can validly be conducted at the exclusion of other processes (1); *procedural questions* control how the process is conducted (2); in most cases national laws are applied to the *substance* of the dispute (3); finally the treatment of the award determines what *effect* the results of the process will have (4).

---

[119]   Over 40 countries and several states within the US have enacted legislation based on the Model Law; for a list cf. www.uncitral.org/uncitral/en/uncitral_texts/arbitration/1985Model_arbitration_status.html

[120]   *Scherk v. Alberto-Culver Co.*, 417 U.S. 506 (1974).

[121]   *Mitsubishi Motors Corp. v. Soler Chrysler-Plymouth, Inc.*, 403 U.S. 614, 105 S.Ct. 3346 (1985). The case was regarded as a historic landmark and has been subject to much discussion; cf. Carbonneau, "The Exuberant Pathway to Quixotic Internationalism: Assessing the Folly of Mitsubishi", 19 *Vand. J. Trans. L.* 265 (1986); Lowenfeld, "The Mitsubishi Case: Another View", 2 *Arb. Int'l* 178 (1986); Park, "National Law and Commercial Justice: Safeguarding Procedural Integrity in International Arbitration", 63 *Tul. L. Rev.* 647, 668-670 (1988); and Robert, "Une date dans l'extension de l'arbitrage international: L'Arrêt Mitsubishi c/ Soler", *Rev. Arb.* 173 (1986).

[122]   Also, a combination of legislation in the United States and a Supreme Court Decision has made it easier to compel arbitration by eliminating appeal from decisions referring a dispute to arbitration and by offering appeal where a federal court assumes jurisdiction in spite of an alleged arbitration agreement, see Sec. 16 of the Federal Arbitration Act and *Gulfstream Aerospace Corp. v. Mayacamas Corp.*, 108 S. Ct. 1133 (1988); both are discussed in Medalie, "The New Appeals Amendment: A Step Forward for Arbitration", 44 *Arb. J.* 22 (1989).

(1) Jurisdiction of the Arbitral Tribunal

The jurisdiction of the arbitral tribunal is based on the arbitration agreement, and its effectiveness depends on the respect awarded to this agreement by the national courts that may come into contact with the dispute. Complications arise when the effect of the arbitration agreement is judged differently by the various bodies that may be called to rule on the jurisdiction of the arbitral tribunal:

- the arbitral tribunal itself will have to decide whether to accept or decline jurisdiction over the dispute;

- once the arbitration has begun, the local courts at the situs of the arbitration may be asked to compel arbitration or may have to deal with actions challenging the jurisdiction of the arbitral tribunal;

- in addition, even without directly intervening in the arbitral process, the courts both at the situs of the arbitration and abroad may be asked to rule over the validity of the arbitration agreement at two different phases of the arbitration:
  - they may have to decide upon their own jurisdiction over the dispute when a *competing lawsuit* is initiated before them, either before or during arbitration proceedings; and
  - after the arbitration has been completed, they may have to judge the validity of the arbitration agreement as an incidental question when asked to determine the validity of the ensuing *award*, either in an action to vacate that award in the country where it was rendered, or in an enforcement action abroad.

In the interest of arbitral autonomy from court intervention, two related legal doctrines have been developed that facilitate the acceptance of jurisdiction by the arbitrator. The doctrine of the "severability" or "autonomy" of the arbitration agreement stipulates that the validity of an arbitration clause contained in another contract can be judged independently from the validity of the rest of the contract.[123] This can be helpful when the contract has been terminated or where its contents render the contract void. However, many times the question at issue is whether a contract was formed at all and if so, which parties are bound by the contract. The latter point is particularly relevant in disputes against corporate respondents where the prospects of recovery in practice may depend on whether corporate affiliates can be joined into the arbitration proceedings.[124] Here, "severability" makes no

---

[123] Cf. the codification of the severability doctrine in Art. 15.2 AAA Rules; Art. 6.4 ICC Rules; Art. 23.1 LCIA Rules; Art. 21.2 UNCITRAL Rules; for more details see Redfern & Hunter, *Law and Practice of International Commercial Arbitration* 154-156 (3rd ed. 1999).

[124] Cf. the Pyramids case where the economic success of the claimants' action depended on

difference in the end result because these questions will generally be answered alike for the main body of the contract and for the arbitration clause.

The other important principle in this area is the doctrine of *Kompetenz-Kompetenz* according to which the arbitrator has the competence to rule over his own jurisdiction. Practically all arbitration rules confer this power on the arbitral tribunal,[125] and many legal systems respect this principle,[126] staying litigation and referring the issue of arbitral jurisdiction for determination by the arbitral tribunal rather than interfering with the arbitral process. However, the doctrine of *Kompetenz-Kompetenz* does not insulate the arbitrator's determination form later review by the courts.

Neither does the New York Convention prevent jurisdictional conflicts from emerging since it only mandates that the national courts of the contracting states respect a foreign arbitration agreement but leaves it to the courts to rule on its validity. Further efforts in the international harmonization or, more precisely, coordination of national court systems are warranted. Hence, it is still possible that a court in one member state and an arbitral tribunal in another conduct parallel proceedings on the same matter and reach conflicting results which might even both be enforceable in a third state: for example a court judgment under the Brussels I Regulation, which excludes arbitration from its ambit,[127] and the arbitral award under the New York Convention.

Another problem of parallel proceedings arises in connection with *multi-party disputes*.[128] A large number of international business transactions are conducted today in a triangular or chain structure involving multiple parties. A classical example are construction projects which include the employer, the contractor and a subcontractor or, more commonly, one or more employers, a consortium of contractors, and scores of sub-contractors. Another example are disputes involving the sale and transportation of goods where seller, buyer, agents, and shippers are linked in a chain of transactions. Even where there is only one entity at each intersection of the structure (i.e. only one employer, one contractor and one sub-contractor) the

---

obtaining an award against the Government of Egypt as "parent" to the state hotel corporation EGOTH.

[125] Cf. Art. 15.1 AAA Rules; Art. 23.1 LCIA Rules; Art. 21.1 UNCITRAL Rules.

[126] Cf. Art. 1466 French New Code of Civil Procedure; Art. 186 (1) Swiss Private International Law Act; Art. 16 (1) UNCITRAL Model Law; see also Redfern & Hunter, *Law and Practice of International Commercial Arbitration* 264-268 (3rd ed. 1999).

[127] Art. 1 of the Regulation states that it "shall not apply to [...] (d) arbitration."

[128] For the problems of multi-party arbitration in general see Austmann, "Commercial Multi-Party Arbitration: A Case-by-Case Approach", 1 *Am. Rev. Int'l Arb.* 341 (1990); Chiu, "Consolidation of Arbitral Proceedings and International Commercial Arbitration", 7 (2) *J. Int'l Arb.* 53 (1990); Redfern & Hunter, *Law and Practice of International Commercial Arbitration* 174-183 (3rd ed. 1999).

situation is complex and creates conflicts of interest. Consolidation may be in the interest especially of the party caught in the center of such a constellation, e.g. the contractor sued for damages by the employer for what he thinks are mistakes of the sub-contractor. For such a party it may be risky, costly and cumbersome to litigate on two fronts, in different fora and with potentially conflicting outcomes. The contractor may in one suit be condemned to pay damages to the employer on the basis of a finding of a mistake in the construction, and he may lose his suit for contribution from the sub-contractor if in that suit it is found that no mistake existed. On the other hand, there are often legitimate interests opposing a consolidation, e.g for some parties it may be more convenient only to deal with its immediate counterpart rather than being involved in a costly and lengthy multi-party arbitration.

Although the arbitration statutes in some countries permit the consolidation of related arbitrations by order of the national courts, under most laws it is impossible to join third parties into an existing arbitration or to consolidate separate arbitrations into one proceeding without the consent of all parties involved. Such consent may be given in advance of the dispute as part of an arbitration clause but it is difficult to draft these clauses so as to cover all the contingencies that can arise in a multi-party context in a way that protects the interests of the party for whom the clause is drafted. And reliance on institutional rules and procedures can be risky as the annulment by the French courts of the ICC award in the consolidated *Sofidif* arbitration illustrates.[129]

(1) Procedure Before the Arbitral Tribunal

Once the arbitration is initiated, there are several ways how national legal systems influence the procedure. These can be divided into the supportive function of the national courts (a) and their supervisory function (b).

(a) Support Function of National Courts

Support to the arbitration process can be required from the national legal systems both at the place of the arbitration and abroad. Certain forms of court assistance at the situs of the arbitration can, in ad hoc arbitrations, substitute some of the support functions of arbitration institutions. Thus, the local courts may be asked to *appoint* a sole *arbitrator* or, in a three-arbitrator panel, the chairman or even a party-appointed arbitrator when the respondent refuses to make his appointment.[130]

---

[129] However, the ICC Rules now provide for consolidation at the request of one party (Art. 4.6), while the LCIA Rules make consolidation conditional upon consent of the interested parties (Art. 22.1 (h)).

[130] Cf. Art. 18 (3) of the English Arbitration Act; Art. 1444 and 1493 of the French New Code of Civil Procedure; Sec. 1035 (3) of the German Code of Civil Procedure; Art. 179 of the Swiss Private International Law Act; Sec. 5 of the United States Federal Arbitration Act 1925; Art. 11 UNCITRAL Model Law.

And they may have to *rule on challenges* against arbitrators and *fill vacancies* on the tribunal.[131] The courts in some countries are better prepared for this task than in other countries, but in any event the fact that the courts have to be involved, possibly with several levels of appeals, may lead to significant delay. However, if the parties have not opted for institutional arbitration and have not even provided for an appointing authority, the assistance of the courts may be the only way to make an arbitration happen at all.

Other support functions are genuine to the courts and can involve local courts as well as courts abroad. These are namely the power to compel the *production of evidence* and to mandate *interim measures of protection.*[132] As to the taking of *evidence*, just like in litigation, it may occur that a document has to be produced or testimony obtained from a party to the arbitration or a third party. In most countries the arbitrators do not have subpoena powers and thus have to request the assistance of courts if they want to compel witnesses to appear before the arbitral tribunal or to compel the production of evidence.[133] Court assistance with the taking of evidence abroad cannot be directly requested via the channels established by the *Hague Convention on the Taking of Evidence Abroad* since it only applies to evidence requested by courts. Nonetheless, apparently many of the signatory states to the Hague Convention lend their judicial assistance to arbitral tribunals sitting in another contracting state.[134] Still, the most common way of compelling the production of evidence in arbitration is *indirectly* through the liberty of arbitrators to draw adverse inferences from the unexcused failure to produce the requested evidence.[135]

This form of indirect compulsion, which postpones the sanction for non-cooperation to the stage where the award is made, cannot be employed for *interim measures of protection* which by definition are urgent and cannot wait until the award is made. Here, two possibilities exist. The arbitral tribunal may itself issue an order, say, for the pre-award attachment of certain assets of the defendant which are in danger of deteriorating or being removed, or it may preliminarily enjoin the respondent from discontinuing work on a construction project. Such an order will usually need the

---

[131] Cf. Art. 24, 27 (3) of the English Arbitration Act; Art. 1463, 1444 of the French New Code of Civil Procedure; Sec. 1037 (3) of the German Code of Civil Procedure; Art. 180 of the Swiss Private International Law Act; Art. 13.3 UNCITRAL Model Law.

[132] As far as the arbitral tribunals' powers to issue interim measures are concerned, cf. Redfern & Hunter, *Law and Practice of International Commercial Arbitration* 345-347 (3rd ed. 1999).

[133] Cf. Redfern & Hunter, *Law and Practice of International Commercial Arbitration* 351 (3rd ed. 1999).

[134] Redfern & Hunter, *Law and Practice of International Commercial Arbitration* 322-323 (3rd ed. 1999).

[135] This is also contemplated in certain arbitration statutes, cf. Art. 1460 in connection with Art. 11 (para. 1) of the French New Code of Civil Procedure.

assistance of the courts to be directly enforced.[136] The other alternative is that the parties directly apply for provisional remedies in the competent courts wherever the provisional measure has to take effect, e.g. at the location of assets to be attached.[137] The latter alternative is in most cases preferable because the delays of having to go through the arbitral tribunal *and* the courts may render the requested interim measures moot, particularly in times where assets can be removed "with a twinkle of a telex"[138]. By-passing the arbitral tribunal to obtain interim relief, however, raises legal problems of competing jurisdiction between the arbitral tribunal and the courts. In some cases the possibility to apply for interim measures directly in the courts is granted by statute.[139] Courts in the United States are split over whether the arbitration agreement excludes the jurisdiction of the courts even for provisional measures.[140] And even where the jurisdiction of courts is not excluded altogether, the issue arises whether courts outside of the seat of the arbitration have jurisdiction to grant interim measures.[141] The safe way to assure the effective availability of interim protection is for the parties to stipulate in the arbitration agreement that interim measures can still be requested in the courts.[142] This is also the path chosen by most standard arbitration rules so that their incorporation by reference obviates the need for any specific contractual arrangements.[143]

---

[136] Indirect enforcement is always possible through contractual means: the party ignoring an interim order can be made responsible for any resulting damage.

[137] A third option is the use of review boards or pre-arbitral referees (see below at p. 201 et seq.) who can issue provisional orders but this has to be agreed in advance by the parties; also, it entails similar – and perhaps even greater – enforcement problems as interim measures ordered by an arbitral tribunal.

[138] Cf. Ebb, "Flight of Assets from the Jurisdiction 'In the Twinkling of a Telex': Pre- and Post-Award Conservatory Relief in International Commercial Arbitrations", 7 (1) *J. Int'l Arb.* 9 (1990).

[139] Cf. Art. 9 UNCITRAL Model Law.

[140] Cf. Ebb, "Flight of Assets from the Jurisdiction 'In the Twinkling of a Telex': Pre- and Post-Award Conservatory Relief in International Commercial Arbitrations", 7 (1) *J. Int'l Arb.* 9 (1990); see also Redfern & Hunter, *Law and Practice of International Commercial Arbitration* 348 (3rd ed. 1999).

[141] For England see the decision of the Court of Appeal declining jurisdiction of English courts on preliminary measures in the Eurotunnel dispute on the basis that the courts of the prospective place of the arbitration had exclusive jurisdiction over the arbitration; cf. Davies, "British Court Cannot Stop Suspension of Channel Tunnel Work", *Financial Times* 10 (January 29, 1992) and Lloyd, "Channel Tunnel Dispute Raises International Issues", *Building* (February 7, 1992).

[142] It may also be advisable to specify that jurisdiction over provisional measures is not limited to the courts at the situs of the arbitration to avoid complications as in the Eurotunnel case, see previous n.

[143] Cf. Art. 21.3 AAA Rules; Art. 23.2 ICC Rules; Art. 26.3 UNCITRAL Rules; Art. 25.3 LCIA Rules.

(b) Supervision by National Courts

The most important supervision over the arbitral procedure is the possibility of judicial review of awards. However, occasionally courts intervene directly in the arbitral process, e.g. when ruling on a challenge against an arbitrator. The ultimate avenue of court supervision of arbitration lies in the possible liability of arbitrators for misconduct, to the extent that such a liability exists.[144] This is a matter of national law, in the first place the law of the country where the arbitration is held and in addition the law governing any contractual arrangement between the arbitrator and the parties.[145] Whether an arbitrator should be protected from liability is much debated among scholars and practitioners, and national laws vary between granting complete immunity,[146] qualified immunity[147] and no immunity[148] to arbitrators. However, it is difficult to gauge the real practical relevance of the immunity issue because little case law exists and under laws that provide for arbitrator liability arbitrators will try to obtain a waiver or an indemnity from the parties.[149]

(2) Substance of the Dispute

National laws also have an impact on the *substance* of the arbitration since most arbitrations are decided according to some national law, in the majority of cases a law selected by the parties. It is, however, also possible to "de-nationalize" the applicable substantive law by specifying that the dispute be decided according to general principles of international trade law (either directly, or as a limiting factor when the agreement stipulates that national law applies, but only to the extent that it is not in conflict with these general principles[150]), the provisions that are

---

[144] For a discussion see Hausmaninger, "Civil Liability of Arbitrators – Comparative Analysis and Proposals for Reform", 7 (4) *J. Int'l Arb.* 7 (1990); for an overview see Redfern & Hunter, *Law and Practice of International Commercial Arbitration* 253-260 (3rd ed. 1999).

[145] Whether that relation can be qualified as contractual is disputed, especially in England; for a position rejecting the contractual nature see Mustill & Boyd, *Commercial Arbitration* 222-223 (2nd ed. 1989).

[146] Mainly Common-law countries; cf. Redfern & Hunter, *Law and Practice of International Commercial Arbitration* 256 (3rd ed. 1999).

[147] E.g. Austria, Netherlands; cf. Redfern & Hunter 254-256.

[148] For Arguments against immunity see Redfern & Hunter 255.

[149] Cf. Redfern & Hunter, *Law and Practice of International Commercial Arbitration* 256 (3rd ed. 1999).

[150] Such "concurrent law" clauses are relatively common in foreign investment agreements with developing nations because they represent a compromise between the desire of the host country to see its national law respected and the desire of the foreign investor to be guaranteed an international "minimum standard" of investor protection; cf. Redfern & Hunter, *Law and Practice of International Commercial Arbitration* 104-106 (3rd ed. 1999).

common to several national systems (*"tronc commun"*[151]), or a basically undefined international "law merchant" (*lex mercatoria*).[152] National courts have upheld arbitral awards that were based on an application of denationalized principles of law.[153] However, it is not necessarily wise to exclude the application of any national laws because that may lead to regulatory gaps since many details of commercial reality are not covered by the very general standards of "general principles" or the "law merchant".[154]

The absence under most arbitration laws of a judicial review of the merits of arbitral awards leaves a large measure of discretion even to arbitrators who do not have the powers of *amiable compositeurs* but are held to decide according to rules of law. This freedom is nevertheless not without limits. The borders between procedural review and substantive review are not entirely clear-cut: even where judicial review is limited to the principally procedural standards established in Art. V of the New York Convention or comparable norms in national arbitration laws, a serious departure from the applicable law[155] may be conceived of as "arbitrariness",[156] as an "excess of powers",[157] or as "beyond the scope of the submission".[158]

---

[151] For an explanation of the term see Rubino Sammartano, International Arbitration Law 513 (1989); see also Redfern & Hunter *Law and Practice of International Commercial Arbitration* 107-110 (3rd ed. 1999).

[152] For a discussion of lex mercatoria and other forms of de-nationalized law see the contribution by various authors in Carbonneau (ed.), *Lex Mercatoria and Arbitration: A Discussion of the New Law Merchant* (1990).

[153] For example the Austrian Supreme Court, the French Court and the English Court of Appeal; cf. Redfern & Hunter, *Law and Practice of International Commercial Arbitration* 122 (3rd ed. 1999).

[154] See Park, "National Law and Commercial Justice: Safeguarding Procedural Integrity in International Arbitration", 63 *Tul. L. Rev.* 647, 670-674 (1988) and Redfern & Hunter, *Law and Practice of International Commercial Arbitration* 112-114 (3rd ed. 1999).

[155] American courts have interpreted the Federal Arbitration Act to allow for vacation of awards when there was a "manifest disregard of the law".

[156] Cf. Art. 36(f) of the Swiss Intercantonal Concordat authorizing the judge to vacate an award that is "arbitrary in that it was based on findings which were manifestly contrary to the facts appearing in the file, or in that it constitutes a clear violation of law or equity" (translation taken from Park, "National Law and Commercial Justice: Safeguarding Procedural Integrity in International Arbitration", 63 *Tul. L. Rev.* 647 n.166 (1988)). Since promulgation of the new Swiss Private International Law Act of 1987, the Concordat, however, only applies to the arbitration if it was expressly elected by the parties; see Park, id.

[157] Cf. Sec. 10 of the United States Federal Arbitration Act; on the interpretation covering a "manifest disregard of the law" see Craig, id. referring to the United States Supreme Court in Wilko v. Swan, 346 U.S. 427, 436 (1953).

[158] Cf. Art. V.1 (c) New York Convention.

There is a

"... thin line between arbitrator excess of authority and a merely incorrect decision on the merits of the dispute".[159]

(3) Effect of the Award

As already mentioned, the award rendered by a private arbitrator will only have the public effect that national legal systems confer upon it. As with court judgments, the two most important effects of an award are its power to preclude re-litigation (its *res judicata* effect)[160] and the capacity to be enforced. Both depend on the recognition of the award by national courts. Only if the *res judicata* effect is recognized, and only if courts are willing to enforce awards, will arbitration achieve binding and lasting dispute resolution. Most countries generally recognize and enforce domestic and foreign arbitral awards but allow for a limited form of judicial review in the courts of the country where the award was rendered and in the country where the award is sought to be recognized. The distinction between these two possibilities of judicial review is important because they involve different types of procedure, frequently different standards of review, are cumulative rather than mutually exclusive (i.e. the same award can be attacked in several fora), and have different kind of consequences.

Judicial review of arbitral awards through the courts of the place *where the award was rendered* can happen in two different procedures. Either the "winner" of the arbitration seeks to have the award confirmed in an *exequatur* proceeding as a basis for local enforcement. Or the "loser" of the arbitration attacks the award in a procedure aimed at vacating the award. The review standard in both procedures may be the same or different, depending on the local law.[161] The effects, however, are different. In the first alternative (confirmation procedure) the effects of a confirmation or refusal of confirmation are limited to the jurisdiction where the award was asked to be confirmed.[162] By contrast, a successful annulment procedure will normally have the effect that the award is finally rendered obsolete and that

---

[159] Park, "National Law and Commercial Justice: Safeguarding Procedural Integrity in International Arbitration", 63 *Tul. L. Rev.* 647, 675 (1988).

[160] On the preclusive effects of awards see Hulbert, "Arbitral Procedure and the Preclusive Effect of Awards in International Commercial Arbitration", 7 *Int'l Tax & Bus. Law.* 155 (1989) and Redfern & Hunter, *Law and Practice of International Commercial Arbitration* 395-397 (3rd ed. 1999).

[161] The – narrow – grounds for refusal of recognition spelled out in Art. V of the New York Convention only apply to the recognition and enforcement of foreign awards; the annulment of domestic awards follows domestic arbitration law which frequently is similar in scope, cf. Sec. 1059 of the German *Zivilprozeßordnung*.

[162] However, it may be possible to seek recognition abroad indirectly through recognition of the *exequatur* judgment ("double *exequatur*").

recognition will be refused in any other country on the basis that the award had been vacated.[163]

Each country has its own standard for judicial review of awards rendered locally. Although some countries still allow for judicial review of the entire merits of the case, in recent times the standard in most countries has been limited to a review for serious procedural mistakes such as lack of jurisdiction (i.e. non-existence of a valid arbitration agreement), improper constitution of the arbitral tribunal, disregard for the terms of the arbitrators' mandate (which may include a "manifest disregard of the law"[164]), corruption, and other serious violations of "due process", or in English terminology "natural justice", comprising mainly the principle of equality of treatment and the right of each party to be heard. Under the laws of some countries, judicial review of awards rendered in the country in arbitrations not involving any nationals or residents can be excluded by agreement of the parties (as in Switzerland[165]), even for violation of the most basic procedural protections.[166] The idea behind such an exclusion is that judicial review can still be obtained at the place where the award is sought to be enforced.[167]

Judicial review in the country *where recognition and enforcement is sought*[168] is much more uniform thanks to recent efforts at harmonizing national arbitration laws and above all due to the success of the New York Convention. Typically, the "winner" of the arbitration will have to obtain, in the courts of the country where recognition and enforcement is sought an *exequatur* which will render the award equivalent to a local court judgment. In *exequatur* proceedings foreign awards are generally not reviewed on the merits but only as to a limited number of procedural defects which in most countries are equivalent to or narrower than the ones listed in Art. V of the New York Convention. And it is generally the burden of the party

---

[163]　See Art. V 1 (e) New York Convention.

[164]　See the famous dictum by the United States Supreme Court in *Wilko v. Swan*, 346 U.S. 427, 436 (1953).

[165]　Art. 192 of the Swiss Private International Law Act.

[166]　In Belgium, the 1985 Arbitration Law excluded the possibility of challenging an award made in Belgium when none of the parties was a natural person having Belgian nationality or residence, or a legal person having its main office or a seat of operations in Belgium (Art. 1717 of the Belgian Code Judiciaire), but in 1998, this provision was amended and now provides for an annulment procedure with the possibility to opt out for non-residents, non-Belgians and legal persons having neither their head office nor a branch in Belgium (Art. 1717.4).

[167]　For a detailed comparative analysis of the standards and procedures for challenging awards see Park, "National Law and Commercial Justice: Safeguarding Procedural Integrity in International Arbitration", 63 *Tul. L. Rev.* 647 (1988) and Redfern & Hunter, *Law and Practice of International Commercial Arbitration* 420- 439 (3rd ed. 1999).

[168]　On recognition and enforcement of arbitral awards generally see Redfern & Hunter, *Law and Practice of International Commercial Arbitration* 443-489 (3rd ed. 1999).

attacking the validity of the award to allege and prove the existence of one of these grounds. The fact that arbitral awards can be challenged both at the place where they were rendered and in each country where enforcement is sought (in many countries through several levels of appeals), provides ample opportunity for tactical maneuvering and can occasion immense transaction costs, both in terms of delays and legal costs and expenses, for the party who has prevailed in the arbitration.

On the other hand, since international arbitration generally proceeds without appeal on the merits, a limited form of judicial review at least as to the most fundamental norms of the procedure is necessary to ensure that "arbitration" will not degenerate into "arbitrariness". Where exactly to strike the balance between the "loser's" interest in procedural fairness and the "winner's" interest in procedural economy and finality, is a difficult question since "one man's delay is another man's due process". Efforts at completely eliminating the first phase of judicial review of arbitral awards, the annulment proceedings at the situs of the arbitration, have been criticized for damaging the control system[169] of international commercial arbitration, which is based on the national courts' supervision of the basic procedural correctness of private arbitration, and for depriving the victim of arbitral corruption or misconduct of an effective remedy: the losing respondent may have to defend against the wrongful award in every country where he has assets, and the situation of a losing claimant is even worse since he lost his chance of pursuing his claim in arbitration and the existence of the award may even prevent him from re-litigating the claims in the national courts.[170] Therefore, despite the potential for abuse, a minimum standard of court review is desirable to ensure the quality of dispute resolution and operates as a safeguard in light of the public effect given the private process of international commercial arbitration.

2. International Conventions

As mentioned above, the legal framework governing international commercial arbitration has been significantly streamlined and harmonized in the direction of greater autonomy of the arbitral process through recent legislative reforms in many countries. However, the most important step on the way towards a "uniform system of international arbitration" has been achieved through a number of international conventions dealing with commercial arbitration, most notably through the 1958 New York Convention on the Recognition and Enforcement of Foreign Arbitral

---

[169] Cf. Reisman, *Systems of Control in International Adjudication and Arbitration: Breakdown and Repair* 107-141 (1992).

[170] On the "dark side of delocalized arbitration" see Park, "National Law and Commercial Justice: Safeguarding Procedural Integrity in International Arbitration", 63 *Tul. L. Rev.* 647, 653-656 (1988).

Awards (New York Convention)[171]. Therefore, a closer look shall be taken at this convention, followed by a brief overview of other significant arbitration conventions.

a. The New York Convention

Despite the limitation suggested by its name, the New York Convention on the Recognition and Enforcement of Foreign Arbitral Awards covers both the enforcement and the jurisdiction aspects of international commercial arbitration.[172] The Convention, initiated by the ICC and sponsored by the United Nations, was opened for signature in 1958. By July 2005, 136 Nations had ratified it, making the New York Convention one of the most successful agreements concluded in the history of the United Nations.[173] The Convention establishes a minimum standard for the treatment of foreign arbitration agreements and foreign arbitral awards by the national courts of the member states but it leaves the regulation of the conduct of the arbitration as such to the member states themselves.

(1) Jurisdiction

Art. II of the New York Convention ensures practically worldwide exclusive jurisdiction to arbitration proceedings based on a valid arbitration agreement:

1. Each Contracting State shall recognize an agreement in writing under which the parties undertake to submit to arbitration all or any differences which have arisen or which may arise between them in respect of a defined legal relationship, whether contractual or not, concerning a subject-matter capable of settlement by arbitration.

---

[171] Cf. Park, "Award Enforcement under the New York Convention", 1 *International Business Litigation & Arbitration* 683 (2001); Van den Berg, *Impoving the Efficiency of Arbitration Agreements and Awards* (1999).

[172] The Convention is designed to apply to all foreign arbitration agreements and arbitral awards, regardless of whether they are from states parties to the Convention and whether they are "commercial" in nature. However, Art. I.3 allows the contracting states to limit the application of the Convention, on the basis of reciprocity, to "convention awards", i.e. awards made in the territory of another contracting state, and to matters regarded as "commercial" by the laws of the respective state.

[173] The United Nations have advanced the aim of a uniform system of international commercial arbitration on three levels: the relationship between the national legal systems and foreign arbitrations is covered by the New York Convention; the relationship between the national legal systems and arbitrations both within their borders and abroad are dealt with by the UNCITRAL Model Law; and the arbitral procedure itself is covered by the UNCITRAL Rules.

2. The term "agreement in writing" shall include an arbitral clause in a contract or an arbitration agreement, signed by the parties or contained in an exchange of letters or telegrams.

3. The court of a Contracting State, when seized of an action in a matter in respect of which the parties have made an agreement within the meaning of this article shall, at the request of one of the parties, refer the parties to arbitration, unless it finds that the said agreement is null and void, inoperative or incapable of being performed.

The recognition of the binding effect of pre-dispute arbitration agreements in Art. II.1 is an important achievement particularly with regard to the situation in countries that traditionally insisted on an express submission of the concrete dispute. Art. II.3 grants exclusive jurisdiction to international arbitration but is premised on the prerogative of the national courts to determine the validity of the arbitration agreement. No provision is made for the possibility that courts in different countries reach conflicting conclusions on this issue, as demonstrated above.[174]

(2) Recognition and Enforcement of Foreign Awards

Art. V of New York Convention ensures the global "currency" of arbitral awards by excluding any review on the merits of foreign awards and by limiting the grounds on which their recognition and enforcement can be refused to a few basic procedural defects:

1. Recognition and enforcement of the award may be refused, at the request of the party against whom it is invoked, only if that party furnishes to the competent authority where the recognition and enforcement is sought, proof that:

   (a) The parties to the agreement referred to in Article II were, under the law applicable to them, under some incapacity, or the said agreement is not valid under the law to which the parties have subjected it or, failing any indication thereon, under the law of the country where the award was made; or

   (b) The party against whom the award is invoked was not given proper notice of the appointment of the arbitrator or of the arbitration proceedings or was otherwise unable to present his case; or

   (c) The award deals with a difference not contemplated by or not falling within the terms of the submission to arbitration, or it contains decisions on matters beyond the scope of submission to arbitration, provided that,

---

[174] For further aspects with regard to the question of jurisdiction, see Gotanda, "An Efficient Method for Determining Jurisdiction in International Arbitrations", 40 *Columbia J. Transnat'l L.* 11-42 (2001).

if the decisions on matters submitted to arbitration can be separated from those not so submitted, that part of the award which contains decisions on matters submitted to arbitration may be recognized and enforced; or

(d) The composition of the arbitral authority or the arbitral procedure was not in accordance with the agreement of the parties, or, failing such agreement, was not in accordance with the law of the country where the arbitration took place; or

(e) The award has not yet become binding on the parties, or has been set aside or suspended by a competent authority of the country in which, or under the law of which, that award was made.

2. Recognition and enforcement of an arbitral award may also be refused if the competent authority in the country where recognition and enforcement is sought finds that:

(a) The subject-matter of the difference is not capable of settlement by arbitration under the law of that country; or

(b) The recognition and enforcement of the award would be contrary to the public policy of that country.

Note that Art. V.1. places the burden of proof for the existence of the limited grounds for refusal on the party opposing the recognition and enforcement[175]. Art. V.1 and V.2 make clear that the determination of the validity of the arbitration agreement and of the award is in the hands of the court deciding over the recognition and enforcement.

Due to a certain divergence between the equally authoritative English and French versions, it is not quite clear whether the refusal to recognize awards that have been vacated by the competent forum as contemplated in Art. V.1 (e) is optional or mandatory. In the much discussed *Norsolor* case, the French *Cour de Cassation* has followed the former approach and granted recognition to an award that was previously set aside by an Austrian Court.[176]

The *Norsolor* decision is in conformity with an important principle of the New York Convention: it creates only a minimum standard and does not pre-empt recognition and enforcement under national laws that might be more favorable than Art. V of the New York Convention. However, there seems to be an emergent issue

---

[175] The refusal grounds set out in Art. V.2 which are more strongly linked to the public interest of the recognition state are worded in a manner that they can be invoked by the court on its own motion.

[176] *Soc. Pabalk Ticaret Siketi v. Soc. anon. Norsolor, Cour de Cassation (Ire Ch. Civ.)*, decision of October 3, 1984, [1985] Dalloz 101 with Note by Jean Robert; cf. account in Redfern & Hunter, *Law and Practice of International Commercial Arbitration* 484 (3rd ed. 1999).

with respect to this provision: while some recent decisions[177] have confirmed the pro-enforceability stance, in 1999 the U.S. Court of Appeals for the Second Circuit refused to enforce two arbitral awards that had been set aside by a Nigerian court, invoking issues of finality and the danger of conflicting judgements.[178]

(3) Comment

The New York Convention represents a remarkable success in the struggle to achieve a universal systems for commercial dispute resolution. Nonetheless this success has its limitations. The harmonization achieved by the New York Convention is incomplete in that the Convention leaves crucial determinations to the national courts who decide on the validity of arbitration agreements and arbitral awards. It provides uniform standards for these determinations but leaves the interpretation and application of the Convention to the national courts. And it does not provide for a mechanism to resolve conflicts between national jurisdictions on matters regarding arbitration. Insofar the New York Convention is a less advanced instrument of harmonization than the Brussels/Lugano Convention (now: Brussels I Regulation) on the Recognition and Enforcement of Judgments which through the jurisdiction of the European Court of Justice has supplied a means for securing the uniform application of its provisions. Since the Brussels I Regulation excludes arbitration from its ambit, no mechanism exists today which could solve the inevitable conflicts arising out of diverging applications of the New York Convention by national courts.

On the other hand, the New York Convention has a much broader geographical scope than the Brussels I Regulation which is limited to a relatively small number of fairly homogenous states. By contrast, the New York Convention has established a truly global system, not only with regard to the number of contracting states but also their geographical, political and economic diversity. Almost all nations of significance for world trade are included. The establishment of a supra-national court for the resolution of jurisdictional conflicts between nations on a global scale would seem desirable but it remains utopian. The New York Convention has to be judged for what it achieved, not for what might be desirable to achieve in a distant future. And for the time being and compared to the existing alternatives, the New York Convention is an extraordinary achievement.

---

[177] Cf. *Hilmarton Ltd. v. Omnium de traitement et de valorisation (OTV)*, *Revue de l'arbitrage* 1994, 327; *Chromalloy Aeroservices Inc. v. Arab Republic of Egypt*, 939 F Supp. 907 (D.D.C. 1996).

[178] Cf. *Baker Marine (Nig.) Ltd. v. Chevron (Nig.) Ltd.*, 191 F.3d 194 (2d Cir. 1999); see account in: Donovan & Rivkin, *International Arbitration and Dispute Resolution* 231, 273/274 (2002) [Commercial Law and Practice Course Handbook Series, PLI Order No. A0-00CT].

b. Other Significant Conventions

The New York Convention is by far the most important international agreement on commercial arbitration, and in practice other conventions only tend to gain relevance where the involvement of government parties calls for a denationalized regime (as offered by the *ICSID Convention*), or where *regional conventions* extend the currency of awards to nations that have not joined the New York Convention.[179]

(1) The ICSID Convention (Washington Convention)

The 1965 Washington Convention on the Settlement of Investment Disputes Between States and Nationals of Other States ("ICSID-Convention" or "Washington Convention")[180] was sponsored by the World Bank in order to facilitate foreign private investment by providing a dependable dispute resolution mechanism that would be acceptable both to host governments and foreign investors. Thanks to the prestige and influence of the World Bank, the ICSID Convention has been ratified by more states than any other arbitration convention. As of May 2005, the Convention had been signed by 155 countries and ratified by 142.[181]

The ICSID system supports dispute resolution in three ways: by creating an arbitration institution to administer the proceedings, by providing a set of conciliation and arbitration rules drafted for this specific type of dispute, and by establishing a denationalized legal framework that insulates ICSID proceedings from national legal systems and ensures the enforcement of ICSID awards in the states parties to the Convention, several of which are not parties to the New York Convention. The legal regime of ICSID arbitration is self-contained and excludes all forms of court intervention in the procedure and any review of ICSID awards by national courts. Instead, the ICSID Convention provides in its Art. 52 for the possibility of a limited review of awards in an annulment procedure where an *ad hoc* Committee of three arbitrators, each of whom is appointed by the President of the World Bank, review the award on the basis of five narrow annulment grounds comprising serious procedural mistakes.[182]

---

[179] The New York Convention was preceded by two other global instruments, the Geneva Protocol of 1923 and the Geneva Convention of 1927, which are still in force today but whose practical relevance has been almost completely superseded by the New York Convention; for a brief description of the history and the limited continuing relevance of these two instruments see Redfern & Hunter, *Law and Practice of International Commercial Arbitration* 66-67, 453-455 (3rd ed. 1999).

[180] Opened for signature March 18, 1965, entered into force October 14, 1966, 575 U.N.T.S. 159.

[181] For the latest status of ratifications, see: www.worldbank.org/icsid/constate/c-states-en.htm.

[182] The Annulment grounds listed in Art. 52 of the ICSID Convention are: "(a) that the Tribunal was not properly constituted"; (b) that the Tribunal has manifestly exceeded its powers; (c)

Once they are final, ICSID awards are directly enforceable in every contracting state "as if it were a final judgment of a court in that State",[183] without the necessity to obtain an *exequatur* and without any possibility of judicial review. One caveat, however, is warranted: although submission to ICSID arbitration by a government implies a waiver of sovereign immunity with respect to the ICSID arbitration, this does not automatically mean that the state has also waived its immunity from execution[184]. It has happened that courts have refused, on grounds of sovereign immunity, to enforce ICSID awards.[185] However, suing a sovereign is always fraught with uncertainty and compared with the alternatives available, ICSID arbitration may offer the most effective way to protect foreign investments, particularly where an express waiver of immunity from execution is obtained.

(2) Regional Conventions

A number of regional arbitration conventions exist, but most are of limited relevance to the practice. The 1961 European Convention on International Commercial Arbitration ("*Geneva Convention of 1961*")[186] was sponsored by the United Nations Economic Commission for Europe and was designed mainly to facilitate East-West trade in Europe. It was ratified by 19 states. With regard to the recognition and enforcement of awards its practical importance is limited because most of the contracting states are also parties to the New York Convention. However, it may facilitate the recognition of an award that was vacated in another state because according to the Geneva Convention of 1961 such a vacation only constitutes a ground for refusal of recognition if the vacation was based on the limited grounds spelled out in the Convention.[187] Unlike the New York Convention the Geneva Convention contains, in its Article IV, fairly detailed default provisions on the

---

that there was corruption on the part of a member of the Tribunal; (d) that there has been a serious departure from a fundamental rule of procedure; or (e) that the award has failed to state the reason on which it is based." Cf. ICSID Basic Documents; Doc. ICSID/15/Rev.1 (2003).

[183] Art. 54 (1) ICSID Convention.

[184] Art. 55 of the ICSID Convention makes clear that the enforcement provisions of the Convention do not derogate from any national laws dealing with sovereign immunity from execution.

[185] Cf. *Liberian Eastern Timber Company v. Government of the Republic of Liberia*, 650 F.Supp. 73 (S.D.N.Y. 1986) and description in Redfern & Hunter, *Law and Practice of International Commercial Arbitration* 480-481 (3rd ed. 1999) with additional references.

[186] Signed in Geneva on April 21, 1961, 484 U.N.T.S. 364 No. 7041 (1963-1964).

[187] Under the Geneva Convention, recognition may only be refused if the award was vacated because of (a) an invalid arbitration agreement, (b) lack of proper notice or inability to present a case, (c) excess of arbitrator authority (d) irregular constitution of the arbitral tribunal; cf. Park, "National Law and Commercial Justice: Safeguarding Procedural Integrity in International Arbitration", 63 *Tul. L. Rev.* 647, 686-688 (1988).

procedure to be followed in case the parties have failed to specify the number of arbitrators and the method for their appointment, the place of the arbitration and the law applicable to the procedure.

The 1975 Inter-American Convention on International Commercial Arbitration ("*Panama Convention*")[188] opens new avenues for enforcement of foreign arbitral awards in a number of Latin American countries that have not ratified the New York Convention.[189] Like the New York Convention, the Panama Convention addresses both jurisdictional aspects and the recognition and enforcement of awards. The latter, Art. 5, is almost identical to Art. V of New York Convention. However, the jurisdiction provision in Art. 1 is "softer" than Art. II of the New York Convention. It only states that a pre-dispute arbitration agreement is "valid" without saying how it is *enforced*. Notably, Art. 1 fails to spell out an obligation of national courts to stay litigation when confronted with an arbitration agreement. As a novelty for international arbitration conventions, the Panama Convention provides in Art. 3 that absent an express selection by the parties, the arbitration shall be governed by the arbitration rules of the Inter-American Commercial Arbitration Commission (IACAC), which were modeled after the UNCITRAL Rules.

3. Advantages of the Legal Framework of International Commercial Arbitration Compared to Transnational Litigation

Due to the enormous variety of controversies encountered in international commerce, it is difficult to state in a general manner the advantages and disadvantages of arbitration compared to litigation in this area. Many things can go wrong in either type of procedure, and it would be distorting to compare, say, a fairly straightforward arbitration between parties who disagree but do not regard themselves at war with each other, to a complex multi-party litigation where the parties fight for their very survival.[190]

However, some generalizations can and have to be made. Arbitration is said to have a number of advantages over transnational litigation, both in regard of its *legal framework* (i.e. how it copes with the problems arising from the lack of

---

[188] English Text reprinted in 14 I.L.M. 336 (1975); for a discussion see Jackson, "The 1975 Inter-American Convention on International Commercial Arbitration: Scope, Application and Problems", 8 (3) *J. Int'l Arb.* 91 (1991).

[189] Thus, the Panama Convention has increased the attractiveness of arbitration venues such as New York that fall into the ambit of both the Panama and the New York Convention because awards made in such a place are enforceable in all member states of the New York Convention plus those signatories of the Panama Convention that have not adhered to the New York Convention.

[190] In particular, it has to be taken into account that some of the worst pitfalls of transnational litigation can be avoided through carefully drafted choice-of-forum clauses or "litigation clauses".

coordination between legal systems) and from a *process* perspective (i.e. the need to serve the interests of the parties and to provide a cost-effective means for conflict-management). Before turning to the question of how these advantages materialize in the experience of the parties, the potential of arbitration to manage the legal complexities of transnational business disputes shall be analyzed in comparison to litigation in national courts. As explained in the previous chapter, dealing with international disputes through national courts creates a number of complications due to the lack of coordination between the legal systems of nations. The following groups of issues were distinguished: jurisdiction over the dispute (a), procedure to be followed (b), the law applicable to the substance of the dispute (c), and the effect that arbitral decisions have abroad (d).

a. Jurisdiction

Arbitration can reduce, albeit not completely eliminate, two serious dangers connected with transnational litigation: forum-shopping and parallel lawsuits. *Forum shopping* is eliminated since the arbitral tribunal will be selected by the parties or, failing agreement, by an institution or appointing authority. The venue of the arbitration, and with it the applicable procedural law, is specified in the arbitration agreement or will be fixed by the institution or the arbitrators themselves.[191] *Parallel lawsuits* are much less likely in arbitration because the courts in most countries are under an obligation, based on local law or treaties like the New York Convention, to decline jurisdiction or stay proceedings when faced with an arbitration agreement, whereas in litigation, the pendency of a lawsuit in another country is not generally accepted as a bar to the exercise of jurisdiction – unless mechanisms like the one contained in the Brussels I Regulation apply. This does not mean that courts generally refuse to respect a pending lawsuit in another country – multiple proceedings are probably the exception in transnational litigation, as well. And even in international arbitration, differing assessments of the validity of an arbitration agreement do sometimes lead to competing procedures. But as a general rule, parallel proceedings can be avoided through properly drafted arbitration agreements.[192]

b. Procedure

An important advantage of arbitration in terms of *neutrality* is that the parties can choose their own judges. Typically, the sole arbitrator or the chairman of a

---

[191] This is a significant advantage over forum selection in transnational litigation because a forum selection clause does not bind the judge: he may decline jurisdiction on the basis of the forum non-conveniens doctrine.

[192] Obviously, "pathological" arbitration agreements exist which, for instance, fail to validly establish the arbitral tribunal's jurisdiction or lack a mechanism for the appointment of the arbitrator(s).

three-arbitrator panel will be from a third country, and the possibility of having party-appointed arbitrators makes it possible for each party to assure that there will be one person on the tribunal who understands their point of view and is capable of communicating that perspective to the other members of the tribunal. In addition, the procedure is usually conducted in a third country. This levels the "playing field" for the parties, although it increases the total transaction costs because now both parties must travel. On the other hand, this increase in costs may be partially offset by savings in translation costs due to the selection of arbitrators who are bilingual or who at least are fluent in the language of the contract.

A significant advantage of international commercial arbitration is the great *flexibility* permitted by its legal framework. Few mandatory rules are imposed, and national arbitration laws as well as international conventions are confined to the establishment of a minimum standard while leaving the details of the procedure to *party-autonomy*. Even most standard arbitration rules are silent on the details of how the actual proceedings are to be conducted. This makes it possible for the parties to tailor the proceedings to the particularities of the dispute and to incorporate ADR elements where suitable. With all of the major institutions now offering rules for international mediation/conciliation as well, this has become even easier.[193]

Another advantage of international arbitration is the *confidentiality* of the procedure which, however, may turn out to be illusory when as a result of a challenge of the award the entire procedure has to be spread out in open court.

An important difference between litigation and arbitration is the amount of *discovery*. Here, international arbitration usually results in a compromise between the fairly extensive possibilities to compel the production of evidence available in the United States and the near total absence of discovery procedures in most Civil Law systems. Depending on which type of litigation it is compared to, arbitration offers either more or less discovery than "normal", and this may be seen as an advantage or a disadvantage, although on balance the flexibility of the framework and the high degree of party-control are viewed as an advantage by most participants.

A potential *disadvantage* of arbitration is the inability of arbitral tribunals to effectively grant *preliminary relief*. If the arbitration agreement is not sufficiently clear on this issue, it may be deemed incompatible with its provisions to ask for preliminary relief directly in the public courts.[194] However, most of the relevant

---

[193]   Inherent in this flexibility and informality is, however, a certain measure of procedural uncertainty: unlike in litigation where detailed rules of procedure exist and where judges and court practice in general have a "track record", arbitration to many parties and counsel appears as something of a "black box".

[194]   Cf. the judgment of the United States Third Circuit in *McCreary Tire & Rubber Co. v. Seat SpA*, 501, F.2d 1032 (3d Cir. 1974); account in Redfern & Hunter, *Law and Practice of International Commercial Arbitration* 348 (3rd ed. 1999).

arbitration laws now expressly provide for the possibility to directly address requests to national courts.[195]

c. Application of Substantive Law

Party-control over the composition of the tribunal permits the appointment of arbitrators with *subject-matter expertise* in the particular applicable law, the relevant trade usages or in the technical matters at issue. Another advantage of arbitration from the perspective of some parties is that arbitrators are less likely than judges to strictly apply statutory provisions which are primarily based on *public policy considerations*. Especially where a contract is governed by American law, arbitration may be a way to avoid double or treble damages, e.g. under antitrust laws.[196] On the other hand, the absence of an appeal on the merits affects the *predictability* of the results: an arbitrator who is familiar with the particular industry or trade may be less likely to issue surprising decisions than a national judge without specialized subject-matter expertise; but once the decision is rendered, an arbitral award can only be corrected for the most extreme mistakes. Finally, a weakness of arbitration lies in the limitations arbitrators face in awarding *specific performance* or *non-monetary remedies*.[197]

d. Effect of Awards

Perhaps the most important advantage of the legal framework of international commercial arbitration is the high degree of *international currency* of arbitral awards. Thanks mainly to the New York Convention, it is generally easier to enforce foreign arbitral awards than foreign court judgments (except perhaps under the regime of the Brussels I Regulation). The ready enforceability of awards has important *indirect effects*: the prospect of an impending enforceable decision enhances the probability of reaching a *negotiated settlement*; thus in many cases, the need for a decision is obviated. And where a decision has been rendered, its effective enforceability creates a strong motivation for *voluntary compliance*, which in turn obviates the

---

[195] Cf. Redfern & Hunter, *Law and Practice of International Commercial Arbitration* 348-349 (3rd ed. 1999).

[196] Cf. Perlman and Nelson, "New Approaches to the Resolution of International Commercial Disputes", 17 *Bus. Law.* 215, 228 (1983).

[197] Particularly injunctive relief may, as a practical matter, not be available in arbitration because injunctions often require for their effectiveness the cooperation of third parties who will normally not be under the jurisdiction of the arbitral tribunal, e.g. where an order prohibiting the transfer of assets has to be addressed not only to the party subject to the injunction but also to the bank where the assets are held, cf. Redfern & Hunter, *Law and Practice of International Commercial Arbitration* 358 (3rd ed. 1999).

need for enforcement proceedings.[198] The finality and international enforceability of arbitral awards is enhanced by the absence, in general, of any *judicial review* on the merits. However, some differentiation is warranted since the absence of judicial review entails a certain lack of control over the quality of decisions, and although appeals may occasion significant delays and costs, they do offer a certain insurance against incompetence or simple error by the decisionmaker. In arbitration, the fact that the decisionmaker has been chosen by the parties themselves, or at least based on an agreed procedure, gives a certain reassurance with regard to the quality of the decision, but the existence of appeals procedures in nearly all court systems shows that a certain measure of judicial error is commonly regarded as inevitable. On the other hand, even the limited forms of judicial review offered in international commercial arbitration can be *abused* by unwilling parties who can drag out the procedures and exploit the delays and costs involved in judicial challenges for extortionary purposes.[199]

4. Conclusion

The comparison of the legal frameworks of international commercial arbitration and transnational litigation shows that with a properly drafted arbitration agreement, the legal framework of international commercial arbitration:

- ensures a competent tribunal and excludes competing procedures practically on a worldwide scale;

- permits to flexibly adjust the procedure to the needs of the parties while guaranteeing the neutrality of the tribunal, a minimum standard of procedural fairness and the confidentiality of the procedure; as well as to achieve a reasonable degree of discovery and to limit judicial review to the most basic questions;

- ensures a reasonably predictable and legitimate decision by a tribunal with expertise in the applicable law, the relevant trade usages or any technical matters at issue;

- achieves results that are final and enforceable on a global scale; the enforceability of awards has the indirect effect of encouraging voluntary compliance

---

[198] Reliable statistics comparing the degree of voluntary compliance of awards in international business disputes do not exist, but according to the information available, a "large majority" of (ICC) awards are complied with voluntarily, cf. email-message from Mr. Emmanuel Jolivet (General Counsel International Court of Arbitration ICC) of April 30, 2004.

[199] Particularly where the annulment or enforcement procedure itself can be followed by several levels of appeal and where the winning party cannot recover its legal costs from the defeated party.

or even an amicable settlement eliminating the need for a decision by the tribunal.

Obviously, these advantages do not materialize in every arbitration, but the framework of international commercial arbitration makes it possible to ensure a high probability that they will.

Nonetheless, sometimes *litigation can be preferable*. Where the enforcement of judgments abroad is either unnecessary (because the defendant has sufficient assets in the jurisdiction of the court that decided the case) or where it is enhanced by mechanisms like the one embodied in the Brussels I Regulation, some of the key advantages of arbitration are less relevant. Also, in certain standard types of cases accelerated procedures like summary or documents-only proceedings may offer a more efficient form of dispute resolution. This consideration is particularly relevant in disputes in the banking field.[200] Another problem may be that in some jurisdictions arbitration agreements are interpreted to preclude interim measures of protection by the courts.[201] And litigation may be the only solution where the assets of the defendant are located in a country that is not party to any relevant international agreement and generally does not enforce foreign arbitral awards.

In sum, it can be said that the legal framework governing and supporting international commercial arbitration has not yet achieved the ideal of a uniform system of international commercial dispute resolution. It is still dominated by national legal systems. However, in contrast to transnational litigation, the way in which the various national legal systems interact is fairly well coordinated, through international conventions and the harmonization of arbitration laws. Although certain discrepancies continue to exist in the way national legal systems treat international commercial arbitration, on balance the system established by the New York Convention offers the most advanced and the most effective legal framework available for international business disputes today.

---

[200] Cf. Park, "When the Borrower and the Banker are at Odds: The Interaction of Judge and Arbitrator in Trans-Border Finance", 65 *Tul. L. Rev.* 1323, 1324-1325 (1991) and Sandrock, "Internationale Kredite und die Internationale Schiedsgerichtsbarkeit", *WM Zeitschrift für Wirtschafts- und Bankrecht* 405, 445 (1994); see also Park, "L'arbitrage et le Recouvrement des Prêts Consentis a des Débiteurs Etrangers", 37 *McGill L.J.* 375 (1992).

[201] However, this problem can be overcome through proper drafting of the arbitration agreement, see Sandrock, id. 447 et seq.

Chapter 3

The Process of International Commercial Arbitration

The process of international commercial arbitration has a distinct "flavor" to it that sets it apart from the procedure in any national court. As one of the leading international practitioners put it:

> "International arbitration is at once serious business and great fun, but it isn't everyone's cup of tea. You may have to structure your arguments under a substantive law you have never considered before, appear in hearing in a remote country before arbitrators trained in three different legal systems who have worked out some weird, fish-and-fowl rules of procedure, which are revealed to you as you go along. If you are truly lucky, your case will depend on your skill in cross-examining a brilliant rogue who insists he can express himself only in Greek or Danish or Thai, and who lengthily answers the question he thinks you ought to have asked, through a befuddled interpreter, all while the jet-lagged chairman's concentration seems exclusively focused upon his watch. Many litigators who perform superbly in their home courts are unable to function in this kind of environment. Coping with such a three-ring circus requires flexibility, tolerance, and a fair dose of humility. You must be ready to play to win while accepting someone else's rules, and to put on a diplomatic veneer on the relentlessness with which you are in fact pursuing your objective."[202]

I. CHARACTERISTIC FEATURES OF THE PROCESS

The process of international commercial arbitration[203] is characterized by two distinctive features, the autonomy of the parties and the arbitrators (to the extent

---

[202] Statement by Jan Paulsson in: "Highly Recommended: International Commercial Arbitration Specialists Elect their Expert", *Legal Business Magazine* 57, 58 (April 1992).

[203] For a detailed analysis of international commercial arbitration, see also Weigand, *Practitioner's handbook on International Arbitration*, 2002 and Yves Derains / Eric Schwartz, *A Guide to the New ICC Rules of Arbitration*, The Hague et al (1999).

the parties make no determinations) to structure the procedure (1) and the frequent blending of elements from different legal traditions (2).

1. Party Autonomy

The conduct of the proceedings in international commercial arbitration is largely governed by party-autonomy. National arbitration laws usually only cover what happens before the arbitration begins, what happens afterwards, and to which extent courts can support or interfere with the proceedings. What actually happens in the arbitration procedure is only addressed by a few basic norms such as the right of the parties to be treated equally and to be heard with their arguments and evidence.

Even standard arbitration rules, such as the ICC Rules, do not treat the actual proceedings in great detail. The rules are mainly concerned with ensuring that the process actually happens and that it leads to a decision. Thus, most arbitration rules have provisions on how the process is initiated, on how the arbitral tribunal is appointed, on costs and the processing of fees and deposits, on the treatment of jurisdictional objections and challenges against the arbitrators, on how to proceed in the event of a default, and on the more formal aspects of the making of the award. How exactly the process will be conducted is left to the parties and, failing agreement, to the arbitrators. Since arbitration rules are made to suit any type of future dispute, they have to be very flexible in order to allow the arbitrators, once they are seized with the actual case, to devise a procedure that is tailored to the concrete dispute. A good example is Art. 14 of the LCIA Rules dealing with the "Conduct of the Proceedings":

> "14.1 The parties may agree on the conduct of their arbitral proceedings, and they are encouraged to do so, consistent with the Arbitral Tribunal's general duties at all times:
>
> (i) to act fairly and impartially as between all parties, giving each a reasonable opportunity of putting its case and dealing with that of its opponent; and
>
> (ii) to adopt procedures suitable to the circumstances of the arbitration, avoiding unnecessary delay or expense, so as to provide a fair and efficient means for the final resolution of the parties' dispute.

Such agreements shall be made by the parties in writing or recorded in writing by the Arbitral Tribunal at the request of and with the authority of the parties.

14.2 Unless otherwise agreed by the parties under Article 14.1, the Arbitral Tribunal shall have the widest discretion to discharge its duties allowed under such law(s) or rules of law as the Arbitral Tribunal may determine to be applicable; and at all times the parties shall do everything necessary for the fair, efficient and expeditious conduct of the arbitration.

14.3 In the case of a three-member tribunal the Chairman may, with the prior consent of the other two arbitrators, make procedural rulings alone."

Art. 14 of the LCIA Rules may appear very general but is actually more specific than many other rules[204] in that it addresses the power of the Chairman to make procedural rulings alone, an issue that otherwise would have to be stipulated by the parties or agreed among the arbitrators.[205] The scarcity of explicit rules on the conduct of the proceedings is reflected by the literature on international commercial arbitration which, albeit plentiful, is mainly concerned with the legal framework within which arbitration is conducted, but rarely deals with "the main event". This is not surprising given the fact that arbitration is a private, confidential procedure and usually happens behind closed doors.

2. The Blend of Civil and Common Law Elements

International commercial arbitration is a "lawyers' show", and the nature of the process will in large measure depend on the legal traditions of the arbitrators and the parties' advocates because it is a natural tendency to conceive of the procedure in terms of patterns familiar from the "home" jurisdiction. The result in most cases is that the procedure is conducted in a blend of Civil Law and Common Law elements,[206] not only by way of a compromise over different procedural attitudes but also as the product of a search for efficient procedures that combine the respective strengths of both systems.[207] The most common blend is that of a fairly extensive written preparation in the Civil Law style, combined with an attempt to reduce hearing time to a minimum, again more in line with Civil Law traditions but motivated primarily by a desire to reduce the enormous costs and logistical difficulties connected with oral hearings extending over many weeks: meeting facilities have to be made available and parties, lawyers, arbitrators, witnesses and experts have to be transported to and accommodated at a place which for most

---

[204] Cf. Art. 15 ICC Rules: "15.1 The proceedings before the Arbitral Tribunal shall be governed by these Rules and, where these Rules are silent, by any rules which the parties or, failing them, the Abitral Tribunal may settle on, whether or not reference is thereby made to the rules of procedure of a national law to be applied to the arbitration; 15.2 In all cases, the Abitral Tribunal shall act fairly and impartially and ensure that each party has a reasonable opportunity to present its case."

[205] Cf. the ICC Rules which do not cover this aspect.

[206] See Lowenfeld, "The Two-Way Mirror: International Arbitration as Comparative Procedure", in: *Studies of Transnational Legal Practice* 163, 165 (Michigan Y.B. Int'l Legal Studies 1985); Smit, "Substance and Procedure in International Arbitration: The Development of a New Legal Order", 65 *Tul. L. Rev.* 1309, 1313 (1991).

[207] See detailed description of the proceedings in Redfern & Hunter, *Law and Practice of International Commercial Arbitration* 312-340 (3rd ed. 1999); see also Wetter, "The Conduct of the Arbitration", 2 (2) *J. Int'l Arb.* 7, 36-38 (1985).

participants will be at a considerable distance from their residence. At the hearing, however, distinctive Common Law elements are frequently encountered, namely the examination and cross-examination of witnesses by the lawyers. But, again in order to enhance the efficiency of the process, the direct examination of witnesses is often replaced by the previous exchange of written witness statements among the participants so as to preserve the valuable hearing time for clarifications and cross-examination. On balance, in most cases the process is probably dominated by Civil Law elements.[208]

The concrete mix of procedural elements, however, depends on the particularities of the case. In complex cases, it is often necessary to prepare the main oral hearing through exchanges of detailed memoranda, large numbers of documents and written testimony, and to conduct several shorter pre-hearing meetings. In other cases, where the parties present conflicting written testimony on a point that is of decisive importance for the outcome of the case, for instance whether a contract was formed, it may be preferable to proceed with the oral hearing as soon as possible and cross-examine the witnesses to test their credibility.

II. THE "TYPICAL" SEQUENCE OF AN INTERNATIONAL ARBITRATION

Even if one excludes specialized arbitrations, amiable composition or contract adaptation, "ordinary" international commercial arbitration comes in an enormous variety, distinguished by the institution involved, if any, and the degree of institutional involvement, by the type of dispute, the technical complexity, the amounts at stake, the involvement of governments, the number of parties, the degree of hostility between the parties, the number of arbitrators, and the cultural backgrounds and legal traditions of the parties, their lawyers and the arbitrators.

However, certain similarities and patterns have developed over the last decades and a certain measure of standardization has been achieved through the activities of arbitral institutions and most importantly through the repeated interaction, in arbitrations and on conferences, of a specialized "bench" and "bar" of international commercial arbitration. Therefore, despite the unique circumstances that make each arbitration different, an attempt shall be made to outline the major steps in the conduct of a "typical" international commercial arbitration. Unless otherwise indicated, the description assumes a dispute that lies somewhere near the center of the spectrum of disputes handled by the ICC, i.e. a dispute with two parties, three arbitrators, average complexity (bearing in mind that the disputes referred to

---

[208] One of the German scholars interviewed said that the procedure in international commercial arbitration resembled to an astonishing measure the procedure before German or Swiss courts.

international commercial arbitration nowadays are generally quite complex), and a total amount in dispute of between USD 2 to 5 million.[209]

1. Initiation

An arbitration commences with the notification of the demand to the defendant[210] or, in the case of institutional arbitration, the receipt of the request for arbitration by the institution.[211] Prior to that, in most cases some sort of attempt at negotiating a settlement will have taken place, and after deciding to commence arbitration the plaintiff will have done the necessary research into the matter and will have prepared his request. Under most rules,[212] the request has to contain information about the parties, the arbitration agreement, any procedural arrangements already made between the parties or proposed by the claimant, the registration fee (in case of institutional arbitration), the relief sought, and an initial statement of the claim which is usually rather cursory.[213] Where the arbitration agreement calls for the nomination of party-appointed arbitrators, the claimant is usually required to present his nomination together with the request for arbitration.[214] Most rules provide a time-limit for the respondent to present his answer which may be required to contain details corresponding to the request, including, under some rules, a detailed statement of defense. Since the time-limits imposed on the respondent tend to be rather short, extensions are frequently granted.

2. Constitution of the Tribunal

The next step, usually after the respondent has presented his answer, will be the constitution of the tribunal. Ideally, the parties are able to agree on the person of

---

[209] In 2004, cases with a value above USD 1 million constituted nearly 60% of the cases.

[210] Cf. Art. 3.2 UNCITRAL Rules.

[211] Cf. Art. 4.2 ICC Rules; Art. 1.2 LCIA Rules.

[212] Cf. Art. 2.3 AAA Rules; Art. Art 4.3 ICC Rules; Art. 1.1 LCIA Rules; Art. 3.3 UNCITRAL Rules.

[213] Cf. Art. 3.3 (e) UNCITRAL Rules which only requires a description of "the general nature of the claim and an indication of the amount involved, if any;" a detailed statement of claim is optional at this stage, see Art. 3.4 (c) UNCITRAL Rules. A similar system is established by the LCIA Rules in Art.1.1 (c) and Art. 15.2. The new version of the ICC Rules has dropped the requirement formerly contained in Art. 3.2. (b), asking the claimant to submit his main statement of case already with the initial request for arbitration. With a view to a rapid initiation of the arbitral process, Art. 4.3 (b) now only asks for a "description of the nature and circumstances of the dispute giving rise to the claim(s)". On the other hand, other than prior versions, Art. 4.3 (c) now requires a statement of the relief sought and, to the extent possible, an indication of amounts claimed.

[214] Cf. Art.8.4 ICC Rules; Art. 1.1 (e) LCIA Rules; under Art. 3.4 UNCITRAL Rules this is optional.

the sole arbitrator or on each member of the tribunal. This is, however, the most unlikely scenario. Frequently, the arbitration agreement lays out a procedure for the selection of the arbitrators. In the case of a three-arbitrator panel the most common approach is that each party appoints one arbitrator, that these two jointly appoint the chairman, and that failing an agreement between the two party-appointed arbitrators, the third arbitrator shall be appointed by the institution administering the arbitration or by an appointing authority. In addition, it is standard practice – in ad hoc and institutional arbitration – that the appointing authority is empowered to nominate a party-appointed arbitrator in the event that a party delays the procedure by refusing to make its appointment. Equally, it is important to supply a mechanism for the replacement of arbitrators and to regulate the question whether any hearings have to be repeated after the replacement of an arbitrator.

If the mechanism contemplated by the arbitration agreement fails to bring about the constitution of the tribunal within a certain time limit, most institutional arbitration rules authorize the institution to go ahead with the appointments regardless.[215] Absent agreement by the parties, many arbitration rules envision the nomination of party-appointed arbitrators and selection of the chairman by the institution.[216] In ICC arbitration, the ICC Court does not make the selection itself but delegates this task to a national ICC committee.[217] Usually this will be the national committee of the seat of the arbitration, typically a "neutral" country with respect to the nationalities of the parties, thus ensuring a chairman who is familiar with the local procedural law (for its importance see above at p. 64 et seq.). The arbitrator(s) so selected then have to be confirmed by the ICC Court. The ICC method has been criticized for its inherent delays. Sources of delay in this process can be the parties who ask for extensions for the nominations of a party-appointed arbitrator,[218] the national committees which may exceed the time-limit set by the ICC, and the ICC Court itself which may reject the national committee's proposal.[219] The average time for the constitution of the arbitral tribunal is estimated at 3-6 months but can on occasions be significantly longer. One of the attorneys interviewed recounted an ICC arbitration where the constitution of the tribunal took 1¼ years. In order to speed things up, Art. 32.1 ICC Rules now authorizes the parties to agree to shorten the various time limits set out in the Rules. However, since Art. 32.2 enables the

---

[215] Cf. Art. 6.3 AAA Rules; Art. 8.4 ICC Rules; Art. 5.4-5 LCIA Rules; see also Art.6-8 of the UNCITRAL Rules with elaborate procedures for non-administered arbitration.

[216] Cf. Art. 8.4 ICC Rules; Art. 5.6 LCIA Rules.

[217] Art. 9.3 ICC Rules.

[218] Cf. Ulmer, "Winning the Opening Stages of an ICC Arbitration", 8 (2) *J. Int'l Arb.* 33, 41-42 (1991).

[219] Where the ICC Court rejects the proposal or where the national committee fails to honor the time limit, the ICC Rules provide that the ICC Court may repeat the request or solicit the proposal of another national committee, Art. 9.3 ICC Rules.

Court to extend any such modified time limit on its own initiative, it remains to be seen whether, in practice, much acceleration will be achieved.[220]

A strong determination to avoid delays in the constitution of the tribunal is reflected in the LCIA rules that mandate the appointment of the entire arbitral tribunal "as soon as practicable" after receipt of the response or expiry of thirty days after receipt by the respondent of the request for arbitration.[221] If the parties have not incorporated a standard set of arbitration rules and failed to provide a mechanism for overcoming deadlocks in the nomination of the arbitrators, in many countries the courts can be asked to make the missing appointments. However, depending on the jurisdiction where the application is made, this procedure can entail significant delays.

3. Pre-Hearing Phase

Once the arbitral tribunal is constituted, the procedure will enter into the "pre-hearing phase". Before the main oral hearing and the taking of evidence can be conducted, a number of preliminary steps have to be taken. Procedural details are determined, preliminary matters are decided, and the issues in dispute, including any counterclaims by the respondent, are elaborated in written exchanges and meetings. Unlike in Common Law procedure where the pleadings tend to be "skeletal",[222] in international commercial arbitration the parties are usually required to present their entire case in writing before the main hearing begins. In particular, it will usually not be sufficient for a respondent to simply deny the claimant's factual allegations. Instead, denials will have to be substantiated, so as to force the respondent to "lay the cards on the table".[223] In order to structure the process by which the main hearing is prepared, it is common to gather the tribunal and the parties at least once for a meeting before the main hearing on the merits. In many cases there will be several (pre-hearing) meetings, one initial gathering, or *"preliminary hearing"*, right at the beginning in order for the participants to get acquainted with each other and to lay out the procedure to be followed in the arbitration, and another meeting following the *written phase*, frequently called *"pre-hearing conference"*, held closer to the date set aside for the hearing on the merits, in order to plan and prepare the main oral hearing.[224]

---

[220]   Cf. Weigand, "Die neue ICC-Schiedsgerichtsordnung 1998", NJW 2081 (1998).

[221]   Art. 5.4 LCIA Rules.

[222]   Smit, "Substance and Procedure in International Arbitration: The Development of a New Legal Order", 65 *Tul. L. Rev.* 1309, 1314 (1991).

[223]   Id.

[224]   Cf. de Boisseson, *Le Droit Francais de l'Arbitrage – Interne et International* No.738 and 776 et seq. (1989); Redfern & Hunter, *Law and Practice of International Commercial Arbitration* 331-334 (3rd ed. 1999); Wetter, "The Conduct of the Arbitration", 2 (2) *J. Int'l Arb.* 7, 36-38 (1985).

a. Preliminary Hearing

The main purpose of the *preliminary hearing*[225] is to provide an opportunity for all participants, including the members of the arbitral tribunal among themselves, to get to know each other, to exchange preliminary views and to work towards a consensus on the exact procedure to be followed in the arbitration. Usually, the arbitrators will be eager to facilitate an agreement between the parties at least on the procedural issues and will go to some lengths to accommodate their concerns. Failing agreement, however, the tribunal decides. The agenda for such a meeting will typically include determinations on the place and the language of the proceedings as well as the form, length, and time limits for the written submissions that will be presented before the main oral hearing. The preliminary meeting will usually be the moment to raise objections against the tribunal's jurisdiction or to discuss challenges against arbitrators. Also, a first discussion of the merits of the dispute will be attempted with a view towards defining and perhaps limiting the issues, or even achieving a settlement.

The preliminary hearing will usually be held early on, as soon as practicable after the exchange of the initial statements between the parties. In ICC arbitration, the timing is influenced by the requirement that the *Terms of Reference* be submitted to the ICC Court for confirmation within two months after the transmission of the file to the arbitral tribunal[226] which, in turn, is supposed to happen immediately after receipt by the ICC Secretariat of the defendant's answer.[227] The Terms of Reference are of great practical importance because they define the mandate, the "mission" of the arbitrators (the French term is *"acte de mission"*) and may later be used as the bench-mark in determining whether the arbitral tribunal exceeded the scope of its authority.[228] Art. 18.1 of the ICC Rules lists the particulars to be included in the Terms of Reference:

a) the full names and description of the parties,

b) the addresses of the parties to which notifications and communications arising in the course of the arbitration may be made,

c) a summary of the parties' respective claims and of the relief sought by each party, with an indication to the extent possible of the amounts claimed or counterclaimed;

---

[225] See the account of Blessing, "Die LCIA Rules – aus der Sicht des Praktikers", 5 *SchiedsVZ* 198, 199-200 (2003).

[226] Art. 18.2 ICC Rules.

[227] Art. 13 ICC Rules.

[228] Cf Art. V.1 (c) New York Convention.

d) unless the Arbitral Tribunal considers it inappropriate, a list of issues to be determined,

e) the full names, descriptions and addresses of the arbitrators;

f) the place of the arbitration; and

g) particulars of the applicable procedural rules and, if such is the case, reference to the power conferred upon the Arbitral Tribunal to act as *amiable compositeur* or to decide *ex aequo et bono*.[229]

By spelling out these particulars, the Terms of Reference "crystallize" the dispute in its essential elements.[230] However, according to lit. (d), revised in 1998, a list of issues to be determined is now only requested if the arbitral tribunal does not deem it inappropriate. This solution constitutes a compromise between those who, with respect to lengthy and unproductive formulation procedures, wished to drop the listing requirement altogether and those who underline the usefulness of an early clarification.[231]

The presiding arbitrator, who is in charge of the organization of the entire procedure, usually has a maximum of two months to prepare the initial gathering. This can involve considerable work:

"As the presiding arbitrator, you are burdened with the entire paperwork necessary for the management of the procedure: telephone conversations with co-arbitrators and counsel about the date for a meeting to establish the Terms of Reference; written confirmation of that date; preparation of the Terms of Reference and circulation of a draft to the co-arbitrators and the parties; consideration of any objections and comments expressed by the other arbitrators and the parties in time for the meeting over the Terms of Reference; preparation of the minutes of the initial gathering; sending of these minutes along with the Terms of Reference to the ICC Court; preparation and discussion of the various procedural orders with the co-arbitrators and the parties; responding to applications for extensions of time limits for written submissions etc."[232]

As mentioned, the preliminary hearing will usually be the moment when the arbitrators rule on preliminary questions. These are issues that set the parameters for the entire procedure and therefore have to be decided by the tribunal before entering

---

[229] Art. 18.1 ICC Rules.

[230] de Boisseson, *Le Droit Francais de l'Arbitrage – Interne et International* No.738 (1989).

[231] See Weigand, "Die neue ICC-Schiedsgerichtsordnung 1998", NJW 2018 (1998); Redfern & Hunter, *Law and Practice of International Commercial Arbitration* 51 (3rd ed. 1999).

[232] Telefax by Professor Otto Sandrock, dated June 19, 1992.

into a discussion of the merits. Examples of such questions are objections to the jurisdiction of the arbitral tribunal, challenges against arbitrators, or the determination of the law governing the procedure and of the law applicable to the substance of the dispute. The tribunal has to decide whether it wants to dispose of preliminary questions through an order or an interim award. This decision is important because in ICC arbitration any award will have to be confirmed by the ICC Court[233] (which can lead to additional delays in the procedure), and because in any event such an award might be attacked in the courts having jurisdiction over the arbitration.

A preliminary question which is not an indispensable threshold issue but still has great practical importance, is whether the tribunal should deal separately with the questions of liability and quantification. It might be more efficient to tackle the quantitative issues only after having made an – affirmative – decision on the issue of liability, usually recorded in an interim award. Whether and when to make this separation is a difficult question because on the one hand quantification issues frequently require the presentation and evaluation of large amounts of evidence, which might be a wasteful effort if in the end no liability can be established. On the other hand the determination of the liability issue sometimes requires the evaluation of the same facts and evidence as the quantification.[234]

Another preliminary question of a more practical nature would be a ruling limiting the admissible evidence to proofs relating to facts deemed relevant by the tribunal on the basis of a preliminary evaluation of the merits. Such a decision requires caution and, in order not to violate the right of the parties to be heard, can only be taken on the basis of a thorough reading of all the factual allegations and legal arguments.[235]

Finally, an important issue for a preliminary hearing are discovery requests by parties asking for the production of documents by the other side. Again, depending on the background of the participants, the tribunal might establish a schedule for the type of limited discovery frequently encountered in international commercial arbitration.

b. Written Phase and Gathering of Evidence

In any international arbitration, extensive documents are exchanged between the parties and presented to the tribunal. The documents initiating the procedure, the request for arbitration and the answer, are intended to outline the claim and the main counter-arguments but they do not go into all details and tend to be comparatively short. Only after the preliminary hearing has set the stage for the procedure by

---

[233] Cf. Art. 27 ICC Rules.

[234] Generally about the separation of liability and quantum see Redfern & Hunter, *Law and Practice of International Commercial Arbitration* 298-300 (3rd ed. 1999).

[235] See Redfern & Hunter, *Law and Practice of International Commercial Arbitration* 300-301 (3rd ed. 1999).

determining the substantive issues and deciding on the procedure to be followed will the parties start to prepare the main hearing and the taking of evidence through the preparation of comprehensive written submissions. These submissions, which are the product of intensive research on factual and legal aspects of the case, consist of documentary evidence, written statements by witnesses and experts (often in the form of sworn affidavits), and another round of memoranda presenting the positions of the parties in more detail than in the initial statements of claim and defense.[236] The bulk of the work is taken up by the investigation and presentation of the facts and the gathering of evidence on the issues that, in the preliminary hearing and particularly through the establishment of Terms of Reference, have been determined to be relevant for the decision of the case. Although it is during the main oral hearing that the tribunal actually "takes" the evidence, it is in the written phase that the evidence is compiled by the parties.

Few provisions in arbitration rules, and even less in national arbitration statutes, deal with the gathering of evidence by and before arbitral tribunals. Again, in practice this is left to party-autonomy and will to a large degree depend on the legal background of the arbitrators, the parties, and perhaps most importantly the parties' lawyers. As in ordinary civil procedure, the way in which evidence is gathered and presented at "trial", generates the most important distinctions between "Civil Law-style arbitration" and "Common Law-style arbitration". And as with other aspects of the arbitral procedure, the result in international commercial arbitration is usually a blend of legal styles as a function of the concrete mix of legal backgrounds prevailing among the participants in a given arbitration.

The four main types of evidence are *documents*, *witness testimony*, *experts*, and *physical inspection* by the tribunal. Documents are presented during the written stage before the hearing while oral evidence (witnesses and experts) and, to the extent practicable, physical evidence will generally be presented at the hearing. In modern arbitration practice, however, oral presentations are to a certain extent substituted by written exchanges before the hearing, through witness statements and expert reports. And often physical inspection will be substituted through an inspection by the expert, as well. Therefore, the bulk of the evidence is gathered during this written phase, before the actual evidence hearing.

---

[236] In order to manage the sometimes huge amounts of documents presented in international arbitrations it may be advisable to agree prior to the main hearing to follow the English technique of assembling "agreed bundles" of documents presented in preparation of the hearing. The documents are not "agreed" as to the veracity of their contents or the admissability or relevance as evidence, but as to their authenticity. This technique allows for uniform numbering of documents which greatly facilitates reference to them in written exchanges and at the hearing because each participant will have a complete set of documents with identical numbering; cf. Redfern & Hunter, *Law and Practice of International Commercial Arbitration* 319-320 (3rd ed. 1999); see also Mustill & Boyd, *The Law and Practice of Commercial Arbitration in England* 285-288 (1982).

A distinction has to be made between "favorable" and "unfavorable" documents. To the extent they are in its control, each party will present the documents that favor its cause (and are unfavorable to the other side). In contractual disputes – and most arbitrations deal with contractual disputes – this voluntary exchange will cover the large majority of documents presented. Sometimes, however, certain key documents will be under the exclusive control of the party for whom they are unfavorable, and the other side may want to request their production by means of discovery requests. English and especially American counsel will usually insist on a certain amount of discovery – not necessarily the same as in American litigation because even American lawyers tend to regard the current practice in America as excessive and in their majority view limits on discovery as an important advantage of international arbitration.[237] On the other hand, lawyers from Civil Law countries sometimes might welcome a certain measure of discovery to escape the narrow constraints on evidence gathering imposed by their own procedural laws.[238] In Germany, for instance, as a practical matter it is virtually impossible to obtain any evidence located in the sphere of the opposing side. As the *Reichsgericht*, the former German supreme court, said:

"… no one should be forced to supply the opponent with the material that the opponent needs to prove his case."[239]

In some cases, this restriction may lead to "tremendously unfair results"[240] which is why arbitration may offer a compromise between the excessive discovery possible under American law and the overly narrow constraints imposed in continental laws.[241] This compromise of allowing a limited form of discovery is exemplified by the International Bar Association's Rules on the Taking of Evidence in International Commercial Arbitration adopted by a resolution of the IBA on June 1, 1999. They were drafted by lawyers from diverse backgrounds and replaced the IBA's Supplementary Rules Governing the Presenting and Reception of Evidence in International Commercial Arbitration issued in 1983.

The enforcement of discovery orders in international arbitration is achieved indirectly: In many countries, orders by arbitral tribunals mandating the production of documents are not enforceable through the courts. And although in England and

---

[237] For empirical evidence see below at p. 108 et seq.

[238] Cf. Fischer-Zernin & Junker, "Between Scylla and Charybdis: Fact Gathering in German Arbitration", 4 (2) *J. Int'l Arb*. 9 et seq. (1987).

[239] "… das Beweisverfahren [ist] nicht dazu da …, um für eine Partei diejenigen thatsächlichen Behauptungen herbeizuschaffen, mit denen sie ihre Rechtsbehelfe zu substantiieren hat." Reichsgericht, *Juristische Wochenschrift* 1892, p.180; (English translation taken from Fischer-Zernin and Junker id. 17).

[240] Fischer-Zernin and Junker id.

[241] Id.

in the United States an arbitral tribunal may ask the courts to enforce a discovery order, in practice this is rarely done. Arbitrators generally prefer to make the parties aware that they might draw adverse inferences from a failure to cooperate with discovery requests.[242]

Sometimes a second type of pre-hearing meeting, called *pre-hearing conference*, is held much closer in time to the actual hearing, perhaps six months to a year after the preliminary hearing. In this case, the *preliminary hearing* has the function of preparing the written phase and the *pre-hearing conference* sets the stage for the main hearing where evidence is taken and the merits are discussed. However, there is no universally accepted terminology: in the practice of the Iran-United States Claims Tribunal, pre-hearing conferences tended to be held earlier, generally after receipt of the statement of defense, and thus performed the function of what is called here preliminary hearing.

4. Hearings on the Merits

Once all written memoranda, documentary evidence and written witness testimony have been exchanged and the report of any expert appointed by the arbitral tribunal has been received, in most cases around one to two years after the initiation of the arbitration,[243] the case is ripe for the main hearing on the merits. Under many arbitration rules, it is possible to conduct an arbitration even without ever having a meeting between the arbitral tribunal and the parties ("documents-only-arbitration").[244] However, this is a rare exception and in most arbitrations at least one meeting is conducted where the parties present proofs and oral arguments to the arbitral tribunal. Hearings can and sometimes must also be held in the absence of a defaulting party because the tribunal cannot simply treat the allegations of the other side as true but has to make a full inquiry into the merits of the case before issuing a default award.[245]

a. Scheduling

The length of the main hearing will vary according to the particularities of the case and the background of the participants. Civil Law arbitrators and lawyers are

---

[242] See also Lowenfeld, "The Two-Way Mirror: International Arbitration as Comparative Procedure", in: *Studies of Transnational Legal Practice* 163, 170-174 (Michigan Y.B. Int'l Legal Studies 1985); Redfern & Hunter, *Law and Practice of International Commercial Arbitration* 319 (3rd ed. 1999); and Wetter, "The Conduct of the Arbitration", 2 (2) *J. Int'l Arb.* 7, 16-20 (1985).

[243] For a discussion of the timing and the delays in arbitration see below at p. 108 et seq.

[244] Cf. Art. 20.6 ICC Rules; Art. 19.1 LCIA Rules; Art. 15.2 UNCITRAL Rules.

[245] See de Boisseson, *Le Droit Francais de l'Arbitrage – Interne et International* No. 779 (1989) and Redfern & Hunter, *Law and Practice of International Commercial Arbitration* 337-338, 383 (3rd ed. 1999).

not accustomed to oral hearings lasting for more than a few days.[246] On the other hand, when all participants are from common-law jurisdictions, it may well be that a hearing over several weeks will be conducted and witnesses are examined, cross-examined and re-examined to the full extent.[247] But in international arbitration, this type of procedure is a "dying breed"[248] because there is a strong pressure to streamline the process and to limit hearing time. Accordingly, a strong arbitrator "will shame the parties into a sensible proceeding".[249] Sometimes this takes the form of a learning experience:

> "... in the course of a very long arbitration ... the American advocates on both sides began by treating it as though it were an American litigation, but by the end of it [they] were perfectly happy to cross-examine between them 10 witnesses in two days and not ask who their great grandfather was..."[250]

As with other stages of the proceedings, the actual procedure will in most cases consist of a blend of Civil Law and Common Law elements, and the relative weight of these elements will depend on the background of the participants. On balance, the Civil Law tradition of more intensive "case management" by the arbitrators and shorter hearings seems to prevail.[251]

In a "typical" arbitration, the main hearing will go through the following stages: brief opening remarks by counsel; testimony by factual witnesses; testimony, if any, by experts; closing of the evidence; legal argument and final pleadings. In more complex cases the main hearing is usually divided into several shorter meetings because it is very difficult to coordinate the schedules of arbitrators, counsel, party representatives, witnesses and experts so as to gather everybody at the same place for longer than a few days at a time. The concrete division of the hearing will depend on the circumstances of the case and on which individuals have to be present at which stage of the proceedings. Hence, there may be special sessions for witnesses and experts and, as mentioned above, there will sometimes be separate hearings on the grounds and on the quantification of the claims.

The venue of the meetings will usually be the official place of the arbitration but it is also possible to hold meetings elsewhere.[252] Sometimes this is recommended

---

[246]   Redfern & Hunter, *Law and Practice of International Commercial Arbitration* 334 (3rd ed. 1999).

[247]   Id.

[248]   Interview with Lord Justice Michael Kerr, March 4, 1992.

[249]   Interview with Michael Kerr, March 4, 1992.

[250]   Interview with Arthur L. Marriott, March 3, 1992.

[251]   Redfern & Hunter, *Law and Practice of International Commercial Arbitration* 334-335 (3rd ed. 1999).

[252]   Cf. Art. 13.2 AAA Rules; Art. 16.1 -2 LCIA Rules; Art. 16 UNCITRAL Rules.

for practical reasons as when certain evidence can only be examined at a particular place. For instance, the tribunal might want to inspect the site in a construction dispute, or a crucial witness might be prevented from travelling to the place of the arbitration.

b. Witness Testimony

Depending on the background of the arbitrators, the witnesses will be questioned either by the tribunal or by the advocates. Frequently, a compromise is worked out whereby the arbitrators commence and then hand over the questioning to the lawyers for cross-examination. In the interest of procedural economy, the main testimony will often be contained in written statements exchanged before the hearing. At the hearing, the witness merely gives a brief summary or a few explanations and is then presented with clarifying questions by the tribunal and some limited form of cross-examination. How much cross-examination there will be is, again, a function of the legal background of arbitrators and counsel. Here, the tribunal has to ensure that Civil Law advocates, who often lack familiarity and the skills needed for cross-examination and who are not accustomed to "witness coaching", will not be placed at a disadvantage. In common-law style arbitration, testimony will be recorded in literal transcripts, whereas Civil Law style arbitration relies more on summaries usually prepared by the presiding arbitrator and presented to the witness for approval and signature.

c. Experts

In many arbitrations certain technical issues can only be judged by the arbitrators with the help of an expert. In the Civil Law tradition it is customary that the arbitral tribunal appoints an independent expert who can examine documents and inspect sites or other physical evidence located in the sphere of any party and may interview witnesses on any side.[253] To a certain extent the expert can fulfill some of the functions that in Common Law litigation are performed by pre-trial discovery.[254] The expert prepares a written report to the tribunal and may be called to appear personally in a hearing to explain his findings and answer questions by the tribunal and parties. In the adversarial tradition of the Common Law, each side appoints their own expert who at the hearing will both be examined, cross-examined and re-examined by the attorneys. The Common Law tradition of hearing conflicting expert evidence has been criticized for a tendency to degenerate in to a "battle of experts" where experts under the pressure of cross-examination are prompted to adopt a partisan stance and where frequently the "winner" is determined less by

---

[253] Cf. Art. 22.1 AAA Rules; Art. 21.1 LCIA Rules; Art. 27.1 UNCITRAL Rules.

[254] Reymond, "Civil Law and Common Law Procedures: Which is the More Inquisitorial? A Civil Lawyer's Response", 5 *Arb. Int'l* (1989).

the substance of their presentation but by their forensic skills and the ability to hold ground when attacked under cross-examination.

d. Pleadings

After all witnesses and experts have been heard, the arbitral tribunal will close the taking of evidence[255] and ask counsel for each side to present their final arguments. This can be done more or less formally. Sometimes a special hearing is scheduled for the pleadings.[256]

5. Making of the Award

The next step is for the arbitral tribunal to hold deliberations in order to discuss the merits of the case and to render a decision. Sometimes this will be preceded by the filing of a "*post-hearing brief*" by one or all of the parties. This may be granted by the tribunal where one party raised a novel point at the pleadings and the other side has had no appropriate opportunity to respond, or else when simply the time scheduled for the final hearing ran out before all pleadings could be finished and the tribunal wanted to avoid having to hold another hearing.[257]

In their *deliberations*, the arbitrators will generally be anxious to reach a unanimous decision in order to bolster the authority of the award, particularly with a view to any potential challenges to its validity or execution. However, where the arbitrators disagree, they will have to *vote*. Generally, the decision will be taken by majority vote and sometimes the arbitrator who was outvoted will write a dissenting opinion. But it is possible and occurs not infrequently that there is no clear majority within the tribunal but that each member of the tribunal advocates a different solution. Arbitration rules provide for two different systems to overcome such deadlocks. The ICC Rules and the LCIA Rules confer, in such a situation, the sole decisionmaking power to the presiding arbitrator.[258] On the other hand, the AAA Rules and the UNCITRAL Rules require in any event a majority decision[259] which in practice forces at least two arbitrators to reach an agreement. Frequently this will mean that the presiding arbitrator will have to make a compromise with one of the two party-appointed arbitrators. In exceptional situations, e.g. where a party-appointed arbitrator refuses to participate in the deliberations and where it

---

[255] The taking of evidence may subsequently be re-opened in exceptional situations, e.g. when new evidence surfaces which could not have been presented beforehand, see Redfern & Hunter, *Law and Practice of International Commercial Arbitration* 339 (3rd ed. 1999).

[256] Cf. de Boisseson, *Le Droit Francais de l'Arbitrage – Interne et International* No. 779 (1989).

[257] Redfern & Hunter, *Law and Practice of International Commercial Arbitration* 339 (3rd ed. 1999).

[258] Art. 25.1 ICC Rules; Art. 26.3 LCIA Rules.

[259] Art. 26.1 AAA Rules; Art. 31.1 UNCITRAL Rules.

would cause excessive costs and delays to appoint a replacement, the deliberations and the making of the award will be undertaken by the two remaining arbitrators as a *"truncated tribunal"*.[260]

Next, the *opinion* has to be drafted and the award officially "made" through the signature of the arbitrators. Contrary to the domestic practice in many countries and to the practice in certain trade or commodity arbitrations, awards in international commercial arbitration are almost always required to be reasoned. The drafting of the opinion can be a major enterprise and, in a large and complex case, can easily consume several weeks of full time work. The division of labor within the tribunal is up to the arbitrators in the concrete case but generally the chairman has to bear the bulk of the burden. Typically, the chairman prepares a first draft, circulates it to his co-arbitrators and then works their comments into the final version. In ICC arbitration the draft award has to be submitted to the ICC Court for review.[261] Once the ICC Court, after scrutiny of the formal aspects, has approved the award, and perhaps after the tribunal incorporates certain changes "suggested" by the ICC Court, the award is ready for signature.

Finally, the award has to be *signed* by the arbitrators in order to be validly issued. Some national laws require the signature of all arbitrators but under most arbitration rules the award has to be signed only by at least two arbitrators to be valid.[262] Where the award is signed may influence the "nationality" of the award because the latter may depend on the place where the award was "made". This can lead to unwanted results. In one case, an arbitration was conducted before a single arbitrator in London but for some reason the arbitrator signed the award in Paris. The House of Lords regarded the award as French although the only connection to France was the act of signing the award. The risk of such a surprise result can be avoided if the arbitrators make sure that the award is "made" at the place of the arbitration as is mandated by most arbitration rules, or through stipulation that the award is deemed to be made at the place of the arbitration no matter where it is signed, as provided in the ICC Rules.[263]

6. Overall Duration of the Process

As shown, arbitration is a sophisticated judicial procedure which entails many steps and therefore by nature requires a substantial amount of work. Usually this means that the procedure will take several years.

---

[260] Redfern & Hunter, *Law and Practice of International Commercial Arbitration* 225 (3rd ed. 1999).

[261] Cf. Art. 27 ICC Rules.

[262] Art. 26.1 LCIA Rules; Art. 32.4 UNCITRAL Rules.

[263] Cf. Art. 25.3 ICC Rules.

a. "Typical" Duration

The great diversity of cases makes it difficult to give an estimate of the average duration of an international arbitration, particularly when the possibility of subsequent judicial review is taken into account. The spectrum of possibilities is fairly large, ranging from "fast-track" arbitration to famous cases such as the "Pyramids" arbitration (see above at p. 37) or the dispute between Klöckner and Cameroon[264] which both lasted for over ten years. As to the "typical" arbitration, the procedural steps usually involved in an arbitration, particularly the constitution of the tribunal, the establishment of the Terms of Reference, at least two rounds of written submissions, the preparation and conduct of the hearings on the merits and finally the making of the award require at least three quarters of a year and often substantially more. However, in the large majority of cases an award is reached around *two to three years* after initiation of the procedure.

b. "Fast-Track Arbitration"

A multi-million dollar ICC arbitration dealing with the redetermination of a commodity price in a long-term supply agreement was brought to conclusion in only two months.[265]

The arbitration clause provided for a 60 days deadline, counting from the initiation of the procedure (without specifying what would happen in case no award would be rendered within the time limit); the procedure took 18 days from the constitution of the tribunal to the notification of the award to the parties, the latter being done on the day of its approval by the Chairman of the ICC Court; during this period, two arbitrations were consolidated, extensive written submissions (over 1,500 pages) were processed, the Terms of Reference were signed by the parties and approved by the ICC Court (again, through its Chairman) and

---

[264] ICSID Case No. ARB/81/2.

[265] The dispute arose out of two parallel contracts with identical arbitration clauses, and the arbitration formally consisted of two separate procedures administered by an identical tribunal; this account is based on an interview with the presiding arbitrator, Hans Smit, on January 21, 1992, the Memorandum on Fast-Track Arbitration issued by the Secretariat of the ICC International Court of Arbitration, dated March 20, 1992 (reprinted in 2 *Am. Rev. Int'l Arb.* 162 (1991)), and the following articles in Vol. 2 No. 2 of the *American Review of International Arbitration* which were written by participants in the procedure: Smit, "Fast-Track Arbitration", 2 *Am. Rev. Int'l Arb.* 138 (1991); Nickles, "Fast-Track Arbitration: A Claimant's Perspective", 2 *Am. Rev. Int'l Arb.* 143 (1991); Bemis, "Fast-Track Arbitration as an Alternative Institutional Procedure", 2 *Am. Rev. Int'l Arb.* 148 (1991); Watkiss, "Fast-Track Arbitration: A Contractual Intermediary's Perspective", 2 *Am. Rev. Int'l Arb.* 150 (1991); Ballem, "Fast-Track Arbitration on the International Scene", 2 *Am. Rev. Int'l Arb.* 152 (1991); Silverman, "Fast Track Arbitration: A Respondent's Perspective", 2 *Am. Rev. Int'l Arb.* 154 (1991); Davis, "Fast-Track Arbitration: An ICC Counsel's Perspective", 2 *Am. Rev. Int'l Arb.* 159 (1991).

the 3-arbitrator panel held one day of hearings during which each party had three hours to present its case; witnesses were present but the parties did not insist in extensive cross-examinations; the written opinion was presented to the ICC Court for approval within 36 hours after completion of the hearing; it was possible to complete the arbitration within an agreed one-week extension of the deadline thanks to the limited scope of issues dealt with (the periodic redetermination of the price in a long-term commodity supply agreement), an unusual degree of cooperation between the ICC, the tribunal and the parties, and a very determined management of the procedure by the presiding arbitrator who, in his own words acted with an "iron fist" but was always concerned to make sure that the parties were involved in the decisionmaking process and were heard with their objections; the draft award which had to be brought by personal courier to Paris was approved by the Chairman of the ICC Court overnight.

The LCIA and the ICC have incorporated provisions providing for shortening of time limits into their Arbitration Rules.[266] The effectiveness of fast-track tools, however, is a function of the participants' willingness to constructively co-operate and it rarely happens that *all* of those involved are equally committed to an accelerated timetable. In practice, not only the parties, but also the arbitral tribunal can slow down the process: under the ICC Rules, for example, the tribunal has the power to re-extend time-limits previously curtailed by the parties.[267]

In addition, fast-track procedures can be very risky: it may either turn out to be impossible to reach an award within the time limit (in the case mentioned above the parties were asked to agree to a one-week extension of the deadline) with the possible consequence that the arbitrators lose their mandate and the arbitration clause becomes inoperative (unless the contract provides for a back-up procedure), or an award can be reached but only at the expense of the due process rights of one of the parties who may later stand a good chance attacking the award in the courts. Another disadvantage of fast-track arbitration is that it makes it harder to reach an amicable solution for the simple reason that there may be no time to conduct settlement negotiations.[268] Also, the potential cost savings should not be over-estimated since the fast-track procedure compresses work that otherwise would be stretched out over several years into a short period of extremely intense activity (in the case

---

[266] Art. 9 LCIA Rules; 32 ICC Rules. However, the ICC has declined to adopt a specific set of procedures allowing for "real" fast-track procedures in situations where only one party claims urgency and presses for departure from the regular time limits while the other party is unwilling to cooperate, cf. Goldstein, International Legal Developments in Review: 1998 Business Transactions & Disputes, International Commercial Arbitration 389, 399-400 (1999); By contrast, the LCIA Rules go further by giving the Court "complete discretion" to curtail certain time-limits irrespective of the parties' consent (Art. 9.3 LCIA Rules).

[267] Cf. Art. 32.2 ICC Rules.

[268] Nickles id. 147.

mentioned, 1500 pages of written submissions were produced!), and the ICC fee schedule, which entitles the arbitrators to earn the full fee upon the rendering of the award, expressly rewards expeditious case management.[269] In any event, fast-track procedures will probably continue to be the exception, and the case outlined above is perhaps even less representative of the general practice of international arbitration than e.g. the "Pyramids" case. According to the Secretary General of the ICC Court, the significance of this case for the ICC was that it demonstrates that, if the parties are serious about expediting the case, the ICC would not be an impediment to a speedy resolution of the dispute; but he emphasized that in practice it is very rare that the defendant wants a quick resolution.[270]

7. Conclusion

Although each arbitration is a unique procedure which in large measure will be tailored to the specific case, certain patterns can be found. The following flow chart gives an overview of the sequence and the distribution of activities over time in a "typical" international commercial arbitration:

Figure 1: Flow Chart – The Arbitral Process

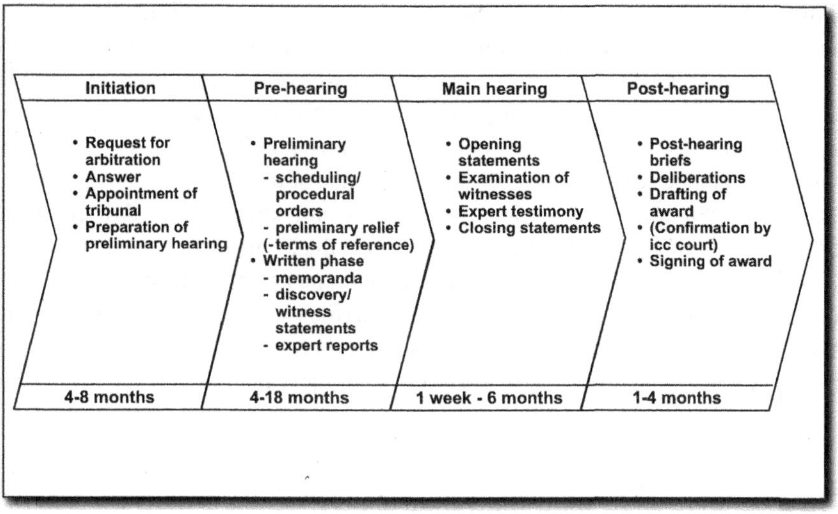

Initiation	Pre-hearing	Main hearing	Post-hearing
• Request for arbitration • Answer • Appointment of tribunal • Preparation of preliminary hearing	• Preliminary hearing - scheduling/ procedural orders - preliminary relief (-terms of reference) • Written phase - memoranda - discovery/ witness statements - expert reports	• Opening statements • Examination of witnesses • Expert testimony • Closing statements	• Post-hearing briefs • Deliberations • Drafting of award • (Confirmation by icc court) • Signing of award
4-8 months	4-18 months	1 week - 6 months	1-4 months

---

[269] Cf. Appendix III to the ICC Rules of Arbitration, Art. 2.2.

[270] Interview with Eric Schwartz, Secretary General of the ICC Court of International Arbitration, Paris, February 25, 1992.

III. THE COST STRUCTURE OF INTERNATIONAL ARBITRATION

In order to find ways of reducing the costs of international commercial arbitration, it is necessary to understand how the costs of arbitration are composed (1), how the most important element of these costs, the fees of counsel and tribunal, are calculated (2), and how costs are allocated between the parties (3).

1. Composition of the Costs of Arbitration

For the purposes of this book, the term "costs of arbitration" shall be understood in a broad sense, covering all transaction costs caused by the procedure and consisting of the *costs of the tribunal* which are identical to the narrower use of the term "cost of arbitration" and are usually subject to an advance deposit paid to the tribunal or the administrating institution (a), and the *costs of the parties* which are incurred by the parties themselves but which may at least in part be subjected to reimbursement by the unsuccessful party to the prevailing party (b).

a. Costs of the Tribunal

The costs of the tribunal comprise the following items:

(1) *arbitrators' fees*[271] *(including any value added tax)*[272] *and expenses;*[273]

(2) *administrative costs* which comprise the fees and expenses[274] of the institution administering the procedure, the administrative costs incurred by the arbitrators themselves and/or the compensation and expenses of a secretary to the tribunal;

(3) *fees and expenses* of any ("neutral") *experts* hired by the tribunal;

---

[271] The calculation of the fees is explained below at p. 91 et seq.

[272] Whether an arbitrator's fee is subject to VAT varies according to the tax laws of the competent jurisdiction. Value added taxes are not accounted for in the fee schedules of most arbitration institutions and therefore have to be budgeted for separately by the parties. Since VAT is also not covered by any security deposits, arbitrators risk having their fees effectively reduced as a result of their VAT liability; for further details on the complex issues arising out of arbitrator's VAT liability see Bühler, Costs in ICC Arbitration: A Practitioner's View, 3 *Am. Rev. Int'l Arb.* 116, 129-130 (1992).

[273] These include mainly the cost of transportation and living expenses; cf. Redfern & Hunter, *Law and Practice of International Commercial Arbitration* 405 (3rd ed. 1999) and Bühler, Costs in ICC Arbitration: A Practitioner's View, 3 *Am. Rev. Int'l Arb.* 116, 132 n.74 (1992).

[274] Some institutions (such as the AAA and the LCIA) assess fees and expenses separately while others (such as the ICC) charge a lump sum irrespective of the actual costs incurred.

(4) *logistical costs connected with hearings* such as conference facilities, the services of any translators and the preparation of transcripts.

b. Costs of the Parties

The costs of the parties are made up of the following:

(1) *lawyers' fees and expenses*, which may include the costs connected with hiring local counsel at the place of the arbitration or counsel specialized in international arbitration in addition to a party's permanent counsel;

(2) *fees and expenses of* any *experts* hired by the parties;

(3) travel and other *expenses of witnesses and individuals representing the party* at hearings;

(4) the costs of *ancillary litigation* relating e.g. to the jurisdiction of the tribunal, to the taking of evidence or to preliminary security measures.

(5) *"indirect" costs* which can be of an internal nature, such as the use of in-house counsel, the disruption of business, the diversion of executive time, the tying up of human resources; or of an external nature, such as damage to business relations or one or both parties' reputation; in the words of the former General Counsel of the American Arbitration Association:

> "... a dispute is by definition non-productive, ... a totally negative thing; you tie up your executives in hearings, it takes on a life of its own; each party gets more intransigent, you cut off your ability to do business again, all kinds of things go wrong that you just can't predict."[275]

(6) *"economic" costs connected with the substance of the dispute* such as the loss of *interest* or currency fluctuations; these are a special category of costs because they can be of a "zero-sum-game" nature: they may not increase the overall costs of the procedure but simply create a burden for one party, typically the owner of a meritorious claim, that corresponds to a benefit to the other party, typically the defendant against such a claim.[276]

Not all of these elements materialize in all cases and not all of these elements have the same weight. For instance, the *fees* of lawyers, arbitrators and experts generally outweigh their *expenses* by a wide margin, and of all the components of

---

[275] Interview with Gerald Aksen, January 21, 1992.

[276] This type of financial consequences does not represent "transaction costs" in the strict sense, and in this regard arbitration indeed is a "zero-sum-game"; however, all other items mentioned are transaction costs and contribute to the fact that arbitration, on balance, is a "negative-sum-game".

the costs of an arbitration, the fees of the *lawyers* – when taken together – almost invariably represent the lion's share. This should come as no surprise since it is the lawyers who typically perform the bulk of the work investigating, analyzing and presenting the case.

2. How Fees are Calculated

The fees of lawyers and arbitrators are calculated in different ways according to the professional standards and practices in the home jurisdictions of the lawyers involved and according to the system of arbitration employed. The two basic forms of calculating the fees are as a function of the time spent or of the amount in dispute, but under most systems some form of a combination method is applied.

a. Fees of Lawyers

Lawyer fees are almost invariably calculated on the basis of the *time worked*, with hourly rates sometimes adjusted according to the monetary importance and complexity of the case. In international cases this is true even for most German lawyers who otherwise operate under a statutory system calculating attorney fees as a function of the amount in dispute.[277]

b. Fees of Arbitrators

The calculation methods for arbitrator fees are more varied. Systems that calculate arbitrator compensation exclusively as a percentage of the amount in dispute *(ad valorem)* are rare but they do exist, for instance under the rules of the German Arbitration Institution.[278] More frequent is a system based on hourly or daily fees regardless of the values involved *(per diem)*, as employed, for instance, by ICSID. However, the most common way of calculating the fees for arbitrators is a *combination method* which is calculated in one of two ways: either it is based on an hourly or daily basis but with a rate calculated in proportion to the amount in dispute, or it is primarily calculated as a percentage of the sum in dispute but will be adjusted in light of the amount and quality of the work performed.

---

[277] Under this system, compensation for lawyers is made up of a maximum of four units of fee ("*Gebühren*") which are calculated as a percentage of the amount in dispute and are triggered by the following tasks: general advice, initiation of procedure, participation in hearings, participation in the taking of evidence, and conclusion of a settlement.

[278] See the fee schedule of the German Arbitration Institution (www.dis-arb.de) which, however, has a comparatively insignificant caseload of international arbitrations; a similar system is employed by the Arbitral Centre of the Federal Economic Chamber Vienna (cf. Art. 24 Rules of Arbitration and Conciliation (Vienna Rules)).

(1) The LCIA and AAA System

An example for the former system is practised by the London Court of Arbitration which for hearing time uses daily fees ranging from £ 800 to £ 2000 and for fractional or overlong days hourly rates between £ 100 and £ 250. The exact fee will be fixed at the time of the appointment of the arbitrators and depends on the circumstances of the case, notably its complexity and the qualifications of the arbitrators.[279] The American Arbitration Association has a similar system: arbitrator compensation is time-based, and although the AAA does not publish a schedule of arbitrator fees, it acts as an intermediary when the fee is negotiated. The result is a similar range of fees as with the LCIA although the AAA asserts that on average, the amount in dispute and accordingly the arbitrators' compensation tends to be less significant in AAA arbitrations than in LCIA or ICC cases.

(2) The ICC System

The most important combination system based primarily on the sums in dispute[280] is that of the International Chamber of Commerce.[281] It establishes a scale with brackets of minimum and maximum amounts combined with additional percentages that decrease as the sum in dispute rises (e.g., a sole arbitrator's fee[282] is calculated as 2% to 11% of the amount in dispute for sums between USD 50,000 and USD 100,000; an additional 1% to 5.5% is added for sums between USD 100,000 and USD 500,000 and so on until the percentage becomes marginal, with a share of 0.01% to 0.056% for amounts over USD 100 million). Within these brackets the fee is determined according to the amount of work done and other factors such as the complexity of the case and the responsibility assumed by the arbitrator.[283] In addition, the ICC rules try to encourage a speedy resolution by taking into account the rapidity of the proceedings[284], thus avoiding any incentive for the arbitrators to drag out the process in order to increase their fees. Another important safeguard

---

[279] See the Schedule of Fees and Costs of the London Court of Arbitration.

[280] While counterclaims advanced by the defendant are always added to the sum in dispute – which can increase the amount substantially and accordingly force the claimant to increase the security deposit – set-off claims, according to Art. 30.5 of the ICC Rules shall be taken into consideration only "insofar as [they] may require the Arbitral Tribunal to consider additional matters". This qualification, however, has very little practical relevance since set-off claims almost always require the tribunal to consider additional matters, cf. Craig, Park & Paulsson, *International Chamber of Commerce Arbitration* § 14.01 ii) (2000).

[281] Appendix III to the ICC Rules of Arbitration; Arbitration Costs and Fees.

[282] The fees for three arbitrator panels are increased, in the discretion of the ICC Court of Arbitration, "up to a maximum which shall normally not increase three times the fee for a sole arbitrator", see Art. 2.2 App. III to ICC Rules.

[283] See Art. 2.2 App. III to ICC Rules.

[284] Id.

is that the determination of the arbitrators' fees remains in the discretion of the ICC Court of Arbitration who evaluates the efficiency of the procedure and is not strictly bound by the bracket. Under special circumstances the ICC Court will go beyond the maximum or minimum figures, e.g., to prevent a windfall to the arbitrators in very simple cases with very high stakes or to avoid hardships in the event of a case that turns out to be very lengthy despite the arbitrators' efforts to accelerate the proceedings.[285]

The ICC's fee schedule has the advantage that it is relatively *predictable* in that it establishes a minimum, and more important from the parties' perspective, a maximum fee which will only be surpassed in exceptional circumstances. The ability of a party to calculate the financial risk of an arbitration is also enhanced by the fact that, before filing its request for arbitration, it can ask the ICC for an estimate of the costs and the advance on costs to be deposited.[286] The general counsel of a multinational industrial conglomerate expressed the importance of the predictability aspect from a "consumer perspective":

"... from the user's perspective the most important requirement for a fee schedule is predictability; the two questions management asks the lawyer are: how long is it going to take and how much is it going to cost ... the ICC schedule has the great advantage that ... it permits the lawyer to tell their client (or the legal department its management) in which range the expected costs will lie; the ICC schedule might not always be just in light of the effort exerted from the arbitrators but ... the predictability is more important ..."[287]

At the same time the ICC system allows for some flexibility to compensate the arbitrators based on the value of their work and to reward an expeditious conclusion of the procedure. In this context it is important to note that, unlike other organizations that fix the arbitrators' rate of compensation in advance, the ICC practices a form of *"performance review"* after the procedure has been concluded.[288] Another way how the ICC encourages a speedy resolution is by paying out the bulk of the fee only after completion of the procedure, leaving the arbitrators with very little revenues while the procedure is going on.[289] Through these means the ICC is

---

[285] Cf. Art. 31.2 of the ICC Rules.

[286] With the introduction of an online cost-calculator, the parties may now also get a direct estimate online (not including arbitrators' expenses): www.iccwbo.org/court/english/cost_calculator/cost_calculator.asp.

[287] Interview with Eric Robine February 21, 1992; translation by the authors.

[288] Interview with Eric Schwartz, Secretary General of the ICC Court of International Arbitration, Paris, February 25, 1992.

[289] Id.

capable to at least partly compensate for the delays occasioned by other features of the ICC procedure, notably the need to obtain the confirmation of the ICC Court for the Terms of Reference, the final award as well as any preliminary or interim awards.

No system of arbitrator compensation is without its drawbacks and the inevitable disadvantage of the ICC system is that it may lead to extreme results, if measured as an hourly compensation, in cases that are resolved very quickly or that take extremely long. However, the ranges given in the ICC fee schedule are sufficiently broad to make it quite rare that an arbitrator will realize a windfall or will be subject to an egregiously low compensation.[290]

c. Fees of Arbitration Institutions

The fees received by the arbitration institutions themselves are also mainly calculated in proportion to the amount in dispute but tend to be limited to a fixed maximum fee which differs from institution to institution.[291] The ICC probably has the highest fees which consist of a *filing fee* of USD 2,500[292] and an *administrative fee* which roughly corresponds to the fee for a single arbitrator and which can be as high as USD 88,800 in the case of an amount in dispute equal to or above USD 80 million.[293]

d. Security Deposits

Most arbitration institutions require a deposit as a security for the costs of the tribunal and the institution. In ICC Arbitration, the former system providing for an "advance on costs" (Art. 9.1.) and authorizing the Secretariat to make the submission of the file to the arbitrator conditional upon payment (Art. 9.3.), has been modified by a mechanism aimed at speeding up the process: while under the previous regulation, only the *Court* could fix an advance intended to cover the costs of the *entire* arbitration and payable by *both* parties, the new Art. 30.1 now

---

[290] Discrepancies between the arbitrators' workload and their compensation are avoided by the schedule developed by the Swiss Chambers of Commerce which at first glance looks as though it were primarily based on the values in dispute but which in essence operates as a time-based system. The arbitrator's fees are taken from a scale of brackets similar to that of the ICC, and within the brackets the fees are likewise determined according to the time spent and the complexity of the case. However, the fees are automatically adjusted upward or downward, regardless of the limits indicated by the bracket, to ensure that the compensation is kept within a fixed minimum and maximum hourly rate; cf. Art. 39, Appendix B Art. 2 and Appendix C of the Swiss Rules.

[291] The American Arbitration Association charges an Initial Filing Fee of up to USD 10,000 (minimum: USD 500) and a Case Service Fee of up to USD 4,000 (minimum: USD 200).

[292] Cf. App. III to ICC Rules, Art. 1.1: "[…] advance payment of USD 2.500 on the administrative expenses […]".

[293] See the ICC's Schedule of Costs.

authorizes the *Secretary General* to ask for a *provisional* advance[294] immediately upon receipt of the arbitration request, to be paid by the claimant *alone* (and intended to cover the costs only until the Terms of Reference have been drawn up)[295]. Thus, neither the Court nor the defendant being required to take any action affecting the transmission of the file, two possible sources of – sometimes considerable – delay have been eliminated.[296] At a later stage, usually after receipt of the answer to the request, the Court fixes the definitive advance, intended to cover the remaining costs. The claimant's contribution to the provisional advance is credited towards his share on the advance on costs.

Thus, under the new ICC Rules, there are two types of payment to be made: the provisional advance, usually paid only by the Claimant and covering the costs of the arbitration until the Terms of Reference are drawn up, and the advance on costs, paid at a later stage in equal shares by both parties, and intended to cover the entire cost of the arbitration.[297]

e. Effect of a Settlement on the Fees

The early termination of the procedure through a settlement or withdrawal of the case invariably leads to very substantial savings. This is obvious for the costs of legal representation and for the tribunal's costs to the extent that the fee system is based on the time worked. But even under the ICC system the fees will be adjusted: since the schedule is based on the assumption that the case ends with an award, the ICC Court tends to reduce both the administrative fee and the fees of the arbitrators in the event of an early termination.[298]

In the practice of the ICC, one third of the *administrative* fee is considered to have been earned after transmission of the file to the arbitrators, and a total of one half is earned once the Terms of Reference have been signed and submitted to the ICC Court for approval.[299] The *arbitrators'* fees will be adjusted taking into account, among other considerations, the amount of time spent by the arbitrators.[300] However,

---

[294] In addition to the payment required to accompany the request under Art. 1.1 of Appendix III.

[295] The provisional advance is determined with reference to the amount of the claim and does not take into account the amounts of any counterclaims, cf. Craig, Park & Paulsson, International Chamber of Commerce Arbitration § 14.01 i) (2000).

[296] See Derains & Schwartz, *A Guide to the New ICC Rules of Arbitration* 306 (1998).

[297] See Greenberg, "An Introduction to Commencing Arbitration under the ICC Rules", *Vindobona Journal of International Commerical Law & Arbitration* 122, 125-126 (2000).

[298] Cf. Art. 2.6 Appendix III to the ICC Rules of Arbitration.

[299] Bühler, "Costs in ICC Arbitration: A Practitioner's View", 3 *Am. Rev. Int'l Arb.* 116, 127 n48 (1992).

[300] Letter from Mr. Eric A. Schwartz, Secretary General of the ICC International Court of Arbitration, to the author, dated June 22, 1992; see also Craig, Park & Paulsson, *International*

where the arbitrators have directly contributed to the achievement of a settlement, the reduction of the fees resulting from the early termination might be partially offset by granting the arbitrators a sort of "settlement bonus".[301] Any excess of the advance on costs over the actual fees will be repaid to the parties.

3. Allocation of Costs in the Award

Under all of the main international arbitration rules, the tribunal has the power to allocate the costs between the parties, i.e. to determine who shall bear the costs of the arbitration and in which proportion. Under all rules the allocation is determined by the tribunal and included in the award, although usually without reasons. A decision on costs will be generally included in the award as far as the *costs of the tribunal* are concerned. Important differences exist with respect to (a) the extent to which the parties' costs can be allocated and (b) the principle according to which this is done.[302]

a. Costs Subject to Allocation

All the main arbitration rules direct the arbitrators to apportion the costs of the *tribunal* including the administrative cost, as well as the "reasonable" (Art 31 (d) AAA Rules, Art 31.1 ICC Rules, Art. 28.3 LCIA Rules) cost of *outside legal counsel*. The *remaining costs of the parties* (executive time, in-house legal advice, etc.) are included in the allowable costs by some arbitration rules (e.g. ICSID, LCIA, ICC[303]) while others (e.g. AAA, UNCITRAL) do not mention or cover them.

The determination of the allowable costs of the procedure is done in two steps: the *arbitrators'* fees are either agreed in advance among the parties and the members of the tribunal or fixed by the arbitration institution, whereas the extent to which the *parties'* costs are subject to allocation will be determined by the tribunal as part of its decision on costs. The practice of arbitral tribunals in determining which legal costs are "reasonable" and therefore subject to allocation is far from uniform. Sometimes the arbitrators simply accept the bills presented by the parties, as long as they are in line with the local practices in the lawyer's "home jurisdiction".

Chamber of Commerce Arbitration § 3.02 iv) (2000) and Bühler id.

[301] Cf. Bühler id. 131.

[302] For a detailed (and, in spite of the 1998 modifications to the Rules still up to date – the basic scheme remaining the same) analysis see Bühler, "Costs in ICC Arbitration: A Practitioner's View", 3 *Am. Rev. Int'l Arb.* 116, 139 et seq. (1992) and Gotanda, Awarding Costs and Attorney's fees in International Commercial Arbitrations, Michigan Journal of International Law 1 (1999); see also Wetter & Priem, "Costs and their Allocation in International Commercial Arbitration", 2 *Am. Rev. Int'l Arb.* 249 (1991).

[303] Cf. the new Art. 31.1 now expressly referring to "reasonable legal and other costs incurred by the parties [...]" (emphasis added). For a detailed discussion, see Derains & Schwartz, *A Guide to the New ICC Rules of Arbitration* 336-337 (1998).

But more often, the amounts will be adjusted, e.g. in accordance with the billing practices at the place of the arbitration or in the arbitrator's "home jurisdiction". Considerations of equity can also play a role, particularly when the legal costs of the winning party appear disproportionate in the circumstances: for instance, it may not seem entirely fair to oblige a third world state enterprise having relied chiefly on in-house counsel to reimburse the legal costs of a Western corporation that was represented by a team of sophisticated lawyers who charge fees of over USD 500 per hour per person. As a result, the amounts recognized for allocation can be substantially lower than the actual costs of the winning party.[304]

b. Principles Governing the Allocation

A number of arbitration rules expressly endorse the principle that *costs follow the event*, also known as the *English Rule*, according to which the costs of the procedure have to be borne by the losing party (e.g. Art. 40.1 UNCITRAL Rules, Art. 28.4 LCIA Rules). Other rules do not provide any guideline (e.g. Art. 31 AAA Rules, Art. 31.1 ICC Rules), and it cannot be said that one particular principle has attained universal recognition in practice.[305]

The simplest and perhaps still the most common approach in international arbitration is that *each party has to bear its own costs*, also known as the *American Rule*, which means that effectively there will be no allocation and that the costs of the tribunal are split evenly between the parties. Where the arbitration rules do not spell out a principle, the arbitrators frequently follow the tradition of their home jurisdiction or considerations of equity, taking into account e.g. the extent to which costs have been occasioned by tactical maneuvering of individual parties. This in turn means that, since most tribunals are composed of arbitrators with different legal backgrounds, the result will often be a compromise between several principles, leading to a solution where the costs are allocated in a more vague proportion to the substantive outcome. Again, a distinction has to be made between the costs of the tribunal which are more likely to be allocated in accordance with the substance of the dispute, and the parties's costs where there may be some hesitation to burden the losing party with the expenses of its opponent which could be perceived as "adding insult to injury".[306]

Since claims are often exaggerated the question arises how to measure the success of a party. Here, arbitral tribunals generally do not simply compare what was claimed with what was awarded, as is the rule, e.g., in German Civil procedure,

---

[304] See the examples in Bühler, "Costs in ICC Arbitration: A Practitioner's View", 3 *Am. Rev. Int'l Arb.* 116, 142-143 (1992).

[305] For a general overview see Smith, "Feature Costs in International Commercial Arbitration", *Dispute Resolution Journal* 30 (February, April 2001).

[306] Cf. Craig, Park & Paulsson, *International Chamber of Commerce Arbitration* § 21.04 iii) (2000).

but tend to examine whether the inflation of claims has led to additional complexity and therefore additional costs.[307]

In sum, in spite of the possibility of cost allocation, a claimant initiating an international arbitration procedure incurs a substantial financial risk even if he can be certain that all of his claims will be upheld: in the best case, the arbitrators will oblige the losing party to bear all of the costs of the tribunal plus the winning party's legal costs to the extent they are deemed "reasonable". All other costs will have to be borne by the winning party regardless of the merits of its case. In addition, in ICC arbitration the winning party will need to recover from the losing party the 50% of the tribunal's cost which it had to disburse as an "advance on costs" because this deposit is actually used to pay the arbitrators' fees and expenses as well as the administrative fee. If the arbitrators do not adhere to the principle that costs follow the event, the winning party is not only burdened with all of its own costs but also has to pay for half of the tribunal's costs. It can be even worse: where the respondent has refused to pay his share of the advance on costs and the claimant was obliged to pay the entire deposit, the claimant will have to run after the respondent to recover that party's 50% share of the tribunal's costs, too.

4. Conclusion: Factors Influencing the Costs of Arbitration

Any party faced with the prospect of having to conduct an international arbitration will have to take into account a number of factors when trying to calculate the financial risk involved. The single most important variable is *time* or, more precisely, the amount of *work done* by both arbitrators and counsel; for counsel this follows from the internationally established practice of determining their fees on an hourly basis; arbitrator fees are also often calculated on a *per diem* basis, but even where the arbitrators' fees are calculated *ad valorem,* the amount in dispute will only determine a bracket of fees, and the actual work done is the most important factor in determining the concrete fee from within the applicable range (see explanation above).

The amount of work done in turn depends on a number of factors such as:

(1) the *nature and complexity of the case* and in particular the *importance of factual and technical issues* and the resulting *number of witnesses and experts*[308] to be examined; a fact-heavy case potentially requires much more preparation by the attorneys and more hearing time than a case depending merely on the decision of a limited number of legal issues;

---

[307] For more details and concrete examples see Bühler, "Costs in ICC Arbitration: A Practitioner's View", 3 *Am. Rev. Int'l Arb.* 116, 140-144 (1992).

[308] Obviously it makes a big difference if there is only one "neutral" expert who is appointed by the tribunal or if there is a "battle" between "partisan" experts presented by the parties.

(2) the *logistical parameters* of the procedure which have a direct impact on costs: this applies to the *number of arbitrators* (having a panel of three arbitrators not only increases the fees and expenses of the tribunal but also creates scheduling problems that may lead to significant delays[309]) as well as to the place of the arbitration;

(3) to a certain extent the costs of the procedure depend on the behavior of the parties, e.g. the intensity of the *involvement of in-house counsel*[310] or the *extent to which claims* and counter-claims have been *exaggerated* for tactical reasons;[311] the *level of antagonism* among the parties also plays a significant role because an efficient arbitration procedure requires a certain degree of cooperation from the parties; if only one party is determined to drag out the procedure or to wage "total war", it will be very difficult to avoid significant delays and costs;[312]

(4) of similar importance for the costs and delays of an arbitration is the *efficiency of case management* achieved by the tribunal, i.e. the capacity of the presiding arbitrator to reach consensus with the parties on process issues and to use his authority within the legal framework in such a manner as to ensure a focused and streamlined procedure that keeps both the volume of the written documentation and the duration of oral hearings to the strictly necessary. Here, the *procedural preferences* of both arbitrators and counsel, particularly the difference between Civil Law-style and Common Law-style arbitration play an important role; substantial costs and delays will be inevitable where the participants follow the pattern of American litigation, with extensive discovery and lengthy oral hearings[313] encompassing protracted direct and cross examinations of witnesses and experts by counsel, as well as the use of

---

[309] One of the respondents told of an arbitration where the chairman, a famous English barrister was so booked out that it was impossible to schedule any meetings for an entire year.

[310] The use of in-house counsel may not only be cheaper in monetary terms but in-house lawyers tend to be more familiar with the economic situation and real interests of a party. Extensive reliance on in-house counsel, however, only saves costs if the in-house level of expertise is sufficient to deal with the intricacies of international arbitration procedures; inexperienced counsel can lead a party – and the entire procedure – into a disaster.

[311] In a value-based fee schedule inflated demands have a direct effect on the costs, but even in time-based systems inflated demands have an impact because counsel will have a natural tendency to do more extensive work on a case of seemingly great magnitude.

[312] The fees of lawyers are almost invariably calculated on a time basis (see above at p. 91) and those of experts do not have the same importance.

[313] Another important aspect is whether hearings are conducted in a few continuous segments or on a "piecemeal" basis with many short meetings stretched over a long period of time; in the latter case, a lot of time gets lost through the need of all participants to again familiarize themselves with the case at the beginning of each meeting.

literal transcripts which in large arbitrations can amount to tens of thousands of pages;

(5) another important factor is the *efficiency of the legal framework* of the arbitration, as determined by the law applicable to the procedure and the arbitration rules, if any, chosen by the parties; a deficient legal framework can cause incalculable delays and costs: when the rules of the game are ambiguous protracted procedural battles before the arbitrators as well as *collateral litigation* in the courts – possibly in various jurisdictions – may ensue; ambiguous procedural rules also entail the danger of subsequent attacks against the award based on alleged violations of the applicable arbitral procedure, a danger that is compounded where the applicable procedural law allows for extensive *judicial review* of arbitral awards;[314] another important aspect of the legal frame is whether the rules of procedure afford the arbitrators sufficient *powers to curtail delay tactics* and procedural maneuvering by the parties; as shown above, the *system for* the *calculation of* the *fees* of the tribunal also has an obvious impact on costs;

(6) last but not least, the amount of work done is in large measure a function of whether the procedure goes all the way to the issuance of an *award or* is terminated early by a *settlement*.

The diversity and number of influencing factors show how difficult it is to make generalized statements on the costs of international commercial arbitration. Nevertheless, a few conclusions can be drawn. Although it is generally difficult to calculate in advance the cost of an arbitration, some systems of institutional arbitration, such as the ICC system, do offer a certain amount of control and predictability at least with respect to the costs of the tribunal. In addition, the parties can exercise some influence on the costs providing for a legal regime that ensures an efficient and effective procedure, by selecting the place of the arbitration which in itself has an important impact for the legal regime governing the procedure, as well as through the selection of arbitrators and certain logistical parameters. However, since time – or more precisely, the amount of work done by arbitrators and counsel – is the most important variable, the most significant savings can be achieved through an early termination of the procedure by means of a settlement.

---

[314] To a certain extent this danger is avoided in ICC arbitration with its clear set of rules and the scrutiny of awards practiced by the ICC Court but from time to time even the practice of the ICC Court is subject to litigation.

IV. RECENT TRENDS IN INTERNATIONAL COMMERCIAL ARBITRATION

The rapid growth of international commercial arbitration in the past decade was accompanied by a few significant developments.[315]

1. Modernization of Arbitration Laws

The last decade brought a wave of modernization of arbitration laws,[316] and in particular widespread acceptance of the UNCITRAL Model Law. It is highly probable that more states will follow the example and incorporate the Model Law in their national laws. The ensuing modernization and homogenization of arbitration laws[317] can be perceived as one of the major trends in the field.

2. Multiparty Constellations

International transactions increasingly involve multiple parties and multiple contracts. Since drafters of arbitration clauses occasionally have been (and still are) unaware of the additional risks and uncertainties resulting from multiparty constellations, and since many international commercial arbitration laws and rules do not regulate multi-party disputes sufficiently, problems are common.[318]

One basic challenge in multi-party arbitration is to ensure consistency of decisions. Ideally, the tribunal should have jurisdiction to deal with all disputes arising between all parties. Four main types of multi-party arbitration have been

---

[315] See, for example, Weigand, *Practitioner's Handbook on International Arbitration* (2002), 90-98.; Hunter, "Anticipating Trends in Dispute Resolution", in de Zylva & Harrison, *International Commercial Arbitration* 15 (2000); Session II, International Commercial Arbitration: Current Trends/Future Possibilities, First Annual Global Center for Dispute Resolution Research Conference, The Hague, April 23, 2004; "The Challenges Ahead" in Bulletin for Dispute Resolution Research, New York: Global Center for Dispute Resolution Research Vol. I, No. 1 (Autumn 2004), at 3-4.

[316] See, for example, Hacking, "Arbitration Law Reform in Europe", 65 (3) *Arbitration: Journal of the Chartered Institute of Arbitrators* 180-185 (1999).

[317] Cf. Weigand, *Practitioner's Handbook on International Arbitration* (2002), 92, who argues that against this background of stability, there is no need for additional international conventions.

[318] For more details cf. Lew, Mistelis & Kröll, *Comparative International Arbitration*, Chapter 16 (2003); Hanotiau, "Complex-Multicontract-Multiparty-Arbitration", 14 *Arb. Int'l* 369-394 (1998); Hardy, "Multi-party Arbitration: Exceptional Problems Need Exceptional Solutions", *Arbitration* 15-20 (2000); Stipanowich, "Arbitration and Multiparty Dispute: The Search for Workable Solutions", 72 *Iowa L. Rev.* 473 at 523 (Mar. 1987); Lew & Smith, "Multiparty Arbitrations", *Stockholm Arbitration Newsletter* (2/2000; Kazutake, "Party Autonomy in International Commercial Arbitration: Consolidation of Multiparty and Classwide Arbitration", 9 *Ann. Surv. Int'l & Comp. L.* 189 (2003).

developed: unified multi-party arbitration[319] and consolidated arbitration,[320] concurrent bilateral arbitration[321] as well as parallel bilateral arbitration.[322] The arbitration clause should explicitly name the form of multi-party arbitration to be conducted.[323]

A significant problem in multi-party arbitration arises from the inherent right of each party to nominate its own arbitrator. Two possible solutions shall be briefly indicated: Firstly, the arbitration clause may provide that all parties on one side of the arbitration, the joint claimants or joint respondents, shall make a joint nomination of one arbitrator; they may also authorize the selected arbitration institution to appoint at its discretion one arbitrator for the party that disagrees. Alternatively, the arbitration clause may provide that all arbitrators shall be appointed by the governing arbitration institution.[324]

3. Focus on Evidence

International arbitration laws and rules tend to give relatively little guidance on the crucial question of the admissibility and taking of evidence. The reason may be two-folded: firstly, the arbitrators and parties are in charge of conducting the arbitration procedure, thereby making the procedure as flexible as possible; and secondly, there is a desire to maintain a neutral stance in the competition between the influence of Civil Law and Common Law.

This has generated an intense debate in the field of international commercial arbitration on the following issues: What evidence is admissible, how and at what stage of the procedure it must be taken and how should it be presented to the

---

[319] All parties are joining in one proceeding to resolve all disputes before a single arbitral tribunal.

[320] Two or more separately commenced arbitrations are consolidated and thereafter proceed before a single tribunal as an unified multi-party arbitration.

[321] Two or more separate arbitrations proceed before the same tribunal at common hearings, thus allowing common issues in the various arbitrations to be considered and resolved together.

[322] Two or more separate arbitrations proceed before the same tribunal but at separate hearings and without any exchange of documentary or witness evidence between the separate proceedings.

[323] Kazutake, "Party Autonomy in International Commercial Arbitration: Consolidation of Multiparty and Classwide Arbitration", 9 *Ann. Surv. Int'l & Comp. L.* 189, 212 et seq. (2003).

[324] The Singapore International Arbitration Centre (SIAC) and the Hong Kong International Arbitration Centre (HKIAC) recognize these problems and provide expressly in their rules that the power of appointment in the absence of agreement shall be exercised by the institution.

arbitral tribunal?[325] In an effort to fill the procedural gap, the IBA has published "Rules on the Taking of Evidence in International Commercial Arbitration".[326] The Rules have been relatively well received and widely used and are likely to shape the future practice.

4. Increasing Role of Alternative Settlement Techniques

Since the first edition of this book, Alternative Dispute Resolution (ADR) – which at that stage already formed an integral part of the legal system in the United States – has become a significant element of the judicial landscape in many other countries in Europe and beyond, and statistics show that the use, for example, of commercial mediation services is rising rapidly. It is no longer considered as misconduct for an arbitrator to go beyond his traditional mandate and structures the process to facilitate settlement.[327] Instead, the discussion now focuses on whether it is a matter of good practice or even a duty of the arbitrator to actively encourage settlement.[328]

Evidently, there is also increasing awareness of the various practical ways in which the arbitrator can re-orientate the process in a direction increasing the chances of settlement. Processes like mediation and conciliation as well as methods like mini-trials or dispute review boards have entered the mainstream discussions and practice, and more and more arbitral institutions offer particular rules on mediation, conciliation or mini-trials.[329]

---

[325] Cf. Böckstiegel (ed.), *Beweiserhebung im Internationalen Schiedsverfahren* (2001); Triebel & Zons, "Befragung von Zeugen vor dem Hearing in Internationalen Schiedsverfahren", IDR 5 et seq. (2004); Weigand, *Practitioner's Handbook on International Arbitration* (2002); von Segesser, "Witness Preparation in International Commercial Arbitration", *ASA Bull.* Vol. 20, Nr. 2, 222 (2002); Böckstiegel, "Presenting Evidence in International Arbitration", *ICSID Rev. – Foreign Investment L.J.* 1, 2 (Spring 2001); Griffin, "Recent Trends in the Conduct of International Arbitration – Discovery Procedures and Witness Hearings", 17 (2) *J. Int. Arb.* 19-29 (2000).

[326] Adopted by a resolution of the IBA Council, June 1, 1999; information online at www. ibanet.org; see also IBA, "Commentary on the New IBA Rules of Evidence in International Commercial Arbitration", *Business Law International*, Issue 2, 3-113 (2000); Bühler & Dorgan, Witness "Testimony Pursuant to the 1999 IBA Rules of Evidence in International Commercial Arbitration", 17 (1) *J. Int. Arb.* 3-30 (2000).

[327] Koch & Schaefer, Can it be Sinful for an Arbitrator Actively to Promote Settlement?", *Arbitration and Dispute Resolution Law Journal*, Part 3, 153-184 (Sept 1999).

[328] Collins, "Do International Arbitral Tribunals have any Obligations to Encourage Settlement of the Disputes before Them?", *Arb. Int'l*, 19 (2003), 333-343. See also detailed discussion in Chapter 4.

[329] Cf. Weigand, *Practitioner's Handbook on International Arbitration* (2002), 97, with further references.

5. Rising Empirical Work on ICA

The body of empirical work on international commercial arbitration is growing. This trend is fostered by academic and practitioners' interest in the subject, the activity of organizations like the *Global Center for Dispute Resolution*[330] and an increasing openness of both arbitrators and arbitration institutions with regard to figures and proceedings. A number of investigations (see below in Chapter Four) into the inner workings of international commercial arbitration have begun to increase the transparency of the field. [331]

V. CONCLUSION

Arbitration in international business fulfills largely the same function that litigation performs in the domestic fields, providing a neutral forum to fairly decide a dispute. In addition, the opportunity to choose the arbitrators, the confidentiality of the arbitral proceedings and the arbitral award, the chance of saving time and money and the easy enforcement of arbitral awards are advantages that can hardly be overestimated in the practice of settling international commercial disputes. Arbitration is a "fundamental service"[332] for international trade.

At the same time, international commercial arbitration is burdened with problems in terms of potentially high transaction costs (direct costs, time lost, tying up of corporate energies) and a limited capacity to produce consensual solutions. In addition, and fully acknowledging the advantages of arbitration, critique with regard to the increasing formalization of the arbitral infrastructure has been expressed:[333]

> "Arbitration has lost that lightness of touch that characterized its early manifestations..., 'ceremonies' are multiplying, 'formalities' are on the increase and much time is spent in mirroring the arts of litigation...."[334]

---

[330] Compare, for example, the recent study *Patterns and Discontinuities in International Commercial Arbitration: The Global Center Survey of Practicioners* (May 24, 2005); the webpage of the Global Center for Dispute Resolution Research can be foud at www. globalcenteradr.org.

[331] Drahozal & Naimark (ed.), *Towards a Science of International Arbitration* (2005), at 3, summarizing the most significant empirical studies of the recent decades.

[332] Weigand, *Practitioner's Handbook on International Arbitration* (2002), 11.

[333] Andrew Okekeiferle, "Commercial Arbitration As the Most Effective Dispute Resolution Method – Still a fact or Now a Myth?", 15 *J. Int. Arb.* No. 4, 81; see also Park, "Arbitration's Protean Nature: The Value of Rules and the Risks of Discretion", 19 *Arb. Int'l* 279 (2003).

[334] Nariman, "International Commercial Arbitration – at the Cross-Roads", *Liber Amicorum Karl Heinz Böckstiegel* 555, at 556 (2001).

Chapter 4

Two Surveys on Arbitration and Settlement

Empirical contributions on international commercial arbitration are still rare because of the difficulties to generate useful empirical data, particularly on the process, the "inner workings" of international commercial arbitration. The confidential nature and the duration of the proceedings make it practically impossible to actually *observe* a large number of international commercial arbitrations. Even a very experienced practitioner will only be able to report on a fairly limited number of arbitrations. The only way to access a meaningful and representative body of arbitration experience therefore is to conduct a survey, backed up by in-depth interviews with leading practitioners.[335]

The first edition of this book comprised one of the first comprehensive empirical studies on the practice of international business dispute resolution. For the first time, empirical evidence was produced on the actual costs of international commercial arbitrations, how these costs accrue, about when, how and why cases are settled, and the specific role of the arbitrators in this process.[336] Ten years later, this survey was complemented by a second survey, prepared for this second edition of the book. Here, we added questions on the different roles of different members of an arbitral tribunal in trying to help the parties settle, the use of separate, "stand-by" mediators during arbitral proceedings, the use of mediation clauses and the role of arbitration institutions in proposing mediation to the parties of an arbitration. At the same time, we repeated some of the questions of the earlier survey in order to see whether the practice of arbitration and/or the attitudes of the participants had changed on certain key issues. The objective of the surveys was to find out the actual function of inter-national commercial arbitration (is it an "alternative" means of dispute resolution?) and to explore to which extent "alternative" settlement techniques could be used to enhance the potential of arbitration to produce amicable, consensual solutions more often, earlier on in the process and with lower transaction costs.[337]

---

[335] Cf. Buehring-Uhle, Scherer & Kirchhoff, "The Arbitrator as Mediator – Some Recent Empirical Insights", 20 (1) *J. Int. Arb.* 81 (2003) on the difficulties to conduct empirical studies in arbitration.

[336] See Buehring-Uhle, *Arbitration and Mediation in International Business* 128 (1996) for information on older empirical studies.

[337] Cf. Buehring-Uhle 127 (1996).

I. DESIGN OF THE SURVEYS

Both quantitative and qualitative elements were included in the studies, which consisted of written questionnaires as well as in-depth personal interviews.

In the first survey, completed in 1994, close to 150 questionnaires were distributed to practitioners all over the world. A total of 91 arbitrators, lawyers and in-house counsel from 17 countries[338] responded, 67 of which from 8 countries were interviewed in person with an average duration of 40 to 50 minutes, while the rest responded in writing.[339] The participants represented elite as well as highly experienced and reputable practitioners, both users and providers, of international commercial arbitration. The sample of the respondents was as diverse as the disputes in international business: just like the process of ICA in general, the survey brought together participants from all sorts of legal and cultural backgrounds.

For the second edition, we conducted a new survey, which was started in the fall of 2001 and completed in 2004. The quantitative analysis is based on 53 completed questionnaires. One might argue that, from a statistical point of view, 53 respondents is not a very large sample. On the other hand, there are probably not more than 200 practitioners worldwide with significant repeat experience in international commercial arbitration, and they form a closely-knit, rather discreet community of very busy people. This community is rather well covered in the sample, and the aggregate experience of this sample group in international business dispute resolution is indeed impressive: the 53 respondents come from 14 countries in all six continents and have participated in more than 3.000 international commercial arbitrations and mediations (over 2.500 arbitrations and over 600 mediations). The group includes both users and providers of dispute resolution services, i.e., in-house counsel, advocates and arbitrators/mediators. A large group of the respondents have been active in various capacities, having acted on some occasions as arbitrators/mediators and in others as counsel to parties in arbitration/mediation. All have had exposure to international commercial arbitration, and 35 have participated in international commercial mediation proceedings.

The group can be segmented by nationalities and, more significant perhaps, by principal legal backgrounds. Americans and Germans were the largest two groups and displayed, on a number of questions, a somewhat different set of experiences and attitudes, which is why we decided to break down the sample in four main segments:

---

[338] USA, Germany, Switzerland, France, England, Colombia, The Netherlands, Spain, Australia, Austria, Denmark, Egypt, Italy, Mexico, Poland, Sweden and Syria.

[339] For a more detailed description of the data collection see Buehring-Uhle 129 et seq. (1996).

Figure 2: Respondents to Survey

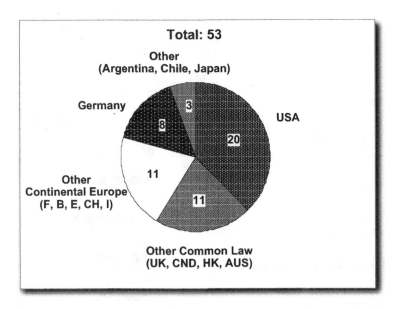

Total: 53

Other
(Argentina, Chile, Japan)

Germany   3

8   USA

20

Other   11
Continental Europe
(F, B, E, CH, I)   11

Other Common Law
(UK, CND, HK, AUS)

II. SUMMARY OF MOST RELEVANT FINDINGS

The findings can be grouped into three topics. The first set of questions dealt with the actual function of ICA (is it an "ADR" technique or simply a form of litigation that actually works in a cross-border setting?) and the transaction costs (is it faster and/or less expensive than cross-border litigation?). These questions were only covered in the first survey because the results were sufficiently clear and did not require additional probing. The second set of questions dealt with the capacity of ICA to facilitate voluntary settlement and the role arbitrators play in this context. These questions were covered in both surveys. We will focus here on the results of the second survey and indicate if there were significant differences between the two surveys. The third set of questions dealt with mediation in the proper sense, and ways to integrate mediation into ongoing arbitration proceedings. These questions were added in the second survey.

1. Function, Costs and Delays

Eliciting the actual advantages of international commercial arbitration in the eyes of the practicioners, the first survey confirmed the initial hypothesis: international commercial arbitration is not perceived as an 'alternative' procedure but as the only litigation mechanism that actually works in a cross-border context and that successfully avoids the pitfalls of litigating transnational disputes in national courts.[340]

Figure 3: Advantages of Arbitration

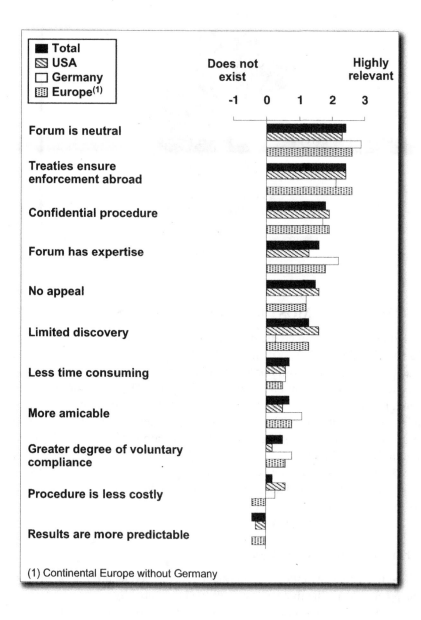

(1) Continental Europe without Germany

---

[340] Cf. Buehring-Uhle 143 (1996).

This is evidenced by the findings why parties actually choose international commercial arbitration instead of litigation: it offers a solution to the specific problems of transnational litigation, without creating a new alternative dispute resolution procedure that is fundamentally different from litigation.[341] The two main advantages of ICA mirror the two fundamental problems of transnational litigation. ICA provides what litigating transnational disputes in national courts appears to lack: the neutrality of the forum and the international enforceability of its decision. Four out of five respondents perceived these two attributes as "highly relevant" or "significant".[342] Next came, in order of relevance, confidentiality of the procedure, the expertise of the tribunal and the absence of appeals. Close to 60% of the respondents considered these to be other important advantages of ICA.[343]

With regard to transaction costs, the practitioners, perhaps surprisingly, held the typical advantages of "alternative" dispute resolution procedures to be less relevant in this context: while 67% of respondents thought that ICA is generally faster than cross-border litigation, only 41% thought it is generally less expensive.[344]

Figure 4: Cost Advantage compared to Litigation

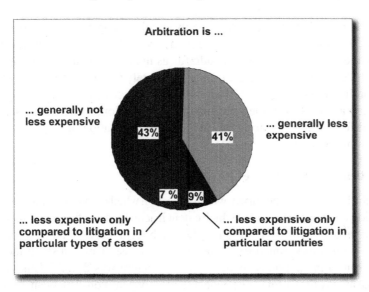

---

[341]   Cf. Buehring-Uhle 141 (1996).

[342]   Cf. Buehring-Uhle 136 (1996).

[343]   The aspect of limited discovery was viewed just as advantageous, but more ambivalent depending whether the respondents compared it to discovery under the rules in civil or Common Law jurisdictions, see Buehring-Uhle, 136-137 (1996).

[344]   US-American respondents were particularly skeptical about the length if the procedure, but more optimistic about lower costs; the vast majority of Germans found ICA both faster and less expensive, see Buehring-Uhle, 146-147 (1996).

Figure 5: Delays compared to Litigation

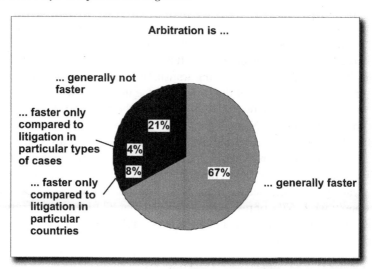

Acknowledging that arbitration commonly entails no appeal on the merits and that normally arbitration does not face congested case dockets as well as the fact that the costs of the procedure are not "subsidized" as in national court procedures, it can be concluded that, on aggregate, ICA is moderately faster but not less costly than litigation in national courts.[345] In light of possible settlement options, significant costs keep accruing until the very end of the arbitration, which opens significant potential for settlement during any stage of the arbitration proceedings that can lead to substantial cost savings.[346]

2. Settlement and the Role of Arbitrators

One of the key issues of the survey was the question whether international commercial arbitration is supposed to, and to which extent it actually does, foster voluntary settlements. A large majority of respondents (86%) thought that facilitating a consensual solution is one of the functions of the arbitral process. This is a slight increase in comparison to the previous survey where the figure was 83%.[347] This view was universal among the German respondents and among the non-American respondents with a Common Law background (England, Canada, Hong Kong, Australia), whereas

---

[345] Cf. Buehring-Uhle 147 (1996).

[346] Cf. Buehring-Uhle 156, 212 (1996).

[347] There are significant variations among respondents from different countries: 100% of the Germans, 95% of the Americans but only 61% of the other continental Europeans, see Buehring-Uhle 157 (1996).

a minority of the Americans (26%) and the non-German Civil Law practitioners (15%) thought that voluntary settlement was not a goal of arbitration.

Figure 6: Settlement as a Function of Arbitration

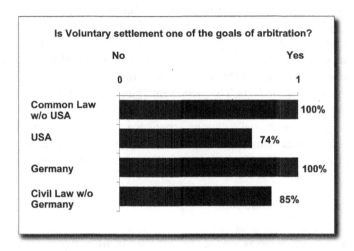

As to the effectiveness of arbitration, some participants (22%) regarded arbitration as an effective means to facilitate voluntary settlement. This was the dominant view particularly among the German participants (58%). Most respondents, however, thought that arbitration was helpful but rather in an indirect way:

Figure 7: Facilitation of Voluntary Settlements

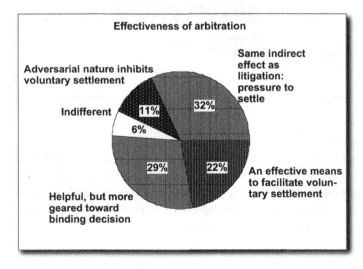

The only significant difference between the two surveys was found in regard to the view that the adversarial nature of arbitration rather inhibits voluntary settlement. Not a single respondent thought this to be true in our earlier survey, whereas now 11% of the respondents endorse this view.

In line with the indirect effect stated by the majority of respondents, the overall settlement rate, i.e., the proportion of international commercial arbitration cases that are settled by the parties before and consequently without the need for an arbitral decision is significant but still a minority (43%). This figure is slightly higher than in the previous survey. The average figure is, however, made up of a widely diverging range of personal experiences (from 5% to 95%), and varies markedly according to the background of respondents. The picture emerging is consistent with the attitudes expressed about the function of arbitration. Those who regard arbitration as a prime means to generate consensual solutions experience a high settlement rate, and vice versa. The differences cannot be explained by the legal background of participants (Common Law versus Civil Law), as the following comparison shows.

Figure 8: Overall Settlement Rate

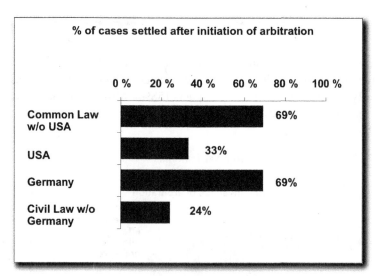

The large divergence of experience between German and American lawyers (69% vs. 33%) might be explained by the rather different practices and traditions of the respective judicial systems, particularly with regard to the function of judicial proceedings and the role of judges (German procedural laws require settlement attempts by the judge, whilst the traditional American image of the judge is one of a detached and impartial decision maker).

With regard to the timing of those settlements that do occur, the participants of the first survey were asked about the distribution of settlements over time. The smallest proportion of settlements occur before the first meeting of the tribunal with the parties. The average estimate of the settlement rate for this first phase was 29%. One third of all settlements (33%) occur during the written phase after the initial hearing and before the main evidence hearings. The largest group of settlements occur fairly late: well over one third of settlements (37%) are achieved only after the taking of evidence has begun (i.e. during evidence hearings or in the post-hearing phase).

Figure 9: Timing of Settlement

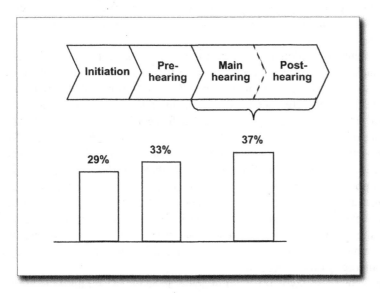

The finding that settlement occurs at all stages of the arbitral procedure but that the likelihood of an agreement increases as the process evolves is in line with many of the answers received in the interviews when discussing the best moment for settlement talks during arbitration. The respondents reported of settlements that were achieved at all moments of the process, from the filing of the claim to the very last minute, after the opinion has been written but before it is notified to the parties.

Opinions varied as to the ideal moment for settlement discussions. Some favored early talks since they promise the largest savings if they succeed and the parties are still more open: they have "invested" less, both in terms of transaction costs and psychological commitment to their case, they are less entrenched in their positions and they may be more open to consider settlement options that go beyond a mere anticipation of the most likely outcome of the arbitration. Others spoke out in favor of a more advanced stage of the proceedings, when the case has been spread out before the parties through written exchanges and the examination of evidence.

Obviously, the more advanced the procedure is, the more information about the strengths and weaknesses of each party's case has been exchanged, and the easier it is for the parties to predict the arbitrators' potential decision. But there is also a psychological element: many arbitrators and counsel insisted that a case had to be "ripe" for settlement; the parties need to have an opportunity to present their case, "flex their muscles", but also to get a feeling for their own vulnerabilities; often, an element of attrition facilitates settlement, since the warring parties sometimes need to get their "pound of flesh" and also for themselves to let some blood before they are ready to lay down their arms.

Several key moments were identified as particularly productive for settlement talks. From a plaintiff's point of view it can be most beneficial (and for the defendant least advantageous) to negotiate right after an impressive statement of claim has been presented (and before the defendant has answered) because it will be difficult at that moment for the defendant to avoid that the discussions will be influenced by the statements in the demand (even if they may not be entirely well founded).

Perhaps the best occasion for both parties to discuss settlement is at the moment of the first (preliminary) hearing, which in ICC arbitration will also be the moment when the Terms of Reference are drawn up and discussed with the parties. At this time, the initial statements of claim and defense will have been exchanged, the issues are determined, the most important arguments have been brought forward, and the parties have had an opportunity to "sense out" the tribunal and each other. The parties know what the dispute is about, they will have a rough idea of the range of possible outcomes, and they might have received some feedback from the arbitrators as to which legal arguments and which facts will play the most critical role. However, it is still early in the procedure, which has the advantage that the bulk of the transaction costs has not yet accrued, but which has the disadvantage that settlement decisions have to be based on rather sketchy information about the likely outcome of the procedure.

This is the reason why others think that it is better to wait until the pre-hearing phase has been completed, i.e. the main memoranda have been produced, discovery has been completed, and everything is ready for the main evidence hearing. At this moment, much more information has been exchanged – and accordingly, more transaction costs have been incurred – and the parties have a much better idea of where they stand, what their strengths and weaknesses are, and what the range of possible outcomes is.

Still others thought that in order to make an informed decision it was necessary to have seen the witnesses and experts and especially the reactions of the tribunal. And indeed, as we have seen, the largest proportion of settlements do occur after the main hearings have begun.

One reason for this – as will be explored in more detail – is that a number of barriers to settlement are more likely to be removed once the parties start to communicate and interact in a direct fashion. Before presenting the survey results with regard to these barriers to settlement, some background observations and statements shall help to illustrate this point.

A frequent barrier to settlement in arbitration is the discrepancy between the parties' assessments of the outcome. Conflicting predictions of the outcome are often a function of a systemic over-optimism that affects the judgment of the parties and frequently also their attorneys when confronting litigation. Surveys about litigation have found that, if both parties' assessments are added, the total chances of winning add up to 150%. Also, the parties often only start to realize the true magnitude of the costs and delays involved once the arbitration is well on its way.

Often there is a general lack of analysis. Parties and attorneys are motivated by an unrealistic picture of the key ingredients of the dispute. They lose perspective of their own interests (e.g. in the continuation of the business relationship) and fail to see the merits of the other side's case. A treacherous dynamic ensues when the attorney is not critical enough of his client's expectations and they reinforce each other in their overconfidence. Parties and lawyers are often not rigorous and critical enough in the quantification of the claim, especially with regard to the damages:

> "... one of the reasons cases don't settle is that lawyers all over the world neglect damages, they do tons of work on liability and they do minuscule work on damages until the last minute, and the key to settle the case is to look hard at the damages and you find it's not really what people thought ..."[348]

A similar lack of judgment often extends to the costs of the procedure which tend to be under-estimated, while at the same time the disputants often feel bound by the "investments" they have made in the procedure: they fail to acknowledge the irrelevance of "sunk costs" for the analysis of the costs and benefits of continuing the arbitration.

Incomplete information leads to mutual distrust and prevents agreement. This is exacerbated by the lack of communication that characterizes many international commercial disputes: in addition to the logistical difficulties created by distances and time zones, the talks are frequently complicated by a language and/or culture gap. Also, effective negotiation usually requires a forum for communication and the simultaneous attention of the parties, and both are frequently missing before the arbitral procedure begins.

Another powerful trap, in which many lawyers get caught, is a perceived need for ever more information in order to make a decision on whether to settle: before taking the responsibility for recommending a settlement, lawyers often feel they need to be very sure about the true chances of winning or losing the case; often they will want to see all the evidence, and ideally the reaction of the arbitrators, before offering an assessment as to the likely outcome of the procedure; but at that time settlement is hindered by the fact that transaction costs keep accruing while the case is spread out in front of the parties who fail to see that even a late settlement can be worthwhile. Instead, at a late stage in the proceedings the feeling is often that "we might as well go all the way and take our chances with an award." On

---

[348]   Interview with Eric Green, May 26, 1992.

the other hand it is often the exchange of information brought about by the arbitral procedure that helps the parties come to terms:

"... sometimes you find that one party really didn't understand where the other was coming from; when you read a carefully prepared statement of claim or a carefully prepared answer you probably get more information than someone was prepared to give you over the phone ... sometimes your legal advice didn't cover everything because sometimes the client doesn't tell the lawyer everything ... so you get educated as the case goes on ... new things come to light that make settlement possible."[349]

Another set of problems is created by the need to follow a dual strategy: settlement talks often only make sense if the parties continue to work on their non-agreement alternatives which in the case of international commercial disputes will usually be an arbitration procedure. The need to follow a two-track approach of pursuing litigation process while at the same time negotiating for settlement entails a certain conflict of goals: vigorous advocacy in pursuit of a "victory" in arbitration requires different tactics and skills than the search for mutually acceptable solutions through negotiation. Some lawyers are equally good as a "litigator" and as a "negotiator", but the fact that the same lawyer follows both tracks can be a disadvantage: a "gladiator" is not always the best "diplomat".

Other human factors that hinder settlement are the unwillingness to give up a position one has once vigorously advocated, particularly since a certain degree of conviction is required in order to effectively present a case:

"... [parties] do not want to take the responsibility to give up the position they have made everybody in their camp believe to be so strong; this hesitation ... is burdening the lawyer before his client, the manager before his board, the executive board before the supervisory board and the supervisory board before the shareholders ... this barrier can be overcome through the involvement of neutrals who "carry the parties over the threshold" by indicating to parties where they are heading in the wrong direction ..."[350]

At the same time, the ongoing costs of the procedure and the impending decision create a pressure which may lead them to more serious negotiations: they have to face the prospect of a protracted procedure and of an imposed decision that is becoming more and more likely and the contents of which become more and more ascertainable. However, a residue of uncertainty remains, which in turn creates a range of probable outcomes within which the parties can search for a negotiated solution. A number of the practitioners interviewed cited the well-known American saying:

---

[349] Interview with Gerald Aksen, January 21, 1992.

[350] Interview with Dr. Bernd Kunth, January 30, 1992 (translation by the author).

"There is nothing like the prospect of hanging to concentrate a man's mind."[351]

In most business disputes the parties are not individuals but organizations that are represented by inside and outside agents. This organizational context creates its own barriers against settlement. First of all, it happens that corporate agents (officers and outside attorneys) simply lack the authority to settle the dispute by way of an agreement. This lack of authority is sometimes real but it is also a frequent tactic to exert further concessions from the other side (the agent negotiates an agreement, then feigns the need to obtain ratification from his principal and comes back with additional demands). The risk is, in both cases, that the other side might react by calling off the talks.

A related problem is that settlement negotiations are sometimes conducted at the wrong level of hierarchy. Whether to settle a dispute is a business decision, and it requires a sense for the overall interests of the organization, a vision of the future, and the kind of detached judgment that is the function of high-level decision-makers.

One arbitrator recalled a procedure where the tribunal had scheduled the evidence hearings deliberately so as to have the two CEOs present for testimony on the same day; the two CEOs who knew each other but had not seen each other for a long time, met in the hallway, started to talk about how unpleasant this whole arbitration was, had lunch together – without the lawyers – and settled the entire case.[352]

A lack of management involvement can prevent amicable solutions that are in the overall/long-term interest of the organization. Officers/agents, especially at a lower level of the hierarchy, are often under an internal pressure not to make concessions. It is always easier to be condemned by a tribunal than to take the responsibility for a settlement. To give up what has been perceived internally as a valid position has to be explained to superior levels in the organization or to constituents such as board members, shareholders or, in the case of state owned entities, to the public. Government representatives are in an especially precarious situation since they are under the obligation not to squander public assets and are often closely scrutinized by the public and by political processes that tend to be motivated by unpredictable political impulses rather than a sober analysis of the situation. In many interviews the respondents emphasized that this was particularly so with representatives from developing countries who risk being exposed to charges of corruption if they make concessions to foreign investors or trading partners:

"… State agencies or government-controlled firms will almost never agree to a settlement, even if the representative of the party must see that the case is hopeless. He will prefer to lose. Had he compromised he would be accused

---

[351] This quote is commonly attributed to Dr. Samuel Johnson, cf. Ballem, "Fast-Track Arbitration on the International Scene", 2 *Am. Rev. Int'l Arb.* 152, 153 (1991).

[352] Interview with a Swiss scholar and practitioner conducted in February of 1992.

of having been bribed to do so…"[353]

This mechanism is illustrated in the following case:

> An experienced arbitrator remembered a large arbitration involving a socialist country where, through consecutive rounds of separate meetings with both parties alone, he got the parties informally to agree to a "very nice settlement"; "… but the representative [from the socialist country] said that although he thought that the solution proposed was good and fair, he could not settle for anything less than 100% because otherwise he may loose his job; so he needed an award, even though he knew that an award would probably give him less than what he was offered in the settlement…"[354]

Sometimes settlement is prevented or delayed by a conscious decision. According to a large number of interviews, one of the main reasons why parties do not exhaust settlement options before resorting to arbitration is that they want to first formalize the dispute by filing for arbitration. This, in turn can have several reasons. First of all, the initiation of arbitration is often motivated by a need to preserve evidence or to avoid the preclusion of a claim. The initiation of the procedure is sometimes a deliberate settlement tactic: it is supposed to create the necessary pressure to get the other side to seriously negotiate. This tactic is not without risk because the initiation of arbitration often has an antagonizing effect and changes the frame for the interaction of the parties. Filing for arbitration can be a two-edged sword:

> "… once you decide to get the matter adjudicated, a dynamic starts that shifts the attention and the energy of the parties from settlement to "winning" the arbitration … but, then again, sometimes you need the pressure of an ongoing arbitration to get the parties to seriously think about settlement …"[355]

> "… the typical scenario that I see is 'Oh well, they are not taking this seriously let's file this complaint to start the arbitration, [then] they'll negotiate' … [but] the other side says 'we can't negotiate now until they have seen our answer and our counterclaims' … plus: 'let's file our request for documents, things like that so they know we're really serious …' – so they file those, and then the other side says 'Geez, this looks like all out war' … and so it takes on a life of its own …"[356]

Against this background, the survey asked respondents to rate several barriers to settlement that related to the organizational dimension, tactical considerations

---

[353] Written response to questionnaire by Ignaz Seidl-Hohenveldern.

[354] Interview with Pieter Sanders, March 2, 1992.

[355] Interview with Arthur von Mehren, April 15, 1992.

[356] Interview with Eric Green, May 26, 1992.

and certain inherent deficiencies of settlement processes in the shadow of the law. Several barriers had some relevance, and none stood out as highly relevant. Also, there were hardly any differences based on the participants' backgrounds, with the exception of the fact that typically the same attorney conducts both the litigation as a whole and the settlement negotiation (the alternative would be to bring in a specialist negotiator to increase the chances of settlement). Only the American participants attributed some relevance to this point, which may be explained by the fact that such a "division of labor" is extremely uncommon outside of the USA.

Figure 10 – Barriers to Settlement

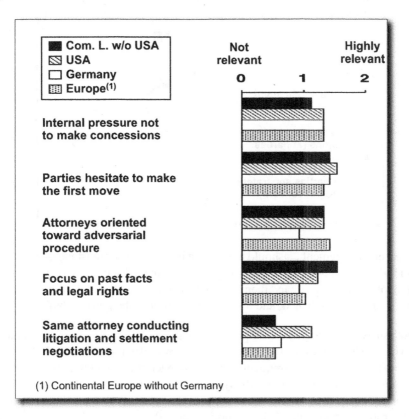

Fundamental differences in attitude towards the function of the arbitral process can also be seen in the way specific settlement techniques are being observed and judged. Obviously, it is "a large step from promoting a settlement to actively participating in the process by which it is achieved."[357]

---

[357] Talbot, "Should an Arbitrator or Adjudicator Act as a Mediator in the Same Dispute?", 67(3) *J. Chartered Inst. Of Arb.* 228 (August 2001).

Figure 11: Frequency of Arbitrator Involvement in Settlement

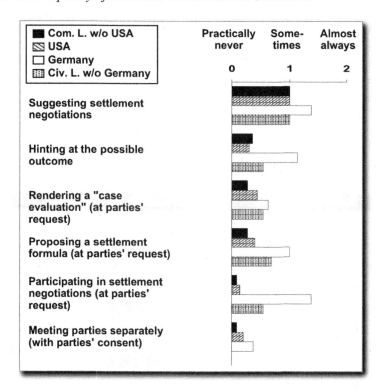

That encouragement ... should not, except in very rare circumstances, involve the arbitrator playing a personal role in the settlement discussions, or assuming the role of a mediator; and then should do so only once the ground rules have been clearly established, and the written consent of the parties obtained.[358]

In both surveys, participants were presented with six of the most common techniques by which arbitrators can try to facilitate a consensual solution and were then asked (a) to indicate how frequently they have encountered them in their personal arbitration experience ("almost always" = 2, "sometimes" = 1, "practically never" = 0) and (b) to give their view as to whether it was acceptable for the arbitrator to go this route ("appropriate = 1, "inappropriate = 0).

The techniques vary according to the role assumed by the arbitrator and the intensity with which the arbitrator becomes involved in the communications and decision making processes of the parties. The least intrusive, and the most frequently encountered way to foster a settlement is simply to suggest to the parties that they

---

[358] Collins, "Do International Arbitral Tribunals have any Obligations to Encourage Settlement of the Disputes Before Them?", 19 (3) *Arb. Int'l* 333-343, at 343 (2003).

go back to the negotiating table and discuss ways to settle the dispute amicably. This technique had been encountered "almost always" by 13 of the respondents and "sometimes" by 30. Only 11 respondents stated they had experienced this "practically never". This distribution of answers leads to an average of "sometimes" (1,02). Not surprisingly, over 90% of respondents (in the earlier survey it was 84%) thought that this was appropriate for the arbitrator to do.

Figure 12: Appropriateness of Arbitrator Involvement

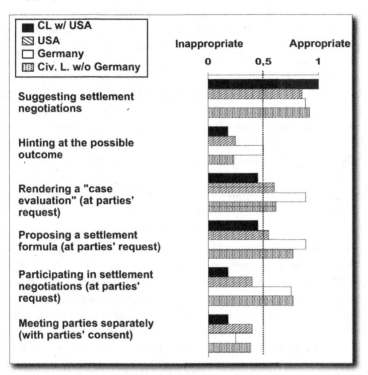

Another frequent, but much more intrusive way to help the parties reach a settlement is for the arbitrator to impart, in a more or less explicit way, his views of the merits of the case. He can do this at his own initiative, by making allusions as to the likely outcome of the case if he were to decide it, or he can be asked by the parties to render a type of informal case evaluation as a guidance for settlement negotiations. Both techniques do not occur very frequently (about halfway between "practically never" and "sometimes") but have a rather different degree of acceptance. A case evaluation at the parties request was regarded as appropriate by a majority of the respondents (62%) – with a somewhat higher acceptance among German and a somewhat lower acceptance among non-American respondents with a Common Law background. Hinting at the outcome, however, is highly controversial. Except for the Germans, who are familiar with this type of behaviour from German judges and who were split evenly as to its appropriateness (a decline compared to 64% acceptance in the previous survey), three quarters of the respondents thought it was not appropriate for the arbitrator to impart unsolicited views on the likely outcome of the case.

The parties can also go further and ask the arbitrator for a concrete settlement proposal. Here, the classical dividing lines between lawyers with Common Law and Civil Law background become apparent. Lawyers with a Civil Law background are more familiar with this type of classical conciliation technique and overwhelmingly (over 80%) regard it as acceptable for an arbitrator to employ, whereas about half of the respondents with a Common Law background rejected such a role.

In contrast to these more traditional ways of promoting settlement, the arbitrator can act as a "real" mediator and get involved in the actual negotiation process. Here we have a significant diversity of experience and attitude among participant groups. Again in line with the common practice in German courts, the German participants were rather familiar with this type of process and had very little objections against this involvement of the arbitrator as mediator (only 25% of German respondents thought this was not appropriate). This stands in stark contrast to the Common Law respondents who have hardly encountered this practice (28 out of 31 have seen it "practically never") and who by a two-thirds majority regard this as inappropriate.

Finally, the arbitrator can go so far as to meet the parties separately, as a means to explore settlement options in a type of "shuttle diplomacy" or even to use the privacy of such a caucus to "talk them to their senses".

> "It sometimes happens, depending on the atmosphere in a specific arbitration, that parties appreciate assistance of the arbitral tribunal in settling the case. As chairman I am prepared to assume this task. However, only if also my two co-arbitrators agree. If the two other arbitrators are not present this simplifies matters. The chairman then hears the parties separately. This means walking from one room for hearing party A to another room for hearing party B. However, only if supported by the co-arbitrators the chairman can pave in this way the ground for a settlement. He may, for example, ask a party 'do you really think that the tribunal will be convinced by this point?' Or may say 'your point on issue three may be convincing but on issue two this may be difficult'. The co-arbitrators, who do not take part in the hearings with the parties are informed and consulted. It is a delicate procedure which presupposes that arbitrators form a team which works together in a friendly atmosphere. If so, my experience shows that it works."[359]

This type of involvement obviously happens much more infrequently (0,2 – close to "practically never"), as it is also a lot more controversial (66% of all participants

---

[359] Interview with Pieter Sanders, March 2, 1992. A similar case is reported by Thomas, "Mediation at Work in Hong Kong", 58 *Arbitration* 29 (1992).

reject it – up from 53% in the previous survey).

With the exception of separate meetings with the parties, settlement efforts by the arbitrators have become more accepted, and the degree of acceptance for the settlement techniques discussed seems to be higher than the frequency of their use.

Figure 13: Acceptance vs. Frequency of Arbitrator Involvement

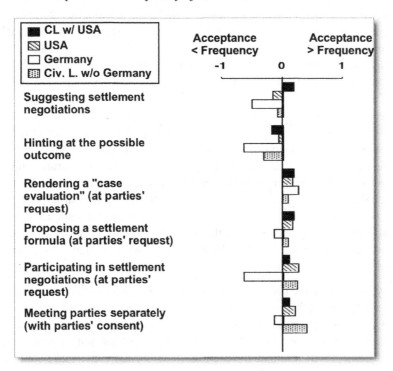

3. Combining Arbitration with Mediation

"An obstacle to mediation is that the participants, the lawyers and the principals, focus too much on two things: First, the limited dispute in front of them – they are not thinking about the larger, bigger picture, it's a limited vision. The other thing is having in their own heads – and being too attached to – what they think is the fair outcome as opposed to entering into a process that might come up with an outcome nobody has thought of."[360]

---

[360] Interview with Rebecca Westerfield, April 25, 2002

In contrast to the questions about the more or less informal or implicit settlement efforts by the arbitrators, we included in the second survey a number of questions concerning the explicit integration of mediation elements in arbitral proceedings. Such explicit "mediation windows" can be conducted by members of the arbitral tribunal in various constellations, as well as by separate mediators, thus avoiding any incompatibilities of the roles of arbitrator and mediator. We found that none of these combinations were encountered very frequently in practice. Overall, the relatively most frequent combination was a mediation attempt by a sole arbitrator or the chairman of a three-arbitrator tribunal, which on average the participants had experienced in about 8% of their arbitration cases in the last three years.

On the other hand it also occurs that the party-appointed arbitrators act as (co-) mediators. Deliberate mediation attempts where all sides agree that the party-appointed arbitrators serve as mediators and in this function "officially" confer with their parties are comparatively rare since it creates a potential conflict with the principle that party-appointed arbitrators are supposed to be completely impartial and should, after their appointment, abstain from any contact to "their" party.

Nonetheless, communications between a party-appointed arbitrator and "his" party can take many different forms, and the existence of inofficial, often very subtle channels of communication was mentioned by many participants in the survey. Not surprisingly, the practitioners interviewed rarely mentioned this communication from the perspective of the arbitrator but rather described how they as counsel communicated with the arbitrator they had appointed. As one attorney who preferred to remain anonymous stated:

> "... you can have the party-appointed arbitrators confer with their parties to give them some allusions and advice about which issues the tribunal deems relevant; this is a very subtle communication, with coded recommendations ('you may want to rethink the following...' – 'I am not quite sure whether this argument will convince the tribunal...') but you have to make sure that the chairman stays clear off these communications and remains "open" and uncommitted so that parties cannot guess which way he will decide..."

Another lawyer emphasized the usefulness of the party-appointed arbitrator as an indirect channel of communication:

> "... although you may not exploit this to unduly influence the arbitrator, it is rather common to have communications between counsel and the arbitrator selected by him; this contact differs according to the arbitrator's personality and it is always oral, usually by means of phone calls, but it is a big advantage of arbitration versus litigation to be able to tell your arbitrator on the phone things that you would not express in a written brief or during a hearing; this is a good medium to launch tentative settlement ideas without exposing yourself to the other party..."

The next most frequent type of mediation element in arbitration was the appointment of an ad-hoc mediator to help the parties settle the case without direct mediation involvement of the arbitrators (6%). The experience, however, varied widely according to the legal background of the participants:

Figure 14: Use of Mediation Techniques during arbitration

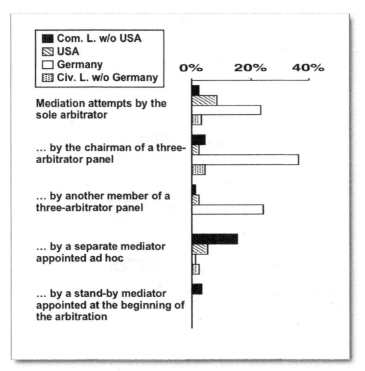

As we can see, explicit mediation attempts by members of the arbitral tribunal (especially the chairman, as seen in more than one third of the cases) are experienced in a significant proportion of cases mainly by German practitioners, once again confirming the existence of a rather specific dispute resolution practice. The use of a separate neutral to conduct the mediation was only encountered to a noticeable degree by the non-American Common Law practitioners (15%).

The relatively infrequent use of a separate or, as it is sometimes called, "stand-by" mediator, to allow for systematic mediation attempts while avoiding a confusion of roles on behalf of the arbitrators stands in contrast to the rather high degree of acceptance of such a practice: only 26% of the participants thought this was inappropriate (interestingly, Americans and Germans showed very similar attitudes, whereas none of the non-American Common Law practitioners and 50% of the non-German Civil Law practitioners thought this was inappropriate). Of the

74% who accepted the use of separate mediators during arbitral proceeding, only 14% doubted the effectiveness of this procedure, while 30% thought it would be appropriate and effective but too unusual/unconventional to be accepted by the parties.

Figure 15: Using Separate Mediator during Arbitration

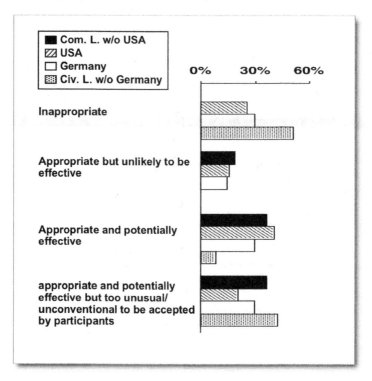

We also wanted to know what the participants thought if an arbitration institution made an explicit suggestion to the parties to try mediation. Three quarters of the participants thought this was appropriate (see Figure 16).

Finally, we also wanted to know what practitioners thought would be the best way to deal with the mediation option while drafting dispute resolution clauses. Only 12% of the participants considered it inappropriate to mention mediation in a dispute resolution clause (4% found it useless). The least intrusive clause is also the most accepted: inserting a good faith obligation of the parties to try mediation. Mediation can be further enhanced by inserting a specific reference to a set of mediation rules or an institution to assist with the appointment of a mediator. This was most popular among the non-German and the non-American participants (see Figure 17).

Figure 16: Arbitration Institution Suggesting Mediation

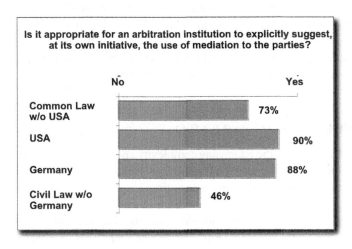

Figure 17: Drafting a Dispute Resolution Clause

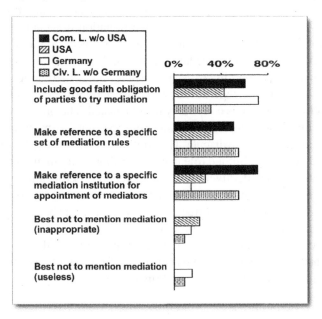

Looking ahead, it might be expected that rising awareness and greater familiarity with settlement techniques will make it an increasingly normal occurrence to experience such elements during arbitration.

Overall we can see a growing acceptance of more or less explicit mediation elements in arbitration proceedings which, however, are used less frequently than their general acceptance might suggest. In line with German judicial tradition, German practitioners favor informal mediation attempts by the arbitrator(s), whereas non-American Common Law practitioners seem to have the most "progressive" attitude toward mediation windows using separate mediators.

III. CONCLUSION TO PART TWO

As Chapter 1 has shown, the increasing complexity and internationalization of world trade create an urgent need for effective conflict management in international business. Litigating international disputes in national courts has severe disadvantages due to a lack of coordination between legal systems. Chapter 2 has explained how the legal framework of international commercial arbitration offers satisfying solutions to most of the problems raised by the deficiencies of transnational litigation. Chapter 3 has demonstrated how the process of international commercial arbitration works in practice and how fees are calculated as a function of the work performed by arbitrators and counsel. The empirical surveys in Chapter 4 have revealed that in the eyes of the parties international commercial arbitration is not an "alternative" type of process but merely a litigation procedure that *works* in an international context. As litigation, arbitration can occasion tremendous costs which keep accruing as the procedure unfolds and have led to a sense of crisis in international arbitration circles. Many disputes are settled amicably although frequently at a rather late stage of the procedure, and most practitioners feel that the potential for settlement is commonly not exhausted. The process of arbitration facilitates voluntary settlements in a number of ways, notably by giving the parties a more realistic picture of the dispute. The arbitrators themselves play an important but, at the end of the day, limited role in bringing about settlements since they face a *dilemma* between the effectiveness of any mediation attempt and the integrity of the arbitral procedure. Inserting mediation windows during arbitration proceedings is steadily gaining support as an effective way to harness the benefits of mediation without causing undue risk to the arbitral process.

Hence, arbitration offers the best legal framework available for the resolution of international business disputes but suffers from high transaction costs and an inherent limitation in the capacity to bring about consensual solutions.

PART THREE:
ALTERNATIVES TO ARBITRATION

The previous Chapters have revealed some of the strengths and weaknesses of arbitration as a method for the resolution of international business disputes. The results of our empirical work have illustrated the close interplay between arbitration and "alternatives" to arbitration in practice. The increasing proceduralization and the associated costs and delays of arbitration and the emergence of conflict management techniques capable to bring about consensual solutions raise the question whether and under which circumstances "alternative" methods might yield more satisfying results. Of particular interest in this context is the process of mediation and related techniques, which under the popular label of Alternative Dispute Resolution (ADR) have begun to enter the mainstream of legal practice.

The development, analysis and refinement of mediation in the United States have been fueled by two interacting but nevertheless separate sources: (1) the pressure created by a judicial system in crisis, and (2) the development of a significant body of interdisciplinary theory and practice of conflict and negotiation. The international discussion of Alternative Dispute Resolution has tended to focus on its "negative" roots – the crisis of the American judicial system – and sometimes overlooked the "positive" scientific roots in the quest for a better understanding of conflicts and the most effective ways for their resolution. In any event, the functioning and the potential benefits of alternative techniques cannot be understood without looking at the findings of an interdisciplinary theory of conflict and negotiation.

At the same time, when discussing alternatives to international commercial arbitration, a look at the growing importance of mediation and other "alternative" techniques in the United States is warranted because many of the symptoms of the "decreasing flexibility" of international arbitration are similar to the symptoms plaguing the American judicial system (and have been linked by critics on both sides of the Atlantic to a process of "Americanization" of international arbitration). And although certain elements of ADR (in particular certain specialized techniques such as simulated jury trials) bear relevance only for the United States, the large majority of procedures developed in the context of domestic American business disputes offer solutions to problems that are increasingly present in international arbitration as well.

Even more important, in our view, are the "positive" roots of alternative dispute resolution. Based on a systematic, scientific analysis of the dynamics of conflict and negotiation, a "technology" for conflict management has been developed that offers an elaborate methodical framework for the analysis of conflicts and for their effective resolution. Since most alternative techniques are either a variant of mediation or a structured form of negotiation, and since mediation itself is essentially a negotiation process assisted by a neutral third party, we believe it is important to understand the dynamics of negotiation and conflict resolution in general before looking at alternatives to arbitration.

In this part of the book we shall therefore first examine the most important interdisciplinary findings on conflict and negotiation theory as the conceptual root for conflict management (Chapter Five), followed by an attempt to describe the workings of mediation and other techniques with potential application to the resolution of international business disputes (Chapter Six). After this description, we look at tools and techniques that support the mediator during business negotiations (Chapter Seven). Finally, a closer look will be taken at the legal framework for "alternative" techniques in the international field (Chapter Eight).

Chapter 5

Conflict and Negotiation Theory as a Conceptual Framework for Conflict Management

Any quest for effective conflict management techniques must be grounded in a concept of conflict (its forms, roots and manifestations), as well as of negotiation as the primary means of peaceful conflict resolution. Various disciplines contributed to the development of a solid theoretical background for the analysis of conflicts and their resolution. The seminal studies on the nature and function of conflict by Lewis Coser[361] and Morton Deutsch[362] can be viewed as a foundation for a scientific panorama about conflict and its resolution. The *socio-legal influence* on conflict (resolution) theory was inspired by the school of legal realism, with Lon Fuller[363] and Karl Llewellyn being prominent supporters. *Political theorists*[364] proposed innovative ideas to adapt formally constitutionalized institutions, ranging from ad-hoc policy-making groups to negotiated rule-making or regionalized decision-making. *Social psychologists*[365] have investigated how human cognitive errors both produce conflict and prevent parties to a conflict from resolving conflicts in rational and efficient ways. Important insight was generated by the work of *game theorists* and *decision scientists* like Howard Raiffa,[366] and studies on the quality

---

[361] Lewis Coser, *The Functions of Social Conflict*, New York: Free Press (1956).

[362] In particular, Deutsch, *The Resolution of Conflict: Constructive and Destructive Processes* (1973), but see also Deutsch & Coleman (eds.) *The Handbook of Conflict Resolution: Theory and Practice* (2000).

[363] Lon Fuller, *The Principles of Social Order: Selected Essays of Lon L. Fuller* (rev. ed. 2001, Kenneth I. Winston (ed.)), (1981, 2001).

[364] See, for example Dahl, *On Democracy*, (1998); Guttman & Thompson, *Democracy and Disagreement*, (1996).

[365] See, for example, Arrow et al. (eds.), *Barriers to Conflict Resolution* (1995); Reason, *Human Error* (1990).

[366] Raiffa/Richardson & Metcalfe, *Negotiation Analysis* (2002); Hammond et al., *Smart Choices: A Practical Guide to Making Better Decisions* (1999).

of outcome of processes such as those by Vilfredo Pareto and Robert Axelrod.[367] *Anthropologists* added a perspective on culture and conflict resolution.[368] The following part of the book will illustrate some insights and observations derived from these disciplines which have a practical value for the process of international commercial dispute resolution.

I. CONFLICT

Conflict is one of the fundamental conditions of the human existence and an inevitable and necessary fact of all social interaction. If managed productively, conflict is an important source of progress and innovation but if left unresolved or if dealt with in a destructive manner it can cause great harm. Before that background, the interest in how to settle disputes – or resolve conflicts – is little surprising. In her reflections about the term, Carrie Menkel-Meadow states:

> "For the purpose of some (perhaps artificial) clarity, I suggest here, as I review the history of the development of the field and its key idea and concepts, that 'disputes' and 'dispute resolution' have been constituted by the legal field, and that 'conflicts' and 'conflict resolution' have been constituted by the broader pastiche of the social sciences (anthropology, political science, international relations, sociology, psychology, history, economics and game theory) and their more multidisciplinary social activist spin-offs ..."[369]

In this book, *conflict* shall be defined as a situation where the perceived interests of two or more persons are opposed in a manner that makes it impossible for all of the respective interests to be fully satisfied. Merrills defines the closely connected term *dispute* as "a specific disagreement concerning a matter of fact, law or policy in which a claim or assertion of one party is met with refusal, counter-claim or denial by another".[370]

---

[367] Axelrod, *The Evolution of Cooperation* (1984); Axelrod, *The Complexity of Cooperation: Agent-Based models of Competition and Collaboration* (1997).

[368] Avruch, *Culture and Conflict Resolution*, (1998).

[369] Menkel-Meadow, *Dispute Processing and Conflict Resolution* (2003), at xvi.

[370] Merrills, *International Dispute Settlement*, 3rd ed. (1998), at 1.

1. Types of Conflicts

In order to conceptualize conflict, several *distinctions* can be made.[371] Looking at the *actors*, one can distinguish conflicts between two parties and multi-party conflicts, between individual actors and between groups, between organizations and within organizations, or "direct" conflicts and conflicts mitigated by agents and representatives. Looking at the *consciousness* of the parties, one can distinguish "manifest conflicts" and "underlying conflicts", the recognition of the latter often being the key to a durable resolution. In addition, conflicts go through different *stages* which can be identified as passing from a mere "conflict structure" through a "conflict situation" until a "manifest conflict" is reached. According to the level of perception and expression by the actors the emergence and *transformation* of conflicts can be seen to go through the stages of "unperceived injurious experiences" to perceived ones ("naming"), and to grievances ("blaming"), until the conflict is manifested through "claiming" and becomes a "dispute".[372] And "dispute resolution" can be seen as part of a more comprehensive notion of "conflict management" that also includes preventive measures dealing with conflicts before they get to be manifested or formalized as disputes.

Conflicts can also be distinguished according to whether they are centered on *interests* or on *rights*, whether they constitute a *competition* between confronting desires or necessities, or are characterized by a *dissent* on norms, values and facts. When conflicting interests cannot be reconciled through trade or compromise, the conflict will often be framed in normative terms: by asserting their rights the parties harness legitimacy and negotiating power based on legal remedies. This process corresponds to the stages of "blaming" and "claiming" in the transformation of conflicts as described in the previous paragraph. The assertion of rights is often perceived as a hostile act and can lead to an escalation of the conflict. But conflicts are almost never purely interest-based or rights-based. The reality of most conflicts is characterized by a complex interrelation between interests and rights because most rights can be understood as standardized manifestations of interests and the interests of a party are in turn influenced by the remedies it possesses.

Looking at the number or the divisibility of *issues* in dispute, "*binary*" situations can be differentiated from "*polycentric*" constellations where many interrelated issues are at stake.[373] Examples for the latter are the allocation of economic resources, the division of a collection of paintings or the assignment of playing

---

[371] The following distinctions are adapted from the very helpful overview of the research on conflict in Folberg & Taylor, *Mediation* 18-37 (1984).

[372] Cf. Felstiner, Abel & Sarat, "The Emergence and Transformation of Disputes: Naming, Blaming, Claiming...", 15 *L. & Soc. Rev.* 631 (1980-81).

[373] Fuller, "The Forms and Limits of Adjudication", 92 *Harv. L. Rev.* 353, 394 (1978); Fuller attributes the term "polycentric" to Polanyi, *The Logic of Liberty: Reflections and Rejoinders* 171 (1951).

positions within a football team. In their pure form polycentric situations resemble a spider web: a pull on one strand will distribute tensions after a complicated pattern throughout the web as a whole.[374] Since no single issue can be resolved without creating repercussions with regard to the other issues, these situations require a more pro-active, creative and forward-looking activity for their resolution than the essentially re-active, binary determination that characterizes adjudication where the decision-maker typically has to choose between the two positions argued before him or a compromise solution that lies somewhere on a direct line between these two positions. The distinction is usually one of degree rather than of category: few controversies are purely one-dimensional, and adjudication almost always has to deal with some sort of underlying conflict or side-issue. But the polycentric elements in a conflict can become so significant and predominant that its resolution requires some form of creative problem-solving that lies beyond the limits of adjudication in its proper form.

A related distinction focuses on the expected outcome and contrasts *"fixed-sum"* (or *"zero-sum"* or *"win-lose"*) situations, where a gain to one party inevitably cor-relates with a loss to the other, with *"variable-sum"* or "non-zero-sum" situations where it is possible that both or all parties can gain[375] (*"positive-sum"* or *"win-win"* situation).[376] Litigation is a classical zero-sum game (or, considering the transaction costs involved, a negative-sum game). Accordingly, the transformation from an interest-based to a rights-based conflict, which occurs when a conflict is framed in legal terms, often reduces a positive-sum situation to a zero-sum game. Most alternative dispute resolution procedures try to reverse this development by shifting the focus back to the interests of the parties.

2. Ways of Dealing with Conflict

As mentioned above, some conflicts never become conscious to the individuals involved. Once realized, there are three basic ways of dealing with conflict: ignorance or avoidance, the use of force or other coercive means, or "procedural resolution" which can be guided primarily by interests or by rights. Procedural resolution includes direct negotiation between the parties, the involvement of a third party as mediator, and adjudication through arbitration or litigation in court. The importance of legal norms increases along this spectrum going from negotia-tion which is principally oriented towards the reconciliation of interests, to court

---

[374]   Fuller, "The Forms and Limits of Adjudication", 92 *Harv. L. Rev.* 353, 395 (1978).

[375]   Or where the parties – as a consequence of the cost of conflict – both lose ("negative-sum" or "lose-lose" situation).

[376]   The equation of positive sum/negative sum situations with "win-win"/"lose-lose" outcomes is not quite correct: in both cases a "win-lose" outcome is still possible. However, a "win-win" outcome can only be achieved in a positive sum situation, and a negative sum constellation will very likely result in losses on both sides.

adjudication, which is characterized by a determination of rights. The resolution will almost always be based on some blend between normative and interest considerations because most arbitrators and even many judges will not exclusively look to the rights of the parties without ever considering the interests at stake, and even in direct negotiations the parties frequently invoke normative principles.

From the perspective of the parties to the dispute and considering their joint interest in increasing the likelihood of "win-win" solutions, the reconciliation of interests is generally preferable because it leads to greater satisfaction with the outcomes, produces lower transaction costs, puts less strain on the relationship and makes a recurrence of the dispute less likely. Where power imbalances exist or where important public policies are at stake, it may be necessary to determine rights. However, in general it is preferable to seek consensual solutions and to reserve the determination of rights for a "back-up" function. In order to avoid deadlocks, and to guarantee lasting results and a minimum standard of legitimacy, interest-based consensual procedures have to be backed up by procedures that determine and enforce rights. In the presence of an effective legal "*back-up*", the parties are bargaining in the "*shadow*" of the law which at the same time provides substantive standards of legitimacy and – in a society based on the rule of law – the most important no-agreement alternative. The efficiency of the result can often further be enhanced if "*loop backs*" are built into the procedure that direct the attention of the parties back to the original focus on interests. This will be explored in more detail in the final chapter of this book.

Effective conflict management therefore has to facilitate consensus while at the same time providing an effective legal back-up. Consensual solutions are the product of *negotiations*. The most important *back-up* is provided by the *legal system* of the society within which the conflict takes place. In international business the parties usually aspire to create a more effective back-up in the form of private arbitration. However, as we have seen in Part Two, in order to perform this back-up function effectively, any system of private arbitration in turn has to be backed up by the legal systems of the states that have a connection to the dispute. Thus, one might speak of two layers of back-ups but for reasons of simplicity the entire system shall be regarded as a single back-up. In an effective system of conflict management, the back-up performs its function both in an indirect manner through the impact it has on the negotiation process, and directly through its actual use which, however, will be an exception rather than the rule. Both the consensual part of the system and the legal back-up reinforce each other and are *interdependent* in their effectiveness because an effective and legitimate back-up will tend to improve the quality of negotiations while effective negotiations perform a filter function by channelling only those cases into the back-up system that are best suited to resolution by determination of rights.

Hence, *negotiation* plays a key role in conflict management, generating solutions that satisfy the interests of the parties and facilitating rational choice in light of the parties' no-agreement alternatives.

II. NEGOTIATION

"For about 15 years of my life, I watched negotiators I was trying to learn from and finally came to the realization that they did not know what they were doing. If something went wrong and I asked 'Well, what went wrong?' they could not tell me. If I asked 'What did you do right?' they could not tell me. The insight I got was that no one knew. You can assemble a group of great people who have taken part in great negotiations for a discussion, and they all come up with completely different reasons for why the negotiation was successful and how it worked."[377]

Without entering into a discussion of the various definitions offered in the literature, for the purposes of this book negotiation shall be defined as any communication between two or more actors directed at achieving a joint decision. The purpose behind this definition is to signal the two elements of the negotiation process which we regard as essential:

– communication

– decision-making.

The word "communication" was chosen because it is broader than "discussion", thus including non-verbal communication. The words "joint decision" have been chosen instead of "agreement" in order to signal that the product of negotiation is at the same time a joint action, a "meeting of the minds", and the exercise of individual choices by each of the parties to the negotiation.

1. Interdisciplinary Research and Theory

The usefulness of theory for the practice of negotiation is sometimes questioned by practitioners. Negotiation belongs to the most complex forms of human interaction. The process of communication, persuasion and choice involves the use of highly personal, somewhat intangible skills, a mixture of shrewdness and intuition that many regard more as an "art" than a proper subject for scientific investigation.

---

[377] Gerard I. Nierenberg, founder and president of the Negotiation Institute and author of several books on negotiation; Cite taken from McDonald & Bendahmane (ed.), *International Negotiation: Art and Science* 45 (1984).

Scientific analysis of negotiation is still a fairly recent phenomenon that has seen a very dynamic development over the last four decades. Particularly in the United States, sociologists, psychologists, mathematicians, economists, political scientists, anthropologists, philosophers and lawyers have been trying to analyze the "inner workings" of negotiation behavior and joint decision-making through empirical and analytical investigations. The methods employed have included psychological experiments,[378] mathematical analysis of strategic competitive interaction and experiments in game theory,[379] case studies[380] and theoretical observations[381] with regard to international negotiations or collective bargaining in labor relations,[382] anthropological observations of conflict resolution in pre-colonial societies,[383] statistical surveys and interviews with lawyers[384] or diplomats,[385] the observation and videotaping of real and simulated negotiations,[386] systematic and repeated class room "laboratories",[387] cross-cultural studies of decision-making behavior[388] and national negotiation styles,[389] conference discussions between academics and practitioners,[390] and in many instances different methods were combined.[391]

---

[378]   Cf. e.g. Rubin & Brown, *The Social Psychology of Bargaining and Negotiation* (1975); according to Zartman & Berman, *The Practical Negotiator* 4-5 (1982), over 1,000 research reports on theories and experiments on bargaining behavior were produced.

[379]   Cf. Schelling, *The Strategy of Conflict* (1960); Axelrod, *The Evolution of Cooperation* (1984); and the works listed in Sebenius, "Negotiation Analysis: A Characterization and Review", 38 *Management Science* 18-26 (1992).

[380]   Cf. Salacuse, *The Global Negotiator*, New York (2003); Sebenius, *Negotiating the Law of the Sea: Lessons in the Art and Science of Reaching Agreement* (1984); or the various case studies contained in Zartman (ed.), *The 50% Solution* (1976); see also Zartman & Berman, *The Practical Negotiator* 4 (1982).

[381]   Goodwin, *Negotiation in International Conflict* (2002); Henrikson (ed.), *Negotiating World Order: The Artisanship and Architecture of Global Diplomacy* (1986).

[382]   E.g. Walton & McKersie, *A Behavioral Theory of Labor Negotiations* (1965).

[383]   E.g. Gulliver, Disputes and Negotiations: *A Cross-Cultural Perspective* (1979) and Nader & Todd, *The Disputing Process: Law in Ten Societies* (1978).

[384]   E.g. Williams, *Legal Negotiation and Settlement* 15-18 (1983).

[385]   Zartman & Berman, *The Practical Negotiator* (1982).

[386]   E.g. Williams, *Legal Negotiation and Settlement* 17 (1983).

[387]   Raiffa, *The Art and Science of Negotiation* 20-34 (1982).

[388]   G. Fisher, *International Negotiation: A Cross-Cultural Perspective* 27-36 (1980).

[389]   E.g. Binnendijk (ed.), *National Negotiating Styles* (1987); see also G. Fisher, *International Negotiation: A Cross-Cultural Perspective* 37-52 (1980).

[390]   Zartman & Berman, *The Practical Negotiator* x-xi (1982) (Foreword by Alvin C. Eurich).

[391]   E.g Raiffa, *The Art and Science of Negotiation* (1982) combining decision analysis and class room experiments or Zartman & Berman, *The Practical Negotiator* (1982) combining interviews, simulations, conference, and reviews of historic and negotiation literature.

It is impossible to give a comprehensive overview of the entire field but in the following, a few of the most practically relevant findings and distinctions of modern negotiation theory shall be summed up.

2. Some Basic Findings and Distinctions

Recent work has done more to bridge the gap between theory and practice by devising more realistic experiments and by devoting more attention to real-life negotiations and the experience of negotiators. Also, there has been important *cross-fertilization between theory and practice*. The Statement of Mission of the Program on Negotiation at Harvard Law School reflects the importance of this exchange:

> "Our method is to shuttle between theory and practice. We subscribe to the credo that there is nothing so practical as good theory, and nothing more stimulating to good theory than engaging in practice."[392]

One can look at negotiation from different angles, each highlighting important distinctions, categories and patterns. The most central distinction (a) runs between integrative and distributive bargaining, reflecting the basic mindset of the negotiators. In addition, questions of strategic choice (b) and the "human factor" (c) are of critical importance. A related distinction opposes "dispute" and "rule-making", revolving around the respective significance of norms in either concept (d). Finally, a closer look at the sources of power (e) and the organizational dimension (f) further underlines the complexity of the matter.

a. Integrative and Distributive Bargaining

One of the most important findings of negotiation theory is the distinction between distributive and integrative bargaining. Distributive bargaining assumes a zero-sum-game and aims at the division of a fixed quantity of benefits: one side's gain is the other's loss. The prototype for distributive bargaining is the situation of a seller and a buyer haggling over the price.[393] Integrative bargaining looks at positive-sum situations where more than one issue is at stake and tries to make use of common interests and differences in valuations or perceptions in order to attain mutual gain.[394]

---

[392] Program on Negotiation, Statement of Mission; available at 513 Pound Hall, Harvard Law School, Cambridge MA 02138, U.S.A.

[393] Raiffa, *The Art and Science of Negotiation* 33 (1982).

[394] The notion of integrative bargaining is generally attributed to Mary Parker Follett, cf. Metcalf & Urwick (ed.), *Dynamic Administration: The Collected Papers of Mary Parker Follett* 32 (1942); see also Davis, "An Interview with Mary Parker Follett", 5 *Neg. J.* 223 (1989). The concept of distributive and integrative bargaining was further developed by

Integrative bargaining is directed at "creating value" ("enlarging the pie") while distributive bargaining pursues the goal of "claiming value" ("dividing the pie"). Few real life situations are pure zero-sum situations that cannot be converted into positive sum by some form of fractioning or linking of issues. Most negotiations are characterized by a mixed situation, with an inherent tension between cooperation and conflict, between creating value and claiming value: once the "pie" has been enlarged, it still has to be divided.

There are three basic ways to attain mutual gain "win-win" solutions: the joint pursuit of shared interests, the creation of economies of scale, and the exploitation of differences between the parties.[395] Value can be created through the pursuit of *shared interests*, e.g. by fostering a good working relationship, by jointly developing an innovative technology, by lining up behind a common ideal, or simply by preventing an escalation of conflict. *Economies of scale* create value by saving costs or making results possible that could not be attained by any of the parties individually. Although that may seem counter-intuitive for those who conceive of negotiations mainly as a form of resolving conflicts of interest, *differences* between the parties can create value in a number of ways.

Differences of preference or of valuation can be exploited through the exchange of concessions which are worth more to the receiving party than to the giving party (a principle that lies at the basis of all trade: the exchange of goods which are valued differently by the individual traders). Exchanges can be facilitated through the conversion of a perceived single-factor problem into a multi-factor problem. This can be done in two directions: by breaking up the problem into sub-units with differentiated valuations and trade-offs for the parties, or by creating linkages with other issues.[396] An important object of differing valuation is *time*. Businesses often operate with different time constraints and a different cost of capital: the same sum of money at a certain moment in the future may have a different value for the receiving than for the paying party. Another area where differences may yield joint gains are *forecasts* of uncertain events. Here, both parties can be satisfied with a contingency arrangement (resembling a bet): If the parties in a negotiation over royalties for a patent disagree over the future profitability of the invention, an arrangement with a low fixed royalty supplemented by a share in the future profits may satisfy both

---

Walton & McKersie, *A Behavioral Theory of Labor Negotiations* (1965) and subsequently taken up by many authors, cf. R. Fisher, Ury & Patton, *Getting to Yes* 70-76 (2nd ed. 1991); Raiffa, *The Art and Science of Negotiation* 131-132 (1982); Lax & Sebenius, *The Manager as Negotiator* 29-45 (1986).

[395] See Lax & Sebenius, *The Manager as Negotiator* 88-116 (1986); see also R. Fisher & Ury *Getting to Yes* (2nd ed. 1991).

[396] Cf. Lax & Sebenius id.; R. Fisher, Ury & Patton id.; Raiffa, *The Art and Science of Negotiation* 131-217 (1982); see also Sander & Rubin, "The Janus Quality of Negotiation: Dealmaking and Dispute Settlement", 4 *Neg. J.* 109-113 (1988).

parties – each believes to have gained more than the other. Similarly, differences in risk aversion may suggest a risk-shifting mechanism resembling an insurance. Other exploitable differences may lie in accounting rules or in *taxation* (a fertile ground for the creation of mutual gains in international business), the *sensitivity to publicity and prestige*, the *significance of precedent*, the *concept of fairness*, the relative importance to the parties of *form versus substance, economic vs. political* considerations, *internal vs. external* considerations, *symbolic vs. practical* considerations.[397]

b. Strategic Choice

The pursuit of a problem-solving strategy encounters a tension between conflict and cooperation, particularly when it is necessary to gain the cooperation of a party pursuing contending strategies. Faced with this tension, which has been called the "toughness-dilemma",[398] the key to a constructive problem-solving strategy is to influence the other side's strategic choice by diminishing the perceived feasibility and attractiveness of contentious tactics while increasing the perceived feasibility and attractiveness of joint problem-solving. *Game theory* has made an important contribution to the conceptualization of the "toughness dilemma" through experiments with the *iterated prisoner's dilemma*:[399]

In this game, two players who cannot communicate with each other are presented with the same choice in repeated rounds: they can either "cooperate" or "defect". The pay-offs to the players are calculated to reward mutual cooperation (e.g. by giving each player three points) and to punish mutual defection (e.g. by giving each player only one point). But, as in real-life negotiations, there is an opportunistic temptation to defect if the other side cooperates: successful exploitation, i.e. defecting while the other cooperates, is rewarded (e.g., with five points for the defector) while unsuccessful attempts at bringing about mutual cooperation are punished (e.g., the "exploited cooperator" gets zero points).[400] The "dilemma" is that although mutual cooperation leaves both players better off in the long run, the danger of being exploited serves as a strong dis-incentive against cooperative

---

[397] For an elaborate analysis of strategies to "invent options for mutual gain" or to "create value" see R. Fisher, Ury & Patton, *Getting to Yes* 56-80 (2nd ed. 1991) and Lax & Sebenius, *The Manager as Negotiator* 88-116 (1986); see also Raiffa, *The Art and Science of Negotiation* 131-217 (1982).

[398] See Zartman, "Common Elements in the Analysis of the Negotiation Process", in: Breslin & Rubin (ed.), *Negotiation Theory and Practice* 147, 156 (1991).

[399] The following account is based on Axelrod, The Evolution of Cooperation (1984) and the discussion of Axelrod's experiments in Lax & Sebenius, *The Manager as Negotiator* 154-160 (1986).

[400] Cf. Axelrod id. 7-11 and Lax and Sebenius 158-159.

moves. The dilemma is aggravated by the fact that the players cannot communicate to agree on a strategy of mutual cooperation.

In order to find out the most successful strategy to maximize individual scores, computer tournaments were held in the United States at which economists, psychologists, sociologists, political scientists and mathematicians from all over the world presented sophisticated computer strategies. To the surprise of many, the most successful strategy was also the simplest. Dubbed "tit-for-tat" it embodied the principle of reciprocity in a *clear* pattern of behavior: it starts with a "*nice*", i.e. cooperative, mode while being *provocable*, i.e. ready to reciprocate any competitive move by the other side but also being *forgiving*, i.e. prepared to continue testing the other side's willingness to engage in a cooperative pattern of positive reciprocity. This strategy of "conditional openness" yielded higher individual scores than even the most intricate opportunistic tactics including those that calculated the other side's defections in order to defect slightly more frequently.[401] The success of "tit-for-tat" conveys a valuable message: in repeated strategic interactions a strategy of reciprocity combined with "conditional openness" tends to be superior to strategies of pure cooperation or pure opportunism.

c. The Human Factor in Negotiation

The analysis of negotiation under economic aspects of value maximization and of strategic choice typically implies assumptions of rationality and equality that carry with it the danger of overlooking the limitations and complexities of the human mind. In the following we shall briefly look at limitations of rationality that are inherent to human nature (1), and the significance of cultural factors (2).

(1) Limits to Rationality

From the perspective of cognitive psychology and behavioural decision theory,[402] systemic deficiencies of judgment can be identified that create obstacles to rational and strategic behavior and to the implementation of prescriptions from negotiation theory.[403] Important psychological traps are the *framing* of judgments, the habitual

---

[401]   See Axelrod id. 27-54.

[402]   Raiffa, Richardson & Metcalfe, *Negotiation Analysis, The Science and Art of Collaborative Decision Making* (2002), 33-52.

[403]   The following account was inspired by Bazerman, Negotiator Judgment: "A Critical Look at the Rationality Assumption", 27 *Am. Behav. Sci.* 211 (1983), cited from: Breslin & Rubin (ed.), *Negotiation Theory and Practice* 197 (1991); See also Neale & Bazerman, *Cognition and Reality in Negotiation* 44 (1991); See generally on psychological barriers to effective negotiation Ross, "Reactice Devaluation in Negotiation and Conflict Resolution", in: Arrow et al., *Barriers to Conflict Resolution* 26-42 (1995) and Kahneman & Tversky, "Conflict Resolution: A Cognitive Perspective", in: Arrow et al., *Barriers to Conflict Resolution* 44-60 (1995).

assumption of a zero-sum situation, nonrational *escalation* of conflict, *systemic overconfidence*, as well as *partisan perceptions*.

A powerful limitation of rationality derives from the way how judgments are influenced by *perceptual frames*.

In an experiment[404] with two comparable groups of roughly 160 participants each, the respondents had to choose between two measures to combat a dangerous epidemic that is threatening to kill 600 people. The first group was presented with the following choice:

(a) if Program A is adopted, 200 will be saved;

(b) if Program B is adopted, there is a one-third probability that all will be saved and a two-thirds probability that none will be saved.

The second group was presented with this choice:

(a) if Program A is adopted, 400 people will die;

(b) if Program B is adopted, there is a one-third probability that no one will die and a two-thirds probability that 600 people will die.

Although, logically, the choices presented to both groups were identical, the difference of judgment was startling: in group one 76% chose Program A and 24% Program B, while in group two Program A was chosen by only 13% and Program B by 87%. Hence, a vast majority in group one preferred Program A which was framed in positive terms: apparently it was more appealing to save 200 persons for sure than to embark on a gamble with equal "expected value". To group two, Program A was framed in negative terms, and the overwhelming majority preferred to take a chance rather than letting 400 people die.

The experiment yielded similar results when replicated in other settings.[405] It demonstrates that judgments can be manipulated simply by framing the problem. This has significant implications for negotiations because traditionally negotiators start out with extreme opening positions and may therefore be led to view any settlement proposals by the other side in a negative frame, as constituting a "loss" compared to their aspiration levels. The mechanism described can be used as a tactical device to "anchor" perceptions. And a mediator may try to use different perceptual frames to facilitate agreement (e.g. by having each side focus on the progress achieved with a settlement proposal compared to the other side's opening demands).

---

[404] Tversky & Kahnemann, "The Framing of Decisions and the Psychology of Choice", 211 *Science* 453 (1981). See also Bazerman id. 198.

[405] Bazerman id.

A significant psychological trap is the fundamental bias towards assuming a *zero-sum situation*. Efforts at introducing problem-solving behavior and integrative bargaining strategies are met with a psychological barrier since they are counter-intuitive: parties to negotiations tend to assume that their interests are diametrically opposed. However, there are important cultural implications since the phenomenon of the *"mythical fixed-pie assumption"* is said to be particulary connected with the value system of Western societies and may therefore be less significant in less competitive cultures.[406]

Another barrier to rational negotiation behavior is the danger of *nonrational escalation of conflict*.[407] Once confrontational measures are adopted and particularly when losses have been sustained in the pursuit of combative strategies, there is a strong pull toward continuing the fight. In addition to the emotional escalation of hostile feelings the parties get trapped in a deceptive thinking of *incrementalism* assuming that if a party held out only a little bit longer with their lawsuit, strike, war offensive etc., the other side would give in. This tendency is reinforced by the *desire to justify past actions* and by a widespread inability to recognize the irrelevance of *sunk costs*. The former phenomenon has multiple aspects: a party that has adopted a confrontational course of action may want to justify the costs that were "sunk" in the confrontation, and where for example a dispute has escalated into a lawsuit, the individuals involved may want to portray the escalation as inevitable and any effort at settlement as impossible.

A well-documented cognitive trap for negotiators is *overconfidence* in the own chances of prevailing in the pursuit of one's alternative to agreement.[408] Psychological research on final-offer arbitration has shown that parties consistently overestimate the likelihood that the arbitrator will agree with their position and accept their final offer. And it is a well known fact in litigation that each side overestimates, often dramatically, its chances of winning.

These *judgment deficiencies* can *reinforce each other* and prevent beneficial agreements: the assumption of a zero-sum game suggests an inevitable confrontation of irreconcilable interests, a negative perceptual frame combines with negotiator overconfidence to induce risk-seeking confrontational strategies, and once a confrontational course has been adopted, an intuitive tendency to escalate the conflict can destroy all prospects of reaching a negotiated agreement.

---

[406] Bazerman id. 201 and Salacuse, *Making Global Deals* 60-63 (1991); see also Nisbett, *The Geography of Thought: how Asians and Westerners Think Differently ... and Why* 75, 194 (2003).

[407] See Bazerman id. 202-203 and Neale & Bazerman, *Cognition and Reality in Negotiation* 65-70 (1991).

[408] Bazerman id. 203-205.

The escalation of conflict is facilitated by *partisan perceptions* and the habitual *reliance on reciprocity* in building relationships.[409] It is well known in the abstract that different individuals perceive the same things differently. But in concrete negotiations the players are frequently unaware of the extent to which *partisan perceptions* lead to conflicting views of the individuals themselves, of their relationship, of the substance of their disagreement, of the relative importance of different issues, and of the values that control their determination. The human mind is governed by a *desire for consistency* in perceptions (cognitive consonance) that leads the individuals engaged in an interaction to observe different events or, where the same event is observed, to focus their attention on different aspects, to concentrate on evidence that supports prior views, to filter and label information so that it is easier to store, to blend out details from memory that are incoherent with the "story", and to reorganize previously stored information in a manner that is coherent with present needs.

Likewise, individuals tend to take their own interests disproportionately into account and are prone to neglect the concerns of the other side. Partisan perceptions are even more damaging to effective interaction when they relate to the relationship itself, to issues such as honesty, good faith, reliability. Invariably, we tend to view ourselves as more honest, consistent and reliable than the other side, or at least as more honest, consistent and reliable than the other side sees us. Differences in perceptions are ominous even where the negotiators share a common cultural background, but they tend to increase where the parties are further apart in culture, religion, background and roles models, as is common in international and cross-cultural negotiations.

This has especially grave consequences when the parties rely on standards of *reciprocity* in shaping their relationship. Positive reciprocity operates on the frequently unrealistic assumption that "good" behavior will be answered by equally "good" behavior, while negative reciprocity lets the other side act first, and then responds to "bad" actions with equally "bad" counteractions. The danger is that partisan interpretation of the other's conduct makes it likely that the other side will fail the test of equally good behavior. And attempts at reacting to negative behavior by responding "in kind" often lead to overreactions since the other side's behavior is perceived as worse than it objectively is (or at least as worse than it was meant to be). This will provoke a reaction which in turn will be perceived as disproportionate by the other side. The result is a spiral of conflict escalation.

---

[409]   The following description is based on R. Fisher & Brown, *Getting Together: Building Relationships as We Negotiate* 24-40 (1988). On the related phenomenon of reactive devaluation see Ross, "Reactice Devaluation in Negotiation and Conflict Resolution", in: Arrow et al., *Barriers to Conflict Resolution* 26-42 (1995).

(2) Cultural Factors

Cultural differences tend to accentuate the impact of the psychological impediments inherent in the negotiation process. They create a significant barrier to effective communication because they exacerbate the potential for misunderstandings and increase the time and attention required for the explanation of issues, positions, and interests.[410] A good part of the literature on cross-cultural negotiation concerns peripheral aspects of *negotiation etiquette* (don't do business over dinner with Mexicans, don't use first names too soon with the French, don't display the soles of your shoes or don't be irritated by moments of silence in conversations with the Japanese etc.) that can be useful to know in order to reduce disturbances, or "cross-cultural noise", in communications but which do not touch the essence of the negotiation process. There are, however, more fundamental ways in which culture affects the psychological patterns of behavior in negotiation.[411] If one thinks of the human mind as an information processor, culture can be understood as the "software" that determines the way information is processed. Communication depends on a minimum of similarity in *"mental programming"*, and disparities in this regard can stand in the way of effective communication, increasingly so when dealing, as is often the case in legal and business negotiations, with abstract concepts.[412]

Another factor that is frequently overlooked is the power of *perception habits*[413] that to a large measure are socially induced and deeply ingrained. In organizing the information and stimuli continually flooding the human mind we are accustomed to perceive new information in a manner that is internally consistent with existing categories, beliefs, and images. Even when new information in reality is incompatible with existing preconceptions, the human mind tends to organize it so as to fit into familiar patterns. International negotiations confront the human mind with new patterns of behavior, new ways of seeing things, and frequently (at least for one party) a new environment. It requires a conscious effort to avoid that this new information will be distorted by old perception habits. Since international

---

[410] G. Fisher, *International Negotiation: A Cross-Cultural Perspective* 7 (1980).

[411] G. Fisher, *International Negotiation: A Cross-Cultural Perspective* 53-57 (1980); Janosik, "Rethinking the Culture-Negotiation Link", 3 *Neg. J.* 385 (1987); see also Salacuse, *Making Global Deals* 42-58 (1991) and Zartman & Berman, *The Practical Negotiator* 227 (1982).

[412] See G. Fisher, *International Negotiation: A Cross-Cultural Perspective* 13-14 (1980); the effects of "mental programming" through culture are discussed in more detail by Hofstede, *Cultures and Organizations: Software of the Mind* 3-19 (1991).

[413] For the following see G. Fisher, *International Negotiation: A Cross-Cultural Perspective* 14 (1980); for a detailed empirical analysis of perception patterns, see Nisbett, *The Geography of Thought: how Asians and Westerners Think Differently … and Why* (2003).

negotiation involves parties from differing cultural backgrounds with disparate perception habits, the number of "perception traps" is multiplied.

An important trap are *implicit assumptions*.[414] Perception, judgment, and communication proceeds on the basis of underlying assumptions and values that are unconsciously taken to be of universal validity even though in reality they differ from culture to culture. Implicit assumptions not only color the meaning we attribute to what the other side says but they also lead us to make *projections* as to what the other side has meant and as to the underlying motives behind that statement. And conversely, we fail to realize that much of what we say with apparently unambiguous words can only accurately be understood in the context of the underlying assumptions and values of our own culture.

Another danger for mutual understanding can be the unconscious *attribution of motives*. Especially in situations of little familiarity and trust between the parties, and even more so in negotiations over a dispute, actions by one side are often interpreted by the other side without taking into account the cultural context in which they occur. The result is often the attribution of bad motives. Ironically, the misattribution of motives will be noticed only when done by the other side: not only do they act in an irritating and suspicious manner but they also refuse to see our own legitimate intentions.[415]

An example for culturally induced attribution of motives in business negotiations is the use of lawyers. In some countries like the United States, the consultation of lawyers and even their presence in negotiations is routine behavior in any dealings of a certain significance. From the perspective of other cultures, the involvement of lawyers is a signal of distrust bordering on a hostile act.[416]

Another factor that greatly influences negotiations are *styles of decision-making*, both on an individual and on a collective level. Individuals will be influenced by their national value systems but also by the institutional culture and the standard procedures of the organizations they represent. When preparing for discussions negotiators have to contemplate *who* has to be influenced (the most senior member of a delegation, its "speaker", or the mid-level technocrats?), and *when* (early on, perhaps before the formal negotiations have started, or better after an initial exchange of views?), *where* (at the bargaining table, over dinner or at the golf course?) and *how* this is best attempted (through open arguments, appealing to general principles or rather to technical details, through the cultivation of personal relationships or through the application of pressure?).[417]

---

[414] G. Fisher id. 14-15.

[415] Cf. G. Fisher id. 15-16.

[416] Cf. the example in Bryan & Buck, "The Cultural Pitfalls in Cross-Border Negotiations", 24 (2) *Mergers & Acquisitions* 61, 62 (September/October 1989).

[417] G. Fisher, *International Negotiation: A Cross-Cultural Perspective* 27-36 (1980); Salacuse, *Making Global Deals* 57-58, 68-69, 84-102 (1991).

Finally, cultural differences can affect the entire *concept of negotiations*. It has been suggested that the very idea of organizing a *meeting expressly* for the purpose of conducting negotiations is a Western concept.[418] And the idea of negotiations as an exercise in joint *problem-solving* is inherent to the American culture – individuals from other cultures might rather see this as an opportunity for *debate* and the presentation of elegant arguments, or the official celebration of an accord that was informally worked out beforehand. And for many Far Eastern cultures the whole notion of openly exchanging conflicting views raises feelings of discomfort.

The differences also relate to the intended product of the negotiation. Americans have a *transaction*-driven concept of negotiations and will tend to view the product as a final and definite determination of an exchange while the Asians are more likely to regard the negotiation as the beginning of a *relationship* and any agreement reached as subject to whatever equitable and practical modifications may make sense in light of future circumstances. An American is likely to view a *compromise* in negotiation as a pragmatic decision based on an analysis of costs and benefits but someone from a more idealistic culture may sense a loss of personal dignity or the denigration of an important principle.[419]

Cultural attitudes may lead to very different *time frames* for the conduct of negotiations: while a German may want to get straight to the heart of the matter, members of other societies might want to first create a personal relationship and may feel that it is appropriate to spend whatever time it takes to build an atmosphere of mutual trust before dealing with the substance at issue. There may be also distinct ideas of how to structure the agenda. For example a French negotiator might be accustomed to a more *deductive* logic and may therefore want to start out with a discussion of the over-arching principles while an English or American negotiator might want to develop such principles in an *inductive* manner on a basis of an analysis of the details of the problem. Culture also influences whether negotiators approach the process with a "zero-sum" or "non-zero-sum" mind frame[420] and whether concessions are made at all and if so, at what moment and what rate.[421]

However, it has to be borne in mind that cultural predispositions are only one factor among many other influences on human behavior, and any prediction of

---

[418] G. Fisher id. 20.

[419] G. Fisher id. 48.

[420] Salacuse, *Making Global Deals* 60-63 (1991); see also Zartman & Berman, *The Practical Negotiator* 225 (1982) referring to Nicholson, *Diplomacy* (1939).

[421] See Binnendijk, foreword to Binnendijk (ed.), *National Negotiating Styles* vi-vii (1987), summing up Chinese negotiation patterns as conceding only at the last minute and continuing to press their cause after a formal agreement was reached, contrasting this style to a "salami-slicing" style where extreme opening positions are gradually given up in a continuous process of slice-by-slice concession making. This, in turn, is contrasted against the rigidity of the Japanese and the French who may enter negotiation without having a fall-back-position.

culturally induced behavior must always be corrected for other factors such as individual personality, gender, age, social class, religion, professional background, and the negotiation environment. And the variations that exist within a cultural group are usually as great as the variations between cultures. Still, the influence of national cultures on negotiator behavior is clearly an instance that has to be taken into consideration in any international negotiation.

d. "Dispute" and "Rule-Making"

The importance of normative arguments varies between negotiations, and a distinction can be made between "*dispute-negotiation*" directed at settling disputes arising out of past events (prototype: settlement in litigation) and "*rulemaking-negotiation*" intended to establish rules governing future conduct (prototype: commercial contract).[422] Since normative considerations tend to play an important role in dispute-negotiations, a related distinction opposes "norm-centered" negotiation to "strategic" negotiation, the latter being characterized by the predominant reliance on bargaining power. However, normative considerations are a common feature of all negotiations, and – as we will see in section *e*. – the "*power of legitimacy*" forms part of a comprehensive notion of bargaining power. The reality is thus characterized by negotiations that are more norm-centered or less norm-centered but rarely completely "norm-free".[423] Dispute negotiations, however, do tend to be heavily norm-centered. To the extent that they are contained in enforceable rules of law, norms take on a much more significant role: the parties are "*bargaining in the shadow of the law*",[424] and legal enforcement procedures provide the yardstick against which no-agreement alternatives are measured. This interaction between the process and the concurrent or subsequent litigation has also been called "*litigotiation*".[425] Legal rights constitute bargaining chips, and enforceability becomes at least as important as legitimacy. Hence there are two dimensions to the discussion of legal rules in dispute negotiation, a *normative dimension* ("what is right?") and a *predictive dimension* ("how will the courts decide?"). Dispute-negotiation and

---

[422] Eisenberg, "Private Ordering Through Negotiation: Dispute-Settlement and Rulemaking", 89 *Harv. L. Rev.* 637, 638 (1976); see also Mnookin & Kornhauser, "Bargaining in the Shadow of the Law: The Case of Divorce", 88 *Yale L. J.* 950, 973 (1979) and Sander & Rubin, "The Janus Quality of Negotiation: Dealmaking and Dispute Settlement", 4 *Neg. J.* 109 (1988). The difference between interest-based and rights-based mediation is discussed below in Chapter 6.

[423] Eisenberg, "Private Ordering Through Negotiation: Dispute-Settlement and Rulemaking", 89 *Harv. L. Rev.* 637, 680-681 (1976); "Mnookin & Kornhauser, Bargaining in the Shadow of the Law: The Case of Divorce", 88 *Yale L. J.* 950, 973 (1979).

[424] See Mnookin & Kornhauser, "Bargaining in the Shadow of the Law: The Case of Divorce", 88 *Yale L. J.* 950 (1979).

[425] Cf. Galanter, "Worlds of Deals: Using Negotiation to Teach about Legal Process", 34 *J. Legal Educ.* 268 (1984).

rulemaking-negotiation are often combined, especially in the context of long-term relations where disputes over past behavior are frequently resolved by redefining the rules governing the relationship. In these cases the use of integrative bargaining techniques can transform dispute-resolution into "deal-making" and create value for both sides.

e. Power in Negotiation

Like power in general, "negotiating power" is not easy to define. It is frequently conceived of as the relative physical strength or as the economic resources of the parties, or "the ability of one side to inflict more damage on the other than it receives in return"[426] but this view seems at the same time too broad and too narrow. It is too broad because it views power in static terms as if the mere preponderance of these resources or capabilities ensure favorable outcomes in negotiation. The possession of fire arms and the ability to kill is of little use to a police officer trying to prevent a suicide. Power in negotiation has to be viewed in dynamic and relative terms, as something that, in order to have *impact*, has to be exercised and that has to have an impact on the other side's *decision*. The suicide example also demonstrates that the static view of negotiating power is too narrow because it overlooks that the human mind can be influenced in many different ways. A more comprehensive notion of negotiating power therefore covers the combined potential of the means of one side to influence the other side's decision.[427]

This notion includes the more subtle and less coercive means of exerting influence such as the use of principles or the relationship, it takes into account that the aim of any negotiation is a *decision* by the other side, and it acknowledges that coercion is a matter of degrees: one side can restrict the options open to the other side but it can hardly eliminate its freedom to make a decision. Since each side has to make a choice between an agreed solution and its alternative course of unilateral action, the ability to influence the other side's decision will to a large extent depend on:

- the relative attractiveness of each side's existing *alternatives to agreement*,

- the ability to change these alternatives, and

- the ability to affect the other side's perception of both side's alternatives.[428]

---

[426] McCarthy, "The Role of Power and Principle", in *Getting to Yes*, 1 *Neg. J.* 59 (1985), cited from: Breslin & Rubin (ed.), *Negotiation Theory and Practice* 115, 121 (1991).

[427] Cf. R. Fisher, "Negotiating Power: Getting and Using Influence", 27 *Am. Behav. Sci.* 149 (1983), cited from: Breslin & Rubin (ed.), *Negotiation Theory and Practice* 127 (1991).

[428] Cf. Lax & Sebenius, *The Manager as Negotiator* 249-258 (1986); Alternatives to agreement are sometimes called "security points"; for a discussion of the use of the notion of security

Hence, the parties' *no-agreement alternatives* are the central category in understanding negotiating power, and most of the factors that enhance negotiating power do so by affecting alternatives to agreement and the manner in which they are perceived:

The *ability to inflict harm* and its correlative, the *willingness to take risks or to sustain costs* can best be understood in their effect on negotiations when measured in terms of the ability to deteriorate the other side's no-agreement alternatives and to withstand the other side's efforts at worsening one's own alternatives. And the relative *physical strength* and *economic resources* of the parties in turn affect power in negotiation by enhancing this capacity to inflict or sustain harm.[429]

A frequent manner of exercising bargaining power is the use of (positive or negative) *commitments*.[430] Positive commitments are offers or promises and are used to make an agreement more attractive to the other side. Negative commitments are more coercive: they take the form of unconditional restrictions of one's own freedom of choice through the irreversible adoption of a bargaining position at the exclusion of other options (unconditional negative commitments), or of threats directed at worsening the other side's no-agreement alternative (conditional negative commitments). The former is usually done by artificially increasing one's costs of accepting any less attractive agreement, thus confronting the opponent with a "take-it-or-leave-it" situation. A negative commitment can be "irresistible": where two trucks are approaching each other on a collision course, one truck driver can force the other to make way by going full speed and throwing the steering wheel out of the window.[431] A more typical manner of gaining leverage in negotiations from commitments are limitations imposed (or purported to be imposed) by constituencies. A union leader who can point out that the union will reject any result below a certain level or a CEO who "has his hands tied" by demanding shareholders may actually be able to claim more than a negotiator with full discretion over the subject-matter.

Negative commitments are a risky strategy, however, because in order to be successful they need to be made visible and credible (what if the other truck driver does not see that the steering wheel went over board, or believes it was a trick?), and they provoke escalation. In theory, the strategy works out for the party who

---

points in different strands of negotiation theory see Zartman, Common Elements in the Analysis of the Negotiation Process, in: Breslin & Rubin (ed.), *Negotiation Theory and Practice* 148-154 (1991).

[429]   Lax & Sebenius, *The Manager as Negotiator* 252-258 (1986).

[430]   On commitments see R. Fisher, "Negotiating Power: Getting and Using Influence", 27 *Am. Behav. Sci.* 149 (1983); Lax & Sebenius, *The Manager as Negotiator* 122-130 (1986); much of the knowledge on commitment was pioneered by Schelling, *The Strategy of Conflict* (1960).

[431]   This example is taken from Schelling, *The Strategy of Conflict* (1960).

commits first because the other side is left with no other choice but to accept or to go with its no-agreement alternative. But in practice it frequently provokes a contests of wills where both parties lock themselves into incompatible and potentially irreversible positions.[432] And finally, take-it-or-leave-it strategies work only if, and only for so long as, the other side acts rationally and considers acceptance (including the loss of face and the precedent set by yielding to pressure tactics) as more attractive than its perceived no-agreement alternative – which it may be in the process of improving.

Conditional negative commitments – threats – are risky because they, too, need to be credible and invite retaliation. To be credible, threats sometimes have to be partially carried out or accompanied by other demonstrative action which in turn produces costs, tends to limit the threatening party's perceived range of options and escalates hostility. What makes threats such a dangerous strategy is that their effectiveness depends on the subjective perceptions and reactions of the other side: threats only serve a useful purpose if they are credible and likely to motivate a favorable decision by the threatened party. And that in turn depends on whether the other side clearly understands what kind of cooperation is requested by the issuer of the threat, regards this cooperation as feasible, and values the expected consequences of this cooperation as more attractive than pursuing its own no-agreement alternative and putting up with the evil threatened. Parties who resort to threats may overlook the need for an upside potential in the choice facing the other side and the necessity for the other side to be able to calculate the feasibility and the consequences of a cooperative solution. In other words, it is necessary to present the other side with a "yesable proposition", with a choice to which it can agree.[433] Finally, the hostile emotions likely to be triggered by threats make it harder to predict how the other side will react.

Power in negotiation can also derive from the ability to invoke standards of *legitimacy*. Even where they are not backed up by an enforcement mechanism, normative arguments can have a very persuasive effect either because the other side shares the principle or because it is concerned about its reputation or other forms of social sanctioning. Invoking normative principles is another albeit more subtle form of affecting no-agreement alternatives or the manner in which they are perceived: they put the other side in the position of losing legitimacy by rejecting an agreement based on accepted normative standards. Legitimacy considerations have an important impact on the effectiveness of commitment strategies: threats and non-conditional negative commitments are more credible and less likely to provoke

---

[432] Even if one party was clearly the first to commit, the other party might nevertheless react with a counter-commitment to provoke a deadlock (even though this strategy is irrational where the first commitment really is irreversible).

[433] R. Fisher, "Negotiating Power: Getting and Using Influence", 27 *Am. Behav. Sci.* 149 (1983).

spiteful reactions if they are backed up by standards of legitimacy, e.g. a commitment never to yield to blackmail or never to forfeit one's basic constitutional guarantees, or simply a threat to sue someone who is going to violate one's rights.[434]

Finally, bargaining power depends in large measure on having the right kind of *information* and good analytical and tactical *skills* as well as the creativity, perceptiveness and communication abilities which are required to assess the respective no-agreement alternatives of each party, to generate solutions, and to influence the other side's perceptions and its eventual decision.[435]

Hence, power in negotiation derives from a number of interconnected factors that can all be understood in the paradigm of shaping the *no-agreement alternatives* and the *perceptions* of the parties. The effective *exercise* of negotiation power requires that all of these factors be taken into account and be used on the basis of a careful analysis of their potential impact on the choice presented to the other side. Negative commitments are especially risky and require particular skill for their use if adverse side effects are to be avoided. It may be preferable to issue a mere – honest – "warning" that objectively alerts the other party of the choice one is facing in the event of a failure to reach an agreement. This preserves maneuvering space and comes across as less offensive and arbitrary than outright threats. But most importantly, the effective use of negotiation power requires looking at both sides of the decision facing the other side: it consists not only of making it harder to say "no" but also of making it easier to say "yes".

f. The Organizational Dimension

In international business, negotiations are generally conducted not between isolated individuals but between companies, governments, and other types of organizations. Since organizations are not monolithic, negotiations *between* organizations will usually be preceded and accompanied by negotiations *within* organizations. And where organizations are represented by negotiation teams, as is frequently the case in international business, there will be another layer of intra-organizational negotiations.[436] The various interests commonly involved can be organized along four layers of negotiations (three of which are internal to the organizations):

- between the organizations,

- within the negotiation teams,

---

[434] Cf. Lax & Sebenius id. 129.

[435] See R. Fisher id. and Lax & Sebenius id. 257.

[436] On the dynamics between internal and external negotiations see R. Fisher, "Negotiating Inside Out: What are the Best Ways to Relate Internal Negotiations with External Ones?", 5 *Neg. J.* 33 (1989); Lax & Sebenius, *The Manager as Negotiator* 345-359 (1986); Rubin & Sander, "When Should We Use Agents? Direct vs. Representative Negotiation", 4 *Neg. J.* 395 (1988).

– between the members of the team and their respective constituencies,

– among the various constituent groups behind the team members.

It is important for each side to understand the particular decision-making style of the other organization and the various particular interests that have to be satisfied. The individuals representing the organizations have to negotiate at least on two fronts and their role sometimes resembles that of mediators trying to reconcile conflicting positions. This task is complicated by the way in which external negotiating positions tend to be developed internally. The usual pattern is that each department, fraction or other constituent group comes to the internal negotiation with its own minimum demands and that difficult choices are avoided by "compromises" that simply add up the demands of each group and consequently lead to a "bottom line" for the external negotiations that is unacceptable to the other side.[437] Even if the designated outside negotiator is aware of this dynamic and tries to exert a moderating influence on his constituents it frequently takes several rounds of shuttling between the inside and outside negotiations until a reasonable position is reached.

Particularly for government representatives the internal negotiation is often the most difficult part of the exercise and sometimes requires outside assistance in form of a neutral opinion, feedback by the arbitrators or even a "rigged award", i.e. an award that on its face looks like the product of a decision by the tribunal but in reality embodies a negotiated settlement. Agreement is further complicated by an inherent tendency for *agents* to be particularly demanding and reluctant to make concessions or even to consider alternative proposals. This is due to the fact that when faced with new issues or counter-proposals, the agent has to make a probability assessment of the principal's reaction, and risk-aversion in this respect can lead to a conservative and inflexible negotiating behavior.[438]

3. Prescriptive Approaches

Although useful in trying to understand the complex reality of negotiations, the descriptive findings outlined in the previous sub-section have only limited value for the practitioner seeking concrete prescriptive advice on how to conduct negotiations or how to structure dispute resolution procedures. This sub-section outlines two comprehensive approaches that organize many of the findings summarized above in a prescriptive analytical framework of high practical value for the search for alternatives to arbitration. Other approaches exist but we consider the concepts of "principled negotiation" and "negotiation analysis" to be the most developed and most influential theories, with the greatest explanatory value and the highest practical usefulness.

---

[437] R. Fisher id. 34; Lax & Sebenius id. 347.

[438] Lax & Sebenius id. 311.

a. Principled Negotiation

"Principled Negotiation", the approach developed by the Harvard Negotiation Project, found its most widely publicized expression in Roger Fisher and William Ury's 1981 best-seller *Getting to Yes*.[439] Written in a simple, non-academic style and directed at a very wide audience, *Getting to Yes* does not reveal the scientific background on which it is based. The wide circulation of *Getting to Yes* and other books,[440] as well as real life intervention and teaching activities conducted around the world under the auspices of the Harvard Program on Negotiation, have made Principled Negotiation probably the single most influential systematic approach to negotiations. Principled Negotiation is contrasted with *positional bargaining* where the parties start by presenting diametrically opposed demands which are then reduced in consecutive rounds of concessions until the parties meet somewhere in the middle on the terms of a lowest common denominator. As explained above, such a zero-sum-game approach frequently leads to inefficient compromise solutions that make both sides equally unhappy and that leave joint gains "on the table". In an attempt to offer a "third way" out of the dichotomy between "tough" and "soft" approaches, *Getting to Yes* provides practical guidelines for the pursuit of "win-win" solutions through integrative bargaining techniques and advocates the use of objective criteria for the principled resolution of the distributive aspects of negotiation.

(1) Main Recommendations

The main recommendations of Principled Negotiation can be summed up as follows:

Separate the people from the problem. The authors suggest to be *tough on the problem* and *soft on the people*. Negotiators should disentangle the substance of their dispute from their relationship and deal with both separately. Trying to "buy" a good relationship by making concessions on the substance (appeasement) is as wrong as trying to extort concessions by taking the relationship as a "hostage". Rather, a *good working relationship* should be regarded as an asset for everyone involved and each side should work towards it through effective communication, active listening, the acknowledgement of emotions, and attempts at understanding

---

[439] R. Fisher & Ury, *Getting to Yes: Negotiating Agreement Without Giving In* (1981), now available in its second edition with Bruce Patton as co-author: R. Fisher, Ury & Patton, *Getting to Yes* (2nd ed. 1991); the book was translated in nearly 20 languages and has sold over two million copies worldwide.

[440] E.g. R. Fisher & Brown, *Getting Together: Building Relationships as We Negotiate* (1988) and Ury, *Getting Past No: Negotiating with Difficult People* (1993); further: Mnookin, Peppet & Tulumello, *Beyond Winning* (2000); Stone, Patton & Heen, *Difficult Conversations* (2000).

the other side's perceptions by trying to "stand in their shoes".[441] This approach was further developed by Roger Fisher and Scott Brown in "Getting Together" (1988)[442] where the authors advocate an *unconditionally constructive* approach to building and managing relationships,[443] and further refined by Ury's "Getting Past No" (1993).[444]

Focus on interests, not positions. Distinguishing between the positions expressed in negotiation and the underlying interests of the parties, the authors suggest the separation of "wants" from "needs". By focusing on what the parties really need they may uncover mutual or complementary interest, an important step towards "win-win" solutions.

Invent options for mutual gain. The next step towards efficient solutions is creativity. Cognitive psychology has established that judgment hinders imagination. The authors therefore advocate a separation between the processes of inventing options and of deciding whether to adopt them. An important technique of separating inventing from deciding are structured brainstorming sessions where a no-criticism rule ensures that evaluations are made only after all ideas, however remote, have been expressed and recorded. Brainstormings can be conducted separately in the negotiating teams or jointly between the parties. In each case the objective is the same: to generate options for an efficient solution that "enlarges the pie".

Insist on using objective criteria. When it comes to dividing the (hopefully enlarged) "pie", the authors suggest to avoid contests of will or the exchange of threats but rather to look for criteria of a fair and principled solution and to agree on the guiding normative standards first as a threshold for an agreement on the substance.[445]

Know your "BATNA" (Best Alternative to Negotiated Agreement). Negotiators should analyze their own (and the opponent's) interests and alternatives in order to realistically assess their relative bargaining power[446] in order to make a reasoned decision whether to accept a solution or to walk away. The purpose is on the one

---

[441] R. Fisher, Ury & Patton id. 17-39.

[442] R. Fisher & Brown, *Getting Together: Building Relationships as We Negotiate* (1988).

[443] The essence of the approach is to only act in ways that are both good for the relationship and good for the individual using the strategy, whether or not the other side reciprocates. The elements of the strategy are a commitment to rationality, reliability, understanding, communication (including the consultation of the other side prior to decisions that affect the relationship), the unconditional acceptance of the other who will be taken seriously in spite of the differences on the substance and regardless of whether he or she responds in kind, and the use of non-coercive modes of influence.

[444] Ury, *Getting Past No: Negotiating with Difficult People* (1993).

[445] R. Fisher, Ury & Patton id. 81-94.

[446] The close connection between bargaining power and no-agreement alternatives is discussed in more detail in sub-section 2e.

hand to avoid resorting to one's no-agreement alternatives when in effect a proposal was on the table that would have better satisfied one's interests, and on the other hand to avoid agreeing to an inferior solution where one would be better off without the agreement. In order to ensure wise decisions in light of changed circumstances or new information the BATNA has to be continually reassessed.

(2) Analytical Tools

A number of simple but helpful analytical tools were developed in order to facilitate the application of these guidelines. Two of the most important tools are the "currently-perceived-choice chart" and the "seven elements".

The *"currently-perceived-choice chart"* is a means of assessing how the other side perceives the choices presented to it. The relative attractiveness of one or more concrete proposals under discussion vis-a-vis the other side's no-agreement alternatives are analyzed by taking a hypothetical course of action (e.g. "shall I agree to proposal x") and listing its respective advantages and disadvantages, as they are likely to be perceived by the other side. Analyzing the decision facing the other side makes it possible to understand how the options presented to the other side (or the other side's perception of this choice) have to be affected in order to come up with a "yesable proposition", a proposal that – in addition to satisfying the interests of the proponent – can be accepted by the other side.[447]

The *seven elements* constitute a *check list* of desirable *objectives* to be considered in preparing for and in conducting negotiations, and in measuring the quality of outcomes. "Effective" negotiation should lead to:

1. a good working *relationship*,

2. effective *communication*,

3. careful analysis of the *interests* of each party,

4. consideration of all relevant *options* (no waste),

5. improvement over each side's *BATNA*,

6. a *legitimate* result which is

7. embodied in wise and lasting *commitments*[448]

---

[447] An example of a "currently-perceived-choice chart" is given in R. Fisher, Ury & Patton id.

[448] Cf. R. Fisher, "Negotiating Inside Out: What are the Best Ways to Relate Internal Negotiations with External Ones?", 5 *Neg. J.* 33, 35-36 (1989).

(3) Comment

The approach pioneered in *Getting to Yes* has been *criticized* for making negotiators vulnerable to exploitation and for being "naive"[449], even misleading[450], in that it neglects the inherent limits of problem-solving as a model of negotiation[451], overemphasizes integrative bargaining and ignores that "the most demanding aspect of nearly every negotiation is the distributional one"[452]. And looking only at one's *best* alternative to agreement may be dangerous: in light of the possible uncertainty of realizing the best alternative it might be at least as important to know one's "WATNA", the *worst* alternative to negotiated agreement.[453] Certain shortcomings in the discussion of the issue of power in negotiations[454] have been acknowledged by the authors themselves and were addressed in more details in subsequent publications[455] and editions of *Getting to Yes*.[456] Another target for attacks is the appeal to objective criteria which some critics say is used in practice more as a bargaining tactic than as an honest basis for a mutually acceptable agreement.[457]

Some of these criticisms seem justified, others may be based on misperceptions. The authors make it clear that they are not preaching an indiscriminately soft approach to negotiations, but they also leave no doubt as to the mission of *Getting to Yes* which is not only a handbook on how to be more successful in negotiations but also an attempt to influence the manner in which negotiations are conducted in general. The underlying commitment to cooperative problem-solving and the attempt to combat the widespread conventional wisdom about how to "win" in negotiation through overreaching and deceptive behavior may indeed have resulted in a perceived overemphasis of the cooperative element in negotiations. However, if understood correctly, principled negotiation is not an ideology of getting to "yes" at any price. Rather it is a strategy to further one's self-interest by developing choices that are better than one's no-agreement alternatives. The inherent danger is that individuals who are already predisposed through their personality towards cooperative strategies might internalize only the positive, problem-solving ele-

---

[449]   White, "The Pros and Cons of Getting to Yes", 34 *J. Legal Educ.* 115-117 (1984).

[450]   White id. 117; Lax & Sebenius, *The Manager as Negotiator* 156 (1986).

[451]   Menkel-Meadow, "Toward Another View of Legal Negotiation: The Structure of Problem-Solving", 31 *UCLA L. Rev.* 754, 829-840 (1984).

[452]   White id 115-116.

[453]   Cf. Singer, *Settling Disputes* 19-20 (1990).

[454]   Cf. McCarthy, "The Role of Power and Principle in Getting to Yes", 1 *Neg. J.* 59 (1985).

[455]   Cf. R. Fisher, "Negotiating Power: Getting and Using Influence", 27 *Am. Behav. Sci.* 149 (1983).

[456]   Cf. R. Fisher, Ury & Patton, *Getting to Yes* 177-187 (2nd ed. 1991).

[457]   White id 117.

ment of principled negotiation and might get caught in a cooperative pathology of appeasement.

The concept of principled negotiation has been continually refined and improved in the years since *Getting to Yes* was first published and particularly the competitive element present in each negotiation has received more careful attention.[458] For the negotiator or mediator who is aware of the potential weaknesses of the approach, principled negotiation continues to provide useful and operational practical advice.

b. Negotiation Analysis

Another prescriptive theory of great practical value both for negotiators and third parties has come to be known as "Negotiation Analysis".[459] It is inspired by economic analysis and its multiple intellectual roots can be found mainly in decision analysis and game theory, with some additional inspirations from organization and management theory.[460] Negotiation analysis draws on the work of many academics from various disciplines. As a prescriptive theory negotiation analysis was pioneered by Howard Raiffa in *The Art & Science of Negotiation* (1982) and was further refined and developed into a more operational system by David A. Lax and James K. Sebenius in *The Manager as Negotiator: Bargaining for Cooperation and Competitive Gain* (1986); it was updated by Howard Raiffa, John Richardson and David Metcalfe in *Negotiation Analysis: The Science and Art of Collaborative Decision Making* (2002).[461] Some essential guidelines are summed up in the following.

(1) The Bargaining Set as Analytical Frame

Interests, Issues, Positions. As in principled negotiation, *interests* are regarded as *the measure (or the raw material) of negotiation.* Interests are distinguished from *issues* that constitute the frame for the discussion and from the *positions* the parties take on these issues. Interests can be intrinsic – of concern in and of themselves – or instrumental, i.e. merely a means to advance intrinsic ends. Negotiations analysis takes a more differentiated stance on whether and when it is recommended to probe for interests in negotiations because in some situations agreement on the overt issues and positions could be reached where emphasis on the parties' underlying

---

[458]   Cf. Ury, *Getting Past No: Negotiating with Difficult People* (1993) and the added passages in subsequent editions of *Getting to Yes.*

[459]   For an overview see Sebenius, "Negotiation Analysis: A Characterization and Review", 38 *Management Science* 18 (1992).

[460]   See Sebenius id. and the foreword to Lax & Sebenius, *The Manager as Negotiator* xiv (1986).

[461]   Raiffa, Richardson & Metcalfe, *Negotiation Analysis, The Science and Art of Collaborative Decision Making* (2002).

interests would only complicate the situation. Also, to insist on positions might sometimes be in the tactical interest of a party.[462]

Alternatives to Agreement. Alternatives constitute *the limits of negotiation* since the parties will rationally only agree to a negotiated solution if it serves their interests better than the pursuit of its no-agreement alternatives. Alternatives to agreement are a subjective and dynamic notion, they can take subtle forms and are subject to real change and to alterations of perception. It is important to take this into account since negotiations are frequently burdened by inflated perceptions of the value of alternative courses of action or the likelihood of their success.

Figure 18: The Bargaining Set

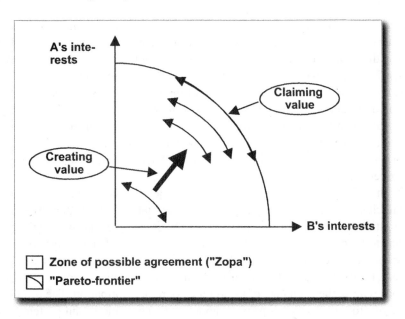

The bargaining range or "Zone of Possible Agreement" ("ZOPA"). Many strategies in negotiation turn around efforts to change the other side's perception of the bargaining range or "Zone of Possible Agreement" ("ZOPA").[463] The bargaining range is defined as the sum of all possible agreements that for both parties are preferable to their respective no-agreement alternatives. The creation of value in negotiations

---

[462]   Lax & Sebenius id. 63-87.

[463]   Raiffa, Richardson & Metcalfe, *Negotiation Analysis, The Science and Art of Collaborative Decision Making* (2002), 110-112, 124-125.

can be measured by the extent to which joint gains are maximized, and this in turn can be graphically illustrated by moving northeast to the "efficiency-frontier" or "Pareto-frontier" which marks the line beyond which no result can be improved for one party without reducing the value attained by the other. The field between the zero-point and the Pareto-frontier defines the "bargaining set" or the "zone of possible agreement". Since parties in real negotiations operate on the basis of incomplete information (particularly in regard of the other side's real interests and alternatives) the "real" zone of possible agreements will usually be unknown to the parties. Rather, they operate on – typically divergent – perceptions of the range and of the location of the Pareto frontier, and much of the negotiation dynamic consists of influencing the other side's perceptions about the bargaining set.[464]

(2) The Negotiator's Dilemma[465]

As mentioned, cooperative and competitive moves, *creating value* and *claiming value* are essential elements of every negotiation.[466] They cannot be neatly separated because the manner in which the parties try to create value sets the parameters for the distribution of that value and, conversely, efforts at securing the lion's share of the "pie" tend to inhibit the expansion of the pie in the first place. Thus, value creation and value claiming are linked by a *fundamental tension*. The ability to create value can be crucial for the success of a negotiation: if the parties do not manage to enlarge the pie, the danger is not only that of an inefficient agreement which leaves potential joint gains "on the table", but the parties risk failing to reach any agreement at all.

On the other hand, even where both parties jointly seek to reach agreements that are close to the Pareto frontier, they will inevitably prefer different points on that frontier. In other words, no matter how much the "pie" has been enlarged, it still has to be divided. The negotiator's dilemma is one of (partially) *conflicting goals*: as we have seen above, value is created through the pursuit of shared interests, the exploitation of differences or through economies of scale. All of these methods require the exchange of a certain amount of information. The problem is that tactics to create value (openness about one's perceptions and preferences, a genuine effort to understand the other side's concerns and to jointly solve problems, willingness to share information and to make creative proposals) can be exploited by the other side, whereas tactics to claim value (manipulating the other side's

---

[464] On the above see Lax & Sebenius id. 42-45 and Sebenius, "Negotiation Analysis: A Characterization and Review", 38 *Management Science* 18, 24 (1992).

[465] Raiffa, Richardson & Metcalfe, *Negotiation Analysis, The Science and Art of Collaborative Decision Making* (2002), 85-86.

[466] For the following see Lax & Sebenius, *The Manager as Negotiator* 33-45, 243-249 (1986); Sebenius, "Negotiation Analysis: A Characterization and Review", 38 *Management Science* 18, 26-34 (1992).

perceptions, deflating its no-agreement alternatives, exaggerating the value of one's own concessions, trivializing the benefits derived from the other's concessions, concealing information, making commitments, holding common values hostage, issuing threats, exploiting cultural expectations, or plainly deceiving the other party) may destroy the atmosphere of trust and cooperation needed for the exchange of information required for value creation. Hence, negotiations present a dilemma because *"competitive moves to claim value individually drive out cooperative moves to create it jointly."*[467]

This dilemma can be illustrated in the categories of game theory by forming an analogy to the famous "prisoner's dilemma" (see above at p. 140): by being cooperative the negotiator can obtain a mutually beneficial outcome, but only if the other party, too, cooperates. Otherwise, the cooperative behavior will be exploited and the other party reaps advantages at the cooperative party's expense. Consequently, anticipated competitive behavior is best matched with competitive strategies. Mutual distrust motivates "pre-emptive strikes", and even if the other party is expected to behave cooperatively, the temptation of opportunistic behavior is strong: why not "play it tough" and exploit that behavior? Thus, competitive behavior seems to be most promising in any event. The problem, however, is that, if both parties behave in this perfectly rational (and in terms of game theory "dominant") manner, any opportunity for joint gains will be missed. The result will be at best a mediocre (or, in the language of economic analysis, "Pareto-inferior") agreement, or no agreement at all, and in the worst case an escalation of conflict causing losses for everyone involved.

The dynamic of the prisoner's dilemma is compounded by the phenomenon of "loss-aversion" in the context of perceptual frames. As we have seen, people are more willing to take chances in the face of impending loss than they are when confronted with a sure gain. In the example of the prisoner's dilemma, the players may see competitive behavior as the "safe" choice, since, at least, it preserves them from immediate exploitation and loss. In this logic, to behave cooperatively would mean risking a sure short-term gain for a *possible* future (joint and) bigger gain – a choice that seems to be counter-intuitive.

Simply *denying the tension* is no solution: ignoring the competitive aspects makes the negotiator vulnerable to exploitation through claiming tactics, whereas neglect of the potential for value creation leads to sub-optimal results, if an agreement can be reached at all.[468] A number of responses seek to overcome this dilemma and pursue more efficient agreements:

- making creating seem better than claiming,

---

[467] Sebenius, "Negotiation Analysis: A Characterization and Review", 38 *Management Science* 18, 30 (1992).

[468] Id. 155-157.

- duplicitous tactics to create unilateral gain,
- the "tit-for-tat" strategy of conditional openness,
- separating inventing from deciding,
- post-settlement settlements,
- single negotiating texts, and
- mediation.[469]

There are a number of ways of *emphasizing value creation* over claiming tactics. This can be done by adopting a cooperative negotiating strategy such as Principled Negotiation with its emphasis on integrative bargaining and objective criteria. However, such strategies require constructive and honest behavior on both sides. If a cooperative negotiator tries to first reach agreement on the principles that should guide the distribution, a hard bargainer can exploit the cooperative party's objectiveness in the discussion over principles to score important points for the distributive part of the negotiation by strategically invoking principles that serve his purposes.

Genuinely cooperative approaches to value creation have to be distinguished from opportunistic tactics of one-sided or *"duplicitous creation"* that try to solve the negotiator's dilemma at the other party's expense. This can be done for instance by generating options that look mutually advantageous but in reality create value only for one party, or by suggesting "neutral" principles which in the concrete circumstances lead to one-sided results. Many duplicitous tactics manipulate the other side's perception of where the real gains of a proposed solution accrue. Opportunistic negotiators sometimes add artificial issues to the problem in order to make cheap concessions in biased trade-offs.

A much discussed technique of eliciting cooperation while avoiding the danger of exploitation is the already mentioned strategy of *conditional openness*. Cooperative negotiation behavior can be protected against exploitation if opportunistic moves are reciprocated with a "tit-for-tat" strategy of being "nice", "provocable", "forgiving" and "clear". However, in real-life negotiations it is often hard to tell what "game" the other side is playing, how many additional rounds will follow, and what will be the respective payoffs of cooperation and exploitation.[470]

A particularly effective way to manage the negotiator's dilemma is by *changing the game* to include *cooperative negotiation structures* that facilitate the creation of value while safeguarding against unilateral exploitation. One way to do this is to *separate inventing from decision-making*.

---

[469]   This list is an adaptation from the list in Lax & Sebenius, *The Manager as Negotiator* 182 (1986).

[470]   Id. 157-164.

Another technique, called *Post-Settlement-Settlement*,[471] reverses the order and tries to first achieve an agreement on how the values at stake shall be divided before engaging the parties in joint value creation (with the benefits accruing to both parties in the previously determined proportions). The danger is, however, that the parties will bargain even harder in the initial round, knowing that the balance struck will affect any future distributions.[472]

Another way to disentangle inventing and deciding is the use of a *Single Negotiating Text (SNT)*[473] or "*One-Text-Procedure*":[474] a tentative draft of a possible solution is presented to the parties who are invited to criticize it freely without having to make any commitments. In consecutive rounds of discussion and criticism, the draft is further adjusted to meet the demands and concerns raised and push the solution towards the "Pareto-frontier", until the final SNT is presented to the parties for a simple yes-no decision over its acceptance. Although typically done with the help of a third party who drafts the initial SNT, suggests the consecutive amendments and determines the final text submitted for ratification, the technique can also be used in face-to-face negotiations.[475]

Potentially the most powerful means of managing the tension between creating and claiming is *mediation*.[476] Many of the techniques which have been listed above can be enhanced by the intervention of a mediator who, for instance, can structure the negotiation so as to emphasize value-creation through integrative bargaining and problem-solving or who may help the parties separate inventing from deciding, or who can formulate a Single Negotiating Text or a Post-Settlement Settlement. In addition, a mediator can facilitate communication, prevent the escalation of conflict, act as a secure channel for sensitive information, enhance the creativity of the parties, e.g. through separate confidential brainstorming sessions with each party, or issue a neutral proposal that spares the parties of the need to be seen to make

---

[471]   Id. 180-181; the concept of Post-Settlement-Settlements was developed by Howard Raiffa; cf. Raiffa, "Post-Settlement-Settlements", 1 *Neg. J.* 9-12 (1985); see also Bazerman, Russ & Yakura, "Post-Settlement-Settlements in two-Party Negotiations", 3 *Neg. J.* 283-291 (1987).

[472]   Lax & Sebenius id.

[473]   Raiffa, Richardson & Metcalfe, *Negotiation Analysis, The Science and Art of Collaborative Decision Making* (2002), 320-326.

[474]   The concept of the Single Negotiating Text originates in international diplomacy and is commonly attributed to Louis Sohn; cf. Acknowledgements to R. Fisher, Ury & Patton, *Getting to Yes* xii (2d. ed. 1991); the procedure is discussed in R. Fisher, Ury & Patton id. 112-116; Lax & Sebenius, *The Manager as Negotiator* 176-178 (1986); Raiffa, *The Art and Science of Negotiation* 205-217 (1982).

[475]   R. Fisher, Ury & Patton, *Getting to Yes* 115 (2nd ed. 1991).

[476]   Raiffa, Richardson & Metcalfe, *Negotiation Analysis, The Science and Art of Collaborative Decision Making* (2002), 311-327; for a brief overview of how a mediator may help overcome the negotiator's dilemma see Lax & Sebenius id. 172-176.

concessions. The many ways how a third party can help overcome the negotiator's dilemma are discussed in more detail in the next Chapter.

c. Comment

Negotiation Analysis and Principled Negotiation are both mature prescriptive theories that build on a vast array of interdisciplinary research and that share many common roots. Both theories have many aspects in common. They both see the purpose of negotiations in doing better through jointly decided action than without agreement, and both regard the interests of the parties as the decisive measure in comparing negotiated outcomes to no-agreement alternatives. And both theories are concerned with achieving efficient results by maximizing joint gains.

III. CONFLICT MANAGEMENT IN CONTEXT

The rising attention conflict management has generated in recent decades mirrors the challenges of national and international actors in connection with the changing frameworks in which they operate. It is both a reaction to the shortcomings of the traditional legal and societal framework and an expression of a more autonomous self-perception of conflict actors: Dissatisfaction and frustration with traditional means of conflict resolution have created a need for more appropriate techniques aiming at providing the parties with control over both the process and the outcome of their transactions. The rising focus on conflict management is by no means limited to international business actors.[477] Parties in almost any relationship – personal, business, or public – are exploring "modern" ways of minimizing the dysfunctional and disruptive effects of conflict. Various entities, business organizations as well as courts and legislative bodies, are using sophisticated conflict management techniques.[478]

A multitude of approaches to the term "conflict management" exist in theory and practice. Instead of comprehensively analyzing controversial interpretations of the term and concept,[479] we will take a more practical approach. Similar to the term "management", referring to multiple tasks such as planning, organizing, leading

---

[477] Altmann/ Fiebinger & Müller, *Mediation: Konfliktmanagement für moderne Unternehmen* (2nd ed. 2001).

[478] For examples of conflict management in business organizations see Lipsky, Seeber & Fincher, *Emerging Systems For Managing Workplace Conflict* 345 (2003) with a list of US corporations and other organizations which were analyzed; see also Slaikeu & Hasson, *Controlling the Costs of Conflict* (1998).

[479] Krüger, *Konfliktsteuerung als Führungsaufgabe* 14 et seq. (1973); and the selected works on conflict management by Costantino & Merchant, *Designing Conflict Management Systems* (1996); Deutsch, *Konfliktregelung – Konstruktive und destruktive Prozesse* (1976); Glasl, *Konfliktmanagement* (2004).

and controlling an organization, "conflict management" serves as a general term for the analysis, prevention, de-escalation, and resolution of conflicts. It comprises strategies and methods as well as procedures and structures. Depending on the organizational context in which conflict management is utilized, its focus will vary on different dimensions and elements: the *user's dimension* of analyzing, preventing, de-escalating, and autonomously resolving conflicts; the *provider's dimension* of training the stakeholders in administering and facilitating the handling of conflicts; as well as the *organizational dimension* of changing the conflict culture within an organization, and lastly, the *procedural dimension* of designing customized processes to be used by the various actors. Ideally, conflict management entails all four dimensions.

Many business and non-business actors are resorting to innovative means of conflict resolution.[480] Within the legal system, where the parties traditionally relied on sources of authority, i.e. the law and the court system, "alternative" processes are now integrated into public adjudication through mandatory or optional mediation programs. Such court-annexed ADR programs exist in the USA[481] as well as in Europe[482] (for example in Germany[483]), where public attention to ADR has triggered the promotion of ADR-related legislation. Controlling and managing conflict in a more autonomous way is becoming a concern for society as a whole.[484]

---

[480] E.g., between 1999 and 2002, Coca-Cola Enterprises developed and implemented an internal workplace conflict management system. The system comprises the institution of an ombudsperson office and the use of mediation and arbitration as methods of handling workplace conflicts and disputes. Lewis, "Conflict Management System for Coca-Cola Enterprises", presentation at the Resolving Conflict Conference, Baltimore, Md., May 24, 2001, cited at Lipsky, Seeber & Fincher, *Emerging Systems for Managing Workplace Conflict* (2003).

[481] Cf. Bergman & Bickerman, *Court Annexed Mediation* (1998), offers an in-depth analysis of selected state and federal programs in the USA.

[482] An important step in establishing ADR in Europe has been the Commission of the European Communities' Green Paper on Alternative Dispute Resolution in Civil and Commercial Law, issued 4/19/2002, available under europa.eu.int/eur-lex/en/com/gpr/2002/com2002_0196en01.pdf; in April 2003, the European Parliament adopted a draft resolution of the Green Paper recommending that a follow-up Green Paper should set out a future Europe-wide model code for ADR encompassing a number of procedural guarantees concerning cross-border disputes, best practice and access to justice.

[483] See, for example, the project on court annexed mediation in the state of Lower Saxony, Germany; Information available at www.mediation-in-niedersachsen.de.

[484] Lipsky, Seeber & Fincher, *Emerging Systems For Managing Workplace Conflict* xii (2003).

IV. CONCLUSION

The purpose of this chapter has been to show that any attempt at improving conflict management in international business and at understanding "alternative" dispute resolution must take into account the results of conflict and negotiation theory.

Conflict is an integral part of any social relationship and a natural element in all forms of cooperation. Conflict has to be managed in ways that satisfy the parties' underlying interests and that lead to legitimate and lasting solutions. The most constructive way of resolving conflicts is by *reconciling interests through consensus*. Consensual solutions tend to be most efficient in satisfying the parties' interests by exhausting the potential for mutual gains, they derive legitimacy from the agreement of the parties, they tend to last longer since the parties will comply more easily with solutions they themselves have developed, and they tend to be less costly in terms of time, actual costs, and strains on the relationship.

Good conflict management depends both on effective negotiation and on the existence of a stable legal framework that provides an effective "back-up". Effective negotiation is burdened by a structural dilemma in the process and by the inherent limits in the capacity of the players to negotiate effectively. Both these types of barriers can be overcome in large measure by means of the "process technology" developed on the basis of modern negotiation theory.

In order to avoid deadlocks, and to guarantee lasting results and a minimum standard of legitimacy, interest-based consensual procedures have to be backed up by procedures that determine and enforce rights. In the presence of an effective legal "*back-up*", the parties are bargaining in the "*shadow*" *of the law*. The law has a double function in negotiations, providing substantive standards of legitimacy and the most important no-agreement alternative or "BATNA". Effective conflict management has to facilitate consensus while at the same time providing a reliable legal back-up, in international business frequently in the form of private arbitration which in turn is backed up by the legal systems of the states that have a connection to the dispute. Both the consensual part of the system and the legal back-up reinforce each other and are *interdependent* in their effectiveness because an effective and legitimate back-up will tend to improve the quality of negotiations while effective negotiations perform a filter function by channelling only those cases into the back-up system that are best suited to resolution by determination of rights.

Consensual solutions are the product of *negotiation*, defined as a process of communication directed at achieving joint decisions. Effective negotiation generates solutions that satisfy the interests of the parties and it facilitates rational choice in light of the parties' no-agreement alternatives. The intuitive "method" of negotiation is inefficient in the vast majority of negotiations since it consists of positional bargaining which assumes a fixed-sum and leads to ineffective patterns of communication. Effective negotiation focuses on interests and attempts to maximize value for both sides while ensuring a legitimate distribution.

Effective negotiation, however, faces a number of significant *obstacles* which are in part inherent in the process of negotiation and in part due to the limited capacity of the parties to negotiate effectively. Inherent in the *process* of negotiation is a *fundamental tension* between cooperation and conflict, between cooperative moves to create value and competitive moves to claim it. Since it is impossible to insulate the creative elements from the distributive elements in negotiation and since the strategies for creating and claiming value are in large measure incompatible, negotiators are faced with a true dilemma: individually rational moves to claim value (and prevent exploitation by the other side) prevent collectively rational moves to jointly create value. This *"negotiator's dilemma"* is a structural problem independent of the ability of the individual negotiators, and it has the tendency to result in inefficient solutions or to prevent agreement altogether. In addition, the *capacity of the players* to negotiate effectively is limited by *psychological, organizational and cultural barriers* and by a widespread lack of skills training in negotiation. Negotiation theory is not only helpful in identifying the barriers to effective negotiation but it has also developed a *"technology"* for conflict manage-ment that can help overcome both the deficiencies of the players and the dilemma inherent in the process.

The *process itself* can be improved by *changing the game* to include constructive negotiation structures that facilitate information exchange and communication and that help manage the fundamental tension between value creation and claiming. The most effective way of changing the game can be *mediation* by a skilled third party who contributes professional process expertise and a measure of objectivity, who improves communication patterns, and who assists the parties in structuring the procedure.

Chapter 6

Alternative Dispute Resolution Techniques

"ADR has changed – and so has our attitude towards ADR."[485]

Alternative Dispute Resolution (ADR) generally refers to any type of procedure that constitutes an alternative to litigation. In a domestic setting this might include arbitration but in the international context, where arbitration has developed into the standard procedure for commercial litigation, it makes more sense to restrict the term *ADR* to procedures that are different from the conventional forms of international commercial arbitration.

Although the use of mediation or conciliation is known in almost all societies, in most countries these techniques traditionally had little practical relevance for the resolution of commercial disputes. Only recently have some jurisdictions and the major arbitration institutions begun to include alternative means of dispute resolution into their procedures.[486]

In certain industries and in certain regions of the world, some form of ADR has long been part of the practice or culture.[487] Most of the countries of the *Far East* have a tradition of using conciliation – as a separate procedure or as an integral part of arbitration – as the dominant method of dispute resolution, even in commercial matters.[488] Conciliation has deep roots in *China* and an overwhelming significance

---

[485] Interview with Professor W. Michael Reisman, April 17, 2002.

[486] On mediation in international business see Salacuse, "International Business Mediation", in: Bercovitch (ed.), *Studies in International Mediation: Essays in Honor of Jeffrey Z. Rubin* (2003); Rau, Sherman & Peppet (ed.), *Processes of Dispute Resolution* 906 et seq. (3rd Ed. 2002); Abramson, "Time to Try Mediation in International Commercial Disputes", 4 *ILSA J. Int'l & Comp. L.* 323 et seq. (1998); Coombe, "The Future: Implementing New Approaches to the Settlement of Transnational Commercial Disputes", 17 *Can.-U.S. L.J.* 533 et seq. (1991).

[487] For the distinction of traditional vs. modern mediation, see below at p. 177 et seq.

[488] For an overview of combined methods see Anchini, *Concitration: The Ultimate Example of ADR*, World Arbitration and Mediation Report 162, 163-164 (2002).

for dispute resolution throughout the entire society, including business relations with foreign investors and traders.[489]

In the United Kingdom, alternative methods of dispute resolution by now have become a standard part of ordinary legal practice. Under the new Civil Procedure Rules, reformed in 1999 and going back to the 1995 "Woolf Report", the courts take a very proactive stance toward settlement. Not only do they encourage the use of mediation, they can even go so far as to penalize a party declining an offer to mediate without good cause – irrespective of the case's outcome.[490] The attitude behind the new Civil Procedure Rules and the courts' practice is reflected in the following statement, issued by Lord Woolf:

"...sufficient should be known about ADR to make the failure to adopt it, in particular when public money is involved, indefensible."[491]

However, the most important development in the evolution of specific ADR techniques for *business disputes* has occurred in the *United States* where the quest for alternatives to litigation has evolved into what some have called a "movement". Many of the considerations which in the United States have led to the development of specific ADR techniques for business disputes increasingly apply to the *international* arena, as well. Any attempt at exploring ways for effective conflict management in international business therefore has to start with an analysis of the techniques developed domestically in the United States. Although it may be possible to avoid the immense costs of American pre-trial discovery, transnational litigation and international commercial arbitration often prove to be protracted, costly, and disruptive. Inter-cultural discrepancies make mutual understanding and constructive settlement negotiations difficult, and simple practical considerations discourage the parties to invest time and money for trans-continental, trans-atlantic or trans-pacific "peace-making missions". Under these circumstances, a procedure that allows for a condensed exchange of data, arguments and evidence, and that makes it possible for senior executives to hear both sides of the story and gain a neutral evaluation of the merits has a great potential for bringing about mutually satisfactory solutions or at least for narrowing the issues and focusing the dispute, thus enhancing the efficiency of any subsequent binding procedures. In the words of the former Secretary General of the ICC Court of International Arbitration,

---

[489] For an overview, placing conciliation within the general dispute resolution framework in China, see Chang, "Resolving Disputes through Conciliation and Arbitration in the Mainland China", 2 *Ann. 2000 ATLA CLE* 1643 (2000).

[490] In *Dunnett v. Railtrack plc* (in administration) [2002] 1 WLR 803 (22 February 2002), the court awarded the costs against the successful defendant for his refusal to consider ADR when asked to by the plaintiff.

[491] Cited in: Newmark, "Agree to Mediate ... or Face the Consequences – A Review of the English Courts' Approach to Mediation", 1 *Schiedsverfahrenszeitung* 23, 25 (2003).

"... one might reasonably assume that in the international domain ADR might have its greatest potential, at least where the parties concerned are in good faith".[492]

The United States can be viewed as a laboratory for innovation in dispute resolution, and consequently, in this Chapter, we shall first take a brief look at the status quo of business ADR in the United States (I.) before presenting the most important common features and principles of ADR techniques (II.). This overview is followed by a more detailed analysis of mediation as the prototype of all ADR techniques (III.) and some comments on other methods such as the mini-trial, fact-finding procedures and preventive structures (IV.). In a conclusion, some strengths and weaknesses of ADR procedures (V.) are presented.

I. BUSINESS ADR IN THE UNITED STATES

In the United States alternative dispute resolution techniques have attained a practical relevance that has converted an initially exotic field into a standard area of the practice of law. Alternative techniques – above all mediation, early neutral evaluation and the mini-trial – have entered the mainstream, to the extent that lawyers who ignore the possibility of employing ADR techniques in the interests of their clients may find themselves at risk of discipline or malpractice liability.[493] Several states have amended their rules of professional conduct for attorneys to include an obligation to be informed about the various techniques and to consider them when advising their clients:

"In a matter involving or expected to involve litigation, a lawyer should advise the client of alternative forms of dispute resolution which might reasonably be pursued to attempt to resolve the legal dispute or to reach the legal objective sought."[494]

In America, corporate ADR has been called a "corporate-consumer revolution"[495] and has resulted in institutional structures like JAMS,[496] a big commercial provider, or the CPR Institute for Dispute Resolution (formerly The Center for Public

---

[492] Schwartz, "International Conciliation and the ICC", 10 *ICSID Rev*. 98, 100 (1995).

[493] Cochran, "Must Lawyers Tell Clients About ADR?", *Arbitration Journal* 8-13 (1993).

[494] Section 2.1 of the Colorado Rules of Professional Conduct, as amended effective 1 January 1993.

[495] Pollock, "The Alternate Route", *The American Lawyer* 70 (1983).

[496] Cf. www.jamsadr.com.

Resources)[497] which works towards the promotion and continuous improvement of dispute resolution techniques between businesses. CPR, founded at the initiative of a group of corporate in-house counsel concerned with the costs of litigation, provides model rules for business mediation, mini-trials and a number of specialized procedures, e.g. for ADR in the oil or securities industries, publishes books and a monthly journal on ADR, provides training in alternative techniques, and assists in the conduct of alternative procedures by providing rosters of qualified neutrals and helping in their selection. By now, more than 4,000 American companies and more than 1,500 American law firms have joined CPR and have signed a pledge obliging themselves to try non-binding procedures such as mediation first before resorting to litigation when faced with a dispute against another CPR member. Similar institutions for corporate ADR have been founded in the United Kingdom (cf. the "Centre for Effective Dispute Resolution" – "CEDR").[498]

A considerable number of American companies have instituted *corporate ADR programs*. A standing ADR policy can improve a party's ability to promote the settlement of disputes in two ways: by encouraging rational choice between litigation and the use of ADR procedures, and by raising the overall ability of the organization to deal with conflict. The use of ADR procedures, such as mediation or mini-trials, can be encouraged by educating the legal and business personnel about these techniques and by making it normal business practice to consider these procedures whenever a dispute arises. Some corporations have appointed an ADR officer to supervise and coordinate the company's ADR activities and some routinely include multi-step dispute resolution clauses in their contracts providing procedures for the early recognition and processing of potential conflicts. Another step is the institution of early-warning procedures and periodic reviews in long-term contracts that alert management of any potential conflicts. Perhaps the most important element of a corporate ADR policy is a high degree of management involvement and control in dispute resolution. Under corporate ADR policies executives are instructed to view dispute resolution as part of their business responsibilities, and procedures are created that involve higher levels of management before, or at least simultaneously to, the involvement of the legal department or the formalization of the dispute.

Corporate *law firms* have also started to embrace ADR as part of their services. Recognizing the difference in training, character and motivation between typical "litigators" and "deal makers", some firms have a negotiation/ADR department or employ specialized outside consultants to conduct settlement negotiations. This is sometimes done in a *two-track approach* while litigation efforts continue. Parallel litigation and settlement efforts can be helpful when a party wants to avoid any sign of weakness or when it hesitates to enter into negotiations because it suspects the other side of exploiting such a situation for delay tactics.

---

[497] Cf. www.cpradr.org.

[498] Cf. www.cedr.co.uk.

An increasing number of corporations – and governments – use the services of *professional negotiation consultants*, either on an ongoing basis to enhance the skills level within the organization or for specific disputes, transactions or relationships (e.g. the formation or unwinding of a strategic alliance).

In the United States, over 90% of all corporate lawsuits are eventually settled without trial, often after years of costly litigation. Empirical research has shown that in the bulk of lawsuits the courts' actual function is not to render a binding decision but to serve as a background for settlement negotiations, for "bargaining in the shadow of the law".[499] Hence the filing of a lawsuit often is simply a pointed way to bring the other side to the bargaining table.

There is a striking contrast between this reality and the lack of attention traditionally devoted by most lawyers to the processes, problems, and skills involved in reaching settlement although trial attorneys are overwhelmingly dissatisfied with the typical ad hoc process of settlement negotiations and parties complain that "compromise comes too late, is too expensive, and is too stressful".[500] Conventional settlement negotiations in the "shadow" of ongoing or imminent litigation proceed in an adversarial setting and are faced with certain inherent drawbacks in addition to the general "dilemma" present in every negotiation. The usual sequence in business disputes is that, after informal and mostly unstructured negotiations between the parties have failed, lawyers are hired to conduct and "win" a lawsuit. After a certain amount of "bloodletting" in terms of pre-trial litigation expenses and in the face of substantial further costs, settlement negotiations are conducted, usually by the attorneys, or at least in the presence and with the direction of the attorneys. These attorneys tend to be "litigators", in many cases they are neither specifically trained nor selected for reaching cooperative agreements, and their character may be dominated by a spirit of competitiveness and "gamesmanship". The litigation context tends to limit the attorneys' horizon of possible solutions to what a court can be expected to order, i.e. generally a monetary sum. Since parties and attorneys have a natural, empirically proven tendency to overestimate their chance of winning in court, agreement – let alone a "win-win" solution – is difficult to reach. Optimizing the process of reaching settlement is the main thrust of ADR. The techniques – with or without the intervention of a neutral – are mostly structures and tools for more effective negotiation.

---

[499] Trubek, Sarat, Felstiner, Kritzer & Grossman, "The Costs of Ordinary Litigation", 31 *U.C.L.A. L. Rev.* 72,89 (1983); The concept of bargaining in the shadow of the law was developed by Mnookin & Kornhauser , "'Bargaining in the Shadow of the Law': The Case of Divorce", 88 *Yale L.J.* 950 (1979).

[500] Edwards, "Alternative Dispute Resolution: Panacea or Anathema?", 99 *Harv. L. Rev.* 668, 669 (1986).

II. COMMON FEATURES OF "ALTERNATIVE" TECHNIQUES

Despite the great variety of alternative techniques, there are certain important common features.[501]

1. Party-Autonomy

ADR methods are premised on the right of the parties to freely dispose over their controversies through voluntary agreement. This liberty implies the freedom to devise any kind of procedure for the resolution of disputes, including the voluntary submission to binding determination by a third party. Where procedures are non-binding, they are *voluntary* in a double sense: both the *participation in the process* and the *acceptance of its results* are subject to a free determination by the parties. This confers upon the parties a sense of *"ownership"* in the resolution of their disputes, an important factor for the high degree of party satisfaction commonly achieved by alternative methods and the main reason why parties – once they have agreed to a solution – in general are found to comply more often and more readily with the results as compared to binding procedures.

2. Flexibility

A result of this party-autonomy is that the parties are free to design the procedure in any way they deem fit and to create tailor-made processes to accommodate the particularities of the dispute. There are no limits to creativity and the parties or their advisors are free to invent dispute resolution mechanisms and to modify them as the process goes along. This flexibility also extends to the possible outcomes which are not limited to the narrow remedies provided for by legal rules but can encompass any combination of material or non-material benefits, transfers and exchanges.

3. Focus on Interests

Since the interests of the parties are the principal benchmark for all conflict resolution, alternative techniques are invariably designed to produce results that best satisfy the parties' interests. These interests can be influenced by the legal rights and remedies that in most cases determine the parties' most important no-agreement alternatives. Many alternative procedures are therefore at least in part "rights-based", as opposed to purely "interest-based", and include an assessment of the parties' legal rights and the probable outcomes of litigation. There is a *complex interaction between rights and interests*: rights influence interests but the realization of rights is no end in itself – any success in litigation in the end has to be measured against a party's broader underlying interests. Litigation limits the

---

[501] See, e.g., Hill, "The Theoretical Basis of Mediation and Other Forms of ADR: Why They Work", 14 (2) *Arb. Int'l* 182 (1998).

scope of the dispute and makes it decidable by framing it in legal terms. At the same time it converts the dispute into a zero-sum game. Although the likely outcomes of any rights-based back-up procedure always have to be taken into account, the real challenge is to shift the focus back to interests in order to realize the potential for mutually beneficial solutions. The focus on interests permits the consideration of issues that do not strictly belong to the dispute if judged from a purely legal perspective. And adding new issues, in turn, makes it easier to "create value" by forming linkages and devising trade-offs. There is a *fundamental dilemma* in ADR: the need to provide a realistic assessment of the prospects of legal back-up remedies conflicts with the goal of directing the focus towards interests in order to reach more satisfying and efficient results.

4. Management Involvement

The focus on the parties' underlying interests is enhanced by the opportunity to efficiently involve the principals directly in the resolution of the dispute. The emphasis on economic aspects helps reverting a legal dispute to a business problem and calls for the use of management skills such as brainstorming and problem-solving in order to produce more efficient results. High-level executives tend to know the interests, priorities and future strategies of the businesses they lead far better than any lawyer can, and if they have sufficient authority to dispose over the controversy, they generally reach agreement faster and with more creative and more forward looking results, sometimes even converting a dispute into a new business deal.

5. Focus on Relationship

Alternative procedures are usually conducted in a less adversarial atmosphere than litigation. Their consensual nature and the focus on the parties' underlying interests make it possible to go to the roots of a conflict while avoiding unnecessary harm to, or even improving, the relationship between the disputants.

6. Confidentiality

Private dispute resolution gives the parties greater control over who will know about the existence of the controversy, how it was resolved (who caved in?) and any trade secrets that may have to be revealed in the course of the negotiations.

7. Limited Transaction Costs

Although there is great variety according to the dispute, the parties, the procedure chosen and the quality of any third-party intervention, alternative procedures generally produce significant savings in terms of the time invested, the direct costs of the procedure and the many indirect transaction costs arising in the context of disputes, such as the diversion of management time and corporate energies, the disruption of business, damage to existing relationships and loss of future business opportunities.

III. MEDIATION – THE PROTOTYPE OF ADR-PROCEDURES

"Any dispute, international or not, is well suited for mediation. I don't care what it is: The best result is when two parties settle the case. The minute they don't settle the case they are entering the area of risk. The lowest level of risk is with a mediator because he works with your concern. To hand your dispute to a judge of some court or three international arbitrators is a high risk."[502]

1. Definition

The involvement of a third party can take a great variety of forms and different degrees of intensity. On a scale of rising intensity of third-party intervention:

– bringing the parties to the negotiation table

– assisting with the negotiation process

– providing a neutral assessment of the situation

– supporting parties in formulating interests and settlement options

– making concrete settlement proposals

– rendering a binding decision (arbitration)

There is no universally accepted definition of mediation. At times, mediation is understood to comprise all forms of third-party intervention short of a binding decision. For the purposes of this book, we suggest the following definition:

Mediation is the non-binding intervention by an impartial third party who helps the disputants negotiate an agreement.

The term "conciliation" is frequently used synonymously to mediation, particularly in the context of international disputes. However, sometimes it is contrasted to mediation and used to denote third-party intervention of a specific quality. For some, conciliation is limited to the act of bringing the parties to the negotiation table, a process others call "facilitation", while for others conciliation is reserved for procedures where the neutral issues a concrete settlement proposal. For the purposes of this book, in order to avoid the use of confusing and not universally accepted distinctions, the terms *mediation and conciliation* shall be *used synonymously.*

---

[502] Interview with Gerald Aksen, April 16, 2002

This definition of mediation (and conciliation) obviously excludes any procedure where the third party has the power to render a binding decision (this would be arbitration).

2.   Traditional Mediation vs. Modern Mediation[503]

Mediation as a traditional form of dispute resolution can be found in societies around the globe and can be traced back to the earliest history of mankind.[504] Cross-cultural and historical studies of mediation are rare, and the diversity of mediation styles and techniques that have been found makes it difficult to make accurate generalizations. However, a few common characteristics suggest distinguishing "traditional" forms of mediation from the more "modern" techniques that have emerged in the last few decades, primarily in the United States. The distinction proposed here is one of ideal types, and there are many shades of gray in-between, but it is important to understand that mediation in the modern sense is a lot more than simply a wise man proposing a compromise.

The characteristic feature that distinguishes "traditional" and "modern" mediation is the social context and the role and standing of the third party. While in modern mediation "ownership" of the process lies with the disputants, and the mediator is simply assisting the parties in developing their own solution, traditional mediation occurs in the context of a coherent social group and is characterized by the dominant role of the third party who is typically a highly respected member of the group and whose suggestions carry great authority with the parties.

Examples of traditional mediation can be found in ancient history where mediation as an institutionalized form of social control and dispute resolution can be found as early as about 3,000 years B.C. in Egypt, Bable, and Assyr. The amicable resolution of disputes had a primordial place in the justice systems of ancient Greece and Rome where an institutionalized system of combined mediation and arbitration appears to have been the preferred means of resolving civil disputes. This form of judicial mediation, particularly in ancient Rome, has had an important influence on civil procedure in continental Europe and can still be found in contemporary court practice, particularly in Austria, Germany, and Switzerland.

Other examples can be found in tribal societies. Ethnological research on conflict resolution in tribal societies in Africa and North America has found a widespread

---

[503]   The following passage was in part taken from Bühring-Uhle, "Traditional Mediation vs. Modern Mediation", *Stockholm Arbitration Newsletter* (Issue 1/2001), online available at www.sccinstitute.com/_upload/shared_files/newsletter/newsletter_1_2001.pdf

[504]   For an interesting enumeration of works from world literature in which forms of mediation played a role (from Homer's *Ilias* and Sophocles' *Ajax* to Shakespeare's *Romeo and Juliet*), see Jacob Bercovitch, "Introduction: Putting Mediation in Context", in Bercovitch (ed.) *Studies in International Mediation: Essays in Honor of Jeffrey Z. Rubin* (2002), 3- 24, at 4.

use of mediation. The informal intervention of a third party who strives to get the disputants to agree to an amicable solution seems to be one of the most widespread forms of dispute resolution and a very important means of social control in these societies. Typically, the third parties are respected members of the community (e.g. elders, priests or other leaders). Their role is to help the parties resolve their controversy but they also represent the community, its values and norms, as well as the communal interest in the restoration of harmony, order and the respect of its laws. The intensity of the third party's intervention ranges from the mere facilitation of discussions to openly binding arbitration. The most common pattern is that the third party listens to both sides and then makes a compromise proposal that is orientated not so much at individual justice but at the restoration of harmonious relations. The social prestige and authority of the third party, the communal values embodied in his proposal, and the collective pressure to restore social harmony create a strong motivation to accept the proposed compromise.

Traditional mediation is also very common in the Far East. In China the preference for mediation (or conciliation – the terms are used interchangeably in the English language literature on Chinese dispute resolution) is deeply rooted in Confucian philosophy and its overriding concern with social harmony.[505] The notion of law is fundamentally different from Western concepts. The Chinese concept of social order is governed by the principles of *"Li"* and *"Fa"*: the Confucian concept of *"Li"*, which ranks above *"Fa"* in the hierarchy of values, comprises the moral standards of correct behavior and good manners in accordance with the supreme goal of harmony with the universe. *"Fa"* denotes the formal system of law imposed by the state and corresponds more closely to Western notions of law but does not have a comparable significance. Conflicts are traditionally resolved through the subtle art of *"Jang"*, the art of compromise. The insistence on individual rights is regarded as a serious disruption of social harmony, and the idea of a lawsuit is an outright scandal. In the interest of the community every individual has to try to avoid that a conflict reaches this stage by seeking a compromise solution that avoids declaring a winner and a loser. This tradition is still very much alive in the People's Republic of China where mediation committees constitute the backbone of the civil justice system. The social (and ideological) control function of mediation and the inherent pressure to accept the mediators' recommendations poses questions as to the voluntary nature of the process. Although not quite as dominant as in China, institutionalized mediation (*"Tschotei"*) plays a very important role in Japan's civil justice system. Traditionally, court-annexed Tschotei is mandatory in family law matters and a widely chosen option in all other civil matters.

---

[505] On the fundamental difference between Western and Eastern patterns of thinking see Nisbett, *The Geography of Thought: How Asians and Westerners Think Differently ... and Why* (2003). See also Chang, at note 490.

Judicial settlement discussions can be interpreted as a distinctive form of traditional mediation. The authoritative position of the third party does not emanate from a particular rank in society or from moral authority but from the official position of the judge, his knowledge of the law and his power to render a binding decision. Judicial settlement discussions are not a form of "communal" dispute resolution since the judge is not necessarily a member of the community but rather an official representative of the state whose task it is to uphold, clarify, and develop the laws of that state. Still, the dominant position of the judge and the way the procedure is centered on a substantive proposal by the third party suggest its inclusion, albeit as a distinctive form, in the category of traditional mediation.

In Germany, the Code of Civil Procedure requires the judge at any stage of the proceedings to pursue an amicable solution. The norm codifies a longstanding tradition in the German judiciary (similar traditions exist in other continental European legal systems, e.g. Austria, France and Switzerland). Empirical research has shown that attempts at promoting an amicable settlement are very common in German courts (conciliation attempts are made in close to 50% of cases). However, the nature of these settlement attempts can hardly be compared to the modern concept of mediation. The conciliation attempt is commonly merged into the regular flow of the judicial procedure, and in the large majority of cases settlement discussions last no longer than five minutes. The discussion tends to focus on the legal merits of each party's case and is frequently dominated by a concrete settlement proposal the judge has developed on the basis of a previous evaluation of the case. This proposal constitutes the background for a discussion where the judge might encourage the parties to look for a solution that better suits their economic interests or where the parties might argue against the judge's legal or factual assessment of the merits of the case. In pressing for an amicable solution, judges commonly point out the uncertainty, delays and costs of continuing litigation, particularly with a view towards possible appeal proceedings. These arguments are sometimes coupled with more or less discrete hints at the likely contents of a judgment in case of a failure to reach a settlement. Consequently, the parties are often under considerable pressure to accept the judge's proposal, and they view settlements in court not so much as the result of an interest-based negotiation but as a substitute for a judgment.

Modern, individualistic (Western or Westernized) societies lack the social context that generated and nurtured the traditional forms of mediation. Consequently, instead of providing dispute resolution through the community, modern mediation – particularly in the field of business disputes, and even more so on an international level – emphasizes the individual interests of the parties who frequently do not belong to a coherent social group. The third party may be a complete outsider. The neutral is asked to intervene not so much on the basis of social standing or moral authority (although that may still be an advantage) but mainly on the basis of his or her skills in dispute resolution, possibly combined with expertise in the subject matter of the dispute. The process is not primarily geared towards a substantive proposal by the neutral but rather towards assisting the parties in devising their own solution. The intervention of the neutral is more "process-driven" than "outcome-driven". Acceptance of a solution is not motivated by social pressure or common values but by the cost-benefit analysis each party performs, comparing options for agreement with non-agreement alternatives. The Mediator, rather than proposing a compromise that "makes the parties equally unhappy", acts as a catalyst for "win-win" solutions that leave both sides better off. Experience, integrity and "wisdom", the hallmarks of the traditional mediator, are necessary but not sufficient to generate solutions that fully realize the value creation potential of a dispute. The modern mediator needs to be versed in the "art and science" (Howard Raiffa) of negotiation and conflict management techniques, which in turn requires formal training and specific professional experience *as a mediator*.

3. How Modern Business Mediation Works

Due to the flexibility of the process, mediation can take any length and any number of forms, depending on the nature of the dispute, the social context, the alternatives or "back-up" procedures available to the parties, the organizational structure and the individuals involved on behalf of the parties, and perhaps most importantly, the person(s) acting as mediator.

This sub-section examines the different stages a modern business mediation typically goes through (a), the eminent role caucuses can play in modern business mediation (b.), the different roles that can be played by the mediator (c), the tactics and tools available in order to facilitate a mutually satisfying agreement (d), as well as the basic distinction between rights-based and interest-based mediation styles (e) and the increasing significance of multiparty mediations (f).

a. *Different Stages of the Mediation Process*

(1) Pre-Mediation Stage

Consent. Mediation is voluntary, both with regard to the participation in the process and with regard to the acceptance of the result. Hence, the most important require-ment to be satisfied before mediation can commence is the *consent* of all parties. However, an *obligation* to participate in mediation can be based on prior agreement between the parties.[506] The usefulness of contractual mediation clauses has been questioned because of the difficulties of enforcing such an obligation, the potential for exploitation through delay tactics, and the fact that a legal obligation cannot substitute the minimum degree of voluntary cooperation needed for mediation to

---

[506] In a few specialized fields of American domestic legislation statutes have been enacted that make mediation mandatory. They are, however, subject to some controversy as to their compatibility with the essentially voluntary nature of mediation. Cf. Nelle, "Making Mediation Mandatory: A Proposed Framework", 7 *Ohio St. J. Disp. Res.* 287 (1992).

have any real chance of success.[507] On the other hand, a previous agreement to at least try to resolve the dispute through mediation can indeed be helpful in overcoming the initial reluctance to make the first step towards an amicable resolution.[508]

Preparation of the Mediation Session. The designation of the mediator, either by the parties themselves or through the involvement of an institution or a professional ADR firm, marks the formal beginning of the mediation procedure. However, before the parties and the mediator can gather for the actual mediation session, a number of things have to happen. First, the session or the series of sessions, depending on the complexity of the dispute, have to be scheduled. Then, except in very simple cases, the mediation session will require advance preparation. In business mediation, the mediator typically asks the parties to present a short written statement of the case (sometimes limited to a specific number of pages), along with a few key documents. The mediator will often have a few short meetings or telephone conversations with each party separately, not only to arrange for the schedule but also to discuss the procedure. In highly complex cases, this preparation can include diagnostic interviews with the parties and their lawyers during which the mediator takes snapshots of the case from various angles in order to gain a first understanding of the main issues before the actual mediation commences. This type of extensive preparation permits to streamline and focus the mediation sessions. Concentrated, short sessions in turn are often a condition for having high-level decisionmakers present in a mediation.

(2) The Mediation Proper

The mediation itself where the parties get together with the mediator can take anything between some hours and over a week, in which case the session is split into several meetings. However, even in complex high-stakes business cases the mediation rarely lasts more than two to three days.

Different models structuring the process into stages have been developed as a basic guideline for the inner process of a mediation. The following model is widely used in the contemporary practice of mediation:[509]

Phase 1: Opening Session. The mediation usually begins with a brief opening stage during which all participants are introduced and the mediator gives a short description of the process and presents the agenda. In this phase, the mediator

---

[507] Cf. Nelle, id.

[508] With the 1998 Alternative Dispute Resolution Act, all United States District Courts are mandated to devise and implement their own alternative dispute resolution program in order to promote the use of ADR in their respective districts (Sec. 651 (b)); According to Sec. 652 (a), the courts shall require that litigants in all civil cases consider the use of ADR at an appropriate stage in the litigation.

[509] For more information, see www.mediationinlaw.org.

has four principal goals: establishing contact with the participants; explaining the process; clarifying the parties' intentions and ability to mediate and negotiating ground rules.

Phase 2: Fact Finding/Information Gathering. The goal of the mediator and parties at this next stage is to set out all information necessary to identify the particular issues to be resolved. This means identifying all relevant facts, including economic, political, relational, and other factors involved in each party's view of the various issues. In the opening statements, each party is afforded a limited time to present its case and the main facts and legal arguments on which it is based. The mediator will usually ask clarifying questions and give an opportunity for each party to rebut the other side's assertions and to ask additional clarifying questions. This fact-finding stage of the process is sometimes structured as a "mini-trial" and can be complemented or preceded by an actual fact-finding mission by the mediator or another neutral.

Phase 3: Working Through Conflict. The third phase constitutes the heart of the process of mediation. The essential task is to explore and elicit relevant aspects and interests underlying the positions defined and information shared by the parties in phase 2. During this stage, often starting from strongly divergent viewpoints, the mediator needs to actively support the parties to recognize and appreciate their own as well as the other party's perception of the issues and generate a clear picture of the motivations and aspirations of the parties. Common knowledge and understanding of these interests – both shared ones and divergent ones – will allow generating mutually beneficial options in the next phase.

Phase 4: Developing and Evaluating Options. Once the parties have ascertained the necessary information and identified their concrete positions and underlying interests, the mediator can help them develop options. In doing so, it is crucial to explore the full range of possibilities. The mediator needs to counteract the tendency of any party to seize upon his or her favorite proposal as the only solution. The parties might discard valuable options simply because they begin to evaluate them prematurely. To counter this, it is preferable to first "brainstorm" options without evaluating them. If the mediator can help the parties defer judgment on any option until a later point, the parties are likely to invent more creative solutions.

Phase 5: Closure. The mediation can lead to a complete settlement, in which case all necessary details should be formulated in the final stage of the meeting. The process can also result in a clear breakdown, in which case the mediator (or any of the parties) might – definitely or temporarily – call off the mediation. Sometimes, the negotiation process can be rescued through a postponement of the mediation and the commitment by each side to consider a continuation at a later date. But it is also possible that some progress has been made and that the mediator wants to continue with an additional round of caucuses. Success in mediation, particularly when the issues are complex and the stakes are high, often hinges on the perseverance of the mediator and his ability to keep the parties committed to the process even when they get the impression that it is going nowhere.

When the negotiations have come to an end, through an agreement or otherwise, the mediation has to be wrapped up in a closure session with all participants. The failure to reach an agreement should not necessarily be viewed as a failure of the process. The goal of mediation – as in any negotiation – should not be agreement at any price, but rational choice. If one or both parties, on the basis of rational analysis, determines that none of the possible agreements serves its interests better than its no-agreement alternative, this should be accepted as a perfectly sensible decision. If a complete agreement cannot be reached, a partial settlement covering certain issues, the stipulation of certain facts or some other form of limiting the scope of the ongoing dispute can constitute a significant advance well worth the effort put into the mediation process. To the extent that the dispute has been resolved, the agreement has to be recorded in a form that establishes commitments that are clearly stated and likely to be complied with. Sometimes the parties reach an agreement in principle without resolving all details. In that case, a framework agreement is recorded on the basis of which the parties work out the details. To the extent that some issues remain unresolved or that additional differences can be expected to arise in the drafting of a detailed settlement, it can be advisable to agree on a procedure for the resolution of theses differences, e.g. through additional mediation efforts or a binding decision by the mediator or a different neutral.

(3) Post-Mediation Phase

Even where the mediation has not led to a complete resolution of the controversy, it often creates a stock of partial agreements and a momentum that in the aftermath to the mediation may lead to a settlement. Sometimes the mediator stays involved and serves as a communication channel or simply as a motivating force, and sometimes the parties reach an agreement by themselves on the basis of the progress made in the mediation. Typical elements of this post-mediation phase are the detailed documentation of the agreement and the control of the follow-up procedure to the extent agreed upon by the parties during mediation.

Figure 19: Flow Chart – The Mediation Process

Pre-mediation	Mediation proper	Post-mediation

• Consent
  - ad hoc; or
  - mediation clause
  (limited
  enforceability -
  but easier
  to make 1st step)
• Appointment of
  mediator
• Preparation of
  mediation
  - scheduling
  - briefs/documents
  - diagnostic
  interviews
	• Opening Session
	  introduction, ground rules/agenda
	• Fact finding / Information Gathering
	  - opening statements
	  - identifying issues
	  - information exchange/mini-trial
	• Working Through Conflict
	  - eliciting and understanding interests
	  - caucuses (where appropriate)
	  - quantitative analysis/LRA
	• Developing and Evaluating Options
	  - brainstorming for creative solutions
	• Closure
	  - (partial) agreement
	  - documentation of outcome
	  - follow-on procedure
		• Detailed docu-
		  mentation of
		  agreement
		  (as far as reached)
		• Follow-on procedure
		  - continuing negotia-
		  tion/mediation
		  - high-low
		  arbitration
		  - final offer
		  arbitration

1 week - 3 months	1 day - 2 weeks	1 day - 3 months

b. Role of Caucuses in Business Mediation

After the main assertions and arguments have been heard, the mediator might break the joint session into private sessions with the parties (caucuses)[510], separate meetings during which each side has an opportunity to speak in confidence with the mediator. Many business mediators regard caucuses as critical for the success of mediation because they create a confidential environment where the parties can reveal in full candor to the mediator their real interests and priorities, and where they can attempt an assessment of the situation without the tactical exaggerations and distortions often present in face-to-face negotiations and hearings before a judge or arbitrator.[511]

Caucuses can be helpful in overcoming the "negotiator's dilemma": as explained above, the creation of value requires that the parties cooperate and disclose information which in turn makes them vulnerable to exploitation by the other side; since no party can be sure that the other side will not behave opportunistically, it is rational to withhold this information; consequently, opportunities to devise a mutually beneficial solution are missed. Caucusing cuts through this dilemma because the

---

[510] Cooley, *Mediation Advocacy* 140-149 (2nd ed. 2002); Moore, "The Caucus: Private Meetings That Promote Settlement", 16 *Mediation Quarterly* 87 (1987)

[511] Empirical research with community mediation has shown that in caucuses direct hostility is less intense, parties are more likely to come up with new proposals and give more information to the mediator, and that problem-solving can easier be initiated in caucuses, but also that the parties are more prone to issue denigrating or even false statements about the opponent and that mediators are more likely to violate the neutrality of the process; see Welton, Pruitt & McGillicuddy, "The Role of Caucusing in Community Mediation", 32 *J. Confl. Res.* 181 (1988); on the pros and cons of caucuses see also Cooley, *Mediation Advocacy* 140-149 (2nd ed. 2002) and Moore, "The Caucus: Private Meetings That Promote Settlement", 16 *Mediation Quarterly* 87 (1987).

mediator can obtain from both sides the confidential information that is needed to craft "win-win" solutions without exposing anyone to exploitation. Caucuses are also extremely useful to brainstorm about possible solutions, for the mediator to question a party's arguments and perceptions, and to sound out how far a party is prepared to go. In addition, the parties can use the mediator as a "testing balloon" to float certain ideas without being associated with them and thus avoiding any impression of being weak.

Frequently, a mediation will have at least two rounds of caucuses before the mediator reconvenes the parties jointly. The mediator will typically use the first round of caucuses to gather more information and to get the full story from each party in order to gain the big picture of the dispute and of possible avenues for its resolution. Subsequent rounds of caucuses are used to narrow the parties' differences and to work toward a more concrete set of options for an agreement. This can evolve into outright *"shuttle diplomacy"* where the mediator goes back and forth between the parties, acts as a messenger, refines the proposed solutions and gradually moves the parties toward agreement. Sometimes there is disagreement *within* one camp about whether and how to pursue settlement. In those cases it can be useful for the mediator to caucus with the members of a negotiating team separately in order to find out where the resistance against settlement lies and to deal with the objections in a targeted manner. Finally, leaving one party by itself while caucusing with the other can also have a value since it gives the resting party an opportunity for reflection and discussion within the team. Sometimes a little time is needed to digest new information and to accept the fact that the own case has weaknesses, to rethink established positions, to revise expectations and perhaps to come up with new proposals.

When the caucuses have reached a point where either agreement is in reach or where additional progress is unlikely, or simply when the mediator senses that direct face-to-face negotiation would be more productive, the parties will be reconvened for a joint session. It may make sense at this point to only gather the parties, without the lawyers, in order to have the real decisionmakers talk to each other in more privacy, perhaps even without the mediator. When difficult decisions have to be made it is often desirable to have as few people at the table as possible. On the other hand, lawyers are often more detached[512] and it is sometimes easier to reach agreement if they get a chance to talk without having the clients present. Which constellation to choose depends on the individuals involved and on the way the negotiations go. It is often a matter of experience and "feeling" for the mediator who, as the process goes along, may sense which constellation might yield the most productive discussions at which moment.

---

[512] For empirical evidence on lawyers' more detached and rational/analytical way of thinking see Korobkin & Guthrie, "Psychology, Economics, and Settlement: A New Look at the Role of the Lawyer", 76 *Texas L. Rev.* 77 (1997).

c. Various Roles of the Mediator

The mediation process and the intervention of the mediator facilitate agreement in a number of different ways. Depending on the circumstances the mediator gets to play any or all of the following roles:

Providing a Forum for Discussions. One of the simplest but most effective ways in which mediation facilitates negotiations is by creating an opportunity and a neutral and "safe" environment for the parties to get together and talk about elements of the case, the background of the people involved, or the history of the dispute.

> "I have, as a mediator, had situations where I don't feel that it has any chance of success because the two decision makers don't know each other, they have never met each other, they come from two different countries, they speak two different languages and they are each nervous about their role because they have been assigned by their companies to settle the case. They are not the executives who did the contract, they are the executives who have to clean up the problem created by somebody else. So what I have done, again with the permission of the lawyers, is to meet alone with the executives at a private dinner where we don't discuss the case at all. We just discuss how they got to where they are, I get them to talk to each other, hopefully they speak English, otherwise we need a translator. ... There is a cultural advantage in many parts of the world getting to know the person on the other side of the table and having tea, having coffee and having dinner with a host. And I have found that amazingly successful. We never discuss the dispute. The most I will do is discuss how the process will work. But we don't discuss the case."[513]

The intervention of a third party is sometimes needed to make negotiations possible in the first place because in addition to the above mentioned reluctance of the parties to take the first step and initiate discussions, the parties are sometimes unable, in the midst of a heated controversy, to agree on such seemingly trivial issues as the place, time and agenda for a meeting. In the words of an experienced business mediator:

> "...we often pad ourselves on the back on our great success in mediation but then when we think about it, we also realize that by getting the parties to the table we may have come a great way to getting them to settle ... it partly is the skill of the mediators but a huge barrier has been overcome if you can get them in the same room together ..."[514]

Facilitator of Discussions. Often the mere presence of a third party at the table curtails aggressions and induces the parties to behave more reasonably:

---

[513] Interview with Gerald Aksen, April 16, 2002

[514] Interview with an American ADR specialist conducted in May of 1992.

" ... even when third parties are not terribly skilled, their mere presence has an impact because with a sort of observer, people start behaving, they act a bit more civil, and that alters their perception ..."[515]

In addition, by laying down the ground rules and presiding over the discussion, the mediator brings order to the negotiation and serves as a guarantor of the integrity of the process. He diffuses tensions, prevents an escalation of conflict and thus maintains a safe environment for constructive discussions. His authority over the process spares the parties from wasting their energies in discussions over logistics and procedure. One of the most important functions as facilitator is to clarify the facts and issues being discussed. Moreover, the mediator can steer the discussions towards the merits of the dispute and force the parties to focus on the strengths and weaknesses of their respective cases, their underlying interests and on objective standards of legitimacy. He can also shift the parties' attention from assigning blame for past actions to devising forward-looking solutions. Finally, a third party who is not involved in the dispute is much better able to structure the discussions and to administer special negotiation structures such as post-settlement settlements or the one-text-procedure. A facilitator is particularly important in multi-party negotiations where it is often practically impossible to organize discussions among the various parties and potential or actual coalitions without the help of a third party who structures the process.

"Lightning Rod" for Emotions. Mediation gives the parties an opportunity to vent their emotions in a controlled and safe atmosphere. By insisting that each side can speak without being interrupted and by discouraging the use of insulting language the mediator can steer the process in such a way that the parties can express their anger and frustrations in front of the mediator and of each other without putting the negotiation process in danger. This confrontation of emotions can be very productive but it entails the danger of escalating the conflict. When this danger outgrows the usefulness of giving the parties an opportunity to let off "steam" and to get a feeling for their respective emotions, the mediator can always interrupt the process and work out the emotional issues with the parties in separate caucuses.

Communications Channel/Translator. One of the most important roles of the mediator is to serve as a conduit for the exchange of information, ideas and proposals in a safe and controlled way. In a caucus, for instance, a party can instruct the mediator to reveal certain information to the other party only under specific circumstances, e.g. a particular concession or acknowledgement. By rephrasing the parties' statements, either in a joint session or shuttling between caucuses, the mediator can also "translate" certain statements into non-partisan language or into a form that reflects the underlying interest rather than mere bargaining positions. Finally, the

---

[515]   Interview with Wayne Davis, August 20, 1992.

parties can use the mediator to present proposals to the other side without revealing their origin.

Catalyst. In modern mediation the main objective is to help the parties craft their own solution. The mediator therefore has to act as a catalyst who enhances the parties' problem-solving skills and their creativity. By focusing the parties' attention the mediator can help them understand the roots of the conflict and the interests of both sides. Problem-solving questions direct the parties to look towards the future and inspire them to come up with solutions that address the underlying concerns behind the conflicting positions. And new ideas can be generated through brainstorming techniques.

Advisor. The mediator is an important resource for the parties providing them with ideas, proposals, feedback, standards of legitimacy, and – where applicable – subject-matter expertise. In addition to offering a neutral assessment of the situation and of the likely ramifications of proposed solutions, including economic, financial and taxation aspects, the mediator can provide the parties with a set of analytical methods and decision-making tools. Through his capacity to hold confidential sessions with everyone involved the mediator is the only one who has a complete picture of the dispute and particularly of the parties' real positions and interests. This enables the mediator to analyze the zone of possible agreement and to indicate to the parties whether they are in "striking range" of an agreement.

Agent of Reality. As an impartial outsider, the mediator is in a unique position to question the parties' assumptions, perceptions and judgments. Thus the mediator can reduce inflated expectations and inject the necessary realism into the process. "Reality-testing" is one of the most powerful techniques for the mediator because it helps overcome the barriers to agreement resulting from partisan perceptions and the systemic overestimation of the parties' no-agreement alternatives. In this context the mediator can use techniques of quantitative analysis to get the parties to conduct a more systematic and realistic analysis of their no-agreement alternatives.

Scapegoat. When it comes to generating movement and concessions or to presenting proposals, a third party can help both sides save face by allowing them to assign the responsibility for a particular move or the acceptance of a solution to the mediator. This way the parties are being reasonable in accepting a neutral proposal that is equally painful for everyone involved, and no one is seen to cave in to the demands of the other. This is particularly important for negotiators who have to justify or "sell" the agreement to their principals or internal constituents.

Draftsman. Once the parties have reached an agreement, the mediator can help articulate the consent in a neutral and balanced terminology and thus avoid squabbles over words. An experienced mediator can prevent the agreement from falling apart in the aftermath by making sure that the commitments are realistic and drafted in unequivocal terms.

Compliance Monitor. Sometimes the mediator is asked to stay involved even after an agreement has been reached in order to monitor the compliance with the terms of the settlement or to resolve any disputes that might ensue in the implementation of the agreement.

Table 1: Roles of the Mediator

Forum for Discussions
mediation provides neutral and safe environment for talks; overcomes logistical barriers (reluctance to take 1st step, difficulty to agree on place, time, agenda)

Facilitator of Discussions
mere presence of 3rd party curtails aggressions; mediator enforces ground rules; avoids disputes over logistics & procedure; clarifies facts & issues; steers discussion (toward interests, future-oriented solutions, objective standards); administers special structures (Single Negotiating Text, Post Settlement Settlement, multi-party negotiations)

"Lightning Rod" for Emotions
parties vent emotions in controlled atmosphere (no interruptions, no insults, no escalation etc.); in front of each other or in caucuses with mediator

Communications Channel/Translator
conduit for information, ideas, suggestions; parties can float proposals without commitment

Catalyst
enhances problem-solving and creativity through targeted questions and brainstorming

Advisor
resource for ideas, proposals, feedback, standards, expertise, neutral assessment, analytical tools, analysis of ZOPA; variation: "confidential listener" (only explores zone of possible agreements)

Agent of Reality
questions parties' assumptions, perceptions, judgments; reduces inflated expectations; injects realism; overcomes partisan perceptions and systemic overconfidence; more systematic analysis of no-agreement alternatives)

Scapegoat
neutral proposal saves face: no one seen to cave in; helps parties "sell" agreement to constituencies

Draftsman
mediator drafts agreement in neutral & balanced terminology; avoids squabble over words; spells out realistic and unequivocal commitments

Compliance Monitor
avoids or resolves disputes over implementation

d. Techniques of the Mediator

The following description of mediator's techniques focuses on aspects of communication and process control. Visualization and supportive tools like Litigation Risk Analysis will be explained in Chapter 7.

Questions. Questions are a powerful tool of the mediator, not only as a means to gather information and to clarify what is said by the parties, but also to create doubts and to stimulate thoughts and ideas. Since the parties are the "owners" of the process and the mediator has no power to impose an agreement, it is often more useful for the mediator to provoke a particular thought in a party (or in all parties) than to express it directly. Questions are vital instruments to steer the discussion, to signal which issues are relevant, to direct the attention of the parties towards exploring interests and options, to engage them in problem-solving, to prompt the parties to rely on objective standards to legitimize their demands, and to challenge partisan perceptions, systemic overconfidence and unrealistic expectations.

Active Listening. Listening is one of the fundamental techniques of the mediator, not only as a means of obtaining information but also as a means of active communication: by rephrasing key statements and asking clarifying questions, the mediator conveys to each party the message of being taken seriously and receiving a full "hearing". It is important for the mediator to show genuine interest and understanding for a party's situation, and by treating all parties equally the mediator can maintain an aura of both empathy and impartiality.

Non-Verbal Communication. The observation of non-verbal communication between the parties is important for the mediator in order to gain information about the conflict (patterns) that might not be revealed by the parties in direct communication. In addition, the non-verbal behavior of the mediator himself might support the resolution process.

Control over the Process. Although both the outcome of the mediation and the participation in the process are at the disposition of the parties, the mediator exercises substantial influence through his de facto control of the process. This control is of a subtle nature and has to be exercised with caution because the parties can opt out of the process at any time. The mediator's process control begins with the logistics of time and place of any meetings and the decision over who sits at the table (the mediator might refuse to act unless the parties send representatives with full authority to settle or unless certain vital constituents or all parties in interest are represented or at least consulted). The selection of the rooms and the seating arrangements are another means of controlling the process. In his role as facilitator the mediator can establish ground rules for the discussion and can restrict the use of unfair negotiation tactics. As a facilitator, he can also shift the parties' attention from winning a fight to jointly solving a problem. The power to structure the discussion not only allows him to focus the parties' minds on particular issues but also to *frame* these issues in ways that are conducive to a resolution of the dispute. This is done through purposeful questions and by paraphrasing the parties' statements and summing up the discussion in ways that emphasize common or complementary interests and the progress already made. His control over the agenda allows the mediator to rank the issues by order of priority and to break them down into sub-issues for easier trade-offs.

Team Work: Co-Mediation. A strategy that is especially useful in large and complex cases is the use of two mediators who as a team can complement each other performing the difficult task of mediation with divided roles. This approach allows combining the expertise and skills of two persons who may even have different professional backgrounds, e.g. a lawyer in tandem with an engineer or an economist. Co-mediation allows the two mediators to concentrate on different tasks: one can actively lead the discussions while the other concentrates on listening and observing the (verbal and non-verbal) communication behavior of the disputants. The division of labor allows each mediator to step back for a while from the exhausting active interaction with the parties and reflect on the conflict and possible solutions. Keeping up to speed with the discussions can be particularly difficult when the parties switch from one issue to the other. In a team, chances are that at least one of the mediators follows the disputants and can bring the other neutral back on track. One of the mediators can focus on the process and the interpersonal aspects while the other is mainly concerned with analyzing the substance of the dispute. Here, different professional backgrounds could come to bear, letting one mediator concentrate on legal and process aspects while the other covers the economic or technical side or handles the quantitative aspects, including the use of computers to conduct decision tree or other types of scenario analysis. Having two neutrals can open up new perspectives if for example one mediator is skeptical, the other encouraging, or one is inventive, the other practical. If a certain mediation strategy has failed, the second mediator can employ a new approach and try to divert the process from a dead end. A team of mediators may also be more creative in the generation of options. The opportunity for mutual check and feedback is a safeguard against misperceptions and unnoticed biases. If performed by the right team, co-mediation may therefore be well worth the expense of involving a second neutral.

Substantive Proposals. The goal in modern mediation is a solution based on a maximum of input by the parties. Although the parties "own" the process, concrete settlement proposals by the mediator can also be a significant step in bringing the parties to an agreement.

> "... if you are trying to mediate a dispute and it seems to be sensible to propose a settlement and say 'look, I've listened to what you've had to say, and I think this would be a fair deal'... then fine, if you think that's going to bring about a settlement, do it! – On the other hand, if you think these are experienced businessmen who have a whole range of considerations to take into account

and what they really want is somebody to help them break the ice, to sit in the same room together after relationships may have broken down, to have an agenda of topics to discuss so they don't have to spend all their time as to whether they should meet in your office or in his office, or the table should be square or round, this sort of nonsense ... it may be that the mediator's role is just confined to that, but who cares? – provided that at the end of the day the settlement gets made ... I mean you've got to be utterly flexible..."[516]

How best to proceed depends on the circumstances of the dispute, and there are good reasons for the mediator to express his opinion rather late in the process and only after having thoroughly discussed the dispute with the parties and having generated other possible options for a settlement. The higher the degree of participation and ownership by the parties, the more likely it is that the settlement will reflect their interests.

Table 2: Techniques of the Mediator

Questions
used to gather information, clarify discussion, signal what's relevant, create doubts, stimulate thoughts; better than saying it explicitly; focus parties' minds on interests, options, standards; attack partisan perceptions, systemic overconfidence, unrealistic expectations

Active Listening
active communication used to demonstrate genuine interest and clarify agenda

Non-Verbal Communication
observation of parties' behavior, reactions

Control over Process
process voluntary but mediator has subtle control over: logistics, participants, room, seating, ground rules; can influence discussions through agenda, framing of issues, ranking, grouping and breakdown of issues; dealing with people-issues separately

Co-Mediation
two mediators can work with divided roles; concentrate on different aspects of the mediation process; permits more thorough observation of parties and process; different professional backgrounds can complement each other; different mediators can have rapport with different parties.

Substantive Proposals
can be decisive for success in mediation; but only after thorough discussion; need to respect party-"ownership", build trust, explore all options before introducing own ideas; goal is maximum party-input

---

[516] Interview with Arthur Marriott, March 3, 1992.

e. Interest-Based and Rights-Based Mediation

In most cases, the back-up mechanism to the mediation process will be litigation or some other form of rights-based adjudication. Most disputes are therefore characterized by a complex interaction between interests and rights. As a result, any form of consensual dispute resolution "in the shadow of the law" has to reconcile the two partially conflicting goals of providing a realistic assessment of the legal remedies that constitute the parties no-agreement alternatives and the need to focus on the parties' underlying interests in order to generate efficient solutions. Depending on which of these two goals the process concentrates on, mediation (and other ADR procedures) can be classified either as more *rights-based* or more *interest-based*, or on the basis of their central objective, as *predictive* or *problem-solving*.[517]

Rights-based mediation tends to be *predictive* because – rather than looking for an abstract legal "truth" – it tries to assess the legal situation as a basis for calculating the parties' respective no-agreement alternatives and therefore needs to make a prediction about the likely outcome of litigation, arbitration or whatever the back-up procedure may be.[518] This goal is manifested by a greater role of counsel in the process and presentations by the attorneys that concentrate on legal arguments in much the same way as in the litigation process itself. What is attempted is a show of strength by the attorneys to give both sides the possibility to make an assessment of where they stand, what their strengths and weaknesses are and what chances they will have at trial or before an arbitral tribunal. A pointed variation of this style of mediation is the *mini-trial* which was invented as a way of giving both sides a "crash course on the merits" of the dispute to serve as a basis for settlement negotiations between senior executives.

Interest-based mediation on the other hand focuses on *problem-solving* techniques in order to find solutions that best satisfy the parties' underlying interest. Here, the process aims at developing options that realize the parties' underlying interests and accordingly the role of the facilitator is that of a moderator, catalyst and a channel of communications.

The functions of problem-solving and prediction do not exclude each other and both play a role in practically all mediations. As mentioned before, there are very few disputes which by their nature are exclusively interest-based or rights-based. Every dispute resolution procedure has to be measured against the parties' interests, and they almost always contain some normative element. What is different is the relative

---

[517] McEwen, "Pursuing Problem-Solving or Predictive Settlement", 19 *Fla. State U. L. Rev.* 77 (1991); for other ways of categorizing mediation, see Riskin, "Understanding Mediator Orientations, Strategies and Techniques: A Grid for the Perplexed", 1 *Harv. Neg. L. Rev.* 7 (1996).

[518] The influence of back-up procedures on mediation is discussed at length by Kolb, "How Existing Procedures Shape Alternatives: The Case of Grievance Mediation", *J. Dispute Resolution* 59 (1989).

weight that legal considerations and predictive techniques have in a given case. How rights-based the process turns out is a function of the extent to which the process occurs in the "shadow" of the law. And this in turn depends on two considerations: (1) how close in time is the dispute to being turned over to an adjudicative process and, above all, when can this process be expected to lead to a definite result? – and (2) how predictable is this process? The closer in time a dispute is toward being resolved conclusively through a legal back-up process, and the less unpredictable this process is, the more the parties' interests and their relative bargaining power are influenced by the likely outcome of the back-up process, and consequently the more important the predictive element in mediation becomes.

However, problem-solving techniques are always important in mediation because legal procedures are at best zero-sum games and frequently lead to inefficient, sub-optimal results. It is therefore always important and worthwhile to search for options that better satisfy the parties' interests, even when it is possible to fairly accurately predict the likely result of litigation or arbitration. The challenge for the mediator is therefore to develop a realistic assessment of the likely outcome of any back-up procedure while still being able to shift the focus toward the interest of the parties and toward "optimal" solutions. Good mediation aims both at accurate predictions and at creative problem-solving.

f. Multiparty Mediation

"As we recognize that many disputes now involve multiple parties ... and many issues, negotiation theorists have appropriately turned their attention to development of theory for multiparty, multiissue negotiations (drawn from legal, business, political and international disputes and conflicts), studying such issues as coalition formation, group dynamics, negotiation in dynamic settings, the role of leadership and coordination, information-processing and the various dynamics of competition, collaboration, cooperation and coordination in multiparty settings."[519]

In *multi-party settings,* mediation is more difficult but at the same time potentially even more beneficial. Negotiations are difficult because the number of relationships (between individuals, between coalitions, and between individuals and coalitions) increases exponentially with each additional party. Obviously, not each of these constellations materializes as a sub-conflict, but the number of cross-claims and sub-disputes does tend to multiply as the number of parties grows. This creates logistical problems in terms of organizing communications. But the real difficulty stems from the fact that the various sub-disputes are often interdependent: like in a spider web, it is impossible to move the various strains without affecting the entire structure.

---

[519]   Carrie Menkel-Meadow, *Dispute Processing and Conflict Resolution*, at xxiv (2003).

Mediation in a multi-party context has several advantages. Due to its voluntary nature, the low transaction costs and the possibility to opt out at any time, mediation is virtually risk-free which makes it easier to persuade the various parties to join the process. And once all the necessary parties have come on board (which can already be facilitated by the mediator), a neutral third party is in a unique position to structure the discussions, and to get a complete picture of the "spider web". Understanding the dispute in its entire complexity, the mediator can orchestrate discussions along the various fault lines of the dispute. In addition he can assess the full potential for value-creation and trade-offs and work towards solutions that would be impossible to achieve in regular negotiation or through litigation or arbitration.

IV. OTHER ADR TECHNIQUES AND COMBINATIONS

Mediation has been introduced in detail due to its status as the prototype of ADR techniques. In the following, variations of mediation and arbitration, significant other ADR techniques as well as early intervention mechanisms shall be briefly introduced. The considerable spectrum of ADR mechanisms constitutes the toolbox for Dispute Resolution Process Design (see Chapter 9).

1. Mini-Trials

A "mini-trial" is a predictive process designed to narrow the differences between the parties' perceptions of their chances in litigation and to bring high-level decisionmakers together for constructive settlement negotiations facilitated, in most instances, by a mediator (sometimes called "neutral advisor"). A mini-trial consists of a structured *information exchange* in which representatives from both sides make brief presentations of their case to a panel of executives from all parties. The executives typically are fairly senior, have not been personally involved in the controversy beforehand, and carry full authority to settle the dispute. On the basis of the information presented and after having heard both sides ("a crash course on the merits of the dispute"), the executives meet for private negotiations and – with or without the help of a third party – try to work out a settlement. The catchword "mini-trial", product of a newspaper headline,[520] is somewhat misleading in that the "information exchange" is a non-binding procedure and does not necessarily involve the intervention of a third-party as the "trier of fact".

The characteristic elements are:

- compressed "trial-like" presentations by attorneys (plus sometimes experts and witnesses) not to a decisionmaking third party, but to top-level representatives of the parties;

---

[520] Henry & Lieberman, *The Manager's Guide to Resolving Legal Disputes* 25 (1985) attribute it to the *New York Times* – Singer, *Settling Disputes* 61 (1990) to the *Wall Street Journal.*

- the involvement of senior management from both sides in an "objective" role;
- the separation of the adversarial task of advocating from the cooperative task of negotiating by assigning these two functions to different actors and different segments of the procedure;
- a strict time limit for the presentations and any discovery, thus forcing the parties to focus on the central issues;
- a strictly confidential setting.

The assistance of a neutral advisor can be of great help in this procedure, but is not an indispensable element of a mini-trial. If conducted without a neutral advisor, the mini-trial is basically a more sophisticated structure for settlement negotiations containing elements of joint fact-finding.

An example of a successful multi-party, multi-million dollar dispute (with the additional complication of involving a government agency) that was solved through a mini-trial without a neutral advisor is the NASA-Spacecom-TRW case. The procedural arrangements were very informal: the parties only agreed on an exchange of briefs and one day of summary presentations by lawyers from each side in front of a panel of four high-ranking officials. After two additional meetings by the four executives, an agreement was worked out that solved the extremely complex technical problems to each party's satisfaction. The savings were estimated at USD 1 million in legal fees alone.[521]

The CPR Institute for Dispute Resolution (formerly The Center for Public Resources) in New York City has developed a model procedure and model mini-trial clause. The CPR model minitrial procedure was revised in 1998. The CPR Institute also assists in the design of tailored mini-trials, and offers help in the selection of a neutral advisor.

Due to the confidential nature of the process it is impossible to tell how many *international* mini-trials have actually been conducted. The general impression from the interviews conducted by the authors is that the concept is only slowly gaining acceptance in international business and arbitration circles.

A frequent argument against the use of mini-trials is that they are viewed as a purely American phenomenon that only makes sense in a legal system with extensive pre-trial discovery.[522] Here, the reasoning goes, a mini-trial is often the only way to condense the results of discovery in order to give parties an overview

---

[521] Green, *CPR Legal Program Mini-Trial Handbook*, cited from: Center for Public Resources, CPR Legal Program, Corporate Dispute Management MH45-MH48 (1982); Hancock, "Corporate Counsel's Primer on Alternative Dispute Resolution Techniques", in: Hancock & Gillan, *Corporate Counsel's Guide to ADR Techniques* 1.001, 1.003, 1.029-1.030 (1989).

[522] Cf. Schlosser, "Alternative Dispute Resolution (uno stimulo alla riforma per l'Europa?)", *Rivista di Diritto Processuale* 4, 1005, 1009 (1989).

of the entire case whereas the extensive written preparation common in European lawsuits makes it possible for the executives to get a picture of the case without incurring the costs of a mini-trial.[523]

This argument is not without merits, as mini-trials in the United States indeed tend to be conducted on the basis of a fair amount of discovery. The reason for this is simple: a mini-trial is a predictive tool intended to permit an assessment of how a court might decide. If the court decides on the basis of facts that have been collected through extensive discovery, the prediction resulting from a mini-trial will only be accurate if most of these facts have been "discovered" beforehand. In other words: the need for discovery is not a function of the nature of the mini-trial but of the procedures for which the mini-trial is intended to offer a preview. Where discovery is part of the system, a good portion of that discovery has to occur before a mini-trial can offer a good prognosis. Conversely, in systems that do not permit discovery, a mini-trial does not require it but will have to be prepared on the basis of other methods, mainly the exchange of documents and memoranda. In international arbitration the amount of discovery depends largely on the background of the parties and their lawyers. However, especially in light of the enormous volume of documents produced in large international disputes, a condensed and structured information exchange can in any event offer an excellent basis for settlement negotiations between high-level executives.

2.   Fact-Finding and Related Procedures

Where the resolution of a dispute depends heavily on technical or scientific questions (e.g. patent, toxic tort and construction cases, or certain issues in anti-trust and securities disputes, or questions of foreign law), the inquiry of a neutral fact-finder can provide the parties with the information and objective evaluation necessary to negotiate a settlement, or with an assessment of certain factual issues.

An example from international practice is the appointment of experts under the rules of the International Centre for Expertise which was established by the International Chamber of Commerce in 1976 in order to provide competent and neutral expertise for complex international transactions in technical, legal, financial and other fields.[524] The Centre, under the newly revised Rules for Expertise,[525] offers three

---

[523]   Schlosser id.

[524]   E.g. desert irrigation, freeze-drying, petrochemicals, tanneries, uranium prices, ship-building, glassmaking etc., Bühler, "Technical Expertise: An Additional Means for Preventing or Settling Commercial Disputes", 6 (1) *J. Int'l Arb*. 135, 150 (1989).

[525]   The Rules, in force as from 1 January 2003, can be found online under www.iccwbo. org/drs/english/expertise/all_topics.asp.

distinct services: the proposal of experts,[526] the appointment of experts,[527] and the administration of expertise proceedings.[528] In the last case, the expert's task consists mainly in making findings in a written report. Those findings, unless otherwise agreed by all of the parties, are not binding.[529] After a period of initial inactivity, the Centre's attractiveness seems to have been growing with every year.[530]

In certain modern industries, the duration of litigation or even arbitration proceedings creates particular problems. For instance, in a micro-electronics patent or a computer software copyright dispute, litigation or arbitration can take longer than the life-cycle of the product concerned: a preliminary injunction can "kill" an entire product line, and a damage award will invariably come too late, at a time when the victim may have already been ruined. Also, the difficulties in communicating complex and highly technical facts to judges or – worse – juries create further delay and uncertainty about the outcome. Most important is probably the danger of exposing highly sensitive trade secrets to competitors or to the public. Fact-finding can solve this problem: if both parties trust a neutral expert, he may be asked to examine each party's product designs *"ex parte"*, i.e. without being accompanied by any representatives from the other side, and determine whether the defendant's product embodies any of the plaintiff's technology – without at any time sharing one party's design with the other's.[531]

Fact-finding can be conducted by a neutral expert or jointly by experts from the parties themselves. In the case of *joint fact-finding* each party appoints an expert and gives the joint-fact finders access to its documents and other pieces of evidence. The fact-finders jointly examine documents, interview witnesses, perhaps conduct on-site inspections, and write a final report in which they include all the facts they were able to agree on. Issues that remained unresolved are covered by separate opinions by each of the party-experts.

The expert findings – whether by joint experts or by a single neutral expert – can have different forms and effects, depending on the mandate given by the parties. Their content can be limited to specific findings on a limited number of issues or they may include recommendations for a settlement, and in each case the result can be either binding, not binding or "semi-binding". Whatever the modalities, in order

---

[526]   Cf. Art. 2-4 ICC Rules for Expertise 2003.

[527]   Cf. Art. 5-8 ICC Rules for Expertise 2003.

[528]   Cf. Art. 9-14 ICC Rules for Expertise 2003.

[529]   Cf. Art. 12.3 ICC Rules for Expertise 2003.

[530]   Cf. Craig, Park & Paulsson, *International Chamber of Commerce Arbitration* § 38.02 (2000).

[531]   For examples of *ex parte* fact-finding or adjudication and other high-tech ADR procedures see Bender, "Alternative Dispute Resolution and the Computer-Related Dispute: An Ideal Marriage?", 7 (5) *The Computer Lawyer* 9, 10-12 (May 1990) and Singer, *Settling Disputes* 69-72 (1990).

to avoid disagreement over the procedure, it is crucial to specify exactly and in advance what effect shall be given to the expert opinion. If the opinion of the expert is meant to be binding, complicated questions arise as to whether such a finding can be treated (and enforced!) as an arbitral award. Due to the essentially non-legal nature of expert appraisals the prevailing opinion does not regard them as arbitral awards and therefore not within the scope of the New York Convention.[532]

If the expert is not empowered to render a final decision, the ultimate solution will be left to the parties' agreement (which may be facilitated by the neutral evaluation of the problem) or to a "downstream" arbitration procedure in which the expert's opinion (unless excluded as evidence by agreement of the parties) tends to have considerable de facto influence since it constitutes competent, neutral and contemporaneous evidence.

3. Variations of Mediation

As the following variations of mediation may run counter to some of the basic principles of the procedure in its pure form, they should be perceived as distinct ADR techniques.

One variation of mediation which frequently can be observed for example in international diplomacy is the so-called 'mediation with clout' or 'partisan facilitation'. These are scenarios where the third parties serve as honest brokers despite the fact that they have a clear self-interest in the resolution of the dispute and might even have a special loyalty to one of the parties to the conflict.[533] Evidently, there are many shades of grey between the classical partisanship of a strategic advisor and the "pure" neutrality of a classical mediator. In essence, how far a formally partial advisor can go in assuming a mediator's role and the success of proceeding in such a capacity depend mainly on the credibility and trust the mediator can establish with both sides.

Another variation of mediation is that a mediator's recommendation can be given "teeth" by stipulating in the mediation agreement that the opinion can be

---

[532] Cf. Craig, Park & Paulsson, *International Chamber of Commerce Arbitration* § 38.02 (2000); see also Bühler, "Technical Expertise: An Additional Means for Preventing or Settling Commercial Disputes", 6 (1) *J. Int'l Arb*. 135 (1989); Derains, "Technical Expertise and 'Referé Arbitral'", in: Sanders (ed.), *ICCA Congress Series* No. 1 183-191 (1983); and Jarvins, "The Role of Conciliation, Contract Modification and Expert Appraisal in Settling International Commercial Disputes", 4 *Int'l Tax & Bus. Law*. 238-246 (1986); the distinction between binding expert appraisal and arbitration is well established in many legal systems, cf. the Dutch institution of "*bindend advies*" or the German institution of "*Schiedsgutachten*" which are considered to have a contractual rather than judicial or arbitral nature, see Sanders id.

[533] See, for example, Smith, "Effectiveness of the Biased Mediator", 1 *Neg. J*. 363-372 (1985), and Zartman & Berman, *The Practical Negotiator* 78-80 (1982) with various examples of interested mediators in international conflicts.

introduced in subsequent judicial or arbitral proceedings, or by providing financial penalties. In the first variety, the parties have to specify exactly which effect they want the neutral's recommendation to have on any subsequent procedure. It can be used as regular evidence, it can be given the status of a rebuttable presumptions (thus affecting the burden of proof), or it can be made conclusive with regard to certain facts, in which case any review by the tribunal would be limited to issues of law. Where the neutral has expert status and particularly where he has made contemporaneous observations of facts (which may have become less accessible by the time of the final proceedings), his findings will carry great weight even where they do not formally bind the tribunal.

Financial penalties can take the form of specified monetary penalties, liquidated damages or actual damages. Actual damages are usually measured as the legal costs occasioned by the judicial or arbitral procedure following the rejection of the mediator's verdict. Again, it is important to specify exactly the triggering event and the method of calculation. The trigger is commonly defined by reference to a margin between the solution proposed by the mediator and the result achieved in litigation or arbitration. Whether any "fee-shift" mechanism indeed makes a difference depends on the way legal costs are normally allocated in the relevant court or arbitration system. Under the "American Rule" where commonly each party has to bear its own costs, no matter who wins, any fee shift represents a significant departure from the normal system and will therefore be perceived as a heavy penalty. Under the "English Rule" or in similar systems where the losing party has to reimburse the winner's legal costs, a fee-shift mechanism only makes a difference where a party "wins" partially in mediation and then fails to improve the result in litigation or arbitration, or where that party scores another partial victory but obtains less than awarded in the mediator's proposal.

4. Variations of Arbitration

The quest for dispute resolution techniques has also generated a number of innovative features to adapt *arbitration* in certain contexts. The most important are "high-low" or "bracketed" arbitration and "final-offer" or "baseball" arbitration.

If the parties argue over monetary figures and want to avoid an extreme solution, they can narrow the range within which the arbitral award can fall by simply agreeing on a bracket between a "high"-figure and a "low"-figure. The figures can or cannot be disclosed to the arbitrator. A disclosure, though, would in effect narrow the range further since, in the view of the arbitrator, choosing one of the corner figures would seem to be an "extreme" solution. This, in turn, might be anticipated by the parties who, expecting the arbitrator to "cut in half" might feel induced to submit extreme figures. Thus, it may be preferable not to disclose the figures to the arbitrator. Within the range, the arbitrator's decision is final. If it falls outside the range, the outcome would nonetheless be the figure which is nearest. A variation of this approach can be to submit a "yes-no" question to the arbitrator and link the two possible outcomes to either the "high" or the "low" figure.

The process of final offer arbitration was designed to counter a perceived tendency of arbitrators to favor compromise decisions. It has been used extensively to solve Major League Baseball salary and public-sector collective bargaining disputes and has been made compulsory for certain public-service disputes in some states in the USA. The parties either submit their final offers to the arbitrator who can only choose between the two alternatives presented, or the arbitrator is asked to fix a sum, but the parties agree that whichever of the two final offers comes closer to the arbitrator's figure, will be the final result (with the option that the arbitrator's figure is valid if he actually "hits" the exact average of the two figures). Like high-low arbitration, final-offer arbitration limits the risks by reducing the possible variance of outcomes, but additionally encourages the parties to adopt reasonable positions which by itself may even lead to settlement in the last moment. However, strategic analysis shows that the procedure favors the risk-taker over the timid and to a certain extent it invites the parties to gamble, since a "moderately extreme" position seems to offer the best risk-benefit ratio.

5. Early Intervention Mechanisms

Contractual negotiation clauses can encourage the parties to deal with differences in a cooperative way and at the earliest possible stage in order to avoid the emergence of full-scale conflicts.

A variety of negotiation clauses exist. *"Negotiate-in-Good-Faith" clauses* require the parties to try to resolve any upcoming dispute amicably before resorting to more confrontational means such as litigation or arbitration. *"Escalation" clauses* provide first for a problem-solving attempt at the operating level, followed (if unsuccessful) by negotiations at a lower management level and finally (if necessary) at the senior management level. The advantage of such a multi-level negotiation structure is that higher-level executives are often more detached from the original conflict and may thus be in a better position to find forward-looking solutions, but an escalation scheme also provides an incentive for the negotiators at the lower level to solve the problem without having to bother their superiors. In a more sophisticated contract a dispute resolution clause can establish a whole sequence of increasingly elaborate negotiation structures backed up by mediation and finally arbitration. To further encourage settlement negotiations, *"cooling-off" periods* can be included which prohibit the initiation of a formal procedure (litigation, arbitration etc.) for a specific period after the emergence of the disagreement.

In Hong Kong, contracts in relation to the construction of the new international airport even contained a four-tiered dispute-resolution clause according to which the engineer's decision was followed – where necessary – by mandatory mediation, a preliminary binding decision by an "adjudicator" and finally arbitration.[534]

Critics might argue that in a good business relationship these successive problem-solving attempts will take place anyway and that in a bad relationship they are useless. In cases of really good or really bad relationships this may be true, but many business relationships fall into a zone between these extremes where there is a general willingness to cooperate, but also certain communication problems and conflicts of interest. Here, a structure that encourages cooperation, de-legitimizes confrontational behavior and sets a precise time frame for the successive steps of dispute resolution, can be of considerable value.

In long-term relationships, conflict prevention begins already with the way the parties initially interact. Particularly where the success of a venture depends on a very high degree of cooperation, as for example in a strategic alliance, writing a good contract is not sufficient to prevent conflicts and disruptions in the envisaged cooperation. When a strategic alliance is formed, it is important to build, from the very first contacts between the future partners, the working relationships that constitute the basis for any successful cooperation:

> "If you look at alliances that worked well and had actually the value material-
> ized that their founders wanted ... it doesn't have that much to do with the
> terms and conditions that were negotiated and agreed to at the outset; it has
> to do with the *pattern of interaction* ... if you have economic, technological
> and business change ... your ability to succeed as an alliance doesn't depend
> on certain financial or technical agreements, it depends on what capacity you
> develop jointly as a pair of partners to deal with opportunities and changes that
> come up; ... alliances that have not succeeded ... [many times] it is because
> there was dysfunctional behavior, distrust, they approach problems as sort
> of an opportunity to either take advantage or avoid being taken advantage
> of, and much of that comes from how the alliance started ... the way they
> do the exploratory discussions and the preliminary agreements not only sets
> the terms but also sets the tone ..."[535]

Negotiation consultants have developed specific *relationship-building* programs that assist the partners in laying the foundation for a close cooperation. These programs are tailored to the situation and differ according to whether the consultants were hired by one side or jointly by both prospective partners. Usually the program begins with a diagnostic phase where the consultants work with the parties separately, prepare them for the negotiation and conduct diagnostic interviews trying to understand the organizations involved (who are the players, which are the

---

[534] Wall, "Hong Kong's Airport Core Programme Dispute Resolution Procedures", 58 *Arbitration* 237 (November 1992); see also Mackie, "ADR in the Hong Kong Airport Project", 5 *World Arb. & Med. Rep.* 104 (1994).

[535] Interview with Elizabeth Gray, January 15, 1992 (emphasis added).

internal constituencies, who stands to benefit from the alliance and who stands to lose, and who might have an interest in sabotaging the relationship?). Next, they develop a plan for the discussions (who is at the table, who is in the background, how are decisions made on each side and who are the chief decisionmakers?). Then key people from both sides get acquainted and develop negotiation and group decisionmaking skills in a 3-4 day launch session, an off-site workshop consisting of role plays with simulated negotiations of fictional, non-related situations and group discussions facilitating an information exchange about the two organizations. Back in separate preparation sessions, the consultants assist each party with the substantive preparation for the negotiation: tasks are assessed, issues are clarified, goals are articulated. Next, the consultants create a "process map" of the negotiation in form of a "flow chart". Finally, the consultants retreat into the background and the actual negotiations are conducted by the parties alone. But the consultants stand on the sidelines, ready to jump in as soon as complications are encountered or resentments start building up. As outsiders, they are in a better posisition to recognize the trouble spots, and not infrequently they serve as a back-channel for communications. The negotiation consultants operate as a mixture between honest broker and coach. By enhancing the problem-solving skills of the parties and facilitating the actual negotiation process, they help improve both the quality and the durability of the cooperation established.

V. CONCLUSION: STRENGTHS AND WEAKNESSES OF ADR PROCEDURES

Rooted in applied negotiation theory, ADR techniques aim at achieving consensual solutions while reducing transaction costs and avoiding harm to relationships. They are based on party-autonomy and try to involve the principals themselves (i.e. in the case of business organizations, management) in the development of interest-oriented, economically sensible solutions which are free of the constraints connected with the zero-sum situation inherent to any litigation procedure. The paradigm for most alternative techniques, which in essence all consist of some form of structured settlement negotiation, is *mediation*. Modern business mediation is process-oriented, providing a structure that helps the parties craft their own solution. Mediation can be interest-based (problem-solving) or rights-based (predictive) and in the large majority of cases has elements of both.

Both the growing practical experiences and the growing body of scientific analysis of ADR will increase the role of ADR in the future of resolving international disputes.[536]

---

[536] Huber & Trachte-Huber, "International ADR in the 1990's: The Top Ten Developments", 1 *Houston Bus. & Tax Law J.* 184-223 (2001); Perritt, "Dispute Resolution in Cyberspace:

1. How Mediation /ADR facilitates settlement

Based on the key factors used to conceptualize the barriers against settlement in arbitration the following table illustrates how mediation and other ADR techniques can facilitate consensual solutions in international commercial disputes.

Table 3: Factors Influencing the Achievement of Settlement

Factors	Barriers to Settlement	How Mediation/ADR Can Help
Uncertainty	uncertainty (+ systemic over-optimism!) about – outcome —» inflated demands – costs —» under-estimated	structured information exchange (in mediation or mini-trial) —» basis for better prediction of outcome —» neutral assessment of costs
Process	"negotiator's dilemma" – hesitation to make 1st step (settlement move seen as signal of weakness) – prevents open communication – incomplete information lack of communication – lack of forum – logistical problems (geography, language) – lack of simultaneous attention – cultural differences dual strategy arb./neg. ("litigotiation") – conflicting tactics ("victory" «—» "peace") – different skills ("gladiator" «—» "diplomat") – same attorney does both litigation/arbitration process – "zero-sum" game – focus on rights/past events – antagonizing effect	"dilemma" overcome: – corporate settlement/ADR policy avoids impression of weakness in concrete case – mediator can hear both parties in private (—» parties can be open) – mediator obtains more information (—» complete picture of conflict) – ADR process as channel for communication – ADR provides structure for settlement talks – focus of attention on entire problem (not just legal dispute) – skilled mediator can bridge cultural gap ADR in "shadow" of arbitration – separation of processes – possible: separation of tasks – potential for "positive-sum" solutions – focus on interests & options to achieve future-oriented problem-solving – strengthening of relationship

Demand For New Forms of ADR", 15 *Ohio St. J. on Disp. Resol.* 675 (2000).

Factors	Barriers to Settlement	How Mediation/ADR Can Help

"Human Factor"	lack of negotiation skills
	lack of analysis → unrealistic picture of:
	  – merits of own/adversary's case
	  – quantification of claims
	  – risk of losing/gains from winning
	  – underlying interests (e.g. in relationship)
	  – real costs of dispute
	  – irrelevance of "sunk costs"
	
	unwillingness to give up positions
	perceived need for ever more information
	"ego" (need to save "face", righteousness)
		mediator injects negotiation skills
		ADR provides analysis:
		  – focused information exchange on merits (reality testing – predictive ADR)
		  – systematic quantitative analysis
		  – decision trees/LRA – costs/benefit analysis
		  – systematic exploration of interests, options & perceived choices
		  – rational analysis of costs
		  – avoidance of "sunk cost syndrome"
		focus on interests; easier to give up position when mediator builds "golden bridge")
		ADR → early and compressed info. exchange
		mediator as "scapegoat", no blame assigned

Organizational Dimension	lack of authority to settle (real or tactical)
	lack of management involvement
	internal pressure against settlement
	
	self-interest of agents (officers/attorneys):
	  – financial interests
	  – desire to justify self/avoid responsibility
		authority to settle = prerequisite for process
		management involvement also prerequisite
		settlement easier to "sell": more satisfying solution, legitimacy through mediator
		direct involvement of principals/management
		  – control over costs
		  – responsibility assumed at top level

Tactical Considerations	desire to formalize dispute to
	  – create pressure towards settlement
	  – avoid preclusion of claim
	  – satisfy insurance requirements
	delay tactics
	desire to create precedent
		arbitration as "back-up"
		  → maintains pressure/guarantees rights
		  → allows for formalization (claims preclusion avoided)
		[no guarantee against delays – minimum of cooperation is prerequisite]
		[difficult to overcome barrier: settlement is different kind of precedent]

2. Costs and Benefits of Mediation / ADR

Alternative dispute resolution techniques have a large number of potential *advantages*, not only with regard to savings in transaction costs but also in terms of the process and the quality of the results. ADR reduces *transaction costs* in many ways. If successful, the procedures save substantial amounts of *time* since they can (and should) be introduced early on in the history of the dispute and are very compressed – a typical business mediation will last between one and three days, compared to an average duration of international arbitration proceedings of more than two years. There are also potentially dramatic savings in *money* since ADR procedures are short in duration and require the participation of a limited number of persons: one representative from each party (ideally high-level executives), usually accompanied by a lawyer or a small team of lawyers who make the presentations and serve as continuous source of advice, possibly a small number of key experts or witnesses and, in most cases, a mediator (or two). However, there are also significant *indirect costs:* ongoing disputes create uncertainty and tie up management time and energies, as well as other corporate resources, and they can have a negative impact on the reputation of a business organization.

The *process* itself has important advantages because in a short and informal procedure it is easier to ensure *confidentiality*. The *flexibility* of the procedures makes it possible to devise a tailor-made process for each particular dispute. In addition, mediation and related procedures tend to have a beneficial effect on the *relationship* between the disputants since they create an opportunity for constructive interaction and demonstrate how differences can be dealt with in a productive way. Most ADR procedures also permit to eliminate misunderstandings and to deliberately deal with "people problems".

Perhaps the most important advantage of mediation and related procedures is that they can lead to *superior results*. A consensual solution has a much higher potential to *reflect* the concrete *interests of the parties* than a decision which is imposed by a judge or arbitrator and is based on abstract legal considerations. Negotiated settlements can devise *creative solutions* that no judge or arbitrator could order. Management involvement ensures that the decision-makers are intimately familiar with the business needs of the parties and long-term interests. This, in turn, entails the potential for "win-win" solutions that create value for both parties, e.g. by converting a lawsuit into a "deal"[537] or by structuring the timing of payments

---

[537] A spectacular example from American domestic practice is the Texaco/Borden mini-trial in which a USD 200 million anti-trust suit was resolved by renegotiating a gas-supply contract that had not even been at issue in the original litigation. The new arrangement provided for the transport of gas to prices favorable to the plaintiff, giving the plaintiff "nine-digit benefits" while still assuring positive cash flows for the defendant; cf. Henry & Lieberman, *The Manager's Guide to Resolving Legal Disputes* 40-42 (1985); Singer, *Settling Disputes* 63 (1990).

so as to exploit differences in the cost of capital or in accounting treatment.[538] A negotiated settlement also carries with it a high degree of *legitimacy* since it is based on the consent of all parties – provided the consent was freely given which in turn depends on the quality of any back-up procedure that has to provide an opportunity for the parties to have their rights respected. Another advantage of ADR procedures is that they can lead to a *solution much earlier* in the life of the controversy and can therefore prevent the dispute taking on a life of its own and causing much greater damage. In addition, negotiated solutions can *get to the roots* of a conflict and therefore lead to *solutions* that are *more complete and more durable*. The parties will also be more likely to accept and comply with a solution when they themselves have participated in its development. Finally, an amicable solution also bears the chance to improve the *reputation* of the parties since it demonstrates the ability to deal with problems in a constructive manner.

ADR procedures can create *benefits even if no complete resolution* of the dispute was reached. They may yield a *partial settlement* or at least an *agreement on* which are the relevant legal and factual *issues*. The subsequent resolution of the entire dispute, e.g. in arbitration, can be further streamlined if certain *facts* are *stipulated* or if the *range of outcomes* is *limited* by fixing a lower and an upper limit (high-low arbitration). And the process as such can improve the *relationship* in any event: substantial progress is made if the parties simply stop treating the dispute as a war and regard the continuation of litigation or arbitration – ideally with a substantially reduced scope – as merely a delegation of the decision to a competent third party. Hence, a mediation attempt may be worthwhile even if it is "unsuccessful".

Compared to these advantages, alternative methods of dispute resolution have only *few weaknesses*, above all the dependency on the cooperation of all parties, and the lack of a coherent legal framework ensuring the finality and enforceability of results. The deficiencies of the legal framework for international ADR and ways how to manage the resulting problems are discussed in Chapter 8. And the dependency on the cooperation of the parties is inherent to the nature of any process aiming at a consensual solution: they should only be tried if there is a reasonable chance of agreement. Apart from the danger of a wasted effort mediation and related procedures entail very limited *risks*. A concern sometimes voiced is that in mediation or in a mini-trial the parties have to give the other side a "free preview" into their best arguments which might result in a tactical disadvantage

---

[538] The time value of money is an important factor since the payment of a sum of money can only be valued correctly if the timing of the payment is considered. In deciding whether to accept a proposed settlement each party will have to make its own calculation based on its own cost of capital. This can lead to differences in valuation which can be used for the creation of value for the parties. Differences in accounting treatment of payments can also create value since booking a payment or a receipt in particular accounting periods may have a different impact on the bottom line of each party. This permits to structure a payment so that it represents a net benefit to the payee that is greater than the net cost to the payor.

at a later trial.[539] However, this argument cuts both ways: each party has to lay its cards on the table. And giving each party a preview of the other side's case can be beneficial even if no settlement is reached since it will render the ensuing litigation or arbitration more focused. Another reservation sometimes expressed is that in complex cases the time allotted to the presentations by the attorneys may not be sufficient to lay out all their arguments.[540] However, the flexibility of mediation makes it possible to provide for a more elaborate exchange of information or, if unforeseen complexities come up, to modify the schedule so as to grant more time for the presentation and discussion of certain issues. And most importantly, there is no danger for the parties since the procedure is voluntary in two respects: the parties are free to leave the procedure at any moment and, above all, they are under no obligation to accept its results.

As the following overview reveals, this – limited – risk will in many instances by far be outweighed by the benefits of ADR procedures.

Table 4: Costs and Benefits of Mediation/ADR

	Costs/Risks	Benefits (in case of a settlement)	Benefits (if no settlement is reached)
Trans-action Costs	*time spent* (2 to 6 days including preparations); possible delay with initiation of arbitration *fees & expenses* of mediator; fees & expenses occasioned by extra work of counsel	*time saved*: average duration of international arbitration above 2 years *savings* as a result of settlement: fees & expenses of tribunal and counsel, indirect costs of arbitration (contingency, executive time, other corporate resources, disruption of business, harm to reputation and relationships)	*savings* in time and other transaction costs resulting from possibility to streamline subsequent arbitration through partial settlement, agreement on relevant issues, stipulation of facts or by fixing of a range for outcome.
Process	[information exchange may create risk of tactical disadvantage in subsequent arbitration – but this is highly unlikely if process is managed correctly]	short & informal process →» easier to keep *confidential* beneficial to *relationship* (constructive interaction; opportunity to deal with "people problems")	still easier to keep *confidential* beneficial impact on *relationship* (war →» delegation of decision)

[539] Cf. Renfrew, "A Survey of Dispute Resolution Methods", in: Hancock & Gillan, *Corporate Counsel's Guide to ADR Techniques* 1.029 et seq. (1989).

[540] Renfrew id.

	Costs/Risks	Benefits *(in case of a settlement)*	Benefits *(if no settlement is reached)*
Result	[no real risk: no obligation to accept settlement —» no risk of unfavorable outcome]	settlement reflects economic *interests* of parties potential to create value through *mutually beneficial solution* (dispute —» deal; differences in cost of capital/accounting treatment of payments) possibility to *get to the roots* of conflict —» solution more *durable* *legitimacy* through consent of parties (effective back-up ensures respect for parties' rights) parties more *likely to comply* with solution positive effect on *reputation* of parties (capacity to solve problems and settle disputes amicably)	partial settlement can produce part of the benefits of a complete settlement

3. What Types of Disputes are Suitable for ADR?

It has been argued that only certain *types of disputes* are *suitable for* resolution through *ADR techniques*. This is correct insofar as dispute resolution techniques should be tailored to the specific circumstances of a dispute and therefore certain techniques can be particularly useful in certain types of cases. It is sometimes argued that mini-trials are best suited to disputes where the facts are difficult to determine or where the law is ambiguous and court decisions unpredictable. Contract cases and especially cases involving long-term business relationships can benefit from the future-oriented approach of interest-based (problem-solving) mediation. And, obviously, the savings attainable are most significant in complex cases involving large monetary amounts. However, none of this justifies the contention that mediation would be unsuitable for other types of dispute. The challenge for appropriate dispute resolution is to find the right procedure for each particular dispute. In this context, the substance of the dispute is less important than the *interests and attitudes* of the parties: where certain legal questions are not yet settled and one of the parties has an interest in creating a binding precedent, the decision of a public court may have to be obtained. And since the success of consensual dispute resolution depends heavily on the cooperation of the parties, a *minimum of trust* and a sincere *interest in* a negotiated *settlement* are crucial. If one party is pursuing litigation purely for tactical reasons or benefits greatly from delaying a resolution,[541] a consensual procedure may simply be exploited for delay. However, the short duration of most ADR procedures creates a natural limit to the delays that can be caused by a frustrated settlement attempt.

Different cultural backgrounds of the parties to a dispute can strongly influence the dynamics of resolution processes. Cross-cultural mediation poses an extra challenge to the already difficult task of the mediator which is why it may turn out difficult to find a qualified neutral to perform this task. Mediators who are multi-lingual or otherwise specifically qualified may be able to build bridges where direct negotiations fail. Thus, when it works the benefits might be even greater than in normal mediation: when communication is difficult, mediation and other specific structures for settlement negotiations may be difficult to perform, but without the help of a mediator or of a deliberate negotiation structure, the communication will be even more difficult.

In sum, there is no particular type of dispute where ADR procedures are a priori unsuitable. In certain contexts, the techniques may be more difficult to carry out but these are situations where settlement negotiations without the help of a mediator or a specialized negotiation structure will be even more difficult. And the risks connected with ADR techniques are limited: the information exchange is mutual and will not normally lead to a tactical disadvantage for one party, and the participants are free to leave the process at any moment or to reject its results. Hence, the worst that can happen is that the effort produces no benefits and the investment is wasted. The investment, however, is limited and will usually constitute a fraction of the likely costs of initiating or continuing litigation or arbitration.

---

[541] In the courts of certain countries, as well as in the practice of international arbitral tribunals, pre-judgment interest may be insufficient to cover the parties' cost of capital, thus creating an economic interest for the defendant to delay payment.

Chapter 7

Tools and Techniques to support Business Mediation[542]

An effective use of certain tools and techniques can significantly enhance the mediation process and improve the outcome. We would like to focus on three tools we find particularly relevant: *Mind Mapping*, useful for collecting and structuring issues relevant to a case, *Litigation Risk Analysis*, supportive in illustrating and evaluating legal aspects of a case, and *Brainstorming*, a familiar but often underestimated technique for generating options for a solution.

I. MIND MAPPING

Mind Mapping – beside being a useful thinking and visualization tool – is an efficient means to enhance the quality of communication during the mediation process. Its basic concept will be briefly described, followed by suggestions on how it can be applied in the mediation process.

1. Basic Concept

The concept of Mind Mapping is based on the results of empirical research dealing with how information is processed and has been directly inspired by the way the human brain functions.[543] The underlying idea is that any information is constantly being associated and connected with other pieces of information.

A Mind Map has four essential characteristics:[544]

– the subject of attention is crystallised in a central image or key word;

– the main themes of the subject radiate from the central image as branches;

---

[542] The authors would like to thank Constantin Olbrisch, Attorney and Mediator, Berlin, for his substantial contributions to this Chapter.

[543] See Buzan, *The Mind Map Book* 53.

[544] See Buzan, *The Mind Map Book* 59.

- these branches comprise key words on the associated lines, with sub-issues represented as sub-branches attached to higher-level branches;
- the branches form a connected nodal structure.

The Mind Map can be created on a sheet of plain paper, using a flipchart or with the support of a software such as MindManager.[545]

2. Application in Mediation

Mind Mapping can be used in mediation right after the beginning of the process, when the issues are collected. The goals of this stage are to gather and document the relevant information and to start structuring the problem. Mind Mapping can support this process, e.g., when the mediator transforms the parties' information into one collective map of the conflict.

Consider a negotiation over a business transaction: Some issues typically addressed are strategic issues, antitrust issues, valuation and methods of pricing, due diligence concerning legal, financial, commercial, tax, environmental, technical, and intellectual property issues, questions regarding human resources, in particular management issues, departments etc. The structure of a Mind Map reflecting these issues could look like Figure 20 opposite.

Mind Maps can be used throughout the whole mediation process. Both communication and documentation tend to be more structured, repetitions can be avoided as well as key issues and subjects identified.

II. LITIGATION RISK ANALYSIS

Litigation Risk Analysis is a tool increasingly used by litigation lawyers in evaluating and preparing cases.[546] Its main purpose is to assess the value of the parties' litigation alternatives to a negotiated agreement (BATNA). In recent years, this tool has been used increasingly by mediators. As will be shown, Litigation Risk Analysis can serve as a useful support for the mediation process, particularly in putting inflated demands into perspective.

1. Basic Concept

Litigation Risk Analysis is based on the concept of *decision trees*. A decision tree maps out every step of the reasoning of a scenario, e.g., a court's (or an arbitral

---

[545] For further information see www.mindjet.com.

[546] For an overview see Victor, "The Proper Use of Decision Analysis to Assist Litigation Strategy", 40 *Bus. Lawyer* 617 (1985); see also Cronin-Harris, "Mainstreaming: Systematizing Corporate Use of ADR", 59 *Alb. L. Rev.* 847, 875 et seq. (1996)

Figure 20: Mind Map

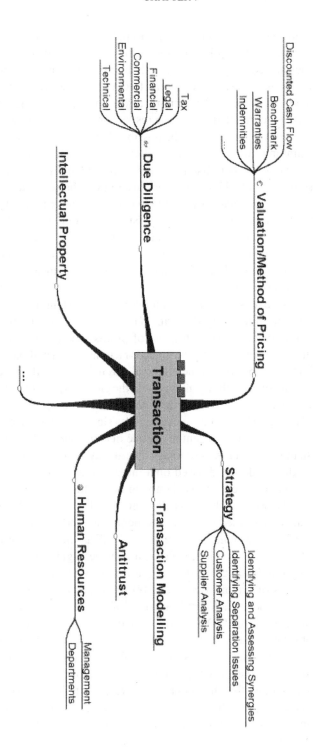

tribunal's) decision, and assigns probabilities to potential outcomes. The analysis consists of three principal steps. First, all relevant *issues*, the alternative answers on each of these issues, the ensuing sub-issues with their possible answers and so forth are identified and recorded like branches in a tree, until all relevant ramifications are covered. Then the reasoning that supports any of the ramifications is recorded next to the branch in the tree that marks the respective issues. In the second step, percentage *probabilities* are assigned to the possible decisions on each of the issues. The process of thinking through all the ramifications of the case and organizing the issues in a decision tree is in itself already helpful in analyzing the case and making the most of the available information. In addition, the percentage values at each intersection of the tree make it possible to calculate, in form of a probability distribution, the likelihood of each of the possible final outcomes. This in turn serves as a basis for the third step, an evaluation of the overall value – or from the defendant's perspective the overall risk – of the case. Assigning a dollar value to the case can provide a rational basis for the decision on whether to make (or to accept) a settlement proposal.

The technique can be illustrated by a simplified example: a long-term distributorship agreement was terminated by the principal without notice, and the agent is claiming USD 2 million in damages for loss of profits. The decision of the case depends on whether (1) a reason had to be given for a termination without notice and if so, whether (2) the reason given by the principal was insufficient. If both questions are answered in the affirmative the agent wins and the ensuing question is how much he will be awarded in damages. This, in turn, depends on whether (3) the damages will be calculated based on lost profits – resulting in a significantly higher award – or on the basis of the investment the agent had made in anticipation of a continuation of the contract. In the former case the damage award may again depend on whether (4a) lost profits will be calculated based on a three year average, resulting in the USD 2 million amount claimed, or based only on the profits of the last year where sales where unusually slow, resulting in a damage award of only USD 1,5 million. If damages are calculated based on the investment made the amount of damages awarded might depend on whether (4b) the tribunal will assume an amortization of the investment over a 10 year period, yielding a damages figure of USD 700,000, or over a 5 year period, leading to a damages award of USD 400,000. Assuming total transaction costs of around USD 400,000 (each party's costs estimated at USD 160,000 – to be borne by each party regardless of outcome – plus the costs of the arbitral tribunal amounting to USD 80,000 – to be borne by the losing party in case of clear defeat, otherwise shared by both parties), an estimate of the probabilities at each ramification of the decision tree permits to calculate a probability distribution of possible outcomes and the ensuing net results for both parties.

The decision tree shows that the plaintiff is more likely to lose than to win even if he has a 2/3 chance of prevailing on the two key issues, i.e. the need for a valid reason for termination without notice and the question whether the reason given

Figure 21: Example – Litigation Risk Analysis

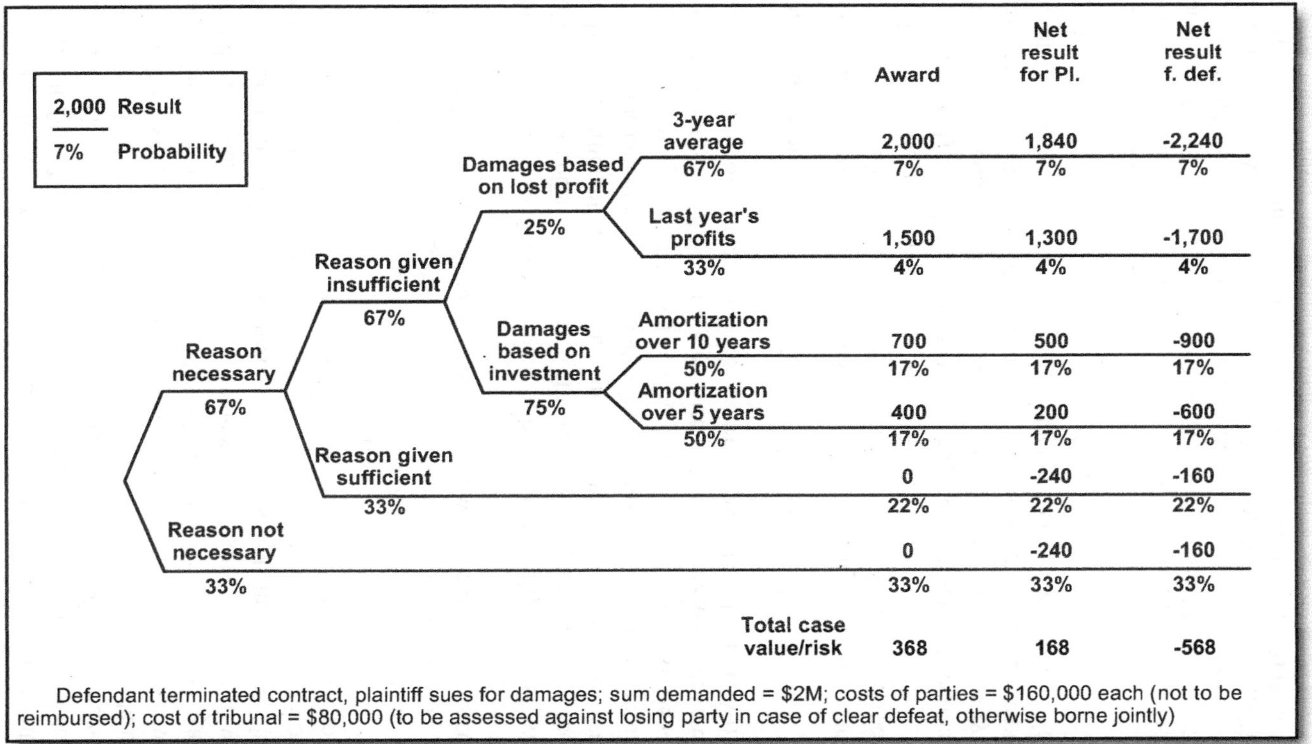

Legend	
2,000	Result
7%	Probability

Decision tree:

- Reason necessary 67%
  - Reason given insufficient 67%
    - Damages based on lost profit 25%
      - 3-year average 67%
      - Last year's profits 33%
    - Damages based on investment 75%
      - Amortization over 10 years 50%
      - Amortization over 5 years 50%
  - Reason given sufficient 33%
- Reason not necessary 33%

	Award	Net result for Pl.	Net result f. def.
3-year average	2,000 / 7%	1,840 / 7%	-2,240 / 7%
Last year's profits	1,500 / 4%	1,300 / 4%	-1,700 / 4%
Amortization over 10 years	700 / 17%	500 / 17%	-900 / 17%
Amortization over 5 years	400 / 17%	200 / 17%	-600 / 17%
Reason given sufficient	0 / 22%	-240 / 22%	-160 / 22%
Reason not necessary	0 / 33%	-240 / 33%	-160 / 33%
Total case value/risk	**368**	**168**	**-568**

Defendant terminated contract, plaintiff sues for damages; sum demanded = $2M; costs of parties = $160,000 each (not to be reimbursed); cost of tribunal = $80,000 (to be assessed against losing party in case of clear defeat, otherwise borne jointly) was sufficient. The analysis also shows that, if only the monetary outcome of the procedure is considered, a *risk neutral* plaintiff would initiate arbitration in any event because the losses connected with a defeat in the arbitration are limited to costs of USD 240,000. This downside risk is outweighed by the upside potential, i.e. the chance of winning a very substantial damages award which may end up in a net benefit of up to USD 1,84 million, resulting in a total net value for the plaintiff's case of USD 168,000. The analysis also shows that a risk-neutral plaintiff would settle if offered more than this net value of USD 168,000 (in this simplified example the effect of the time lag of any payment is neglected; in reality, the plaintiff would have to face a delay of easily two to three years until he gets his money. This, in turn, would suggest further reducing the acceptable settlement amount according to the plaintiff's cost of capital to the extent it exceeds any interests to be expected in the arbitral award). Conversely, the defendant faces a calculated litigation risk of USD 568,000 making it rational to settle for a payment of anything below that figure (although, again, this figure would need to be downward adjusted in order to reflect the time lag of any payments, in accordance with the defendant's cost of capital).

Litigation Risk Analysis can be enhanced by the use of flipcharts as well as specifically designed decision analysis software. The software-based process is significantly more efficient since inputs can easily be altered, and the software usually executes the calculations automatically. Various software solutions are offered by different providers, emphasising different aspects of the process. Generally available decision analysis software packages are: DATA by TreeAge Software Inc., KnowledgeTools, @RISK, Precision Tree, Expert Choice, DPL1, and HIVIEW.

2. Use in Mediation

In mediation, the merits of Litigation Risk Analysis primarily lie in the clarification of the expected values of the parties' alternatives. Additionally, the tool can significantly enrich the process of mediation itself. [547]

Decision tree analysis helps gain maneuvering space in settlement negotiations by reducing the over-confidence of the parties. A mediator can use this type of analysis to foster agreement by structuring the discussion and forcing the parties to concentrate on concrete issues and the influencing factors and probabilities for

---

[547] For decision analysis and mediation see: Aaron, "The Value of Decision Analysis in Mediation Practice", 11 *Neg. J.* 123 (1995); Eidenmueller, "Prozessrisikoanalyse", *ZZP*, 5 et seq, 23 (2000); Eidenmueller, in: Duve, Eidenmueller, Hacke, *Mediation in der Wirtschaft – Wege zum professionellen Konfliktmanagement* 232 (2003); McGuire, "Practical Tips for Using Risk Analysis in Mediation", *Dispute Resolution Journal*, 15 et seq, 21 (May 1998); Hoffer, "Decision Analysis as a Mediator's Tool", 1 *Harv. Neg. L. Rev.* 113 et seq (1996); Neuenhahn, "Erarbeiten der Prozessrisikoanalyse und deren Einsatz in der Mediation", *ZKM* 245, 246 (2002).

each of them. Breaking down the case and discussing each issue separately already tends to reduce the differences in assessment and often makes it possible at least to identify the issues that really matter. In addition, it helps overcome a significant barrier to early settlement negotiations. Attorneys have a natural reluctance to take settlement decisions based on incomplete information. They frequently prefer to wait until the first steps in litigation have shed more light on the strengths and weaknesses of their case. However, at that point the savings that can be realized through a settlement are much smaller because the parties have already "sunk" considerable costs into litigation. Decision tree analysis helps overcome this obstacle since it makes better use of the information available and allows the parties to make rational assessments of the litigation prospects. This permits the parties to take responsible settlement decisions at an earlier stage.

The use of Litigation Risk Analysis during mediation proceedings also enhances the communication and understanding between lawyers and clients because the clients are capable of following the legal argument more easily. Since they can estimate the risks and chances of the case themselves instead of having to rely exclusively upon their lawyers' advice, the clients are enabled to better support and control their lawyers. If the client is enabled to follow the legal argument, he may cushion his lawyer's strategic behavior to the extent that the client prefers a more cooperative approach to the negotiation process. Thus, in lawyer-dominated disputes, the tool can serve as a means to canalise and moderate the lawyers' input as well as to make use of their knowledge and capabilities in the best possible way.[548]

In the privacy of caucuses the mediator can elicit each parties' own appraisal on concrete issues. Where necessary, he can challenge these assessments and thereby gradually narrow the gap between the positions which, however, requires a high degree of familiarity with all legal aspects relevant at any juncture of the decision tree. If the mediator manages to reduce the discrepancy between the probability estimates of the parties to the point where the gap approaches the transaction costs, settlement becomes likely. However, even where no complete settlement can be reached, it can be a major advancement to reduce the scope of the dispute to a few key issues or a limited range of outcomes, particularly when the parties are able to agree on a streamlined procedure for their resolution, e.g. a "high-low" arbitration based on agreed upper and lower limits for the final award.

A barrier to a negotiated settlement can be the need for an approval of the agreement by a constituency not participating in the mediation process. With the help of Litigation Risk Analysis the outcome of the mediation can be justified more convincingly. By referring to the decision tree, its structure and the respective

---

[548]   Hoffer, "Decision Analysis as a Mediator's Tool", 1 *Harv. Neg. L. Rev.* 113, 129 (1996).

probabilities, the path towards and the motives for the agreement can be presented in an efficient, well structured and transparent way.[549]

3. Case Study

The following real-life example illustrates the tool's potential effectiveness in mediation.[550] The case dealt with a damage claim based on breach of duty during the acquisition of a major share package of a large German building company. The dispute occurred between a Dutch company, the HBG Hollandsche Beton Group (in the following: "HBG") and a German company, the AGIV AG (in the following: "AGIV") in the year 1998 and was settled by means of mediation in the year 2000.

HBG was an international building company that intended to expand in the German market. AGIV was a holding company with stakes in various industrial areas. In December 1996, AGIV sold the majority of shares (75 %) in Wayss & Freytag AG to HBG. The purchase price amounted to DEM 260 million and was based on a due diligence executed in December 1996. The contract provided for a price adjustment of up to DEM 55 million depending on the company's results for 1996. 1996 turned out to be disastrous, and the purchase price was reduced to DEM 205 million. In the following years 1997 and 1998, Wayss & Freytag AG again experienced severe losses, which led to HBG having to inject several million German marks to save the company. The reasons for these losses were seen in actions that had been taken in the time before the sale to HBG.

In May 1998, a report by a renowned international consulting company surfaced. It was dated 1996 and highlighted the risk of losses in the amount of several million German marks for the following years. The report had been presented to the board of Wayss & Freytag AG immediately before the execution of the due diligence in December 1996. HBG had not been informed about this report.

In May 1999, HBG filed a lawsuit claiming more than DEM 200 million in damages. The claim was based on the following allegations: insufficient information during the due diligence and fraudulent misrepresentation by the AGIV board. In May 2000, the first court session was held. AGIV denied knowledge of the report in 1996. As had been expected, the judge raised the issue of attributing the knowledge of Wayss & Freytag AG about the report to AGIV since AGIV was the controlling shareholder at that time. The judge also emphasised the risks of the lawsuit, stressing the point that due to the uncertain legal position the case might be

---

[549]   See Sander/Goldberg, "Fitting the Forum to the Fuss: A User-friendly Guide to Selecting an ADR-Procedure", 10 *Neg. J.* 49, 56 (1994).

[550]   The case and the ensuing mediation were presented in public on the occasion of a workshop hosted by the German Institute for Arbitration, Deutsche Institution für Schiedsgerichtsbarkeit in Bad Godesberg, Germany, in October 2001. All information presented in the text is derived from materials made public.

taken to the court of appeal as well as to the court of ultimate resort, which could take ten years. He urged the parties to explore settlement options.

Previous negotiations had led to a gap of DEM 100 million: while AGIV was willing to offer up to DEM 20 million, HBG claimed at least DEM 120 million. In light of the uncertainty of the suit and the heavy transaction costs, the parties took the case to mediation in August 2000, which was carried out by Professor Horst Eidenmueller. The mediation took four days and resulted in a comprehensive settlement. Participants were members of both parties' top management, their lawyers and experts. The first day was spent with presentations of the different views on the dispute as well as a first search for interest-based "win-win" solutions. The second day was spent with a comprehensive Litigation Risk Analysis that made it possible to break down a very large and complex case to a few decisive legal issues.

The Litigation Risk Analysis had been thoroughly prepared in advance and was conducted mainly in caucuses. The mediator assisted the process by explaining the relevant case law and illustrating the resulting risks. As a professor of German business law, the mediator could assist the parties and the lawyers in assessing the probabilities of the various ramifications in the decision tree. From HBG's point of view, the expected value of the litigation now appeared to be in the order of DEM 160 million. Taking into account the necessary risk adjustments and the litigation costs, the net value of the litigation turned out to be more like DEM 110 million, less than half the amount initially claimed.

Based on the results of the Litigation Risk Analysis, the mediation went on for another two days and resulted in the following settlement: AGIV agreed to pay DEM 55 million to compensate losses resulting from the sale plus another DEM 6 million compensating different other claims. Additionally, the parties agreed on various real estate deals as well as on a joint press release. In the end, after the final settlement agreement had been signed in December 2000 and adding in several related deals, DEM 71 million were paid.

In the aftermath, representatives of the parties explicitly recommended the use of Litigation Risk Analysis and announced never again to proceed to litigation without having executed a Litigation Risk Analysis.

4. Comment

Decision tree analysis has inherent *limitations*. The quality of the results depends on the quality of the input which consists of the lawyers' legal analysis of what the issues are and their "educated guesses" of how they will be resolved ("garbage in – garbage out"). The precise calculation of monetary values may suggest a scientific accuracy that would be illusory. And litigation risk analysis only deals with one particular aspect of the conflict: the calculation of judicial no-agreement alternatives. It frames the entire dispute in terms of the negative-sum game of litigation and does little to clarify the interests of the parties or to expand the options for a resolution of the dispute. And the non-monetary consequences of a lawsuit (e.g.

precedential value, publicity, damage to existing or potential relationships, diversion of management energies) are also ignored.

Still, the assessment of the likely outcome of litigation (or arbitration) plays a highly significant role in every settlement negotiation, and systematic quantitative analysis is a good way to make this process more rational and to narrow the gap between conflicting predictions.

III. BRAINSTORMING

During a mediation process, brainstorming can serve as a very useful tool to widen the parties' perspective on the potential outcome of the case and to enhance the process of looking for creative solutions.

1. Basic Concept

The concept of brainstorming is based on the insight that ideas stimulate ideas, and that seemingly unrealistic approaches often lead to unexpected solutions for a problem.[551] With the guidance of a facilitator, participants familiar with a specific problem are requested to generate ideas and options.

The procedure is based on three features:

– cross stimulation;

– suspended judgement;

– formality of the setting.

Cross stimulation denotes the effect that ideas lead to other ideas. Even if misunderstood, an idea from one person stimulates other people's thoughts. During a brainstorming session, it becomes possible to create ideas that might not have seemed to exist at first sight. The session continues until a satisfactory number of ideas, depending on the complexity of the agenda, have been reached.

Suspended judgement stands for the "no criticism rule". In a brainstorming session, it is essential to separate the process of creating ideas from the evaluation of these ideas. Evaluation uses other areas of the brain and limits creativity, thus blocking the process of inventing new ideas. The background, again, is that even unrealistic ideas might bear a new approach that can be developed further and lead to more realistic options. Extreme ideas are therefore expressly invited. All ideas should be visibly recorded, e.g., on a flip chart or using an overhead projector.

---

[551] Generally on brainstorming and creativity techniques see de Bono, *Lateral Thinking*, 130 et seq (1970).

Formality of the setting stands for the rigid frame in which a brainstorming session should be conducted. Brainstorming should be experienced as a break from routine activities. Ideally, the session is conducted in a specific room or an otherwise unusual setting (e.g., standing up). Paradoxically, the formal frame does not impair the creativity, but instead enhances the quality and informality of ideas to be created.[552]

2. Application in Mediation

Brainstorming can be especially useful in the option gathering stage, either in joint brainstorming sessions with all parties present, or in separate brainstorming caucuses. The mediator serves as a facilitator, acting as a catalyst, recording (without exception) all ideas mentioned and ensuring compliance with the brainstorming ground rules, especially the "no criticism rule".

---

[552]   De Bono id. 133.

The Legal Framework for (International) ADR

While there have been significant improvements in making the mediation process more efficient, less progress has been made in the establishment of an internationally recognized framework for Alternative Dispute Resolution. A "law of ADR" is in the process of being formed on a domestic scale, and so far this process has taken shape only in those countries where ADR-procedures have begun to play a role in practice. Probably the most important body of law, in the form of state statutes and court decisions, has evolved in the United States, but even there the "law of ADR" is not fully developed, with only some of the most litigious issues covered and with frequently conflicting rules being promulgated by different courts and state legislatures.[553] A more uniform picture could emerge in the US as the states adopt the "Uniform Mediation Act", a Model Law regulating core issues of mediation, drafted in 2001 by the National Conference of Commissioners on Uniform State Laws. In October 2004, the European Commission proposed a directive of the European Parliament and the Council on aspects of mediation in civil and commercial matters, which is a remarkable step towards establishing and harmonizing a legal framework for mediation in Europe.[554]

A comparative study of the legal treatment of the various forms of alternative procedures in the major legal systems of the world would go beyond the scope of this work. Also, such a comparative study would not provide answers to the issues arising out of the use of alternative procedures in *international* business disputes. Evidently, a specific "law of *international* ADR" has yet to be developed. Apart from the UNCITRAL Model Law on International Commercial Conciliation (see below), intended to serve as a point of reference for states enacting mediation legislation, a number of model rules for international mediation procedures exist (see below). These are standard provisions to be incorporated into an agreement by

---

[553] There is a certain irony in the fact that the trend towards de-legalization of dispute resolution has ended up producing a new field of legal practice, see Menkel-Meadow, "Pursuing Settlement in an Adversary Culture: A Tale of Innovation Co-opted or 'The Law of ADR'", 19 *Florida St. L. Rev.* 1 (1991).

[554] For an in-depth analysis, see Eidenmueller, "Establishing a Legal Framework for Mediation in Europe: The Proposal for an EC Mediation Directive", *SchiedsVZ* 124 (2005).

way of reference, and are therefore of a purely contractual nature. In the absence of adequate international treaties and national statutes that deal with the recognition of agreements reached in "foreign" mediation, alternative procedures are subject to the full range of legal problems arising out of the multiplicity of legal systems that affect international trade. The natural answer to this problem may be the attempt to structure ADR procedures so as to benefit from the legal frame of international commercial arbitration.

In this Chapter we shall first take a look at some of the *model procedures* offered by different institutions (I), before examining the various *legal issues* arising out of alternative procedures in an international context (II). The Chapter ends with the suggestion to use *the legal framework of* international commercial *arbitration* in order to avoid the uncertainties and problems described in this chapter (III) and a short conlusion (IV).

I. MODEL CONCILIATION AND MEDIATION PROCEDURES

A number of institutions have developed model rules for conciliation/mediation procedures[555] and mini-trials. With the exception of the UNCITRAL Model Law, addressing the legislatures of the different states, the rules can be incorporated by private parties into commercial agreements, either separately or in connection with an arbitration clause that provides for a "back-up" procedure in case the conciliation attempt fails. So far, the use of these model ADR procedures has been relatively limited.

1. ICC ADR

In 2001, the International Chamber of Commerce has issued its ADR Rules, replacing the 1988 ICC Rules of Optional Conciliation.[556] The term "ADR" refers to "amicable dispute resolution", thus excluding arbitration from its scope and instead referring only to "proceedings which do not result in a decision or award of the neutral which can be enforced at law".[557] The two lines of service – arbitration and ADR – are each administered by a separate secretariat based at the ICC headquarters in Paris. However, there are a number of ways in which the different processes can be combined, for example by providing for arbitration after the ADR-attempt has failed, as is reflected in one of the suggested ICC ADR-clauses. These clauses

---

[555] For a comparative overview, cf. Baker/Ali, "A Cross-Comparison of International Mediation Rules", *Dispute Resolution Journal* 72 (2002).

[556] ICC Conciliation was resorted to rather infrequently. For example, in 1999, only seven conciliation request were received as opposed to 529 requests for arbitration; cf. Craig/ Park/Paulsson, *International Chamber of Commerce Arbitration* § 38.01 (2000).

[557] Cf. *Guide to ICC ADR*, Introduction.

range from low to high commitment, starting with "Optional ADR" and ending with "Obligation to submit dispute to ADR, followed by ICC arbitration as required". The two intermediate levels are: "Obligation to consider ADR" and "Obligation to submit dispute to ADR with an automatic expiration mechanism".[558] The ADR Rules permit the parties to agree upon whatever settlement technique they consider appropriate to help them resolve the dispute at hand. In the absence of such an agreement, mediation is the fallback procedure.[559] The process is entirely voluntary for all parties where there is no previous agreement to refer to the Rules. In this case, any party or parties wishing to commence ADR proceedings may send in a written request of which the ICC promptly informs the other side.[560] If there is no positive reply within a period of 15 days, the request is deemed to have been declined.[561] Where there *is* an agreement to refer to the Rules – either contained in a pre-existing contract or brought about by a positive response to the other side's request – all of the parties are held to at least attend the first meeting with the neutral, where the procedure to be followed is discussed.[562] Ideally, the parties themselves jointly designate a neutral; where they are unable to do so, the ICC makes an appointment through an ICC National Committee or otherwise. In doing so, the institution tries to accommodate the wishes of the parties as to certain qualifications of the neutral.[563] The neutral has a certain measure of discretion with regard to procedural matters but always has to keep the principles of fairness and impartiality and the wishes of the parties in mind.[564] The ADR proceedings terminate, *inter alia*, upon the signing by the parties of a settlement agreement, withdrawal of the neutral or one of the parties (after the initial meeting has been completed), and the expiration of any time limit set for the proceedings.[565] A settlement agreement is binding upon the parties in accordance with the applicable law which they may choose in their agreement.[566] Regardless of the settlement approach, the neutral has no power to bind the parties. However, the parties are at liberty to contractually agree to abide by the neutral's opinion, evaluation or recommendation.[567]

---

[558] Cf. "Suggested ICC ADR Clauses", ICC ADR Rules.

[559] Cf. Art. 5.2 ICC ADR Rules.

[560] Cf. Art. 2.B.1 ICC ADR Rules.

[561] Cf. Art. 2.B.2 ICC ADR Rules.

[562] Cf. Art. 5.1 ICC ADR Rules; *Guide to ICC ADR* Art. 2.

[563] Cf. Art. 3.1 ICC ADR Rules.

[564] Cf. Art. 3.2 ICC ADR Rules.

[565] Cf. Art. 6.1 ICC ADR Rules.

[566] Cf. *Guide to ICC ADR* Art. 6.1 a).

[567] Cf. *Guide to ICC ADR* Art. 5, "Combination of Settlement Techniques".

The cost of ICC ADR consists of three elements: ICC administrative expenses, the fees of the neutral as well as his or her reasonable expenses.[568] The processes are intended to be rapid and therefore relatively inexpensive.[569] In the absence of an agreement of the parties to the contrary and subject to any mandatory provisions of the applicable law, the ADR proceedings are private and confidential. The Rules regulate the issue of confidentiality in detail.[570]

During the first full year of operation for ICC ADR (2002), cases with amounts at stake ranging from USD 30,000 to 6 million were handled. The ICC received applications from Europe, the United States, Latin America and the Middle East. However, ICC ADR is not yet resorted to very often: in 2003, only 8 cases were introduced under the ADR rules as opposed to 580 under the Rules of Arbitration.[571] On the other hand, it can be expected that more applications will be filed over the years as ICC ADR-clauses inserted into contracts in or after 2001 will become applicable to the conflicts arising within the framework of those contracts.

2. AAA Mediation

Like the ICC, the American Arbitration Association ("AAA") administers non-binding procedures as well. In 2003, the AAA's International Centre for Dispute Resolution (ICDR) as well added a new section to its International Dispute Resolution Procedures, providing expressly for *international* mediation.[572] The Rules have largely the same content as the ICC and UNCITRAL Rules, addressing issues such as the mediator's limited authority,[573] confidentiality,[574] privacy[575] etc. The AAA generally encourages mediation and does not raise additional fees for parties who, during a pending arbitration, attempt to mediate their dispute under the ICDR's auspices. Further, the AAA has a longstanding practice to suggest, at the beginning of an arbitration, that the parties attempt to reach an amicable solution by means of mediation.

---

[568] Cf. Art. 4 ICC ADR Rules.

[569] Cf. *Guide to ICC ADR*, Characteristics of ICC ADR 2).

[570] Cf. Art. 7.1-4 ICC ADR Rules.

[571] Information received from Emmanuel Jolivet, General Counsel International Court of Arbitration ICC, email-message of April 30, 2004.

[572] Cf. www.adr.org/International.

[573] Cf. M-10 International Mediation Rules.

[574] Cf. M-12 International Mediation Rules.

[575] Cf. M-11 International Mediation Rules.

3. LCIA Mediation

The London Court of International Arbitration also has developed a set of rules dedicated expressly to mediation[576] which have last been amended in June 2004. The rules do not differ in any significant way from those already described.

4. UNCITRAL Conciliation

The United Nations Commission for International Trade Law ("UNCITRAL") has, in 1980, published a set of conciliation rules for non-administered conciliations.[577] The rules provide for a completely voluntary process,[578] confidentiality,[579] and broad discretion for the conciliator(s) to conduct the process.[580] As in the ICC rules[581] and unless the parties agree otherwise, the mediator is prevented from acting as an arbitrator, counsel or witness in related subsequent arbitrations.[582] Acknowledging that "conciliation is being increasingly used in dispute settlement practice in various parts of the world, including regions where until a decade or two ago it was not commonly used",[583] the UNCITRAL Commission recently drafted a Model Law on International Commercial Conciliation intended to serve as a template for uniform legislation supporting the increased use of conciliation throughout the world. The Model Law, reflecting the spirit of the UNCITRAL Conciliation Rules, was promulgated by the General Assembly on 19 November 2002.[584] It is accompanied by an explanatory "Draft Guide to Enactment and Use of the UNCITRAL Model Law on International Commercial Conciliation".[585]

---

[576] Cf. www.lcia-arbitration.com

[577] GA resolution no. 35/52 dated Dec. 4, 1980; UN Doc. A/35/17; www.uncitral.org/uncitral/en/uncitral_texts/arbitration/1980Conciliation_rules.html

[578] Cf. Art. 1.2 – the parties may modify or exclude any of the provisions anytime – under the ICC ADR Rules, by contrast, the consent of the ICC is needed (Art. 1 ICC ADR Rules); Art. 2; 15 c), d) UNCITRAL Conciliation Rules.

[579] Cf. Art. 10; 14 UNCITRAL Conciliation Rules.

[580] Cf. Art. 7 UNCITRAL Conciliation Rules.

[581] Cf. Art. 7.3-4 ICC ADR Rules.

[582] Cf. Art. 19 UNCITRAL Conciliation Rules. For a more detailed discussion of the UNCITRAL Conciliation Rules see Herrmann, Conciliation as a New Method of Dispute Settlement, in: Sanders (ed.), ICCA Congress Series No.1 145-165 (1983). See also Donahey, International Mediation and Conciliation, in: Roth, Wulff & Cooper, The Alternative Dispute Resolution Practice Guide (1993).

[583] Draft Guide to Enactment and Use of the UNCITRAL Model Law on International Commercial Conciliation, 3 (see below).

[584] Document A/res/57/18; www.uncitral.org/uncitral/en/uncitral_texts/arbitration/2002Model_conciliation.html .

[585] Document A/CN.9/514; www.uncitral.org/pdf/english/texts/arbitration/ml-conc/ml-conc-e.pdf. For further discussion of the texts, cf. Dobbins, "UNCITRAL Model Law on Inter-

5. World Bank/ICSID Conciliation

Very detailed provisions have been created under the Convention for the Settlement of Investment Disputes Between States and Nationals of Other States.[586] The International Centre for the Settlement of Investment Disputes (ICSID) administers these proceedings and appoints the conciliator(s). Only few conciliations have been administered by ICSID so far,[587] but ICSID has only recently begun to process more significant numbers of cases which has also to do with the very limited scope of its jurisdiction. Before the formation of the Centre, the World Bank, or more precisely its President, had mediated a number of investment conflicts relating to projects financed by the Bank. To channel and institutionalize this kind of activity, which was not part of the mainstream tasks of the Bank, was one of the considerations that had led to the formation of the Centre.[588]

6. CPR Minitrial Procedure

The CPR Institute has developed Model Minitrial Procedures for the US and Canada on the one hand and Europe on the other hand. The CPR procedures have many characteristic elements of a mini-trial: information exchange before a "neutral advisor" plus two executives with full settlement authority, immediate negotiations, and a flexible role of the neutral who gives an oral or written opinion and may mediate the negotiations as well as propose settlement terms.

II. LEGAL ISSUES ARISING OUT OF INTERNATIONAL ADR

In light of the multiple legal systems and their lack of coordination described throughout this book, effective dispute resolution in international disputes needs a legal framework ensuring that:

- The ADR-procedure is being conducted and that, parallel, competing procedures (no matter where) are excluded;

---

national Commercial Conciliation: From a Topic of Possible Discussion to Approval by the General Assembly", *Pepperdine Dispute Resolution Journal* 529 (2003); Sekolec & Getty, The UMA and UNCITRAL Model Rule: An Emerging Consensus on Mediation and Conciliation, Journal of Dispute Resolution 175 (2003); Niggemann, IDR 143 (2004).

[586] ICSID Conciliation Rules, cf. www.worldbank.org/icsid/basicdoc/partE.htm.

[587] In one case, an account has been published, cf. Nurick & Schnably, "The First ICSID Conciliation: *Tesoro Petroleum Corporation v. Trinidad and Tobago*", 1 *ICSID Rev.- F.I.L.J.* 340 (1986).

[588] Cf. Parra, The Role of the World Bank in the Settlement of International Investment Disputes, paper before the ABA National Institute on the Resolution of International Commercial Disputes (November 5-6, 1987).

- a result is reached within a reasonable time, with an adequate standard of procedural fairness, ensuring confidentiality and the neutrality of any third-party decision-maker;

- the result is final (i.e. it excludes any subsequent procedure no matter where) and enforceable worldwide.

1. Nature and Effects of ADR Clauses

a. Ensuring Participation

In the ADR agreement, the parties establish the roadmap for the resolution of future disputes arising out of their transaction or within the general framework of their business relationship.[589] Since ADR processes are based on voluntary participation, the parties may want to increase the likelihood that the ADR procedure will be used by inserting into their contract a clause expressly providing for an ADR process in the event of a dispute. The question whether the agreement to conduct an ADR process is substantive or procedural in nature is subject to controversy. Only one point is not disputed: regarding its effect to exclude parallel litigation, the agreement is of a procedural nature, and procedural matters are invariably regulated by the *lex fori*.[590]

Since in international business standard contract terms are widely used, the question arises whether an ADR process can be agreed upon by merely accepting the other party's standard terms. So far, this question has not been sufficiently addressed with regard to international ADR proceedings.[591]

ADR procedures are a consensual means of dispute resolution, depending on a minimum of cooperation from all parties involved. They are most successful when the parties participate on a voluntary basis. Hence, one of the most important problems in the practice of alternative procedures is to *get the parties to participate*. This may be difficult when the parties have reached a point where negotiations have come to an impasse, and confidence in the parties' ability to reach an agreement is lost. Not infrequently the parties fail to perceive their interest in a settlement because they simply miscalculate the benefits of pursuing litigation or other alternatives to settlement (in negotiation jargon, they over-estimate their "BATNA"). In such a situation, even a reluctant participation in a mediation or a mini-trial can serve as an "eye-opener" and create a dynamic that, against all odds, might result in a

---

[589] Hacke, ADR-Vertrag (2001).

[590] Heß & Sharma in: Haft/Schliefen (eds.), *Handbuch Mediation*, § 26 Column No. 64 (2003).

[591] Cf. Eidenmüller, "Vertrags- und verfahrensrechtliche Grundfragen der Mediation: Möglichkeiten und Grenzen privatautonomen Konfliktmanagements", in Breidenbach et al. (eds.), *Konsensuale Streitbeilegung* 58 et seq. (2001) only from the perspective of German law.

settlement. It may therefore make sense to provide for a mandatory ADR procedure prior to litigation or arbitration.

In this context, however, the question arises as to whether an obligation to participate is enforceable. The matter is widely disputed[592] and, above all, raises issues of practicability. The alternatives to direct enforcement are indirect means such as damage payments for breach, and even more indirectly, the exclusion or suspension of other procedures and remedies.[593] Even if the parties make express provisions for enforcement, it may be up to the courts to determine the existence and the consequences of a breach of an ADR clause. Since there are only few precedents, it amounts to speculation to try to predict how the courts in various countries might interpret and enforce such clauses.[594] In addition, there is a significant potential for ancillary litigation over the actual content of such an obligation, i.e. whether it is sufficient to be physically present at the procedure or whether some effort to reach an agreement is required and if so how this effort is to be measured. Even in the United States, where the law on this point is most developed, the matter is far from being settled, although there have been a few decisions ordering damage payments and, at least in one case,[595] the specific enforcement of an ADR clause.

---

[592] See the discussion in Singer, *Settling Disputes* 84 (1990) and Carrel, "An ADR Clause by Any Other Name Might Smell as Sweet: England's High Court of Justice Queens Bench Attempts and Fails to Define what is not an Enforceable ADR Clause", *Journal of Dispute Resolution* 547 (2003); on the practical aspects, see also the discussion above at p. 167.

[593] Art. 13 of the UNCITRAL Model Law on International Commercial Conciliation provides that „[w]here the parties have agreed to conciliate and have expressly undertaken not to initiate [...] arbitral or judicial proceedings [...], such an undertaking shall be given effect by the arbitral tribunal or the court [...] except to the extent necessary for a party, in its opinion, to preserve its rights." For a discussion of this clause see Eidenmüller, „A Legal Framework for National and International Mediation Proceedings", *International Journal of Dispute Resolution* 14, 16 (BB-Beilage 7 zu Heft 46/2002).

[594] Some clues might be derived from decisions regarding the enforcement of renegotiation clauses. German courts have occasionally imposed damage payments for failure to participate in renegotiations, see Nelle, *Neuverhandlungspflichten* 23 et seq. (1994); see also the various contributions in Horn (ed.), *Adaptation and Renegotiation of Contracts in International Trade and Finance* (1985). In a recent decision of the English High Court of Justice Queens Bench Division, a very broad ADR clause was enforced (*Cable & Wireless Plc v. IBM United Kingdom Ltd.* [2002] 2 All E.R. 1041 (Q.B. 2002)). However, the requirements for enforceable ADR-clauses remain unclear, see Carrel, „An ADR Clause by Any Other Name Might Smell as Sweet: England's High Court of Justice Queens Bench Attempts and Fails to Define what is not an Enforceable ADR Clause", *Journal of Dispute Resolution* 547 (2003).

[595] *AMF v. Brunswick*, 621 F. Supp. 456 (E.D.N.Y. 1985). A recent District Court decision has extended the analysis used in Brunswick by saying that the Federal Arbitration Act (FAA), providing for enforcement of arbitration clauses in its Section 2, conceptually embraces all alternative means of dispute resolution, including mediation, cf. *Allied Sanitation Inc. v. Waste Mgmt. Holdings Inc.*, 97 F. Supp. 2d 320 (E.D.N.Y. 2000).

One way of motivating the parties not to sue shortly after negotiations or ADR processes have failed is the stipulation of a "cooling off" period during which no party may commence litigation. The effect of such a clause is not to force the parties back to the "table" but rather to create "breathing space" giving the parties time to reconsider and to work toward a consensual resolution. Whether the courts in different countries would respect such a provision is, again, a matter of speculation.

b. Excluding Competing Procedures

One of the main concerns with regard to the legal frame for alternative dispute resolution procedures is the need to *avoid parallel, competing procedures*, which in the context of international disputes can occur in several countries at the same time and which can result in conflicting outcomes. In addition, the exclusion of competing procedures serves as an indirect means of "enforcing" the agreement to use the procedure chosen.

An agreement to conduct an ADR procedure can explicitly state,[596] or may be interpreted as, a contractual obligation not to initiate any other procedure that might conflict with the agreed process.[597] A breach of this obligation not to sue may lead to a claim for damages, but it is doubtful whether it will actually oblige a court to decline jurisdiction over a matter brought before it. An obligation of the court to decline jurisdiction exists in most countries in the case of an arbitration clause but it is based on express statutory provisions. This recognition could be extended to non-binding procedures by statute,[598] and courts have gone so far as to include non-binding procedures under the notion of "arbitration" or to stay proceedings to force the parties to honor a contractual ADR clause on the basis that litigation in breach of an ADR clause would amount to an "abuse" of the court procedure.[599]

---

[596] While with Art. 16 of the UNCITRAL Conciliation Rules, the parties undertake not to initiate parallel proceedings, Art. 9 of the LCIA Mediation Procedure expressly allows the parties to initiate or continue such proceedings, unless they have agreed otherwise. Neither the ICC ADR Rules nor the AAA International Mediation Procedure contain similar provisions.

[597] However, such an interpretation might become less likely with the existence of Art. 9 LCIA Mediation Procedure since this provision shows that the exclusion of parallel proceedings is not an automatism parties reasonably can expect.

[598] Art. 13 of the UNCITRAL Model Law on International Commercial Conciliation contains a regulation providing for stay of arbitral and judicial proceedings when the parties have agreed to conciliate and have expressly undertaken not to resort to such measures.

[599] *AMF v. Brunswick*, 621 F. Supp. 456 (E.D.N.Y. 1985) considered non-binding ADR to be within the meaning of "arbitration" in accordance with the U.S. Federal Arbitration Act. For more details and further references to (in part unreported) cases from the United States and Australia (spelling out the "abuse" argument) see Rawding, „ADR: Bermuda's International Conciliation and Arbitration Act 1993", 10 *Arb. Int'l* 99, 101-103 (1994). The "abuse of process" argument in favor of enforcing mediation clauses is also advanced by Brown & Marriott, *ADR: Principles and Practice* 328-329 (1993). In an Australian case, the NSW

However, this would not prevent courts in other jurisdictions from hearing the case. An international convention that would mandate the recognition of the exclusive effect of agreements providing for mediation and other non-binding ADR procedures does not exist and cannot be expected in the near future. Arbitration conventions, notably Art. II of the New York Convention on the Recognition and Enforcement of Foreign Arbitral Awards, only cover clauses providing for "arbitration".

c. Suspension of Limitation Periods

In some cases, the parties may be concerned that, while they are attempting to settle their dispute amicably, some or all of their claims will be precluded due to the expiration of limitation periods. They therefore should include a clause like the one suggested by the CPR Institute, reading as follows:

> "All applicable statutes of limitation and defenses based upon the passage of time shall be tolled while the procedure(s) specified in this Article ... is pending. The parties will take such action, if any, required to effectuate such tolling."[600]

Even such a clause, however, cannot safeguard against all risks since it may not be enforced by the relevant forum court. [601]

2. Conducting the Procedure

In contrast to adjudicatory processes of dispute resolution, the parties are rather free in designing the conduct of the ADR procedure. The principle of party autonomy is of paramount importance. Time, place, language, admissible evidence, style of the third party neutral etc. are some of the many aspects that the parties ideally

---

Supreme Court found an agreement to conciliate – which had specified the procedure to be followed – as sufficiently concrete to be enforceable and ordered the stay of an arbitration proceeding that had been commenced in defiance of said agreement to conciliate, *Hooper Bailie Associated Ltd. v. Natcon Group Pty Ltd.*, (1992) 28 NSWLR 194; see discussion by Newton, "Australian Update: ADR makes Further Gains", 5 *World Arb. & Med. Rep.* 109 (1994).

[600] Cf. www.cpradr.org.

[601] The UNCITRAL Model Law on International Commercial Conciliation deals with the problem by suggesting an optional "Article X" for "States that might wish to adopt a provision on the suspension of the limitation period": "(1) When the conciliation proceedings commence, the running of the limitation period regarding the claim that is the subject matter of the conciliation is suspended. (2) Where the conciliation proceedings have terminated without a settlement agreement, the limitation period resumes running from the time the conciliation ended without a settlement agreement." In Germany, the new sections 203 and 204 Civil Code (BGB) provide for suspension of the limitation period in connection with ADR procedures, for details see Eidenmüller, "Die Auswirkungen der Einleitung eines ADR-Verfahrens auf die Verjährung", 4 *SchiedsVZ* 163 (2003).

agree on before the proceedings commence. Generally, the parties conclude a contract with the ADR neutral which incorporates all these issues. Addressing all possible scenarios and facets of the conduct of the ADR proceedings from a legal perspective goes beyond the scope of this book. We will therefore focus on two core issues: the professional conduct of the neutral and a minimum due-process standard in ADR proceedings.

a. Conduct of the ADR Neutral

One of the parties' main concern during the ADR proceedings is the quality of service of the ADR neutral.[602] Absent binding and enforceable rules on professional conduct and ethics of international ADR neutrals, the parties are confined to agree on professional standards in a contract with the third party neutral.[603] Such standards include disclosure of conflicts of interests, experience and required qualifications, as well as impartiality and neutrality.[604] In practice, such obligations seem very difficult to enforce and sanctions, if any, against a neutral in breach of his contractual obligations would be limited to damages.[605] Sometimes, the only way out may be for the dissatisfied party to drop out of the mediation. Given this limited scope of the "legal arsenal", it is advisable for the parties to spend considerable time choosing an ADR neutral who fits their standards of conduct and ethics.

b. Minimum Due-Process Standard

Another legal issue deals with the question whether the general rules of due process must be followed in international ADR processes. So far, this question has been addressed in the national context only.[606] The concern for procedural

---

[602] Eidenmüller, "A Legal Framework for National and International Mediation Proceedings", *Journal of International Dispute Resolution* 14, 17 (BB- Beilage 7 zu Heft 46/2002).

[603] Heß & Sharma in Haft/Schlieffen (eds.), *Handbuch Mediation*, § 26 Column No. 66 (2003); Eidenmüller, "Vertrags- und verfahrensrechtliche Grundfragen der Mediation: Möglichkeiten und Grenzen privatautonomen Konfliktmanagements", in Breidenbach et al. (eds.), *Konsensuale Streitbeilegung* 92 (2001).

[604] Cf. Sec. 9 of the UMA, Art. 5 and 6 of the UNCITRAL Model Law, and questions 20 and 21 of the Green Paper of the European Commission.

[605] Eidenmüller, "A Legal Framework for National and International Mediation Proceedings", *Journal of International Dispute Resolution* 14, 17 (BB- Beilage 7 zu Heft 46/2002); Eidenmüller, "Vertrags- und verfahrensrechtliche Grundfragen der Mediation: Möglichkeiten und Grenzen privatautonomen Konfliktmanagements", in Breidenbach et al. (eds.), *Konsensuale Streitbeilegung* 77 et seq., 92 (2001); Heß & Sharma in Haft/Schlieffen (eds.), *Handbuch Mediation*, § 26 Column No. 33 (2003).

[606] Cf. Heß & Sharma in Haft/Schlieffen (eds.), *Handbuch Mediation*, § 26 Column No. 47 et seq. (2003); Eidenmüller, "Vertrags- und verfahrensrechtliche Grundfragen der Mediation: Möglichkeiten und Grenzen privatautonomen Konfliktmanagements", in Breidenbach et al. (eds.), *Konsensuale Streitbeilegung* 45, 76 (2001).

fairness is less urgent in non-binding procedures since the parties do not submit to the decisionmaking power of a third party and are free to terminate the proceedings if they are dissatisfied with the process. In this case, the ADR process simply fails and there is no settlement agreement that might subsequently be attacked. The issue can become relevant, however, in cases where the parties do conclude the procedure and come to an agreement but where, with hindsight, one of them considers the process to be flawed.

3. The Importance of Back-up Dispute Resolution Processes

ADR procedures are non-binding in that no third party is empowered to render a final decision. It is exclusively up to the parties to control the outcome of their dispute. The influence of the legal framework on the quality and predictability of any ADR settlement agreements is indirect but nonetheless important: to the extent that an effective back-up is available, the parties will find it easier to make their rights respected in an ADR settlement because each of them knows that they have a solid adjudication "BATNA". Hence, in non-binding ADR procedures the ultimate resolution of the dispute can only be ensured by providing for an effective, binding *back-up procedure*, or at least by making sure that the ADR procedure does not pre-empt any existing back-ups such as court litigation. This is the inverse problem to the danger that ADR agreements may not be recognized to the extent they preclude competing procedures.

The availability of a back-up and in particular the effectiveness of an arbitration agreement can be thwarted when the completion of the ADR proceedings is regarded by a court or an arbitral tribunal as a precondition to commencement of litigation or arbitration. Such a policy opens the door for dilatory maneuvers by a reluctant defendant seeking to drag out the ADR process indefinitely in order to avoid a resolution of the claim.[607] The problem can, however, be solved in the ADR clause itself simply by providing reasonable time limits for the ADR procedure which can only be extended by agreement of all parties, and by making it clear that the parties are free to pursue other remedies once the period set aside for mediation has lapsed.[608]

4. Maintaining Confidentiality

A serious issue in practice is how to protect the *confidentiality* of the ADR procedure. Although some national laws touch upon the question of whether the content of the ADR process is admissible evidence in subsequent court or arbitration proceed-

---

[607] Cf. Perlman & Nelson, "New Approaches to the Resolution of International Commercial Disputes", 17 *Bus. Law.* 215, 242, 248 (1983).

[608] Cf. "Suggested ICC ADR Clauses", which provide for a 45-day period of settlement attempts after which the parties are free to pursue other options.

ings,[609] many issues remain unaddressed. The parties can extend the scope of confidentiality by means of contractual obligations. Most model ADR rules provide that all communications, representations, admissions, proposals, actions (in short: everything that happened in the course of the procedure) remain confidential and may not be introduced into any subsequent judicial or arbitral procedure.

However, whether a court will respect such an agreement or whether it will simply order, as a matter of public policy and judicial authority, the disclosure of any pertinent documents or the testimony by any of the participants in the ADR procedure, will depend on the laws and legal practice in the respective jurisdiction.[610] Since there are few express legal rules or precedents, it is difficult to predict what a court in a given case might do. It may therefore be well worth considering at least to avoid any written documentation of the process.[611]

5. Enforcing the Result

If the parties do reach a settlement in a non-binding procedure, their agreement will have the legal nature of a contractual obligation. This means that it is not in the same way *final* as a court judgment or an arbitral award since it does not have a *res iudicata* effect and can therefore not preclude any subsequent proceedings in the same matter. And it is also not directly *enforceable* but has to be fully litigated as a contractual claim.

Under some laws, settlements can have similar effects as judgments or arbitral awards if they are recorded in a public instrument or meet certain other formal requirements.[612] Generelly, such provisions only cover domestic settlements, and do not ensure that the enforceability of the settlement will be recognized in other

---

[609] The UMA contains many provisions that privilege mediation communication. Art. 10 of the UNCITRAL Model Law contains an unspecific exception on the admissibility of evidence in other proceedings. The German Code of Civil Procedure contains a provision in its sec. 383 Para.1. No. 6, Para. 3 barring mediators from testifying in court provided they belong to certain privileged professions like attorneys, doctors, judges etc.

[610] For the situation in Germany see Eidenmüller, *Vertrags- und Verfahrensrecht der Wirt-schaftsmediation* 23-29 (2001): Generally, the parties may agree to keep certain information confidential and courts are bound to respect such agreements.

[611] The ICDR (AAA) and LCIA Mediation Rules expressly exclude written transcripts of the Procedure: M-13 AAA International Mediation Rules; Art. 10.5 LCIA Mediaton Rules.

[612] Cf. Sec. 1053 of the German *Zivilprozessordnung* (ZPO – Code of Civil Procedure). The settlement may even be directly enforceable without the need of an *exequatur* if it is recorded in an enforceable public instrument before a notary public (Sec. 1053 para. 4). The enforceability of settlements reached in mediation – on a domestic basis – has been provided for in the arbitration statutes of Bermuda and of several American states (e.g. California), see Rawding, "ADR: Bermuda's International Conciliation and Arbitration Act 1993", 10 *Arb. Int'l* 99, 100-101 (1994) and Sanders, "Unity and Diversity in the Adoption of the Model Law", 11 *Arb. Int'l* 1, 28 (1995).

jurisdictions. There are only a limited number of international agreements that mandate the recognition and enforcement of foreign *enforceable* public instruments (other than court judgments and arbitral awards). An example is Art. 57 of the Brussels I Regulation according to which authentic instruments and court settlements which are enforceable in a member state have to be recognized and enforced in the same procedure as a judgment from that state.

Some procedures provide "teeth" to the recommendations of the neutral by making them admissible in subsequent proceedings or by establishing penalties in case the party who rejected the recommendation does not attain, in the subsequent litigation or arbitration procedure, a certain minimum result relative to the recommendation issued by the neutral. It is, again, a question of the respective national law and practice, which will often be non-existing or in its infancy, whether such sanctions are recognized by the courts. In particular, it is far from sure that a court in a given country will allow itself to be restricted in its evaluation of the evidence and attribute the exact evidentiary weight to the findings of the mediator or expert that the parties had intended. And contractual penalties are subject to restrictions under many laws.

While the UMA does not address the enforceability issue at all, the UNCITRAL Model Law, in its Article 14, leaves it to the implementing states to determine the appropriate enforcement methods. This potentially leads to an undesirable and internationally impractical variety of different enforcement mechanisms.[613]

So far, the legal issues and their resolution depend for the most part on the *lex fori*, i.e. the legal regime in force where litigation takes place. In theory, the parties can determine the forum via choice-of-forum clauses. Selecting an "ADR friendly" forum, in principle, allows the parties to control the legal issues, especially the enforcement of the ADR settlement, in favor of the ADR processes. Practice, however, often looks different: firstly, choice of forum clauses are limited[614], and secondly, the attitude of a forum towards ADR processes is only a minor factor in considering the forum; costs and the predictability of the decision are usually more important.[615]

6. Conclusion

The discussion of the legal issues raised by international commercial ADR procedures has revealed the following picture:

---

[613] Eidenmüller, "A Legal Framework for National and International Mediation Proceedings", *Journal of Dispute Resolution* 14, 18 (BB- Beilage 7 zu Heft 46/2002).

[614] For example under the doctrine of *forum non conveniens* or consumer protection provisions, cf. Eidenmüller, "A Legal Framework for National and International Mediation Proceedings", *Journal of Dispute Resolution* 14, 18 (BB- Beilage 7 zu Heft 46/2002).

[615] Eidenmüller, "A Legal Framework for National and International Mediation Proceedings", *Journal of Dispute Resolution* 14, 18 (BB- Beilage 7 zu Heft 46/2002).

– there is no effective way yet to compel participation and to ensure that the procedure is conducted; competing procedures can be excluded contractually (unless the mediation is integrated into an ongoing international arbitration protected by the New York Convention);

– to preserve their rights, the parties are advised to provide for a suspension of the limitation period themselves;

– there is less concern about the way the process is conducted and about neutrality of the ADR neutral since the procedure is in the hands of the parties;

– parties can extend the scope of confidentiality by means of contractual obligations; most model ADR rules provide that all communications, representations, admissions, proposals, actions remain confidential and may not be introduced into any subsequent judicial or arbitral procedure; if no settlement is reached, it cannot be guaranteed that the courts in a given country will respect the confidentiality of the ADR procedure;

– the quality of the result is in the hands of the parties who can veto any solution but the lack of an effective back-up makes it harder for a party to have its rights respected;

– it cannot be ensured that a result is reached, and care has to be taken not to cut off any back-up procedures that may be needed if no settlement is reached; the finality of the result is not guaranteed, and subsequent proceedings in the same matter cannot be excluded; the resulting settlement only has the binding force of a contractual obligation and accordingly may require full litigation for its enforcement (except in the rare case that it is recorded in an enforceable public instrument and benefits from an international agreement warranting enforcement abroad).

The weaknesses of the legal framework of international ADR constitute serious disadvantages. Of particular relevance are the limitiations to exclude competing procedures and to guarantee the finality and enforceability of the results.[616] These flaws can render the entire procedure futile and, worse still, may even have the effect of precluding other methods of resolving the dispute. As long as national

---

[616] As explained above, the situation is somewhat different under the system of the Brussels I Regulation which among its member states ensures that litigation operates as an effective back-up procedure and which provides for the enforcement of foreign public instruments. Articles 13 and 14 of the UNCITRAL Model Law on International Commercial Conciliation, providing for a stay of proceedings and enforcement of settlement agreements, are partly "without teeth", allowing for broad exceptions (stay of proceedings) and leaving the specific procedures to be followed up to the countries (enforcement).

legal systems will not have fully developed the structures necessary to support ADR procedures, and as long as the treatment of ADR procedures will not be coordinated between different jurisdictions, international ADR procedures entail legal risks, at least to the extent they are conducted outside of the established framework of international commercial arbitration.

III. INTEGRATING ADR INTO ARBITRATION FRAMEWORK

Providing for arbitration in the event of a failure of settlement negotiations may already make sense from a pure process perspective because it creates an effective back-up that guarantees a resolution of the dispute and serves as an incentive to reach a fair solution on agreed terms. In addition, arbitration offers the best legal framework for international commercial dispute resolution. This raises the question to which extent the legal shortcomings of international ADR procedures can be solved if these procedures are integrated into the framework of an arbitration procedure. Due to the principle of party autonomy and the great flexibility of the arbitral procedure, there are no general objections against providing for mediation or any other non-binding settlement procedure either before the initiation of arbitration proceedings or at any point thereafter. In particular, the enforceability of an arbitral award will not be endangered by the fact that the arbitration procedure was preceded or accompanied by mediation attempts as long as the arbitrators maintain their impartiality and the procedure was "in accordance with the agreement of the parties."[617] However, care must be taken to specify exactly how the ADR procedure is intended to be conducted and how it relates to the arbitration process. Whether and how the issues raised above can be solved through the use of the framework of international commercial arbitration shall be discussed in the following.

1. Initiating / Excluding Competing Procedures

The legal framework of arbitration does not make it more likely to obtain specific enforcement of an obligation to try mediation but it does make it easier to indirectly compel the participation in a settlement procedure prior to arbitration through financial penalties or by suspending the beginning of the actual arbitration procedure.

Arbitrators can be expected to respect a penalty clause in the arbitration agreement as long as the clause is precise enough as to the content of the obligation and the computation of the penalty. A simple but effective way to give "teeth" to an ADR clause is to instruct the arbitrators to consider any failure to make a good faith effort at settlement as a key factor in the allocation of the costs and to expressly authorize them to order the uncooperative party to reimburse the legal costs of the other party. The suspension of the arbitration procedure, e.g. through a

---

[617] Cf. Art. V 1. (d) of the New York Convention.

"cooling off" period, is also likely to be respected by an arbitral tribunal and may serve as an incentive to engage in serious negotiations, but care must be taken not to undermine the arbitration clause.

In any event it is important to specify in the dispute resolution clause whether the parties are required to go through the ADR procedure before filing a request for arbitration or whether they can initiate the arbitration right away, with the possible consequence of setting in motion a specified period during which a mediation or other settlement procedure has to be conducted before the arbitral tribunal will be constituted. In the event the parties want to allow for discovery in preparation of the mediation they will have to determine the extent of the discovery permitted and the ensuing obligations of the parties.

An arbitration clause is capable of excluding competing procedures within the entire realm of the New York Convention. This protection functions independently of whether the arbitration clause provides for pre-arbitral mediation.

As to the relation between the arbitration itself and the alternative procedure, they are not to be viewed as competing with each other but the arbitration will only be conducted – or continued – in the event of a failure to reach a mediated settlement within a specified time after initiation of the mediation.

If all parties to a multi-party dispute are subject to an arbitration agreement, mediation may be the best vehicle to achieve – ideally – a settlement, or at least a voluntary consolidation or a more manageable structure for a separate resolution of the various conflicts contained within the multi-party dispute. Where the applicable law allows for a mandatory consolidation of the arbitration the tribunal might be authorized in the arbitration agreement to suspend the proceedings temporarily to pressure the parties to participate in mediation. A party forced into an arbitration procedure against its will might find a mediated solution to be the "lesser of the two evils".

2. Conduct of the Procedure

As mentioned, the legal framework of arbitration permits to flexibly adjust the procedure to the needs of the parties while guaranteeing the neutrality of the tribunal, a minimum standard of procedural fairness, as well as to achieve a reasonable degree of discovery and to limit judicial review to the most basic questions. The arbitral framework makes no difference to the confidentiality of any settlement: the parties are under a contractual obligation but there is no way to actually prevent violations.

Integrating the ADR procedure into an arbitration opens the possibility to request the arbitrators to issue interim measures of protection. However, this does not make a great difference in practice because, as mentioned, such measures face enforcement difficulties, are not available against third parties and require that the tribunal be already constituted, which is unlikely in pre-arbitral ADR. Hence, even within the framework of arbitration is it advisable to permit the parties to request preliminary relief in the courts.

3. Quality of Results

The combination with arbitration offers an advantage with respect to the quality and predictability of negotiated solutions since it presents an effective back-up procedure allowing the parties, if a satisfactory agreement cannot be reached, to enforce their rights through a reasonably predictable and legitimate decision by a tribunal with expertise in the applicable law, the relevant trade usages or any technical matters at issue.

4. Effective Termination of the Dispute

As mentioned above, in a combined ADR-arbitration clause it is important to include time limits for any pre-arbitral ADR procedure in order to avoid that the arbitration clause is undermined by fruitless settlement attempts and delay tactics.[618]

The finality and the enforceability of any agreement reached in the ADR procedure can be enhanced by requesting the arbitral tribunal to issue a consent award or "*award on agreed terms*". Such an award will have the same effect and status as any regular arbitral award and will benefit from international currency under the New York Convention.[619] A consequence of the issuance of an arbitral award is the termination of the tribunal's mandate and the obviation of the arbitration agreement.[620] In order to cover any future disputes that may arise out of the execution or non-performance of the recorded settlement the parties will therefore have to include a new arbitration clause.[621] Arbitrators are free to refuse the issuance of a consent award at least to the extent that the settlement was not entered into voluntarily or if the terms of the settlement are grossly unfair or violate public policy under the applicable law. However, these are rare exceptions, and it can be regarded as part of the mission of arbitrators to record a settlement when they are asked to do so by the parties.[622]

An award on agreed terms, of course, requires that the tribunal be in place. Hence, to the extent that a settlement contains obligations to be performed in the future and which are capable of being directly enforced (e.g. future money payments

---

[618] Cf. the examples given in the "Suggested ICC ADR Clauses".

[619] Berger, *International Economic Arbitration* 582 (1993); Redfern & Hunter, *Law and Practice of International Commercial Arbitration* 383-385 (3rd ed. 1999); van den Berg, *The New York Convention of 1958* 49-50 (1981); Wegen, *Vergleich und Klagerücknahme im Internationalen Prozeß* 397 (1987).

[620] At least to the extent that the matters referred to arbitration have been disposed of.

[621] Cf. Berger id. 587.

[622] Berger id. 583-585.

but not, in many jurisdictions, the obligation to refrain from competition) it may be worthwhile to pursue the constitution of the tribunal solely for the purpose of obtaining a consent-award – the extra expense might be justified by the added security.

It should be noted that even in the form of a consent award the ADR settlement agreement raises legal issues.[623] A core question is whether the arbitration procedure must commence before the ADR process is conducted or whether it is sufficient to initiate arbitration only in the event that the ADR process fails. It might seem very technical to differentiate these two options, but the importance cannot be underestimated: If arbitration is initiated first, the New York Convention shields not only the arbitration process but also the ADR process from parallel transnational litigation, as they are both part of the arbitration procedure. In this case, however, it is disputed whether the minimum rules of due process in arbitration apply to the ADR proceedings also.[624] If that were to be the case, there could be more grounds for challenging the award, e.g. if the mediator used private caucuses with the parties[625] or if the roles of mediator and arbitrator were assumed by the same person.[626]

In the event of a failure to reach an agreement the arbitral framework presents a significant advantage. Not only because it guarantees a decision but also because an arbitral tribunal is bound by the arbitration agreement and is therefore more likely than a national court to respect any covenants with respect to the exclusion of any statements or events from admission into evidence or, conversely, the admissibility of and the weight accorded to the opinion rendered by a mediator or a neutral expert in the preceding ADR procedure.[627] Finally, as with the duty to participate in mediation, an arbitral tribunal is also more likely than a court to enforce any financial penalties for rejection of the neutral's proposal on the basis of fee-shift provisions.

5. Advantages of Using the Arbitral Framework

If done right, the integration of non-binding (or "semi-binding") settlement procedures into an arbitration agreement within the realm of the New York Convention will make it possible to solve most of the problems raised by ADR procedures in a transnational context:

---

[623] Rau/Sherman & Peppet, *Processes of Dispute Resolution: The Role of Lawyers*, 936 et seq. (3rd ed. 2002); Eidenmüller, "Vertrags- und verfahrensrechtliche Grundfragen der Mediation: Möglichkeiten und Grenzen privatautonomen Konfliktmanagements", in Breidenbach et al. (eds.), *Konsensuale Streitbeilegung* 81 et seq., 93 (2001).

[624] Eidenmüller id. 84 et seq.

[625] Eidenmüller id.

[626] Cf. Bühring-Uhle, 366 et seq. (1996); Eidenmüller id. 86 (2001).

[627] Cf. Perlman and Nelson, "New Approaches to the Resolution of International Commercial Disputes", 17 *Bus. Law.* 215, 249-250 (1983).

- through indirect enforcement mechanisms it can help to ensure the participation of unwilling parties in the ADR procedure, and to exclude competing parallel procedures;

- it provides a binding back-up procedure with a guaranteed standard of fairness and neutrality; the confidentiality of the procedure is guaranteed in a limited but significant respect since statements, actions, and events occurring during the ADR procedure can be excluded from evidence at least in the subsequent arbitration proceedings;

- the arbitration "back-up" not only ensures in the event of no-agreement a reasonably predictable and legitimate decision but it also has an effect on the quality of any results achieved in mediation because it provides the parties with an effective back-up to enforce their rights;

- the arbitration "back-up" guarantees that a resolution of the dispute will be reached and that it will be final and enforceable; in "semi-binding" ADR procedures, the arbitration back-up secures the enforcement of sanctions;

Disadvantages deriving from the combination of ADR procedures with arbitration do not have to be feared – as long as the clause is drafted carefully so as to avoid undermining the arbitration agreement.

The integration of mediation or other alternative settlement procedures into the framework of arbitration hence permits to have the "best of both worlds" by combining the process advantages of ADR with the legal framework of international commercial arbitration. Whether such a combination should be adopted in a particular case depends on an assessment of whether the additional costs are worth the potential benefits that can be derived from a successful mediation. In light of the benefits of effective conflict management, a mediation attempt will in most situations be well worth the limited investment it requires.

IV. CONCLUSION

Even on a domestic level, the legal framework governing alternative dispute resolution procedures is, at best, in the process of being developed. Model ADR rules exist, both for domestic and international disputes, but they are of a purely contractual nature. In light of the absence of an international law of ADR, alternative procedures are therefore subject to the full range of problems that can arise in a multi-jurisdictional context, particularly the inability to exclude competing procedures and to guarantee the finality and enforceability of the results. The legal problems arising out of the use of alternative procedures in transnational disputes can best be solved by integrating the process into the framework of international commercial arbitration. Many institutional arbitration procedures and model rules for ad hoc arbitration allow the inclusion of non-binding procedures such as preliminary fact-finding and particularly mediation within the framework of arbitration.

How arbitration and mediation can be combined in practice will be examined in Part Four in a more detailed fashion.

PART FOUR:
SYNTHESIS

The key points of this book so far can be summed up as follows: Part One shows that conflict management poses a growing challenge for international business and that, in a multi-jurisdictional context, litigation in national courts is not the most effective answer. Part Two explains how international commercial arbitration solves most of the problems connected with the multiplicity of legal systems but reveals that it has shortcomings comparable to those of domestic litigation in terms of its high transaction costs and limited capacity to bring about consensual solutions. Reconciling the interests of the parties is the most constructive way of resolving private business disputes. Part Three shows how modern business mediation and related techniques facilitate consensual solutions with a potential to create value through mutual gains for the parties. However, international ADR has its own drawbacks since it still has a rather poorly developed legal framework. Most of the problems can be solved when alternative procedures are integrated into the flexible legal framework of international commercial arbitration. The empirical work conducted by the authors shows that most international arbitrators are aware of this potential, but that uncertainty exists as to when and how to integrate the various techniques.

By way of a synthesis, the final Part of this study looks at how procedures can be designed that combine the benefits of arbitration and mediation.

Chapter 9

Designing Procedures for Effective Conflict Management

In international business relations, no single procedure exists that is suitable for each and every type of dispute. Even more than in the domestic field, dispute resolution procedures have to be tailored to meet the particularities of the conflict, the type of transactions involved, as well as the legal, economic, social, and cultural backgrounds of the various participants. However, as explained above, good conflict management should in any event aspire to satisfy the interests of the parties by combining a structured, interest-based negotiation with an effective back-up procedure that guarantees a final and principled resolution of the dispute. As we have seen, the goal of ensuring a constructive negotiation process is best achieved by interest-based mediation while arbitration remains the most effective back-up procedure in a multi-jurisdictional context.

Arbitration may be combined with mediation in a number of ways. The empirical work has shown that more or less "intuitive" settlement and mediation attempts by the arbitrator are not uncommon in the practice of international arbitration.

This practice is reflected in the WIPO Arbitration Rules which expressly state in article 65 (a):

"The Tribunal may suggest that the parties explore settlement at such times as the Tribunal may deem appropriate."

To some practitioners, settlement attempts are indeed part of the essence of the arbitrator's mandate:

"An arbitrator, is an arbitrator, is an arbitrator, whose function it is, not merely to adjudicate the dispute but also to help resolve it amicably with the co-operation of the parties. ... 'Arbitration' must never be considered as excluding from its purview the settlement of a dispute before the arbitrator: because this is the essence of the spirit of arbitration."[628]

---

[628] Nariman, "The Spirit of Arbitration, The Tenth Annual Goff Lecture", 16 *Arb Int'l* 261, at p. 267 (2000).

However, in the eyes of many, the roles of arbitrator and mediator are incompatible, and in the vast majority of cases the settlement activities performed by arbitrators present a rather low intensity of third-party intervention in the negotiation process. The reason behind this restraint is a fundamental *dilemma* between the effectiveness of mediation and the procedural integrity of arbitration:

> "The pitfalls that are likely to be encountered by direct involvement in the settlement process are pretty obvious, but their importance cannot be overemphasised. ... All arbitrators, international and domestic alike, owe a duty to the parties to perform their part in resolving the dispute in respect of which they have been appointed in as fair, efficient and cost-effective a way as is reasonably possible. Any steps that may lead to a challenge to the arbitrator will delay the resolution of the dispute, and will increase costs. Any steps that may lead to the setting aside of the award will do so exponentially."[629]

This chapter first examines the arbitrator's dilemma in more detail and then looks at ways of overcoming it through strategies of combination or integration that aim at realizing the full potential of mediation without compromising the integrity of the arbitral procedure. Finally, we shall attempt to develop a systematic approach to process design for international business disputes.

I. THE ARBITRATOR'S DILEMMA

As we have explained, arbitrators who want to facilitate a negotiated settlement face a dilemma between the effectiveness of the mediation attempt and the integrity of the arbitral procedure. The root of this dilemma is the danger of confusing two potentially incompatible roles.

In mediation, the quest for an efficient and value-creating solution makes it necessary to explore the interests behind the parties' legal positions. The neutral therefore may have to ask the parties for confidential information that is not supposed to influence his decision as an arbitrator. Another important element of effective mediation is "reality-testing" – the mediator has to confront and put into question the parties' positions on the merits in order to narrow the difference between them and to deflate exaggerated demands. Both reality-testing and exploring the parties' real interests can work particularly well when the mediator meets the parties separately. Finally, in order for mediation to be effective, the intermediary frequently has to build a more personal relationship with the parties.

By contrast, the task of adjudicating a dispute requires a high level of detachment and emotional distance from the parties as persons as well as from their interests and

---

[629] Collins, "Do International Arbitral Tribunals have any Obligations to Encourage Settlement of the Disputes Before Them?", 19 (3) *Arb. Int'l* 333-343, at 337 (2003).

positions. The integrity of the adjudicative process is imperiled when contentions by one side remain unchallenged by the other side or when the arbitrator obtains information that he must disregard when deciding the dispute; and his impartiality is threatened when he expresses his thoughts on the merits before having seen all the evidence and legal arguments.

As a consequence, the arbitrator will tend to be rather cautious in expressing his views and eliciting sensitive information. This, in turn, reduces the effectiveness of his mediation attempts. In addition, the prospect of dealing with the person who may later have to decide the dispute can discourage the parties from being honest and candid to the mediator, thus further weakening the effectiveness of the mediation process.

This confusion of roles and the resulting interference between the processes can only be overcome if mediation and arbitration are conducted as two distinct processes. The most effective way to achieve a clear separation is to have different persons perform the two tasks. In this case, the risk of compromising the procedural integrity of arbitration and the danger of a challenge against the arbitrator or against the award on the grounds of a confusion of the two roles are eliminated. An additional advantage of having two neutrals is that the quality of both processes can be improved, especially if the two are chosen accordingly, e.g. a process expert as mediator and a legal or technical specialist as arbitrator.

However, the empirical findings on mediation attempts by the arbitrator (see Chapter Four), as well as the example of the I.B.M.-Fujitsu arbitration (see below), reveal that, in practice, it is not infrequently the same person that performs elements of both tasks. In personal interviews, a whole number of arbitrators reported that they resort to a broad array of settlement techniques and still revert to the role of a decisionmaker without fearing to compromise their impartiality.

One might argue that the two tasks can be separated not only through the structure of the process but, above all, in the mind of the arbitrator: he has to conduct mediation and arbitration clearly as separate processes and must make sure that his behavior – and that of the parties – will be adjusted accordingly. At any moment of the procedure it must be clear in which capacity he is acting. And in his mind he must try to build a "Chinese Wall": when he reverts to the role of arbitrator, he must disregard any information that is *immaterial* to a decision on the basis of the applicable law; he will also have to disregard any *material* information that was obtained in private caucuses and therefore could not be challenged by the other side.[630]

---

[630] Cf. Sec. 2B (3) of the Hong Kong Arbitration Ordinance (1997), which mandates that the arbitrator discloses to the other parties all information obtained in confidence to the extent he considers the information material to the arbitration proceedings; such a disclosure, however, might violate the confidentiality of the caucuses if the parties are not in advance made aware of this possibility. Also, it is recommendable to grant an opportunity for comment to the party whose confidential information is about to be disclosed before disclosing the information to the other side.

What causes lawyers most concern is the idea of the mediator privately caucusing with each side. The right to know and be able to answer an opponent's case is fundamental to most notions of justice. But what if one side has no way of knowing what the other side might have said, and what influence that might have on the mediator turned arbitrator?[631]

Beside the problem of dealing with information gained during caucus, the mediator turned arbitrator must distance himself in his mind from any views he may have expressed in the course of the mediation in order to render an impartial decision on the basis of the – admissible and properly presented – evidence.

> "...the arbitrator ... must remain capable of ruling against one party; this requires hardness and distance to the parties; already in normal arbitration, arbitrators must resist an urge to split the baby, to soften the results, e.g. in the quantification of damages; this is much harder after having acted as a mediator ... the skills [he needs as] a mediator in order to "add value" are: to empathize with the parties, to find and emphasize common ground between them ... to question their assumptions and test their sense of the reality ... and to divert the focus of the discussion away from the purely legal aspects ... to be able to jump back and forth requires a rare strength of character ..."[632]

The hybrid role of the mediator-arbitrator is so demanding that many practitioners prefer to err on the side of caution:

> "When acting as a mediator, I have no doubt about my own impartiality should I later find myself as the arbitrator in the same matter. However, if I am acting as counsel, I may well be concerned about the appropriateness of such a structure and may be sceptical about the mediator/adjudicator's ability to remain impartial. It is a bit like one of those irregular verbs: *I* am impartial, *you* are capable of being impartial; *he* is probably biased."[633]

In sum: faced with the complexity of the arbitrator's dilemma, in many scenarios it may be strongly advisable to have different persons perform the tasks of mediator and arbitrator.[634] In the next section, different strategies for combining the processes will be analysed.

---

[631] Elliott, "Med/Arb: Fraught with Danger or Ripe with Opportunity?", 62 (3) *J. Chartered Inst. Arb.*, 176 (1996).

[632] Interview with an American in-house counsel conducted in April of 1992.

[633] Oghigian, "The Mediation/Arbitration Hybrid", 20 (1) *Journal of International Arbitration* 75, 75-80 (2003).

[634] An intermediate option exists where the tribunal is comprised of three arbitrators. Here, the separation of the tasks can be partially achieved by entrusting only certain members of the tribunal with the task of mediating a settlement. The different constellations in which members of the tribunal can have different roles in this process are discussed in the empirical

II. STRATEGIES OF INTEGRATING THE PROCESSES

"An increasing number of variations on the med/arb process are emerging: mediate first and if mediation fails, arbitrate; start arbitration proceedings and allow for mediation at some point during the arbitration; mediate some issues and arbitrate others; mediate, then arbitrate some unresolved issues, then turn to mediation; mediate, if unsuccessful ask for an "advisory opinion" by the mediator which is binding as an award unless either party vetoes the opinion within a limited period of time. Another med/arb variation growing in popularity is mediation, if unsuccessful, followed by a final offer by each side, coupled with limited argument, following which the mediator turned arbitrator must choose one or other of the offers."[635]

Among the rich panorama of possible ways to combine and integrate the processes, four concepts will constitute the focus of our analysis: *pre-arbitral mediation* (1.), *post-arbitral mediation* (2.), *complete integration* between arbitration, mediation and other ADR processes as in the IBM/Fujitsu case (3.), and *explicit integration of mediation windows* in the arbitral process (4.).

1. Pre-Arbitral Mediation

a. Concept

The most common combination of mediation and arbitration is pre-arbitral mediation. Pre-arbitral mediation can occur at two different stages of the dispute: mediation can either be used as an immediate precursor to arbitration, as a last attempt to settle the dispute before a request for arbitration is filed. This is the situation envisaged by many of the institutional mediation or conciliation rules. Or mediation comes earlier in the life of the dispute as part of a multi-step ADR scheme which provides for mediation as a routine procedure that has to be conducted within a fixed period after negotiations have reached a certain level without resolving the dispute.

The advantage of pre-arbitral mediation, in any event, is that it may make it possible to avoid arbitration proceedings altogether. In this regard, pre-arbitral mediation performs a filter function. A multi-step ADR clause has the additional advantage of ensuring early attention to an evolving dispute, making it easier to get to the roots of the conflict and to remedy the problem before damages grow out of proportion. By contrast, the timing of the classical model of pre-arbitral conciliation has a number of drawbacks which might explain why ICC ADR is resorted to in a

---

Chapter Four. The advantage is that at least one or two members of the tribunal preserve their complete impartiality by staying free of the dual role. However, those members of the tribunal who do mediate will still have to build separate compartments in their mind.

[635] Elliott, "Med/Arb: Fraught with Danger or Ripe with Opportunity?", 62 (3) *J. Chartered Inst. Arb.* 175 (1996).

comparatively small number of cases. When the parties are preparing for an impending arbitration, their minds are set on preparing and winning a fight. They may at that point have too one-sided a view of the probable outcome of the arbitration and may not realize the likely transaction costs. Also, there is always the danger that one party, usually the defendant, exploits pre-arbitral mediation for delay tactics. In addition, at this moment it is particularly difficult to initiate the procedure, i.e. to take the first step and to agree on the person of the mediator. Perhaps the most significant problem is that the parties simply lack the necessary information on the merits of the dispute:

> "...usually it only makes sense to negotiate settlement once the arbitration has commenced because beforehand there is a psychological block and parties also simply don't know enough about the strengths and weaknesses of their respective cases..."[636]

> "... the parties don't want mediation when they are preparing for arbitration because they are too convinced of their case and think they'll win ... at a certain stage of the dispute, the parties want a decision in an adversarial procedure; they go to great lengths trying to settle, but when they come to the conclusion that they can't settle, they want a binding decision, so there you just don't have room for mediation; in the course of the arbitration procedure, it starts again, parties realize that they didn't have a very clear idea of their case and now they can consider settlement again ..."[637]

> "...sometimes parties aren't ready to settle their case until they're staring an arbitration 'in the eye'."[638]

Hence, once a dispute has reached the stage where the parties are preparing to litigate before an arbitral tribunal, a mediation effort might have a greater potential for success if it is conducted not before the initiation of the arbitration but afterwards.[639]

b. Comment

A pre-arbitral mediation may be conducted by a separate neutral or by the same person who starts out as a mediator and, in the event of no agreement, continues as arbitrator. Especially where going through mediation is a precondition for arbitration, it is generally assumed that statements and admissions made during the mediation

---

[636] Interview with Eric Robine, February 21, 1992 (translation by the authors).

[637] Interview with a Swiss scholar and practitioner conducted in February of 1992 (translation by the authors).

[638] Interview with Peter J. Engstrom, April 24, 2002.

[639] This is one of the essential ideas behind "mediation windows" which will be explained below.

process cannot later be taken into account in the arbitration.[640] In order to avoid the problems associated with the arbitrator's dilemma, it is often held that the mediator may not personally take part in the subsequent arbitration.[641]

In practice, however, the concept of the same person first serving as mediator and subsequently acting as arbitrator can be described as gaining popularity[642]. In certain Asian arbitration legislations, this possibility has even been expressly recognized. For example, the Singapore International Arbitration Act of 2001 provides in section 17:

> (1) If all parties to any arbitral proceedings consent in writing and for so long as no party has withdrawn his consent in writing, an arbitrator or umpire may act as a conciliator.

> (4) No objection shall be taken to the conduct of arbitral proceedings by a person solely on the ground that that person had acted previously as a conciliator in accordance with this section.[643]

Some commentators explain this explicit approval of the dual role with the particular Asian culture, and argue that the silence of most other institutional rules as to the possibility of the arbitrator playing a dual role indicates that role separation is clearly favored. Others assume that what is not prohibited will, in certain circumstances, be permissible.

When both processes are conducted by the same person, concerns about the procedural integrity of the arbitration can be allayed to a certain extent by granting the parties the right to opt out of the arbitration part of the procedure if they do not feel comfortable with the dual role of the neutral ("med-arb opt-out"). This way the parties can avoid being submitted to a binding decision by the mediator if, based on his conduct in the mediation, they have doubts about his impartiality, or if they have disclosed highly sensitive information that might expose them to the

---

[640] Berger, "Integration of Mediation Elements into Arbitration", 19 (3) *Arb. Int'l* 387-403, at 393 (2003) with further references.

[641] Cf. Berger id. 394 (2003), referring to Art. 19 of the UNCITRAL Conciliation Rules (The parties and the conciliator undertake that the conciliator will not act as an arbitrator or as a representative or counsel of a party in any arbitral or judicial proceedings in respect of a dispute that is the subject of the conciliation proceedings) and Art. 12 of the UNCITRAL Model Law on International Commercial Conciliation (Unless otherwise agreed by the parties, the conciliator shall not act as an arbitrator in respect of a dispute that was or is the subject of the conciliation proceedings or in respect of another dispute that has arisen from the same contract or legal relationship or any related contract or legal relationship).

[642] Cf. Berger id.; Schneider in: van der Berg (ed.) *International Dispute Resolution, Towards an International Arbitration Culture* 57, 69 (2000).

[643] The same wording can be found in Sec. 2B (4) of the Hong Kong Arbitration Ordinance (1997).

danger of an unfavorable decision. An opt-out clause can have a beneficial effect on the mediation: the parties may feel less inhibited and lay open more candidly their real interests or their bottom line since they can always "pull the brake" in case no settlement is reached. On the other hand, an opt-out clause creates the risk of eliminating the back-up procedure.

2. Post-Arbitration Mediation

a. Concept

In a second, inverse combination, an arbitration may turn into a mediation. We will at this point focus exclusively on "pure" post-arbitration mediation while the scenario where an ongoing arbitration is *suspended* and may *continue* after the mediation will be described below (mediation window). One variant of post-arbitration mediation is the so-called envelope technique, as described by Berger and Oghigian:

> "… sealed envelopes with signed copies of the full and final award are placed on the table and the arbitrator, without revealing the content of the award, asks the parties whether they both wish to mediate their dispute with him acting as the mediator subject to each parties' right to stop the proceedings, call for a termination of the mediation and take the award."[644]

In post-arbitral mediation, it may be recommendable for the neutral to ask the parties – when switching from arbitrator to mediator – to be fully vacated of the office as arbitrator. Oghigian gives an account of a number of successful post-arbitration mediations and highlights possible advantages of this serial combination:

> "In short, I was able to play a much more effective role as a mediator where I was vacated of my responsibilities and duties as an arbitrator and could, by agreement and voluntarily, bring out the interests and weaknesses of the parties in order to expand the dialogue and achieve settlement. A final advantage of this modus operandi is that it avoids another common problem of med/arb: if it is understood that the mediator will become the arbitrator in due course, the parties may well use the process to present their position not with a genuine view to achieving a settlement but rather, tactically, to lay the groundwork for the subsequent adjudicatory phase of the process."[645]

---

[644] Berger, "Integration of Mediation Elements into Arbitration", 19 (3) *Arb. Int'l* 387-403, at 395 (2003).

[645] Oghigian, *Discussion On Arbitrators Acting as Mediators*, (2001), at 45.

b. Comment

Just like pre-arbitral mediation, post-arbitral mediation is based on a rather strict division of both procedures. It follows the logic of the "Post-Settlement Settlement" and by-passes the arbitrator's dilemma. At the same time, especially in cases where the award is written (without the content being revealed) before the mediation commences, another conflict arises since the arbitrator

> "has not only conducted the arbitration but has also rendered a final decision in favour of one side, making it even more difficult for him to take an unbiased approach to the conduct of the mediation process."[646]

It is because of this conflict that, again, a clear separation between the two roles seems preferable even in the case of post-arbitration mediation. This can be achieved by inserting a mediation window (see below at 4.) between the rendering of a decision and the formal issuance of the award.

3. Complete Integration: The IBM-FUJITSU Example

A complete integration of full-intensity mediation and arbitration was employed in the much-discussed I.B.M.-Fujitsu[647] arbitration. The case demonstrated that arbitrators can play many roles and that the entire range of ADR techniques can be integrated into the framework of international commercial arbitration to design a procedure that is tailored to the particularities of a controversy.

The dispute had a long history. In the early 1970s Fujitsu began to develop I.B.M.-compatible operating system software for Fujitsu mainframes. At that time, I.B.M. did not claim any copyrights for such software, and there were doubts whether computer software could be the subject of copyrights protection at all. However, in the late 1970s I.B.M. began to register copyrights for new releases of its operating system software, and when it became clear that U.S. copyrights law did indeed protect computer software, I.B.M. alleged that Fujitsu's operating system software

---

[646] Berger, "Integration of Mediation Elements into Arbitration", 19 (3) *Arb. Int'l* 387-403, 395 (2003).

[647] For more details see Mnookin/Greenberg, "Lessons of the IBM-Fujitsu Arbitration: How Disputants Can Work Together to Solve Deeper Conflicts", 18 *Dispute Resolution Magazine* (1998), Mnookin, "Creating Value through Process Design", 11 (1) *J. Int'l Arb.* 125 (1994), and Bühring-Uhle, "The IBM-Fujitsu Arbitration: A Landmark in Innovative Dispute Resolution", 2 *Am. Rev. Int'l Arb.* 113 (1991); see also Johnston, "The IBM – Fujitsu Arbitration Revisited – A Case Study in Effective ADR", 7 (5) *The Computer Lawyer* 13-17 (1990); Albert, "An Alternative Approach to Computer Pirating Disputes, the Mnookin-Jones Settlement: *IBM v. Fujitsu*", 3 *Temple Int'l & Comp. L.J.* 113 (1989); Coulson, "Significance of the IBM-Fujitsu Software Award", in: American Arbitration Association, *Arbitration and the Law* 1987-1988 224-224 (1988); Note, "Neutrals Deployed Several Kinds of ADR to Solve IBM-Fujitsu Copyright Dispute", *Alternatives*, Vol. 5 No. 11 (November 1987).

violated I.B.M.'s copyrights and claimed damages amounting to several hundred million dollars.

In 1983 the two companies agreed to a settlement providing for a lump sum payment and subsequent semi-annual license fees to be paid by Fujitsu in exchange for immunity from further copyright claims by I.B.M. and the permission to continue to use a number of "Designated Programs". The settlement also addressed the need for Fujitsu to follow I.B.M.'s innovations in order to continue to offer I.B.M.-compatible computer products. On a mutual basis the parties agreed to make available to each other the external (interface) information needed as a basis for independent development of compatible operation programs.[648] However, the 1983 settlement was not specific enough. When attempts at negotiating a more operational arrangement failed, I.B.M. in 1986 initiated arbitration proceedings under an arbitration clause contained in the 1983 settlement.[649]

The arbitrators experimented with the whole array of dispute resolution techniques. At a "responsible executive meeting" early on in the procedure lawyers and experts presented the parties' views before the arbitrators and one senior executive from each side. This mini-trial did not lead to a resolution of the fundamental differences. The panel therefore suggested that the parties try and negotiate the two major areas of disagreement (scope of I.B.M.'s copyrights, amount of "external information" to be exchanged) with the two party-appointed arbitrators acting as mediators. The mediation efforts benefited from the combined expertise of the arbitrators-turned-mediators in computer technology and dispute resolution. They employed the full arsenal of mediation techniques, including private caucuses with each party. However, in order to maintain complete neutrality, they conducted all mediation activities jointly and refrained from *ex parte* communications between one of them and the party that had appointed him.

The mediation resulted in a basic settlement in the spring of 1987. It represented a breakthrough in the two principal areas of the controversy and laid the foundation for the resolution of the entire dispute. With respect to existing software it was agreed that Fujitsu would compensate I.B.M. with a lump sum payment for a "paid-up license" covering all past and future use of the programs. With regard to the external information to be exchanged the 1987 settlement provided for the

---

[648] Thus, the 1983 settlement already laid the ground for the solution finally resulting from the subsequent arbitration: (1) Fujitsu may continue to use certain of I.B.M.'s existing operating system programs in return for monetary compensation, and (2) the companies agree on a technology transfer that would enable both to maintain compatibility of its operating system software.

[649] I.B.M. appointed John L. Jones, an American computer industry executive. Fujitsu nominated Robert H. Mnookin, an American professor of law and ADR expert, founder of the Stanford Center for Conflict and Negotiation and since 1993 director of the Program on Negotiation at Harvard Law School. The two party-appointed arbitrators selected the Canadian Donald MacDonald as chairman who, however, retired before the first award was rendered.

creation of a "Secured Facility" regime under which each party would have limited access to the other's programming information in exchange for an annual access fee. The basic structure of the Secured Facility regime was already laid out in the 1987 settlement: just like in certain arms control treaties, specified personnel from one side would have access to the sensitive research facilities of the other, and a neutral "Facility Supervisor" would – under the guidance of the arbitrators – ensure that only information covered by the agreement leaves the Facility.

However, the 1987 settlement was only a framework agreement. The determination of the exact amount of the paid-up license, as well as the scope of the information covered by the Secured Facility regime, the amount of the annual compensation and the task of compliance monitoring, were left to the arbitration panel. When the chairman of the tribunal resigned in May of 1987 the parties decided not to have him replaced but instead to reduce the panel to the two party-appointed arbitrators who had conducted the mediation element of the procedure. In the event of a disagreement they were authorized to engage, on an ad-hoc basis, a third arbitrator to break the tie. At the same time the arbitrators' appointment was extended for another 15 years, thus creating a standing dispute resolution panel in order to monitor the implementation of the Secured Facility regime, and to resolve all disputes arising out of its operation.

The arbitrators postponed the calculation of the paid-up license and decided to first deal with the future-oriented rule-making task of determining the details of the Secured Facility regime. In September of 1987 the panel issued a partial award containing the framework for the creation of the Secured Facility regime. Although this award already included fairly elaborate ground rules, the determination of the exact types of information subject to the supervised exchange and the fixing of the annual access fee was only achieved through further interaction between the panel and the parties. In a revolving process, teams of technical experts negotiated with the input of "guidelines" from the panel, narrowed the dispute, resubmitted unresolved issues to the panel for partial determinations and further "guidelines" and then continued to negotiate, leaving only a limited number of issues for final determination by the arbitrators.

In determining the amount of the paid-up license the arbitrators followed one of the fundamental rules of negotiation theory, the maxim to insist on using objective criteria and to try to first agree on guiding principles as a threshold for the decision of the substance of the dispute. Hence, before dealing with the concrete facts relating to the I.B.M. programs used by Fujitsu, the arbitrators requested the parties to produce statements on the principles that should govern the calculation of the lump sum license fee. The parties were then given the opportunity to present evidence on the vast quantity of designated programs (Fujitsu produced a "price report" with 22 volumes of appendices), and seven days of hearings were held to discuss the facts. Once again the arbitrators did not render a final decision but preferred to rely on further interaction with the parties: on the last day of the hearings the arbitrators presented their basic approach as to the principles guiding the computation of the lump sum fee and then asked the parties to each develop a calculation model which would make it possible for the arbitrators to calculate the license fee as a function of the factors announced by the panel. When the models were presented, the arbitrators discussed them with parties and gave them an opportunity for further modification. Finally, the arbitrators "fed" both models with the data derived from the panel's factual determinations and, based on a comparative analysis of the results, made their final determination.

The Secured Facitlity regime was dismantled in 1997, ten years after its inception. In the eyes of the parties, it had served its purpose in light of a number of changes, both in the relevant technology and in the relationship between the two companies.

The case was exceptional in many ways, not only with respect to the stakes and complexity but also because in the course of the proceedings the arbitrators were given a mandate that went well beyond the scope of ordinary dispute resolution: against the background of a multi-jurisdictional dispute and an area of the law still in a developing stage, the arbitrators assumed a rulemaking function and were asked to formulate the computer software copyrights law to be applicable among the two parties for a specific period of time. And they were given continuing jurisdiction to decide any subsequent disputes.

The procedure employed by the two arbitrators was remarkable, too. Almost the whole spectrum of dispute resolution techniques was used at some point: structured negotiations, mini-trial, mediation, final-offer arbitration, negotiated rule-making facilitated by the arbitrators, compliance monitoring by neutral experts, and ongoing dispute resolution by a standing panel of two arbitrators with an option to engage a third arbitrator on an ad-hoc basis. Throughout the dispute, a complex relation existed between negotiation and adjudication. The breakthrough occurred when two of the arbitrators were allowed to transform themselves temporarily into mediators and facilitated the agreement that formed the foundation for all subsequent determinations: the decision to settle all claims relative to existing programs through a lump sum payment, and the decision to create a Secured Facility regime to allow for a controlled exchange of future programming data. These two key elements of the final solution could not have been *ordered* by the arbitrators. Later, when the details of these two decisions had to be worked out, a revolving procedure emerged which oscillated between negotiation and adjudication: step-by-step, through consecutive rounds of negotiations alternating with "guidance" from the arbitrators and the adjudication of threshold-issues, the parties managed to narrow the dispute and dispose of most issues, until a hard core of data and figures remained that had to be determined by the arbitrators.

The I.B.M.-Fujitsu arbitration illustrates the potential for creative process design. The arbitrators focused on the underlying interests of the parties and were able to turn a judicial procedure into a future-oriented problem solving process that went beyond the confrontation of necessarily abstract legal issues to the roots of the concrete conflict. The final solution contained a high degree of consensual elements and created value for the parties not only by resolving a destructive and costly controversy but also by creating the basis for a controlled technology transfer considered beneficial by both parties. The maximization of consensus was achieved in a continuous revolving process in which facilitated negotiation alternated with limited arbitral decision-making. The entire procedure was conducted by the same neutrals who carried out a highly intensive form of mediation but managed to keep this process separate from the judicial process of arbitral decision-making.

In sum, the complete integration of these various elements is a process with high risks but also potentially high returns. In the words of a senior in-house counsel who participated in the procedure:

> "... the I.B.M.-Fujitsu arbitration showed that it is possible for the arbitrator to facilitate agreement where possible and to break log jams through adjudication ... there can be serious problems but it can also be the optimal process, it all depends on the personality of the neutral who needs a very rare skill and a strong character and absolutely needs a very high degree of confidence from both parties ..."

4. Mediation Windows

> "During a complex international business case, I can see where individuals may want to focus on a portion of the case, stop the arbitration and engage in mediation since everyone, including the parties and the principals, will have a better sense of what the case is actually beginning to look like."[650]

a. Concept

As we have seen above, settlement facilitation efforts by arbitrators during an on-going arbitration are a common feature of the practice of international arbitration. By contrast, a full-scale mediation as a separate procedure in the "shadow" of an on-going arbitration is less usual though not entirely uncommon. The flexibility of the legal framework of arbitration makes it possible to explicitly introduce a mediation segment at any moment of the procedure.

An explicit "mediation window" does not necessarily disrupt the arbitration since there are long periods during any arbitration where no hearings are conducted and the participants simply prepare for the next step in the proceedings. Setting aside a few days for a mediation attempt – the maximum duration will be one or two weeks – is therefore possible without causing a noticeable disruption. In particular, a mediation window does not necessarily require any changes in the schedule for

---

[650] Interview with Rebecca Westerfield, April 25, 2002

hearings etc., and it might even be beneficial to conduct the mediation with the prospect of a scheduled series of hearing days in order to create an incentive to settle and thus avoid the expense and delays connected with going through the scheduled procedure.

The possibility of inserting a separate mediation procedure into an ongoing arbitration is expressly recognized by Rule 8 of the (National) Commercial Arbitration Rules of the American Arbitration Association (AAA), as amended and in effect as of July 1, 2003. In this provision, the AAA even provides for a financial incentive for mediation efforts during ongoing arbitrations in that it waives the fee it usually charges for administering the mediation. In the international version of the rules, there is no corresponding provision, but in its introduction to the International Mediation Rules, the AAA declares that the same principle applies.

The interviews conducted by the authors revealed that the inclusion of a "window" for the purpose of conducting a more or less structured settlement attempt is actually taking place in the practice of international arbitration. Practitioners from different countries recounted a variety of situations where an ADR segment was inserted into an on-going arbitration. Such a mediation window can lead to very substantial savings, as the following case illustrates:

> "... it was an international ICC arbitration, about a resort hotel, it involved an international construction manager and the developer operating in Asia made up of individuals from various countries, including an American; counsel were both London solicitors ... the legal fees were already enormous and I don't know which one suggested that they wanted to have a facilitated settlement meeting prior to the next arbitration hearing, I think it was an evidentiary hearing ... [the parties] knew what mediation was, they knew it would be inexpensive, quick and that it would not in any way prejudice them in the [ongoing] arbitration, that it was simply a way to see whether the rest of the arbitration with its enormous cost could be cut off ... and we settled the case, it took a day and a half, it was a mini-trial ... one of the most memorable moments, of some importance, was a call to the Secretariat of the ICC Court of Arbitration to see how much of the ICC fee would be refunded ... as both counsel pointed out, the panel had not had to do much work ... so there was some bargaining going on, and the person we talked to had to check with someone and they had to call one of the panel members' clerks to see what the panel was going to do, and it took a couple of hours, and word came back, and I think they made a fair return ... the ICC was able to give a break on their [administrative] fee, and then they had to check with the head of panel about how much that would be [reduced] ..."[651]

---

[651]   Interview with Eric Green, May 26, 1992.

When a mediation window is conducted by a different person, the two processes can still be integrated to a high degree, and the efficiency of the entire procedure improved, if the two neutrals cooperate. This can be done by allowing the mediator to observe the arbitration, e.g. by reading the most important briefs and participating as a tacit observer in preliminary meetings or even the main (evidence) hearing. The mediator would get informed about the dispute and could stand by in case the parties decide to inject a mediation attempt. Such a *stand-by mediator* was successfully employed in a construction dispute administered by the American Arbitration Association:

"In a complex multi-party construction dispute with eight parties and claims and counterclaims totalling close to USD 9 millions, three arbitrators were appointed and up to 50 hearing days were anticipated. When confronted with a suggestion by the AAA to try mediation, the parties felt that the potential for settlement had been exhausted and that any additional delay had to be avoided. Still, the head of the local AAA office administering the arbitration thought the parties might benefit if they had a mediation option available in case an opportunity for settlement talks arose during the course of the arbitration. In order to have a mediator available while not losing any time on the way to the arbitration hearing, a retired judge was appointed as a mediator who would "shadow" the arbitration proceedings as an initially passive observer, getting informed about the case and being ready to step in as soon as the parties thought mediation attempts might make sense. At a pre-hearing conference the arbitrators, after listening to brief presentations of each party's case, issued a procedural ruling allowing for limited discovery to be held in the remaining two months before the hearings. Watching the parties' presentations, the mediator gained a compressed overview of the issues in dispute and an impression of the various parties. In the afternoon, the arbitrators left the floor to the mediator who met with the main parties and was able to persuade them to try mediation. Although they were not able to settle at that meeting, the mediator – through periodic phone calls – stayed in touch with the parties during the discovery period. At no time did the arbitrators and the mediator discuss the merits of the case. On the day the main hearing was to commence, the parties could be persuaded to insert a mediation attempt. Here, the breakthrough occurred. After giving each side a chance to give a summary presentation of its case, the mediator met with all parties and engaged in intensive negotiations and shuttle diplomacy. After 1 1/2 days, he was able to broker an agreement not only between the two main parties in dispute but also among the various subcontractors. Getting the sub-contractors to agree and to materially contribute to the settlement was indispensable in reaching a solution that actually terminated the entire dispute. The compensation for the mediator, who had spent a total of four days observing the arbitration and conducting the mediation and who charged the same per diem fee as the arbitrators, could easily be covered by the deposit the parties had made with the AAA to cover the costs of the arbitration. The savings achieved through the mediated settlement were estimated at between USD 500,000 and 750,000."[652]

A mediation window could lead to various types of *results:* ideally, the entire dispute is settled, and the parties may ask the arbitrator to render a consent-award on the basis of the agreement reached. The settlement would then be enforceable and have international currency like any arbitral award. If a complete agreement cannot be reached, the mediation might at least serve to streamline the ensuing arbitration: the parties might be able to agree on a concrete determination of the issues, on a stipulation of certain facts, or even on a partial resolution of the dispute, reducing the task left to the arbitrator.

Even after the arbitrator has resumed his function there might still be a role for the mediator if the parties agree to continue with a second mediation attempt after the arbitrator has broken an impasse, e.g. by rendering an interim award on a particular threshold issue such as liability. The mediator might even be asked to stand by until after the arbitrator has rendered a final award: in accordance with the idea of Post-Settlement Settlements and Post-Arbitral Mediation (see above), the mediator (again subject to a time limit) could try to work with the parties to improve the result so as to reach a solution that both parties prefer to the one reached by the arbitrator. The arbitrator would wait with the issuance of the final award for an agreed period of time, thus giving the parties an opportunity to come up with an improved result.

An important issue in this context is how to introduce the mediation window since – as with all settlement initiatives – the parties may hesitate to make the first move. The parties are often afraid that they might appear weak if they actively seek an amicable resolution. One possibility to overcome this problem is to use arbitration rules that expressly provide for such a step, or to expressly mention the possibility of mediation windows in the arbitration clause. Another option is to have the arbitral tribunal approach the parties with this idea (or for a party to ask the tribunal to do this in order for the party itself not to be exposed). Perhaps the best way to introduce the idea of a mediation window is to have a standard procedure in place at the arbitration institution:

"... if the idea of a mediation segment were to be introduced, the way it would have to be done is an institutionalized process that, following the terms of reference, or whatever stage, the ICC would send a letter to the parties

---

[652]   This report is based on Mackenzie, "'Shadow Mediation': A Breakthrough Tactic Resolves Claims and Saves Dollars', *Florida Constructor*, March/April 1991, p.7, and telephone interviews with Marc Sholander, Head of the Orlando office of the AAA, on July 2 and 20, 1992.

saying 'at this stage, as a matter of routine, we ask whether the parties would be interested in having a mediator appointed who is not the arbitrator and has nothing else to do with the case and will have nothing to do with it if the mediation fails' – because parties should not feel that it is particular to their case, that they're offending the arbitrator..."[653]

In order to find out how this idea is received by practitioners in international commercial arbitration, the participants in the survey were asked in the interviews whether they thought it was appropriate for an arbitration institution to suggest, at its own initiative, the use of mediation to the parties. The response was overwhelmingly positive: 75% of the 53 individuals who commented on this issue considered this appropriate.

b. Comment

Inserting a mediation window into an ongoing arbitration procedure will be worth the extra expense more often than might be thought. In many instances it might indeed open a "window of opportunity". Regardless whether a stand-by or an ad hoc mediator will fulfil the mediator's task, the pitfalls and tradeoffs of the various roles can be avoided through the clear separation of roles inherent in the concept of mediation windows.

5. Conclusion

The tension between the effectiveness of any mediation attempt and the integrity of the arbitral procedure can only be resolved through a clear separation of the two processes. Depending on the concept of integrating arbitration and mediation, there are different ways of achieving this separation of processes while still creating an integrated dispute resolution procedure. A fully integrated procedure like the one employed in the I.B.M. – Fujitsu arbitration can be an ideal way to combine the benefits of mediation and arbitration but it is likely to remain reserved for cases in which exceptional circumstances put the neutral(s) in a position to achieve the separation of processes required to cope with the arbitrator's dilemma.

It has to be borne in mind that private meetings of an arbitrator with a party are regarded as inappropriate by a large number of practitioners, scholars and institutions. It can be argued that such a practice constitutes a violation of the principles of natural justice:

"[the] combination of mediation/arbitration by the same person reveals the Achilles' heel in terms of natural justice: everyone should be able to be heard and whatever may be said to the mediator by a party should also be heard by the other party .... From a practicioner's perspective, the problem might

---

[653] Interview with Stephen Bond, February 19, 1992.

be better expressed as: the mediator who has now become an arbitrator may have developed a skewed view of position which my client may not have an opportunity (or ability) to set right. It is a variation of the classic tautology: I can't tell you what you don't know because I don't know what you don't know". [654]

Therefore, especially when caucuses are conducted, the procedure requires the express – preferably written – consent of the parties, in order to avoid the danger of a challenge against the arbitrator or the ensuing award.[655] However, great caution is warranted since even a written waiver may not completely eliminate the danger of a challenge in the courts. It has been argued that since the principles of natural justice cannot be set aside by an agreement of the parties, the validity of the award cannot be assured by means of a written consent to the double role of the neutral.[656] On the other hand, if the parties agree with the mediator/arbitrator that the content of any private communication has to be disregarded in the arbitral decision, the essential idea that a party has the right to be "heard" on any issues on which the decision might be based is, at least theoretically, moot. This view, of course, requires a high degree of confidence in the ability of the neutral to build "watertight" compartments in his or her mind. And in any event, regardless of the preferences or opinions of the tribunal, the parties and their lawyers: some degree of legal risk to the award remains since this point is far from being settled in the many jurisdictions that may become relevant in any given case.

In the large majority of cases, therefore, full-intensity mediation in the shadow of arbitration will only be advisable if it is conducted by a second neutral.

As far as *timing* of mediation attempts is concerned, emerging conflicts generally should receive early attention. However, it is never too late to attempt an amicable resolution, and the possibility of a mediation window should be borne in mind at any time during an arbitration. As explained above, the moment immediately before the initiation of an arbitration may not be the most appropriate stage of the dispute to conduct a mediation since the parties are preparing to litigate and focus on how to win rather than on how to reconcile their interests. When the dispute has reached this point it may be preferable to formalize the dispute by initiating arbitration proceedings and, once the preparatory phase of the arbitration has produced an

---

[654]   Oghigian, "The Mediation/Arbitration Hybrid", 20 (1) *Journal of International Arbitration* 75-80, at 76-77 (2003),

[655]   It may even be advisable to ask the parties for a written waiver of challenges that might be based on the dual role of the arbitrator; cf. Sec 17 (4) of the Singapore International Arbitration Act of 2001 cited above at p. 242 and Sec. 2B (4) of the Hong Kong Arbitration Ordinance (1997)

[656]   Eidenmüller, "Vertrags- und verfahrensrechtliche Grundfragen der Mediation: Möglichkeiten und Grenzen privatautonomen Konfliktmanagements", in: Breidenbach et al. (eds.), *Konsensuale Streitbeilegung* (2000), p. 86

exchange of information that permits the parties to better gauge their respective strengths, revert to settlement talks in a mediation window.

Finally, there is an important practical aspect to be considered: the *skills* of the arbitrator to act as mediator. Even assuming that the arbitrator is permitted and willing to make the transition from one process to another, he will not necessarily be capable to perform this task without proper training.

"The skills required, while complementary, are different and need to be underpinned with training and experience and, at the very least, an appropriate 'mindset'. For the process to work the parties must have confidence not only in the process but also in the capacity of the third party. For the future it is likely that dispute resolution professionals will be required to display a broader range of skills".[657]

III. A DYNAMIC APPROACH TO DISPUTE RESOLUTION PROCESS DESIGN

The preceding section has shown that there is no single answer to the question of how best to integrate mediation and arbitration in order to combine their respective benefits. The final section of this study attempts to develop a systematic approach to the challenge of designing flexible procedures that meet the requirements of any given dispute. Since international business disputes come in an enormous variety, such a systematic approach can only consist of rather general rules of thump. Still, a set of guidelines and a general understanding of the dynamics underlying dispute resolution process design can be of significant help in approaching this challenge.

1. The Task of Dispute Resolution Process Design

Designing dispute resolution procedures entails the conscious use of the arsenal of methods and tools offered by modern conflict management "technology". The task presents itself at different moments in the life of a dispute and confronts different players.

Independent of any specific dispute, business organizations should be prepared to deal in a flexible, constructive and cost-effective manner with any conflict that might arise in the course of their business. This begins with the education of management and relevant staff. Another useful step is the establishment of guidelines and standard procedures, e.g. ensuring that disputes are brought to the attention of management early enough, or a general commitment to the use of consensual dispute resolution techniques such as mediation before resorting to adjudication, or the development of

---

[657] Talbot, "Should an Arbitrator or Adjudicator Act as a Mediator in the Same Dispute?", 67(3) *J. Chartered Inst. Arb.* 228, at 229 (August 2001).

model procedures for the processing of disputes with particular types of clients/suppliers. When a transaction is planned it is the task of the parties and their advisors to include provisions for conflict management before any concrete dispute arises. The more complex and long-term oriented economic exchanges are, the greater is the need for flexible structures that provide for early attention to emerging conflicts or prevent conflicts altogether.

Once a conflict has emerged, the parties and their advisors have to find ways of limiting damages, preventing escalation and dealing with the roots of the conflict. When the conflict develops into a formal dispute, the challenge is to find a cost-effective way to ensure a fair and final resolution instead of getting locked into a confrontation that blocks interest-based outcomes. This should also be of concern for any third party who gets involved in the resolution of the dispute, particularly the arbitral tribunal, but also the arbitral institution or any mediator brought into the procedure. Since consensual solutions can be beneficial to the parties even if reached at an advanced stage of an arbitration, all participants are held to continue exploring the potential for a settlement until the very end of the procedure. Even after an award has been rendered it is no mistake to contemplate whether the result reached can be further improved through an agreement.

2. Guiding Principles

The yardstick for success in commercial dispute resolution is the interests of the parties. A fair and lasting reconciliation of the parties' interests should therefore be the ultimate goal, and dispute resolution process design should aspire to develop cost-effective procedures that ensure a final resolution while realizing the potential to create value for the parties. Since the parties themselves know best what is in their interest, it should be the parties themselves who fashion the solution on a consensual basis. Only where consensus cannot be reached, a final resolution has to be guaranteed through a binding decision issued by a third party.

Hence, the guiding principle for dispute resolution process design should be to maximize the consensual element in any solution and to have third-party decision-making available, but limited to an indispensable minimum.

3. Basic Elements of the System

In accordance with the guiding principle stated above the two main elements of the proposed system for dispute resolution process design are *interest-based negotiations* and a *rights-based adjudication* procedure as a *back-up* in case no agreement is reached.

The best way to achieve consensus is through negotiation. Since interests are the yardstick for commercial dispute resolution the *negotiations* should be primarily *interest-based*. There are a number of ADR techniques, most notably mediation, that can improve the effectiveness of negotiation. They should therefore be considered when structuring the negotiation element of the system. We have shown above that arbitration is the most effective *back-up* available in international commercial disputes. Litigation, the prototype of rights-based adjudication, has to be considered as an option in specific contexts where arbitration is not available or where international mechanisms have improved the legal framework for transnational litigation.

There are two intermediate steps between these two principal elements: *rights-based negotiation* as a filter to adjudication and *loop-backs* as a way to revert to interest-based negotiation.

Rights-based negotiations are an important *filter* to adjudication. Rather than incurring the costs of going through an adjudication procedure the parties try to anticipate its result in negotiations. These negotiations typically take the form of an exchange of legal arguments and a confrontation of conflicting predictions about the outcome of the back-up procedure. This form of "bargaining in the shadow of the law"[658] characterizes conventional settlement negotiations. It can be enhanced through certain forms of predictive ADR, most notably mini-trials and related mediation structures. In practice, interest-based and rights-based negotiation are blended into one process which in the shadow of an impending adjudication is dominated by rights-based negotiation. However, it is important to make this distinction, mentally and through the structure of the process, in order not to lose sight of the ultimate goal of dispute resolution process design – a consensual solution that reconciles the interests of the parties on the highest possible level. Both interest-based and rights-based negotiations can be brought to their maximum effectiveness through the assistance of a mediator. In mediation, too, it is important to distinguish problem-solving and predictive techniques in order to accomplish the two objectives of realizing the interests of the parties and having their rights respected.

A *loop back* is a structure that permits the participants of a rights-based adjudication procedure to revert to interest-based negotiation, always in line with the guiding principle to maximize consensus and to minimize third-party decisionmaking.[659] Examples for loop backs are mediation windows in arbitration and post-arbitration-mediation which try to improve the result of adjudication through negotiation.

4. Dynamics of the System

Based on the objective of maximizing consensus and limiting arbitral decision-making to the indispensable, the elements described above can be viewed as a dynamic system that combines mediation and arbitration and where interest-

---

[658] The term goes back to Mnookin & Kornhauser, "Bargaining in the Shadow of the Law: The Case of Divorce", 88 *Yale L. J.* 950 (1979).

[659] Ury, Brett & Goldberg, *Getting Disputes Resolved* (1988) 52-53 have a slightly different use of the term loop back. They include predictive ADR procedures like the mini-trial since they try to bring the parties back to the path of negotiations before a back-up procedure is initiated. In our eyes the term loop back is more useful to denote structures that do not try to prevent a confrontation in litigation but try to depart – to "loop back" – from it.

based negotiation merges into rights-based negotiation followed, if necessary, by adjudication which, however, is limited to deciding threshold issues. This permits, by way of a loop back, to revert to interest-based negotiation. The dynamic can be illustrated through a circle:

Figure 22: The Dynamics of Dispute Resolution Process Design

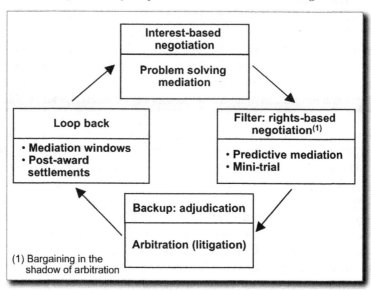

This process can be continued through several rounds in a revolving dynamic resembling a spiral until the potential for consensus has been exhausted and either a final settlement is agreed by the parties or the remaining issues are left for decision by the tribunal.

PART FIVE:
CONCLUSION

There is a growing need for effective conflict management in international business. Transnational *litigation* has serious shortcomings in meeting this demand. Most of the deficiencies of transnational litigation can be overcome with the legal framework of international commercial *arbitration* which, in a multi-jurisdictional context, offers the best guarantee for the final resolution of business disputes. Empirical analysis reveals that in international practice arbitration has the same function that litigation fulfills in a national context. The formality, the costs and the duration of international commercial arbitration are often comparable to those of litigation in national courts and can reach extreme proportions. Empirical analysis also reveals that arbitration as a litigation procedure faces inherent limitations in its capacity to bring about consensual solutions. Although a substantial number of arbitrations end with a settlement, this tends to happen at a fairly advanced stage of the procedure and mainly as a result of the parties' becoming more realistic and more aware of the costs as the procedure unfolds. When arbitrators try to actively facilitate a negotiated settlement they are faced with a dilemma between the effectiveness of their mediation attempts and the integrity of the arbitral procedure.

This limitation is significant because consensual solutions are the best way to reconcile the interests of business actors. And the *interests* of the parties should be the yardstick for success in the resolution of commercial disputes. Rooted in conflict and negotiation theory, modern business *mediation* and related dispute resolution techniques offer a variety of methods to overcome the limitations inherent in direct negotiations. They provide cost-effective ways to facilitate consensual solutions with a potential to create value for the parties through mutual gains. The direct involvement of senior management in the settlement process hands control over the dispute back to the parties. The savings in transaction costs can be dramatic. However, in order to guarantee a final resolution consensual procedures have to rely on a binding "back-up" procedure, and in international commercial disputes the most effective back-up is arbitration.

Based on party-autonomy, the law governing international commercial arbitration is flexible enough to permit the integration of mediation and other alternative methods in the framework of arbitral proceedings. However, in order for mediation to be fully effective without compromising the integrity of arbitration as a judicial procedure, the two processes have to be clearly separated. In many instances, it will be indispensable to involve a separate mediator. This step is worthwhile even if a mediation window is inserted at a fairly advanced stage of the arbitration.

There is no single answer to the challenge of *designing procedures* for effective conflict management. Dispute resolution procedures have to be tailored to the circumstances. The goal of effective conflict management is to maximize consensus while guaranteeing an enforceable decision in case no agreement is reached. Therefore, the extent to which a dispute is decided by the arbitrator should be reduced to the indispensable. This can be achieved through the conscious use of modern conflict management technology. In this context, interest-based mediation plays a central role, both as a filter before arbitration and – in the "shadow" of an ongoing arbitration – in the form of mediation "windows" that redirect the attention of the parties toward their interests.

The term "alternative" dispute resolution is misleading: mediation and related, interest-based negotiation structures should be the principal means of dispute resolution, while arbitration and other forms of litigation serve as back-up mechanisms. Mediation and arbitration, therefore, should not be seen as mutually exclusive alternatives but as complementary elements of an integrated system of modern dispute resolution process design.

Appendix 1

List of Individuals who Participated in the Surveys or Contributed in Interviews or through Correspondence

(incl. positions held as of the time of the interview/correspondence)

Marjorie Aaron
Principal
Endispute
Cambridge, MA, USA

Anonymous
(Member of the Committe on Corporate
Counsel of the American Arbitration
Association)
USA

Howard J. Aibel
Solo Practitioner
New York, NY, USA

Gerald Aksen
Partner, Thelen Reid,
New York, NY, USA

José María Alcántara
Partner, Abogados Marítimos y
Asociados
Professor of Maritime Law
Madrid, Spain

Jane Andrewartha
Partner, Clyde & Co
London, UK

Ignacio Arroyo
Partner, Ramos & Arroyo
Professor of Commercial Law
Barcelona, Spain

Markham Ball
Partner, Morgan, Lewis & Bockius
Washington, DC, USA

Axel Baum
Partner, Hughes, Hubbard & Reid
Paris, France

Charles A. Beach
Counsel, Exxon Corporation
Irving, TX, USA

Pierre Bellet
Former President, Tribunal de
Commerce,
Paris, France

Klaus Peter Berger
Professor, University of Cologne
Cologne, Germany

Marc Blessing
Partner, Bär & Karrer
President of the Swiss Arbitration
Association
Zürich, Switzerland

Karl-Heinz Böckstiegel
Professor of International Business Law
Director, Inst. for Air and Space Law,
Univ. of Köln
Köln, Germany

Matthieu de Boissesson
Partner, Gide Loirette Nouel
Paris, France

Stephen R. Bond
Partner, White and Case
Paris, France

Stephen M. Boyd
Independent Arbitrator
Washington, DC, USA

Stephan Breidenbach
Professor of Law, European University
Viadrina
Frankfurt (Oder), Germany

Lucas Briner
Senior Vice President, Zürich Chamber
of Commerce
Zürich, Switzerland

David Bristow
Partner, Fraser, Milner, Casgrain
Toronto, Canada

William Brown
Partner, Donovan, Leisure, Newton &
Irvine
New York, NY, USA

Andreas Bucher
Professor of Law, University of Geneva
Geneva, Switzerland

Peter S. Caldwell
Independent Arbitrator and Mediator
Hongkong

Thomas Carbonneau
Professor, Tulane Law School
New Orleans, LA, USA

James H. Carter, Jr.
Partner, Sullivan & Cromwell
New York, NY, USA

Abraham Chayes
Professor of law, Harvard Law School
Cambridge, MA, USA

Antonia Handler Chayes
Principal
Endispute
Cambridge, MA, USA

Edward Chiasson
BLGCanada.com
Canada

Anthony Clapes
Senior Counsel, I.B.M
White Planes, NY, USA

William Laurence Craig
Partner, Coudert Frères
Paris, France

Wayne Davis
Principal
Conflict Management Group
Cambridge, MA, USA

Yves Derains
Partner, Derains & Ass.
Paris, France

Horst Eidenmüller
Professor of Law, European University
Viadrina
Munich, Germany

Peter D. Ehrenhaft
Partner, Miller & Chevalier, Chartered
USA

John Feerick
Professor of Law
Dean, Fordham University Law School

Roger Fisher
Professor of Law
Director, the Harvard Negotiation
Project
Harvard Law School

Vincent Fischer-Zernin
Partner, Weiss & Hasche
Hamburg, Germany

Jason Fry
Partner, Clifford Chance
London, UK

Emmanuel A. Gaillard
Partner, Shearman & Stearling
Professor of Law, Univ. of Paris XII
Paris, France

Alfred C. Gaedertz
Partner, Gaedertz Vieregge Quack Kreile
Wiesbaden, Germany

Walter Gans
Special Counsel, Kaye Scholer
New York, NY USA

Ottoarndt Glossner
Lawyer
Frankfurt, Germany

Berthold Goldman
Professor Emeritus, University of Paris II
Paris, France

Jack Goldsmith
Professor of Law, University of Chicago
Chicago, USA

Germán González Cajiao
Lawyer and Consultant
Santa Fé de Bogotá, Colombia

Richard Graving
Professor, South Texas College of Law
Houston, TX, USA

Elizabeth Gray
President, Conflict Management, Inc.
Cambridge, MA, USA

Eric Green
Founding Partner, Endispute
Boston, MA, USA

George J. Grumbach, Jr.
Partner, Cleary, Gottlieb, Stean &
Hamilton
New York, NY, USA

Klaus Günther
Partner, Linklaters & Alliance
Germany

Mohamed M. Hassan
Vice-Chairman of the Intenational Court
of Arbitration,
International Chamber of Commerce
Cairo, Egypt

Hans-Georg Haeseler
General Counsel
Linde AG
Wiesbaden, Germany

Richard W. Hulbert
Partner, Cleary, Gottlieb, Steen &
Hamilton
New York, NY, USA

J. Martin H. Hunter
Partner, Freshfields
London, GB

William E. Jackson
Partner, Milbank, Tweed, Hadley &
McCloy
New York, NY, USA

Sigvard Jarvin
Counsel, Jones, Day, Reavis & Pogue
Paris, France

Richard K. Jeydel
Secretary and General Counsel,
Kanematsu USA, Inc.
New Jersey, USA

Peter Jousssen
General Counsel, Thyssen Industrie AG
Essen, Germany

Peter Kaskell
Senior Vice President
Center for Public Resources
New York, NY, USA

Gabrielle J. Kaufmann
Partner, Baker & McKenzie
Geneva, Switzerland

Sir Michael Kerr
Barrister
President, London Court of International
Arbitration
London, GB

Richard Kreindler
Partner, Shearman & Sterling, Frankfurt,
Germany
USA

H.J. Kruse
Chief Executive Officer, Hapag-Loyd AG
Hamburg, Germany

Bernd Kunth
Partner, Freshfields Bruckhaus Deringer
Düsseldorf, Germany

Pierre Lalive
Counsel, Lalive Budin & Partners
Professor of law
Geneva, Switzerland

Klaus Lamberth
Partner, Capelle, Lamberth, Flehinghaus
& Engel
Düsselforf, Germany

Senge Lazareff
Partner, J.C. Goldsmith
Paris, France

Jürgen Lebuhn
Partner, Lebuhn & Puchta
Honorary Professor, University of
Aachen
Hamburg, Germany

Richard E. Lerner
Associate General Counsel
American Arbitration Association
New York, NY, USA

Julian D. M. Lew
Partner, S.J. Berwin & Co.
London, England

Rodrigo Llorente Martínez
Abogado (Lawyer)
Santa Fé de Bogotá, Colombia

Richard S. Lombard
Vice President & General Counsel,
Exxon Corp.
New York, NY, USA

Andreas F. Lowenfeld
Professor of Law, New York University
New York, NY, USA

Harold G. Maier
Professor of Law, Vanderbilt University
Law School
USA

Philippe Malinvaud
Professor of Law, University of Paris II
Paris, France

Gianni Manka
Partner, Piergrossi Villa Manca
Graziadei
Italy

Arthur L. Marriot
Partner, Wilmer Cutler & Pickering
London, England

Lars Matsson
Director, General International Area,
Digital Equipment Corporation
Acton, MA, USA

Richard J. Medalie
Partner, Medalie & Ferry
Washington DC, USA

Arthur von Mehren
Professor of Law, Harvard Law School
Cambridge, MA, USA

Robert B. von Mehren
Partner, Debevoise & Plimpton
New York, NY, USA

Alexander v. Meybom
Partner, Wessing Berenberg Gossler
Zimmermann
Düsseldorf, Germany

Howard Miller
Professional Mediator
Marine Mediation
Long Island, NY, USA

Robert H. Mnookin
Professor, Harvard Law School;
Director, Harvard Negotiation Project
Cambridge, MA, USA

Ramon Mullerat
Partner, Mullerat
Spain

Michael J. Mustill
Vice-Chairman ICC International Court
of Arbitration
London, UK

Jean-Claude Najar
General Counsel, GE Oil&Gas
USA

Horacio Grigera Naon
Special Counsel, White & Case,
Washington, USA
Argentina

Fritz Nicklisch
Professor of Law
Heidelberg, Germany

William W. Park
Professor, Boston University Law
School
Counsel, Ropes & Gray
Boston, MA, USA

Antonio R. Parra
Counsel
International Centre for Settlement of
Investment Disputes (ICSID)
Washington, DC, USA

Jan Paulsson
Partner, Freshfields
Lecturer of Law, Univ. of Paris
Paris, France

Wolfgang Peter
Partner, Pirenne, Python, Schifferli,
Peter & Partners
Geneva, Switzerland

Allan Philip
Partner, Pontoppidan, Philip & Partnere
Professor of Law
Copenhagen, Denmark

Michael Charles Pryles
Partner, Minter Ellison Barristers &
Solicitors
Professor of Law, Monash Univ.
Melbourne, Australia

Howard Raiffa
Professor, Harvard Business School
Boston, MA, USA

Alan Rau
Professor of Law, University of Texas at
Austin
USA

Greg Reid
Partner, Linklaters & Alliance, Paris,
France

W. Michael Reisman
Professor of Law, Yale Law School
New Haven, USA

Harald Rieger
Counsel, Kaye Scholer, New York/
Frankfurt
Frankfurt, Germany

Claude Reymond
Partner, Reymond, Bonnard, Maire,
Barman, Freymond
Adjunct Professor of Law
Lausanne, Switzerland

David Rivkin
Partner, Debevoise & Plimpton
New York, NY, USA

Eric Robine
General Counsel, GEC Alsthom S.A.
Paris, France

William D. Rogers
Partner, Arnold & Porter
Washington DC, USA

José Carlos Fernández Rosas
Professor
Spain

Maurice Rosenberg
Professor, Columbia University Law
School
New York, NY, USA

Mauro Rubino-Sammartano
Professor of Law
Chairman, Mediterranean and Middle
East Istitute of Arbitration
Milan, Italy

Pieter Sanders
Professor Emeritus, Erasmus Univ.
Rotterdam
Schiedam, NL

Otto Sandrock
Professor Emeritus, University of
Münster
Partner, Hoelters & Elsing
Düsseldorf, Germany

Sami Sarkis
Attorney at Law
Damascus, Syria

Toshio Sawada
Attorney
Tokio, Japan

Richard A. Schiffer
Managing Director, IDR Europe Ltd.
London, GB

Peter Schlosser
Professor of Law
University of Munich
Munich, Germany

Jörg Schmeding
Partner, White & Case Feddersen
Hamburg, Germany

Eric Schwartz
Secretary General
Internation Court of Arbitration
Fance

James Sebenius
Professor, Harvard Business School
Boston, MA, USA

Ignaz Seidl-Hohenveldern
Preofessor Emeritus, University of
Vienna
Vienna, Austria

Marc Sholander
American Arbitration Association
Orlando, Florida, USA

Jose Luis Siqueiros
Professor of Law
Counsel, Barrera, Siqueiros y Torres
Landa S.A.
Mexico DF, Mexico

Lucien Simont
Professor Emeritus, Université Libre de
Bruxelles
Brussels, Belgium

Spiros Simitis
Professor of Law, University of
Frankfurt
Frankfurt (Main), Germany

Hans Smit
Professor of Law, Columbia University
New York, NY USA

Ezekiel Solomon
Partner, Allen, Allen & Hemsley
New York, NY, USA

Sir Laurence Street
Commercial Mediator and Arbitrator
Sidney, Australia

Joseph Sweeney
Professor, Fordham Law School
New York, USA

Tadeusz Szurski
President, Court of Arbitration at the
Polish Chamber of Foreign Trade
Warzawa, Poland

David Tavender
Senior Partner, Fraser Milner Casgrain
Toronto, Canada

Claude R. Thompson
Senior Partner, Fasken Martineau
DuMoulin
Toronto, Canada

Frank-Rainer Toepfer
Partner, Baker & McKenzie
Germany

Johannes Trappe
Partner, Wessing Berenberg Gossler
Zimmermann
Hamburg, Germany

Rolf Trittmann
Partner, Freshfields Bruckhaus Deringer
Germany

Rudolf Tschäni
Partner, Lenz & Staehelin
Zurich, Switzerland

Albert Jan Van den Berg
Partner Stibbe & Simont
Professor of Law, Erasmus Univ.
Rottedam
Amsterdam, NL

Hans van Houtte
Professor, Institute of International
Trade Law, Univsersity of Leuven
Belgium

Eberhard Vetter
General Counsel, Klöckner-Humbolt-
Deutz AG
Köln, Germany

Francisco Orrego Vicuna
Professor of Law, University of Chile
Chile

Andrew Vollmer
Partner, Wilmer, Cutler & Pickering
Washington, DC, USA

William Weitzel
Partner, Cummings & Lockwood
Greenwich, CT, USA

Jacques Werner
Partner, Werner & Associés
General Editor, Journal of International
Arbitration
Geneva, Switzerland

Kurt Wessing
Partner, Wessing Berenberg Gossler
Zimmermann
Düsseldorf, Germany

John A. Westberg
Partner, Westberg & Johnson
Washington DC, USA

Rebecca Westerfield
JAMS
San Francisco, USA

John Wilkinson
Partner, Donovan, Leisure, Newton &
Irvine
New York, NY, USA

Tony Willis
Independent Mediator/Arbitrator
UK

Frank T. Zotto
Associate Vice President-Case
Administration
American Arbitration Association
New York, NY, USA

List of Institutions

American Arbitration Association
(AAA)
Corporate Headquarters
335 Madison Avenue, Floor 10
New York 10017-4605
U.S.A.

Phone   +1 (212) 716-5800
Fax   +1 (212) 716-5905
E-mail   Websitemail@adr.org
Web   www.adr.org

Arbitration Centre of Mexico (CAM)
Centro de Arbitraje de México
World Trade Centre, Montecito 38,
Floor 14, Office 38, Col. Napoles
Mexico, D.F. C.P 03810
Mexico

Phone   +52 (55) 5488 0436
Fax   +52 (55) 5488 0437
E-mail   camex@camex.com.mx
Web   www.camex.com.mx

Cairo Regional Centre for International
Commercial Arbitration (CRCICA)
1, Al Saleh Ayoub Street
Zamalek,
11211 Cairo
Egypt

Phone   +20 (202) 7351 333
Fax   +20 (202) 7351 336
E-mail   info@crcica.org.eg
Web   www.crcica.org.eg

Centre for Effective Dispute Resolution
(CEDR)
International Dispute Resolution Centre
70 Fleet Street
London EC4Y 1EU
United Kingdom

Phone   +44 (20) 7536 6000
Fax   +44 (20) 7536 6001
E-mail   info@cedr.co.uk
Web   www.cedr.co.uk

China International Economic and Trade
Arbitration Commission (CIETAC)
6/F Golden Lang Building
32 Liang Ma Qiao Road
Chaoyang District
Beijing
China

Phone   +86 (10) 6464 6688
Fax   +88 (10) 6464 3500
E-mail   CIETAC@public.bra.net.cn
Web   www.cietac.org.cn

German Institution of Arbitration (DIS)
Deutsche Institution für
Schiedsgerichtsbarkeit e.V.
Beethovenstraße 5-13
50674 Köln
Germany

Phone   +49 (221) 285 520
Fax   +49 (221) 285 52222
E-mail   dis@dis-arb.de
Web   www.dis-arb.de

Institute of Arbitrators and Mediators
Australia (IAMA)
Level 1, 450 Little Bourke Street
Melbourne, Victoria 3000
Australia

Phone   +61 (03) 9607 6906
Fax   +61 (03) 9602 2833
E-mail national@iama.org.au
Web   www.iama.org.au

International Bar Association (IBA)
271 Regent Street
London ,W1B 2AQ
United Kingdom

Phone   +44 (20) 7629 1206
Fax   +44 (20) 7409 0456
E-mail member@int-bar.org
Web   www.ibanet.org

International Chamber of Commerce
(ICC)
38 Cours Albert 1er
75008 Paris
France

Phone   +33 (1) 49 53 28 28
Fax   +33 (1) 49 53 28 59
E-mail webmaster@iccwbo.org
Web   www.iccwbo.org

International Centre for Settlement of
Investment Disputes (ICSID)
1818 H Street, N.W.
Washington, D.C. 20433
U.S.A.

Phone   +1 (202) 458-1534
Fax   +1 (202) 522-2615
Web   www.worldbank.org/icsid/

International Institute for Conflict
Prevention and Resolution (CPR)
366 Madison Avenue, 14th floor
New York, NY 10017-3122
U.S.A.

Phone   +1 (212) 949 6490
Fax   +1 (212) 949 8859
E-mail info@cpradr.org
Web   www.cpradr.org

JAMS
JAMS Home Office
1920 Main St. at Gillette Ave.
Suite 300 Irvine, CA 92614
U.S.A.

Phone   +1 (949) 224 1810
Fax   +1 (949) 224 1818
E-mail info@jamsadr.com
Web   www.jamsadr.com

London Court of International
Arbitration (LCIA)
70 Fleet Street
London
EC4Y 1EU
England

Phone   +44 (20) 7936 7007
Fax   +44 (20) 7936 7008
E-mail lcia@lcia.org
Web   www.lcia-arbitration.com/

Netherlands Arbitration Institute (NAI)
Nederlands Arbitrage Instituut
Secretariaat NAI
Aert van Nesstraat 25 J/K
3012 CA Rotterdam
PO Box 21075
3001 AB Rotterdam
Nederlands

Phone   +31 (10) 281 6969
Fax   +31 (10) 281 6968
E-mail   secretariaat@nai-nl.org
Web   www.nai-nl.org/english/

Singapore International Arbitration
Centre (SIAC)
City Hall, 3 St. Andrew's Road
Singapore 178958
Singapore

Phone   +65 6334 1277
Fax   +65 6334 2942
Web   www.siac.org.sg

Standards Council of Canada (SCC)
270 Albert Street, Suite 200
Ottawa ON
K1P 6N7
Canada

Phone   +1 (613) 238-3222
Fax   +1 (613) 569-7808
E-mail   info@scc.ca
Web   www.scc.ca/en/index.shtml

Arbitration Institute of the Stockholm
Chamber of Commerce (SCC Institute)
Jakobs Torg 3
P.O. Box 16050
10321 Stockholm
Sweden

Phone   +46 (6) 5551 0050
Fax   +46 (6) 5663 1650
E-mail   arbitration@chamber.se
Web   www.sccinstitute.com/

World Intellectual Property Organisation
(WIPO)
Arbitration and Mediation Center
34, chemin des Colombettes
P.O. Box 18
1211 Geneva 20
Switzerland

Phone   +41 (22) 338 8247
Fax   +41 (22) 740 3700
E-mail   arbiter.mail@wipo.int
Web   http://arbiter.wipo.int/center/

Zurich Chamber of Commerce (ZCC)
Bleicherweg 5
P.O. Box 3058
8022 Zürich
Switzerland

Phone   +41 (1) 217 4050
Fax   +41 (1) 217 4051
E-mail   direktion@zurichcci.ch
Web   www.swissarbitration.ch

Bibliography

Aaron, Marjorie C., "The Value of Decision Analysis in Mediation Practice", 11 (2) *Neg. J.* 123 (1995)

ABA Subcommittee on Alternate Means of Dispute Resolution, "The Effectiveness of the Mini-Trial in Resolving Complex Commercial Disputes: A Survey" (1986), in: Hancock & Gillan, *Corporate Counsel's Guide to ADR Techniques* 3.001-3.029 (1989)

Abramson, Harold I., "Time to Try Mediation in International Commercial Disputes", 4 ILSA *J. Int'l & Comp. L.* 323 (1998)

Albert, "An Alternative Approach to Computer Pirating Disputes, the Mnookin-Jones Settlement: *IBM v. Fujitsu*", 3 *Temple Int'l & Comp. L.J.* 113 (1989)

Altmann, Gerhard / Fiebinger, Heinrich / Müller, Rolf, Mediation: *Konfliktmanagement für moderne Unternehmen*, Weinheim, Basel (2nd ed. 2001)

Anchini, Concitration: *The Ultimate Example of ADR, World Arbitration and Mediation Report* 162, 163-164 (2002)

Appel, Mark, Partnering – New Dimensions in Dispute Prevention and Resolution, *Arbitration Journal* 47 (June 1993)

Arnaldez, Jean-Jacques et al. (eds.), *Collection of ICC Arbitral Awards 1996-2000*, ICC Publishing S.A., Paris (2003)

Arrow, Kenneth et al. (eds.), *Barriers to Conflict Resolution*, New York: W.W. Norton (1995)

Arrow, Kenneth / Mnookin, Robert / Ross, Lee / Tversky, Amos / Wilson, Robert (ed.), *Barriers to Conflict Resolution*, New York, London (1995)

Augsburger, David, *Conflict Mediation Across Cultures. Pathways and Patterns*, Louisville, Kentucky (1992)

Austmann, Andreas, "Commercial Multi-Party Arbitration: A Case-by-Case Approach", 1 *Am. Rev. Int'l Arb.* 341 (1990)

Avruch, Kevin, *Culture and Conflict Resolution*, Washington, DC (1998)

Axelrod, Robert, *The Evolution of Cooperation*, New York (1984)

Axelrod, Robert, *The Complexity of Cooperation: Agent-Based models of Competition and Collaboration*, Princeton (1997)

Baker, Mark C. / Ali, Arif Hyder, "A Cross-Comparison of Institutional Mediation Rules", *Dispute Resolution Journal* 72 (2002)

Ballem, John Bishop, "Fast-Track Arbitration on the International Scene", 2 *Am. Rev. Int'l Arb*. 152 (1991)

Barin, Babak, *Carswell's Handbook of International Dispute Resolution Rules*, Scarborough, Ontario (1999)

Bartlett, Christopher / Goshal, Sumantra, *Managing Across Borders*, Cambridge, MA (2nd ed 2002)

Basedow, Jürgen, "Das Amerikanische Pipeline Embargo vor Gericht", 47 *Rabels Zeitschrift* 147 (1983)

Bazerman, Max, "Negotiator Judgment: A Critical Look at the Rationality Assumption", 27 *Am. Behav. Sci*. 211 (1983)

Bazerman, Max / Russ, Lee / Yakura, Elaine, Post-Settlement-Settlements in Two-Party Negotiations, 3 *Neg. J*. 283 (1987)

Bemis, Knox, "Fast-Track Arbitration as an Alternative Institutional Procedure", 2 *Am. Rev. Int'l Arb*. 148 (1991)

Bender, David, "Alternative Dispute Resolution and the Computer-Related Dispute: An Ideal Marriage?", 7 (5) *The Computer Lawyer* 9 (1990)

Bercovitch, Jacob (ed.), *Studies in International Mediation: Essays in Honor of Jeffrey Z. Rubin*, New York (2003)

van den Berg, Albert Jan (ed.), *ICCA Congress Series* No. 4, 81 (1989)

van den Berg, Albert, *Impoving the Efficiency of Arbitration Agreements and Awards: 40 Years of Application of the New York Convention*, ICCA Congress Series No. 9, The Hague (1999)

Bergemann, Niels / Sourisseaux, Andreas, *Interkulturelles Management*, Berlin (3rd ed. 2002)

Berger, Klaus Peter, "Integration of Mediation Elements into Arbitration", 19 (3) *Arb. Int'l* 387-403, 393 (2003)

Berger, Klaus Peter, *International Economic Arbitration*, Deventer, Boston, (1993)

Berger, Klaus Peter, *Private Dispute Resolution in International Business*, The Hague (2006)

Bergman, Edward J. / Bickerman, John G., *Court-Annexed Mediation: Critical Perspectives on Selected State and Federal Programs*, Chicago (1998)

Bierbrauer, Günter / Falke, Josef / Giese, Bernhard / Koch, Klaus-F. / Rodinger, Hubert (ed.), *Zugang zum Recht* (1978)

Bilder, Richard B., "Some Limitations of Adjudication as an International Dispute Settlement Technique", 23 *Virginia Journal of International Law* 1-12 (1982)

Binnendijk, Hans (ed.), *National Negotiating Styles*, Washington D.C. (1987)

Blessing, Marc, "Die LCIA Rules – aus der Sicht des Praktikers", 5 *SchiedsVZ* 198 (2003)

Blessing, Marc, "The Zurich Mini-Trial Procedure", 2 (1) *J. Int'l Arb.* 67 (1985)

Böckstiegel, Karl-Heinz (ed.), *Beweiserhebung im Internationalen Schiedsverfahren*, Cologne (2001)

Böckstiegel, Karl-Heinz, "Presenting Evidence in International Arbitration", ICSID Rev. – *Foreign Investment L.J.* 1, 2 (2001)

de Boisseson, Matthieu, Address to CPR Annual Meeting, Seabrook SC (May 1988), in: Center for Public Resources, *CPR Practice Guide: Transnational Disputes*, A104 (1988)

de Boisseson, Matthieu, *Le Droit Francais de l'Arbitrage – Interne et International*, Paris (1989)

Bond, Stephen, "The Rules of Arbitration of the International Chamber of Commerce" 37, in: Barin, *Carswell's Handbook of International Dispute Resolution Rules* (1999)

de Bono, Edward, *Lateral Thinking: A Textbook of Creativity*, London, (1970)

Born, Gary, "Planning for International Dispute Resolution", 17 (3) *J. Int'l Arb.* 61-72 (2000)

Breidenbach, Stephan / Coester-Waltjen, Dagmar / Heß, Burkhard / Nelle, Andreas / Wolf, Christian (Eds.), *Konsensuale Streitbeilegung: Akademisches Symposium zu Ehren von Peter Schlosser*, Bielefeld (2000)

Breslin, William / Rubin, Jeffrey (ed.), *Negotiation Theory and Practice*, Cambridge, Mass. (1991)

Brett, Jeanne, *Negotiating Globally: How to Negotiate Deals, Resolve Disputes, and Make Decisions Across Cultures*, San Francisco (2001)

Brown, Henry / Marriott, Arthur, *ADR: Principles and Practice*, London (1993)

Brus, Marcel M. T. A., *Third Party Dispute Settlement in an Interdependent World: Developing an International Framework*, Dordrecht, Boston, London (1995)

Bryan, Robert / Buck, Peter, "The Cultural Pitfalls in Cross-Border Negotiations", 24 (2) *Mergers & Acquisitions* (1989)

Bühler, Michael, "Costs in ICC Arbitration: A Practitioner's View", 3 *Am. Rev. Int'l Arb.* 116 (1992)

Bühler, Michael, "Technical Expertise: An Additional Means for Preventing or Settling Commercial Disputes", 6 (1) *J. Int'l Arb.* 135 (1989)

Bühler, Michael / Dorgan, Carroll, "Witness Testimony Pursuant to the 1999 IBA Rules of Evidence in International Commercial Arbitration", 17 (1) *J. Int'l Arb.* 3 (2000)

Bühring-Uhle, Christian, "The IBM-Fujitsu Arbitration: A Landmark in Innovative Dispute Resolution", 2 *Am. Rev. Int'l Arb.* 113 (1991)

Bühring-Uhle, Christian, *Arbitration and Mediation in International Business*, The Hague, London, Boston (1996)

Bühring-Uhle, Christian, "Traditional Mediation vs. Modern Mediation", *Stockholm Arbitration Newsletter* (Issue 1 / 2001), online available at http://www.sccinstitute. com/_upload/shared_files/newsletter/newsletter_1_2001.pdf

Bühring-Uhle, Christian / Scherer, Gabriele / Kirchhoff, Lars, "The Arbitrator as Mediator – Some Recent Empirical Insights", 20 (1) *J. Int'l Arb.* 81-90 (2003)

Buzan, Tony, *The Mind Map Book*, London (1993)

Carbonneau, Thomas (ed.), *Lex Mercatoria and Arbitration: A Discussion of the New Law Merchant*, New York (1990)

Carbonneau, Thomas, "The Exuberant Pathway to Quixotic Internationalism: Assessing the Folly of Mitsubishi", 19 *Vand. J. Trans. L.* 265 (1986)

Carrel, Alyson, "An ADR Clause by Any Other Name Might Smell as Sweet: England's High Court of Justice Queens Bench Attempts and Fails to Define what is not an Enforceable ADR Clause", *Journal of Dispute Resolution* 547 (2003)

Cauley de la Sierra, Mimi, "How MNCs Handle Disputes in Strategic Alliances", *Business International* (June 15, 1992)

Center for Public Resources, CPR Legal Program, *Containing Legal Costs: ADR Strategies for Corporations, Law Firms and Government* 33-43 (1988)

Center for Public Resources, CPR Legal Program, *Corporate Dispute Management: A Manual of Innovative Corporate Strategies for the Avoidance and Resolution of Legal Disputes* 105 (1982)

Center for Public Resources, *CPR Practice Guide: Transnational Disputes*, A104 (Fall 1988)

Chang, Jesse, "Resolving Disputes through Conciliation and Arbitration in the Mainland China", 2 *Ann. 2000 ATLA CLE* 1643 (2000)

Chayes, Antonia Handler / Wofford, John, *Managing the Corporate Legal Function: the Law Department, Outside Counsel, and Legal Costs*, New York (1985 & 1990)

Chiu, Julie, "Consolidation of Arbitral Proceedings and International Commercial Arbitration", 7 (2) *J. Int'l Arb.* 53 (1990)

Cochran, Robert, "Must Lawyers Tell Clients About ADR?", *Arbitration Journal* 8 (1993)

Collins, Michael, "Do International Arbitral Tribunals have any Obligations to Encourage Settlement of the Disputes Before Them?", 19 (3) *Arb. Int'l* 333-343 (2003)

Cooley, John, *Mediation Advocacy*, Notre Dame, IN (2nd ed. 2002)

Coombe, "The Future: Implementing New Approaches to the Settlement of Transnational Commercial Disputes", 17 *Can.-U.S. L.J.* 533 (1991)

Costantino, Cathy A. / Sickles Merchant, Christine, *Designing Conflict Management Systems; A Guide to Creating Productive and Healthy Organizations*, San Francisco (1996)

Coulson, "Significance of the IBM-Fujitsu Software Award", in: American Arbitration Association, *Arbitration and the Law* 1987-1988 224-224 (1988)

Craig, William Laurence, "The Uses and Abuses of Appeal From International Arbitration Awards", in: Southwestern Legal Foundation, *Private Investors Abroad – Problems and Solutions in International Business* Ch. 14 (1988)

Craig, William Laurence / Park, William / Paulsson, Jan, International Chamber of Commerce Arbitration, New York, (3rd ed. 2000)

Cremades, Bernardo, "Overcoming the Clash of Legal Cultures: The Role of Interactive Arbitration", 14 *Arb. Int'l* No. 2 157 (1998)

Cronin-Harris, C., "Mainstreaming: Systematizing Corporate Use of ADR", 59 *Alb. L. Rev.*, 847 (1996)

Dahl, Robert, *On Democracy*, New Haven, CT (1998)

Davies, "British Court Cannot Stop Suspension of Channel Tunnel Work", *Financial Times* 10 (January 29, 1992)

Davis, Albie, "An Interview with Mary Parker Follett", 5 *Neg. J.* 223 (1989)

Davis, Benjamin, "Fast-Track Arbitration: An ICC Counsel's Perspective", 2 *Am. Rev. Int'l Arb.* 159 (1991)

Delaume, Georges, "ICSID Arbitration: Practical Considerations", 1 (1) *J. Int'l Arb.* 101-125 (1984)

Derains, Yves, "Technical Expertise and 'Reféré Arbitral'", in: Sanders (ed.), *ICCA Congress Series* No.1 (1983)

Derains, Yves / Schwartz, Eric A., *A Guide to the New ICC Rules of Arbitration*, The Hague (1999)

Desax, Marcus, "The Zurich Mini-Trial: A New Option for International Dispute Resolution", 3 (1) *Alternatives* 1 (1985)

Deutsch, Morton, *Konfliktregelung – Konstruktive und destruktive Prozesse*, München, Basel (1976)

Deutsch, Morton, *The Resolution of Conflict: Constructive and Destructive Processes*, New Haven (1973)

Deutsch, Morton / Coleman, Peter (eds.) *The Handbook of Conflict Resolution: Theory and Practice*, San Francisco (2000)

Dezalay, Yves / Garth, Bryant, *Dealing in Virtue: International Commercial Arbitration and the Construction of a Transnational Legal Order*, Chicago (1998)

Dobbins, Robert, "UNCITRAL Model Law on International Commercial Conciliation: From a Topic of Possible Discussion toe Approval by the General Assembly", *Pepperdine Dispute Resolution Journal* 529 (2003)

Donahey, Scott, "International Mediation and Conciliation", in: Roth, Wulff & Cooper, *The Alternative Dispute Resolution Practice Guide* (1993)

Donne, Michael, "Laker Creditors 'to be paid by Christmas'", *Financial Times* 1 (September 7, 1985)

Donovan, Donald Francis / Rivkin, David W., *International Arbitration and Dispute Resolution* (2002)

Drahozal, Christopher, "Commercial Norms, Commercial Codes, and International Commercial Arbitration", 33 *Vanderbild Journal of Transnational Law* 79-134 (2000)

Drahozal, Christopher / Naimark, Richard (ed.), *Towards a Science of International Arbitration*, The Hague (2005)

Duve, Christian / Eidenmueller, Horst / Hacke, Andreas, *Mediation in der Wirtschaft – Wege zum professionellen Konfliktmanagement*, Köln, Frankfurt (2003)

Ebb, Lawrence F., "Flight of Assets from the Jurisdiction 'In the Twinkling of a Telex': Pre- and Post-Award Conservatory Relief in International Commercial Arbitrations", 7 (1) *J. Int'l Arb.* 9 (1990)

Edwards, Harry, "Alternative Dispute Resolution: Panacea or Anathema?", 99 *Harv. L. Rev.* 668 (1986)

Eidenmüller, Horst, "Prozessrisikoanalyse", *ZZP* 5 (2000)

Eidenmüller, Horst, "A Legal Framework for National and International Mediation Proceedings", *Journal of International Dispute Resolution* 14, 17 (BB- Beilage 7 zu Heft 46 / 2002)

Eidenmüller, Horst, *Vertrags- und Verfahrensrecht der Wirtschaftsmediation*, Cologne (2001)

Eidenmüller, Horst, "Vertrags- und verfahrensrechtliche Grundfragen der Mediation: Möglichkeiten und Grenzen privatautonomen Konfliktmanagements", in Breidenbach et al. (Eds.), *Konsensuale Streitbeilegung* 58 et seq. (2001)

Eidenmüller, Horst, "Die Auswirkung der Einleitung eines ADR-Verfahrens auf die Verjährung", 4 *ScheidsVZ* 163 (2003)

Eidenmüller, Horst, "Establishing a Legal Framework for Mediation in Europe: The Proposal for an EC Mediation Directive", *ScheidsVZ* 124 (2005)

Eisemann, Frédéric, "Conciliation as a Means of Settlement of International Business Disputes: the UNCITRAL Rules as Compared with the ICC System", in: *The Art of Arbitration (Liber Amicorum for Pieter Sanders)* 124 (1982)

Eisenberg, Melvin Aron, "Private Ordering Through Negotiation: Dispute-Settlement and Rulemaking", 89 *Harv. L. Rev.* 637 (1976)

Elliott, David C., "Med / Arb: Fraught with Danger or Ripe with Opportunity?", 62 (3) *J. Chartered Inst. Of Arb.*, 176 (1996)

Epstein, Lee / King, Gary, "The Rules of Inference", 69 *University of Chicago Law Review* (2002)

Eyzaguirre Echeverria, Rafael / Siqueiros, José Luis, "Arbitration in Latin American Countries", in: Van den Berg (ed.), *ICCA Congress Series* No. 4, 81 (1989)

Felstiner, William / Abel, Ricard / Sarat, Austin, "The Emergence and Transformation of Disputes: Naming, Blaming, Claiming...", 15 *L. & Soc. Rev.* 631 (1980-81)

Fine, Erika / Plapinger, Elizabeth, "Introduction to ADR", in: CPR Legal Program, *Containing Legal Costs: ADR Strategies for Corporations, Law Firms and Government* 9 (1988)

Finz, I. Leonard, "The Hi-Lo Contract: Trial by Chance", 48 *N.Y. State Bar J.* 186 (1976)

Fischer-Zernin, Vincent / Junker, Abbo, "Arbitration and Mediation: Synthesis or Antithesis?", 5 (1) *J. Int'l Arb.* 21 (1988)

Fischer-Zernin, Vincent / Junker, Abbo, "Between Scylla and Charybdis: Fact Gathering in German Arbitration", 4 (2) *J. Int'l Arb.* 9 (1987)

Fisher, Glen, *International Negotiation: A Cross-Cultural Perspective*, Yarmouth, Maine (1980)

Fisher, Glen, *Mindsets: The Role of Culture and Perception in International Relations*, Yarmouth, Maine (1988)

Fisher, Roger, "Negotiating Inside Out: What are the Best Ways to Relate Internal Negotiations with External Ones?", 5 *Neg. J.* 33 (1989)

Fisher, Roger, "Negotiating Power: Getting and Using Influence", 27 *Am. Behav. Sci.* 149 (1983)

Fisher, Roger / Brown, Scott, *Getting Together: Building Relationships as We Negotiate*, New York (1988)

Fisher, Roger / Ury, William / Patton, Bruce, *Getting to Yes*, New York (2nd ed. 1991)

Folberg, Jay / Taylor, Alison, *Mediation*, San Francisco (1984)

Frick, Joachim, *Arbitration and Complex International Contracts*, The Hague, New York (2001)

Fuller, Lon, "The Forms and Limits of Adjudication", 92 *Harv. L. Rev.* 353 (1978)

Fuller, Lon, *The Principles of Social Order: Selected Essays of Lon L. Fuller* (rev. ed. 2001, Kenneth I. Winston (ed.)), Oxford (1981, 2001)

Galanter, Marc, "Worlds of Deals: Using Negotiation to Teach about Legal Process", 34 *J. Legal Educ.* 268 (1984)

Glasl, Friedrich, *Konfliktmanagement*, Bern (8th ed., 2004)

Glossner, Ottoarndt, "Enforcement of Conciliation Settlements", 11 *Int'l Bus. Law.* 151 (1983)

Goldberg, Stephen / Sander, Frank / Rogers, Nancy, *Dispute Resolution: Negotiation, Mediation and Other Processes*, Boston (1992)

Goldstein, Marc J., "International Legal Developments in Review: 1998 Business Transactions & Disputes", *International Commercial Arbitration* 389 (1999)

Goodwin, Deborah, *Negotiation in International Conflict* (2002)

Gotanda, John Y., "Awarding Costs and Attorney's Fees in International Commercial Arbitrations", 21 *Mich. J. Int'l L.* 1 (1999)

Gotanda, John, "An Efficient Method for Determining Jurisdiction in International Arbitrations", 40 *Columbia J. Transnat'l L.* 11-42 (2001)

Green, Eric (Ed.), "CPR Legal Program Mini-Trial Handbook", in: Center for Public Resources (ed.), *CPR Corporate Dispute Management* MH35 (1982)

Green, Eric / Marks, Jonathan / Olson, Ronald, "Settling Large Case Litigation: An Alternate Approach", 11 *Loy. L.A. L. Rev.* 493 (1978)

Greenberg, Simon, "An Introduction to Commencing Arbitration under the ICC Rules", *Vindobona Journal of International Commerical Law & Arbitration* 122 (2000)

Griffin, Peter R., "Recent Trends in the Conduct of International Arbitration – Discovery Procedures and Witness Hearings", 17 (2) *J. Int'l Arb.* 19 (2000)

Gulliver, Philip, *Disputes and Negotiations: A Cross-Cultural Perspective*, New York (1979)

Guttman, Amy / Thompson, Dennis, *Democracy and Disagreement*, Cambridge, MA (1996)

Hacke, Andreas, *ADR-Vertrag: Vertragsrecht und vertragliche Gestaltung der Mediation und anderer alternativer Konfliktlösungsverfahren*, Heidelberg (2001)

Hacking, David, "Arbitration Law Reform in Europe", 65 (3) *Arbitration: Journal of the Chartered Institute of Arbitrators* 180-185 (1999)

Haft, Fritjof / Schlieffen, Katharina von (Eds.), *Handbuch Mediation*, München (2003)

Hall, Edward, "The Silent Language in Overseas Business", *Harv. Bus. Rev.* 87 (May-June 1960)

Hall, Edward, *The Silent Language*, New York (1959)

Hammond, John et al., *Smart Choices: A Practical Guide to Making Better Decisions*, Cambridge (1999)

Hancock, William, "Corporate Counsel's Primer on Alternative Dispute Resolution Techniques", in: Hancock & Gillan (ed.), *Corporate Counsel's Guide to ADR Techniques* 1.001 (1989)

Hancock, William / Gillan, (ed.), *Corporate Counsel's Guide to ADR Techniques* (1989)

Hanotiau, Bernard, "Complex-Multicontract-Multiparty-Arbitration", 14 *Arb. Int'l* 369 (1998)

Hardy, Clive, "Multi-party Arbitration: Exceptional Problems Need Exceptional Solutions", *Arbitration* 15 (2000)

Hausmaninger, Christian, "Civil Liability of Arbitrators – Comparative Analysis and Proposals for Reform", 7 (4) *J. Int'l Arb.* 7 (1990)

Henrikson, Alan K. (ed.), *Negotiating World Order: The Artisanship and Architecture of Global Diplomacy*, Wilmington (1986)

Henry, James / Lieberman, Jethro, *The Manager's Guide to Resolving Legal Disputes*, New York (1985)

Hill, Richard, "The Theoretical Basis of Mediation and other Forms of ADR: Why they Work", 14 (2) *Arb. Int'l* 182 (1998)

Hoddinott, Alfred, "Alternative Resolution of International Disputes: Practical Observations on a Mini-Trial", in: CPR Legal Program, *Containing Legal Costs: ADR Strategies for Corporations, Law Firms and Government* 377 (1988)

Hoellering, Michael, "Is a New Practice Emerging From the Experience of the American Arbitration Association?", lecture, ICC Court of Arbitration, Paris (October 24, 1985)

Hoffer, David P., "Decision Analysis as a Mediator's Tool", 1 *Harv. Neg. L. Rev.* 113 (1996)

Hofstede, Geerd, *Cultures and Organizations: Software of the Mind*, London (1991)

Horn, Norbert (ed.), *Adaptation and Renegotiation of Contracts in International Trade and Finance*, Frankfurt/M. (1985)

Huber, Stephen / Trachte-Huber, Wendy, "International ADR in the 1990's: The Top Ten Developments", 1 *Houston Business & Tax Law Journal* 184-223 (2001)

Hulbert, Richard, "Arbitral Procedure and the Preclusive Effect of Awards in International Commercial Arbitration", 7 *Int'l Tax & Bus. Law.* 155 (1989)

Hunter, Martin, "Anticipating Trends in Dispute Resolution", in: de Zylva & Harrison, *International Commercial Arbitration* 15 (2000)

International Bar Association (IBA), "Commentary on the New IBA Rules of Evidence in International Commercial Arbitration", *Business Law International*, Issue 2, 3-113 (2000)

Jackson, Howell et al., *Analytical Methods for Lawyers*, New York (2003)

Jackson, Joseph Jr., "The 1975 Inter-American Convention on International Commercial Arbitration: Scope, Application and Problems", 8 (3) *J. Int'l Arb.* 91 (1991)

JAMS, "Facilitative and Evaluative Mediation: An Overview", (unpublished paper 1994)

Janosik, Robert, "Rethinking the Culture-Negotiation Link", 3 *Neg. J.* 385 (1987)

Jarvins, Sigvard, "The Role of Conciliation, Contract Modification and Expert Appraisal in Settling International Commercial Disputes", 4 *Int'l Tax & Bus. Law.* 238 (1986)

Jessup, Philip C., *Transnational Law*, New Haven (1956)

Johnston, "The IBM – Fujitsu Arbitration Revisited – A Case Study in Effective ADR", 7 (5) *The Computer Lawyer* 13-17 (1990)

Kahneman, Daniel / Tversky, Amos, "Conflict Resolution: A Cognitive Perspective", in: Arrow et al., *Barriers to Conflict Resolution* 44 (1995)

Kazutake, Okuma, "Party Autonomy in International Commercial Arbitration: Consolidation of Multiparty and Classwide Arbitration", 9 *Ann. Surv. Int'l & Comp. L.* 189 (2003)

Koch, Christopher / Schaefer, Erik, "Can It Be Sinful for an Arbitrator Actively to Promote Settlement?", *Arbitration and Dispute Resolution Law Journal*, Part 3, 153-184 (Sept 1999)

Koch, Klaus-Friedrich, "Konfliktmanagement und Rechtsanthropologie. Ein Modell und seine Anwendung in einer ethnologischen Vergleichsanalyse", in: Bierbrauer, Falke, Giese & Rodingen (ed.), *Zugang zum Recht* 86 (1978)

Kolb, Deborah, "How Existing Procedures Shape Alternatives: The Case of Grievance Mediation", *J. Dispute Resolution* 59 (1989)

Korobkin, Russell B. / Guthrie, Chris, "Psychology, Economics, and Settlement: A New Look at the Role of the Lawyer", *Texas Law Review* 77 (1997)

Kriesberg, Louis, *Constructive Conflicts*, Oxford (1998)

Krüger, Wilfried, *Konfliktsteuerung als Führungsaufgabe*, Munich (1973)

Lalonde, Marc, "The New LCIA Rules", in: Barin, *Carswell's Handbook of International Dispute Resolution Rules* 71 (1999)

Langbein, John, "The German Advantage in Civil Procedure", 52 *U. Chi. L. Rev.* 823 (1987)

Lax, David / Sebenius, James, *The Manager as Negotiator*, New York (1986)

Lecuyer-Thieffry, Christine / Thieffry, Patrick, "Negotiating Settlement of Disputes Provisions in International Business Contracts", 45 *Bus. Law.* 577 (1990)

Lew, Julian / Mistelis, Loukas / Kröll, Stefan, *Comparative International Arbitration*, The Hague, New York (2003)

Lew, Julian / Smith, Herbert, "Multiparty Arbitrations", *Stockholm Arbitration Newsletter* (2 / 2000)

Lipsky, David B. / Seeber, Ronald L. / Fincher, Richard, *Emerging Systems For Managing Workplace Conflict*, San Francisco (2003)

Lloyd, Humphrey, "Channel Tunnel Dispute Raises International Issues", *Building* (February 7, 1992)

Lowenfeld, Andreas, *International Litigation and Arbitration*, St. Paul, MN (2nd ed. 2002)

Lowenfeld, Andreas, "The Mitsubishi Case: Another View", 2 *Arb. Int'l* 178 (1986)

Lowenfeld, Andreas, "The Two-Way Mirror: International Arbitration as Comparative Procedure, in: Studies of Transnational Legal Practice", 163 *Michigan Y.B. Int'l Legal Studies* (1985)

Macaulay, Stewart, "Non-Contractual Relationships in Business: A Preliminary Study", 28 *Am. Sociological Rev.* 55 (1963)

Mackenzie, "'Shadow Mediation': A Breakthrough Tactic Resolves Claims and Saves Dollars", *Florida Constructor* (March / April 1991)

Mackie, Karl, "ADR in the Hong Kong Airport Project", 5 *World Arb. & Med. Rep.* 104 (1994)

Mackie, Karl, "Arbitration by the Thousands – the London Grain and Feed Trade Association (GAFTA) Machinery", 44 *Arbitration* 13 (1977)

McCarthy, William, "The Role of Power and Principle in Getting to Yes", 1 *Neg. J.* 59 (1985)

McDonald, John / Bendahmane, Diane (ed.), *International Negotiation: Art and Science*, Washington, D.C. (1984)

McEwen, Craig, "Pursuing Problem-Solving or Predictive Settlement", 19 *Fla. State U. L. Rev.* 77 (1991)

McGuire, James E., "Practical Tips for Using Risk Analysis in Mediation", *Dispute Resolution Journal* 15 (May 1998)

Medalie, Richard, "The New Appeals Amendment: A Step Forward for Arbitration", 44 *Arb. J.* 22 (1989)

Menkel-Meadow, Carrie, *Dispute Processing and Conflict Resolution*, Ashgate Dartmouth (2003)

Menkel-Meadow, Carrie, "Pursuing Settlement in an Adversary Culture: A Tale of Innovation Co-opted or 'The Law of ADR'", 19 *Florida St. L. Rev.* 1 (1991)

Menkel-Meadow, Carrie, "Toward Another View of Legal Negotiation: The Structure of Problem-Solving", 31 *UCLA L. Rev.* 754 (1984)

Mentschikoff, Soia, "Commercial Arbitration", 61 *Col. L. Rev.* 847 (1961)

Merrills, John G., *International Dispute Settlement*, 3rd ed., Cambridge (1998)

Metcalf, Henry C. / Urwick, Lionel (ed.), *Dynamic Administration: The Collected Papers of Mary Parker Follett*, New York (1942)

Millhauser, Margaret, "Alternative Dispute Resolution: An Overview of Basic Procedures", in: Hancock & Gillan, *Corporate Counsel's Guide to ADR Techniques* 1.037 (1989)

Mnookin, Robert, "Creating Value through Process Design", 11 (1) *J. Int'l Arb.* 125 (1994)

Mnookin, Robert, "Why Negotiations Fail: An Exploration of Barriers to the Resolution of Conflict", 8 *Ohio St. J. Disp. Res.* 235 (1993)

Mnookin, Robert / Kornhauser, Lewis, "Bargaining in the Shadow of the Law: The Case of Divorce", 88 *Yale L. J.* 950 (1979)

Mnookin, Robert / Peppet, Scott / Tulumello, Andrew, *Beyond Winning: Negotiating To Create Value in Deals and Disputes*, Cambridge, Mass. (2000)

Mnookin, Robert / Greenberg, Jonathan, "Lessons of the IBM-Fujitsu Arbitration: How Disputants Can Work Together to Solve Deeper Conflicts", 18 *Dispute Resolution Magazine* (1998)

Mode, Paul / Siemer, Deanne, "The Litigation Partner and the Settlement Partner", in: Hancock & Gillan, *Corporate Counsel's Guide to ADR Techniques* 10.001 (1989)

Montagnon, "World Bank Steps Into Egyptian Tourism Row", *Financial Times* 4 (August 5, 1988)

Moore, C., "The Caucus: Private Meetings That Promote Settlement", 16 *Mediation Quarterly* 87 (1987)

Moore, "Laker Settlement Stalled by Demand for U.S.$ 60 Million Fee", *Legal Times* 1 (June 10, 1985)

Morse, Duane / Powers, Joan, "U.S. Export Controls and Foreign Entities: The Unanswered Questions of Pipeline Diplomacy", 23 *V. J. Int'l L.* 537 (1982)

Murray, John / Rau, Allan Scott / Sherman, Edward F., *Processes of Dispute Resolution*, San Francisco (1989) (3rd ed. 2000)

Mustill, Michael / Boyd, Stewart, *The Law and Practice of Commercial Arbitration in England*, London (1982)

Myers, James, "Why Conventional Arbitration is not Effective in Complex Long-Term Contracts", in: Nicklisch, *The Complex Long-Term Contract: Structures and International Arbitration* 503 (1987)

Nader, Laura / Todd, Harry, *The Disputing Process: Law in Ten Societies*, New York (1978)

Naimark, Richard, "Building a Fact-based Global Database: The Countdown", 20 *J. Int'l Arb.* 105 (2003)

Narayanan, Prakash / Menon, Raghubir, "Presentation of Evidence in International Commercial Arbitration – A Comparative Study", 4 (2) *The Vindobona Journal of International Commercial Law and Arbitration* 105-121 (2000)

Nariman, F.-S., *International Commercial Arbitration – at the Cross- Roads, Liber Amicorum Karl Heinz Böckstiegel* 555-566 (2001)

Nariman, "The Spirit of Arbitration, The Tenth Annual Goff Lecture", 16 *Arb. Int'l* 261, at p. 267 (2000)

Neale, Margeret / Bazerman, Max, *Cognition and Reality in Negotiation*, New York (1991)

Nelle, Andreas, "Making Mediation Mandatory: A Proposed Framework", 7 *Ohio St. J. Disp. Res.* 287 (1992)

Nelle, Andreas, *Neuverhandlungspflichten*, Munich (1994)

Nisbett, Richard E., *The Geography of Thought: How Asians and Westerners Think Differently ... and Why*, New York (2003)

Neuenhahn, Hans-Uwe, "Erarbeiten der Prozessrisikoanalyse und deren Einsatz in der Mediation – Bericht über einen Workshop anlässlich des Mediations-Kongresses", *ZKM* 245 (2002)

Newmark, Christopher, "Agree to Mediate... or Face the Consequences – A Review of the English Courts' Approach to Mediation", 1 *Schiedsverfahrenszeitung* 23 (2003)

Newton, David, "Australian Update: ADR Makes Further Gains", 5 *World Arb. & Med. Rep.* 109 (1994)

Nicholson, Harold, *Diplomacy* (1939)

Nickles, Peter, "Fast-Track Arbitration: A Claimant's Perspective", 2 *Am. Rev. Int'l Arb.* 143 (1991)

Nisbett, Richard, *The Geography of Thought: How Asians and Westerners Think Differently ... and Why*, New York (2003)

Nurick, Lester / Schnably, Stephen, "The First ICSID Conciliation: *Tesoro Petroleum Corporation v. Trinidad and Tobago*", 1 *ICSID Rev.- F.I.L.J.* 340 (1986)

Odams, Martin / Higgins, Joanna (ed.) *Commercial Dispute Resolution*, London (1996)

Oghigian, Haig, "The Mediation / Arbitration Hybrid", 20 (1) *J. Int'l Arb.* 75 (2003)

Okekeiferle, Andrew, "Commercial Arbitration as the Most Effective Dispute Resolution Method – Still a Fact or Now a Myth?", 15 *J. Int'l Arb.* No.4, 81

Park, William, "L'arbitrage et le Recouvrement des Prêts Consentis a des Débiteurs Etrangers", 37 *McGill L.J.* 375 (1992)

Park, William, "National Law and Commercial Justice: Safeguarding Procedural Integrity in International Arbitration", 63 *Tul. L. Rev.* 647 (1988)

Park, William, "The *Lex Loci Arbitri* and International Commercial Arbitration", 32 *I.C.L.Q.* 21 (1983)

Park, William, "When the Borrower and the Banker are at Odds: The Interaction of Judge and Arbitrator in Trans-Border Finance", 65 *Tul. L. Rev.* 1323 (1991)

Park, William (with A. Bjorklund & J. Coe), "International Commercial Dispute Resolution", 37 *International Lawyer* 445 (2003)

Park, William, "Award Enforcement under the New York Convention", 1 *International Business Litigation & Arbitration* 683 (2001)

Park, William, "Arbitration's Protean nature: The Value of Rules and the Risks of Discretion", 19 *Arb. Int'l* 279 (2003).

Parra, Antonio, "The Role of the World Bank in the Settlement of International Investment Disputes", paper before the ABA National Institute on the Resolution of International Commercial Disputes (November 5-6, 1987)

Paulsson, Jan, "Delocalization of International Commercial Arbitration: When and Why it Matters", 32 *I.C.L.Q.* 53 (1983)

Perlman, Lawrence / Nelson, Steven, "New Approaches to the Resolution of International Commercial Disputes", 17 *Bus. Law.* 215, 242, 248 (1983)

Perritt, Henry Jr., "Dispute Resolution in Cyberspace: Demand For New Forms of ADR", 15 *Ohio St. J. Disp. Resol.* 675 (2000)

Peter, Wolfgang, "Arbitration and Renegotiation Clauses", 3 (2) *J. Int'l Arb.* 29 (1986)

Polanyi, Michael, *The Logic of Liberty: Reflections and Rejoinders*, London (1951)

Pollock, Ellen Joan, "The Alternate Route", *The American Lawyer* 70 (September 1983)

Prodolliet, Simone, *Interkulturelle Kommunikation*, Luzern (2000)

Proppe, Helmut / Krapp, Thea, "Außergerichtliche Verfahren – Alternative zur Ziviljustiz?", *Jur. Arbbl.* 65 (1990)

Raiffa, Howard, *Decision Analysis: Introductory Lectures on Choices under Uncertainty*, New York (1968)

Raiffa, Howard, "Post-Settlement-Settlements", 1 *Neg. J.* 9 (1985)

Raiffa, Howard, *The Art and Science of Negotiation*, Cambridge, Mass. (1982)

Raiffa, Howard / Richardson, John / Metcalfe, David, *Negotiation Analysis, The Science and Art of Collaborative Decision Making*, Cambridge, Mass. (2002)

Rau, Alan / Sherman, Edward / Peppet, Scott (eds.), *Processes of Dispute Resolution*, New York (3rd ed. 2002)

Rawding, Nigel, "ADR: Bermuda's International Conciliation and Arbitration Act 1993", 10 *Arb. Int'l* 99 (1994)

Reason, James, *Human Error*, Cambridge (1990)

Redfern, Alan, "Jurisdiction Denied: The Pyramid Collapses", *Journal of Business Law* 15 (1986)

Redfern, Alan / Hunter, Martin, *Law and Practice of International Commercial Arbitration*, London (3rd ed. 1999)

Reisman, Michael, *Systems of Control in International Adjudication and Arbitration: Breakdown and Repair*, Durham, NC (1992)

Renfrew, Charles, "A Survey of Dispute Resolution Methods", in: Hancock & Gillan, *Corporate Counsel's Guide to ADR Techniques* 1.029 (1989)

Reymond, Claude, "Civil Law and Common Law Procedures: Which is the More Inquisitorial? A Civil Lawyer's Response", 5 *Arb. Int'l* 357 (1989)

Riskin, Leonard L., "Understanding Mediator Orientations, Strategies and Techniques: A Grid for the Perplexed", 1 *Harv. Neg. L. Rev.* 7 (1996)

Robert, Jean, "Une date dans l'extension de l'arbitrage international: L'Arrêt Mitsubishi c / Soler", *Rev. Arb.* 173 (1986)

Rodner, James, "International and National Arbitration: A Fading Distinction", 19 (5) *Journal of International Artbitration* 491 (2002)

Rogers, Nancy H. / McEwen, Craig A., "Employing the Law to Increase the Use of Mediation and to Encourage Direct and Early Negotiations", 13 *Ohio St. J. Disp. Resol.* 831 (1998)

Röhl, Klaus, *Rechtssoziologie*, Cologne (1987)

Ross, Lee, "Reactice Devaluation in Negotiation and Conflict Resolution", in: Arrow et al., *Barriers to Conflict Resolution* 26 (1995)

Roth, Bette, "The UNCITRAL Model Law on International Commercial Arbitration", in: Weigand, *Practitioner's Handbook on International Arbitration* 1165 (2002)

Roth, Bette / Wulff, Randall / Cooper, Charles, *The Alternative Dispute Resolution Practice Guide*, Scarborough (1993)

Rubin, Jeffrey / Brown, Bert, *The Social Psychology of Bargaining and Negotiation*, New York (1975)

Rubin, Jeffrey / Sander, Frank, "When Should We Use Agents? Direct vs. Representative Negotiation", 4 *Neg. J.* 395 (1988)

Rubino Sammartano, Mauro, *International Arbitration Law*, Deventer, Boston (1989) (2nd ed. 2001)

Salacuse, Jeswald W., "International Business Mediation", in: Bercovitch (ed.), *Studies in International Mediation: Essays in Honor of Jeffrey Z. Rubin* (2003)

Salacuse, Jeswald W., *Making Global Deals: Negotiating in the International Marketplace*, Boston (1991)

Salacuse, Jeswald W., *The Global Negotiator*, New York (2003)

Sander, Frank, "Varieties of Dispute Prrocessing", Address Delivered at the National Conference on the Causes of Popular Dissatisfaction with the Administration of Justice, 70 F.R.D. 111 (1976)

Sander, Frank / Goldberg, Stephen, "Fitting the Forum to the Fuss: A User-friendly Guide to Selecting an ADR-Procedure", 10 *Neg. J.* 49 (1994)

Sander, Frank / Rubin, Jeffrey, "The Janus Quality of Negotiation: Dealmaking and Dispute Settlement", 4 *Neg. J.* 109 (1988)

Sanders, Pieter (ed.), *ICCA Congress Series* No. 1, Deventer, Boston, London (1983)

Sanders, Pieter, "Unity and Diversity in the Adoption of the Model Law", 11 *Arb. Int'l* 1 (1995)

Sandrock, Otto, "Internationale Kredite und die Internationale Schiedsgerichts-barkeit", *WM Zeitschrift für Wirtschafts- und Bankrecht* 405 (1994)

Schelling, Thomas, *The Strategy of Conflict*, Cambridge, Mass. (1960)

von Schlabrendorff, Fabian, "Resolving Cultural Differences in Arbitration Proceedings", *International Financial Law Review* 38-38 (Mar 2002)

Schlosser, Peter, "Alternative Dispute Resolution (uno stimulo alla riforma per l'Europa?)", *Rivista di Diritto Processuale* 4, 1005 (1989)

Schwartz, Eric, "International Conciliation and the ICC", 10 *ICSID Rev.* 98 (1995)

Scott, Robert, "Conflict and Cooperation in Long-Term Contracts", 75 *Cal. L. Rev.* 2005 (1987)

Scott, Robert, "Risk Distribution and Adjustment in Long-Term Contracts", in: Nicklisch (ed.), *The Complex Long-Term Contract* 51 (1987)

Sebenius, James, *Negotiating the Law of the Sea: Lessons in the Art and Science of Reaching Agreement*, Cambridge, Mass. (1984)

Sebenius, James, "Negotiation Analysis: A Characterization and Review", 38 *Management Science* 18 (1992)

von Segesser, Georg, "Witness Preparation in International Commercial Arbitration", *ASA Bull.* Vol. 20, No. 2, 222 (2002)

Seidman Diamond, Shari, *Reference Guide on Survey Research, in Federal Judicial Center, Reference Manual on Scientific Evidence* (2nd ed.), St. Paul (2000)

Sekolec, Jerney / Getty, Michael, "The UMA and UNCITRAL Model Rule: An Emerging Consensus on Mediation and Conciliation", *Journal of Dispute Resolution* 175 (2003)

Shearer, Robert / Maes, Jeanne / Moore, Carl, "Partnering – A Commitment to Common Goals", *Dispute Resolution Journal* 30 (1995)

Shell, Richard G., *Bargaining for Advantage: Negotiation Strategies for Reasonable People*, New York (1999)

Silverman, Moses, "Fast Track Arbitration: A Respondent's Perspective", 2 *Am. Rev. Int'l Arb.* 154 (1991)

Singer, Linda, *Settling Disputes: Conflict Resolution in Business, Families, and the Legal System*, Boulder, Col. (1990)

Slaikeu, Karl / Hasson, Ralph, *Controlling the Costs of Conflict*, San Francisco (1998)

Smit, Hans, "Fast-Track Arbitration", 2 *Am. Rev. Int'l Arb.* 138 (1991)

Smit, Hans, "Substance and Procedure in International Arbitration: The Development of a New Legal Order", 65 *Tul. L. Rev.* 1309 (1991)

Smith, Adam, *The Wealth of Nations* (E. Cannon ed. 1937) (1776)

Smith, Murray, "Feature Costs in International Commercial Arbitration", *Dispute Resolution Journal* 30 (2001)

Smith, W., "Effectiveness of the Biased Mediator", 1 *Neg. J.* 363-372 (1985)

Staughton, C., "Common Law and Civil Law Procedures: Which is more Inquisitorial? A Common Lawyer's Response", 5 *Arb. Int'l* 351 (1989)

Stipanowich, Thomas J., "Arbitration and Multiparty Dispute: The Search for Workable Solutions", 72 *Iowa L. Rev.* 473 (Mar. 1987)

Stitt, Allan, *Alternative Dispute Resolution for Organizations*, Toronto (1998)

Stone, Douglas / Patton, Bruce / Heen, Sheila, *Difficult Conversations*, New York (2000)

Talbot, Peter, "Should an Arbitrator or Adjudicator Act as a Mediator in the Same Dispute?", 67 (3) *J. Chartered Inst. Of Arb.* 228 (2001)

von Thulen Rhoades, Rufus, *Practitioner's Handbook on International Arbitration and Mediation* (2002)

Triebel, Volker / Zons, Jörn, "Befragung von Zeugen vor dem Hearing in Internationalen Schiedsverfahren", *IDR* 5 (2004)

Trubek, David / Sarat, Austin / Felstiner, William / Kritzer, Herbert / Grossman, Joel, "The Costs of Ordinary Litigation", 31 *U.C.L.A. L.Rev.* 72 (1983)

Tversky, Amos / Kahnemann, Daniel, "The Framing of Decisions and the Psychology of Choice", 211 *Science* 453 (1981)

Uff, John, "The Predictability Factor in International Arbitration", in: Odams & Higgins (eds.) *Commercial Dispute Resolution* 144 (1996)

Ulmer, Nicolas, "Winning the Opening Stages of an ICC Arbitration", 8 (2) *J. Int'l Arb.* 33 (1991)

Ury, William, *Getting Past No: Negotiating with Difficult People*, New York (1993)

Ury, William / Brett, Jean / Goldberg, Stephen, *Getting Disputes Resolved*, San Francisco, London (1988)

Vagts, Detlev, "Dispute-Resolution Mechanisms in International Business", 203 *Recueil des Cours* 17 (1987-III)

Verdross, Alfred / Simma, Bruno, *Universelles Völkerrecht*, Berlin (3rd ed. 1984)

Victor, Marc, "Evaluating Legal Risks and Costs with Decision Tree Analysis", Ch. 12 in: West Group / American Corporate Counsel Association, *Successful Partnering Between Inside and Outside Counsel* (2000)

Victor, Marc, "The Proper Use of Decision Analysis to Assist Litigation Strategy", 40 *Bus. Lawyer* 617 (1985)

Wall, Colin, "Hong Kong's Airport Core Programme Dispute Resolution Procedures", 58 *Arbitration* 237 (1992)

Walton, Richard / McKersie, Robert, *A Behavioral Theory of Labor Negotiations*, New York (1965)

Watkiss, David K., "Fast-Track Arbitration: A Contractual Intermediary's Perspective", 2 *Am. Rev. Int'l Arb.* 150 (1991)

Wegen, Gerhard, *Vergleich und Klagerücknahme im Internationalen Prozeß*, New York (1987)

Weigand, Frank-Bernd, "Die neue ICC-Schiedsgerichtsordnung 1998", *NJW* 2081 (1998)

Weigand, Frank-Bernd, *Practitioner's Handbook on International Arbitration*, Copenhagen (2002)

Weintraub, Russell, *International Litigation and Arbitration: Practice and Planning*, Durham, NC (3rd ed. 2001)

Welton, Gary / Pruitt, Dean / McGillicuddy, Neil, "The Role of Caucusing in Community Mediation", 32 *J. Confl. Res.* 181 (1988)

Wetter, Gillis, "The Conduct of the Arbitration", 2 (2) *J. Int'l Arb.* 7 (1985)

Wetter, Gillis / Priem, Carl, "Costs and their Allocation in International Commercial Arbitration", 2 *Am. Rev. Int'l Arb.* 249 (1991)

White, James, "The Pros and Cons of 'Getting to Yes'", 34 *J. Legal Educ.* 115 (1984)

Wilberforce, Richard, "Written Briefs and Oral Advocacy", 5 *Arb. Int'l* 348 (1989)

Williams, Gerald, *Legal Negotiation and Settlement*, St. Paul, MN. (1983)

Wilmore, Katherine Birmingham / Teitz, Louise Ellen, "Parallel Proceedings – Sisyphean Progress", 36 *Int'l Law.* 423 (2001)

Wirth, Markus, "Ihr Zeuge, Herr Rechtsanwalt! – Weshalb Civil-Law-Schiedsrichter Common-Law-Verfahrensrecht anwenden", 1 *SchiedsVZ* 9 (2003)

Zartman, William (ed.), *The 50% Solution*, Garden City (1976)

Zartman, William, "Common Elements in the Analysis of the Negotiation Process", in: Breslin & Rubin (ed.), *Negotiation Theory and Practice* 147 (1991)

Zartman, William, "Negotiation: Theory and Reality", in: McDonald & Bendahmane (ed.), *International Negotiation: Art and Science* 2 (1984)

Zartman, William / Berman, Maureen, *The Practical Negotiator*, New Haven (1982)

Zeisel, Hans / Kaye, David, *Prove It with Figures: Empirical Methods in Law and Litigation*, New York (1997)

de Zylva, Martin Odams / Harrison, Reziya (ed.), *International Commercial Arbitration*, Bristol (2000)

Index

P
Panama Convention, 63
Park, William W., v
partisan facilitation, 199
partisan perceptions, 142, 144
polycentric vs. binary disputes,
133-134
positional bargaining, 154, 166
post-arbitration mediation, 254
post-settlement-settlement, 163, 255
pre-arbitral mediation, 251
prisoner's dilemma, 140, 161
process design, *see* dispute resolution
process design
Pyramids Arbitration, 37

R
relationship building, 202
Reisman, W. Michael, 169
res judicata, 25, 54
Robine, Eric, 93, 252

S
Sanders, Pieter, 118, 122
Sandrock, Otto, 77
SCC (Stockholm Chamber of
Commerce), 281
Schiedsgutachten, 199
Schwartz, Eric, 95
settlement, *see* settlement in
arbitration
shadow of the law, *see* bargaining in
the shadow of the law
SNT (Single Negotiation Text), 163
Sofidif arbitration, 38, 49
Solomon, Ezekiel, 20
strategic alliances, 5, 26
submission agreement, 33

T
terms of reference, 36, 262
tronc commun, 53
Tschotei, 178

U
UNCITRAL
 – arbitration rules, 63, 84
 – conciliation rules, *see* conciliation

W
WATNA, 157
Westerfield, Rebecca, 123, 259
World Bank as conciliator, 61, 228

Z
zero-sum-game, 110, 138, 154
ZOPA, 159, 189
Zurich Mini-Trial Rules, *see* mini-trial

INTERNATIONAL ARBITRATION LAW LIBRARY

1. Moshe Hirsch, *The Arbitration Mechanism of the International Center for the Settlement of Investment Disputes* (ISBN 0792319931)
2. Aida B. Avanessian, *Iran-United States Claims Tribunal in Action* (ISBN 1853339024)
3. Isaak I. Dore, *The UNCITRAL Framework for Arbitration in Contemporary Perspective* (ISBN 1853335738)
4. Christian Bühring-Uhle, Lars Kirchhoff, Gabriele Scherer, *Arbitration and Mediation in International Business* (ISBN 9041122567)
5. Vesna Laziæ, *Insolvency Proceedings and Commercial Arbitration* (ISBN 9041111158)
6. Joachim Frick, *Arbitration in Complex International Contracts* (ISBN 9041116621)
7. Katherine Lynch, *The Forces of Economic Globalization: Challenges to the Regime of International Commercial Arbitration* (ISBN 9041119949)
8. Christoph Liebscher, *The Healthy Award: Challenge in International Commercial Arbitration* (ISBN 9041120114)
9. Hamid G. Gharavi, *The International Effectiveness of the Annulment of an Arbitral Award* (ISBN 9041117172)
10. Abdullah Sayed, *Corruption in International Trade and Commercial Arbitration* (ISBN 9041122362)
11. Gabrielle Kaufmann-Kohler and Thomas Schultz, *Online Dispute Resolution. Challenges for Contemporary Justice* (ISBN 9041123180)
12. Christopher R. Drahozal and Richard W. Naimark (eds), *Towards a Science of International Arbitration: Collected Empirical Research* (ISBN 9041123229)
13. Ali Yeşilırmak, *Provisional Measures in International Commercial Arbitration* (ISBN 9041123539)
14. Bernard Hanotiau, *Complex Arbitrations: Multiparty, Multicontract, Multi-issue and Class Actions* (ISBN 904112442X)